A Guide to Special Education Law

Elizabeth A. Shaver, J.D. and Janet R. Decker, J.D., Ph.D.
Editors

EDUCATION LAW ASSO
No. 97 in the K-12 Se

© 2017 by the Education Law Association
Cleveland, Ohio 44115-2214
Phone: 216-523-7377 / Fax: 216-687-5284
www.educationlaw.org

A Guide to Special Education Law
#97 in the ELA K-12 Series

Printed in the United States of America
ISBN-10: 1-56534-183-X
ISBN-13: 978-1-56534-183-8

Education Law Association Publications

Founded in 1954, the Education Law Association is a nonprofit, nonadvocacy member association that seeks to improve education by promoting interest in and understanding of the legal framework of education and the rights of students, parents, school boards, and school employees.

Both authors and editors who collaborate on ELA publications include many of the best-known experts in their fields: deans, professors of education or law, school administrators, and attorneys specializing in education law.

Whether you're doing research as an educational administrator, attorney, or student—or you are a professor selecting high-quality and affordable textbooks—help yourself succeed by choosing education law publications from ELA's bookstore on our website, www.educationlaw.org.

Citations for This Text

Bluebook format: Author(s) of chapter, *Title of Chapter*, *in* A GUIDE TO SPECIAL EDUCATION LAW (Shaver & Decker, eds. 2017).

APA format: Author, A. A., & Author, B. B. (2017). *Title of chapter*. In E. Shaver & J. Decker (Eds.), A Guide to Special Education Law. (pages of ch.). Cleveland, OH: Education Law Association.

Editors

Elizabeth A. Shaver (Lead Editor) is an Associate Professor of Legal Writing at The University of Akron School of Law, where she teaches legal writing, education law, and special education law. She regularly publishes and presents on education law topics, and her scholarship on special education law has been cited to the United States Supreme Court. Before joining Akron Law in 2009, Professor Shaver worked both in private practice and as in-house counsel. Professor Shaver received her B.A., magna cum laude, from Vanderbilt University and J.D., cum laude, from Cornell Law School, where she was a member of the *Cornell Law Review*.

Janet R. Decker (Editor) is an Assistant Professor at Indiana University, where she teaches school law courses. Dr. Decker's research comprises three intersecting strands: informing special education policy and practice, increasing the legal literacy of teachers and administrators, and examining discriminatory practices at charter schools. She holds a J.D. and Ph.D. from Indiana University. Dr. Decker became interested in special education policy when she taught students with autism at the Princeton Child Development Institute.

Authors

Sean Bielmeier, Ph.D. Student, Educational Leadership & Policy Studies, University of Wisconsin-Madison, Madison, WI

Susan C. Bon, J.D., Ph.D.: Professor, Educational Leadership & Policies, University of South Carolina, Columbia, SC

Susan G. Clark, Ph.D., J.D.: Professor, Educational Foundations and Leadership, The University of Akron, Akron, OH

Jean B. Crockett, Ph.D.: Professor, School of Special Education, School Psychology, and Early Childhood Studies, University of Florida, Gainesville, FL

Janet R. Decker, J.D., Ph.D.: Assistant Professor, Educational Leadership & Policy Studies Dept., Indiana University, Bloomington, IN

Cathleen A. Geraghty-Jenkinson, Ph.D.: Assistant Teaching Professor, School Psychology Program, University of California, Riverside, CA

Julie F. Mead, Ph.D.: Associate Dean for Education and Professor, Educational Leadership and Policy Analysis, University of Wisconsin-Madison, Madison, WI

Allan G. Osborne, Jr., Ed.D.: Principal (Retired), Snug Harbor Community School, Quincy, MA

Mark A. Paige, J.D., Ph.D.: Associate Professor, Department of Public Policy, University of Massachusetts-Dartmouth, N. Dartmouth, MA

Charles J. Russo, J.D., Ed.D.: Joseph Panzer Chair of Education and Director of Ph.D. Program in Educational Leadership in School of Education & Health Sciences; Research Professor of Law, University of Dayton, Dayton, OH

Elizabeth A. Shaver, J.D.: Associate Professor of Legal Writing, The University of Akron School of Law, Akron, OH

Jennifer A. Sughrue, Ph.D.: Professor, Dept. of Educational Leadership, Technology, and Research, Florida Gulf Coast University, Ft. Myers, FL

Philip H. Swartz, Ph.D.: Teacher, Vineyard STEM School, Ontario-Montclair School District, Ontario, CA

Stanley L. Swartz, Ph.D.: Professor, Department of Educational Leadership and Technology, and Department of Special Education, Rehabilitation and Counseling, California State University, San Bernardino, CA

Mitchell L. Yell, Ph.D.: Fred and Francis Palmetto Chair in Teacher Education Special Education, Educational Studies, University of South Carolina, Columbia, SC

The editors would like to express their appreciation to Julie Mead for suggesting and compiling the Case Appendix, to Suzanne Eckes for providing guidance in the development of the book, and to Pamela Hardy for offering excellent editorial assistance.

Table of Contents

Chapter 1
Special Education Legal Literacy

Chapter 2
The American Legal System

Chapter 3
Fundamentals of Federal Disability Law

Chapter 4
Discrimination under Section 504 of the Rehabilitation Act and Americans with Disabilities Act

Chapter 5
Qualifying for Special Education Services under IDEA

Chapter 6
IEPs, Least Restrictive Environment, and Placement

Chapter 7
Related Services under the IDEA

Chapter 8
Secondary School Transition Planning

Chapter 9
Disciplining Students with Disabilities

Chapter 10
Parental Rights

Chapter 11
Procedural Safeguards: Resolving Family-School Disputes

Chapter 12
Current Issues in Special Education

Appendix

Topical Index

x

Chapter 1

Introduction: Special Education Legal Literacy

Janet R. Decker and Elizabeth A. Shaver

A Guide to Special Education Law pools the experience and expertise of special education legal experts from across the U.S. into one valuable resource. In their current roles as special education attorneys and university professors, the authors navigate the complex maze of federal and state legislation, regulations, and case law. They also must stay abreast of the constant changes in special education law.

In the following chapters, the authors provide a clear and concise explanation of the current status of special education law. Importantly, they translate the law for those who do not have a legal background. Each chapter also offers practical recommendations. By heeding the authors' useful guidance, special education directors, teachers, paraprofessionals, parents, and others will be better prepared to address the many legal dilemmas they face.

Why this Book is Needed

Special education lawsuits are the most common type of litigation filed against schools.[1] In order to prevent lawsuits and ensure the rights of students with disabilities are not violated, school employees must be legally literate. They must be able to "spot legal issues, identify applicable laws or legal standards, and apply the relevant legal rules to solve legal dilemmas."[2] Yet, national studies have found that the majority of teachers and principals lack effective legal training and, therefore, remain uninformed about the legal rights of students, especially students with disabilities.[3]

This lack of special education legal literacy is concerning because teachers and administrators are often the first people who must respond to legal dilemmas. Many times, the immediacy of the situation or district policy prevents them from contacting an attorney. Additionally, without legal training, school employees may fail to recognize when it is imperative to seek legal advice. If they inadvertently violate the law, little can be done to rectify the situation after the fact. On the other hand, when educators do identify a legal dilemma, some may be so fearful of the law that they "fail to act when they should and overreact when they should not."[4] Indeed, "...too many teachers view the law as a source of fear and anxiety—an invisible monster lurking in the shadows of the classroom, hallways, or playground, waiting to ensnare any educator who makes an innocent mistake."[5] Increasing special education legal literacy could reduce fear and, ultimately, protect the legal rights of students with disabilities.[6]

Special education legal literacy also is an imperative for any parent of a child with a disability.[7] Many children with disabilities begin to receive services after their third birthday and will remain eligible, depending on state law, until their early twenties.[8] Over those many years, parents will encounter different issues and aspects of special education law, which could include issues regarding school discipline, the provision of "related services" to a child with a disability, transition services to assist a child in transitioning from school to work, and other issues.[9]

It is particularly important that parents be familiar with special education law because the law accords parents such an important role in the process of developing their child's special education programming.[10] And, parents often report that they feel intimated in their discussions with school personnel, who might discount their opinions as stemming from "emotion rather than reasoned judgment about appropriate educational services for the[ir] child."[11] Special education legal literacy is essential for parents who wish to fully participate in their child's educational programming and need the "know-how" to support their opinions.

Students with disabilities are guaranteed a unique set of protections and entitlements through federal laws, including the Individuals with Disabilities Education Act (IDEA), Section 504 of the Rehabilitation Act (Section 504), and the Americans with Disabilities Act (ADA). In addition to understanding these laws, educators must also be well-versed in state and federal statutes, regulations, and case law.

Despite the legal mandates, many educators and administrators receive little to no training in special education law. Most university preparation programs do not require school leaders or teachers to complete any formal coursework in special education law.[12] As a result, research has documented that educators and administrators are woefully underprepared and lack the knowledge about special education procedures and law that is needed to fulfill their job responsibilities.[13] School employees are aware of this deficit and respond that they would like more training in special education law.[14]

This book is designed to provide that necessary training in special education legal literacy. When school employees, parents, and others are better informed about the legal rights of students with disabilities, they can prevent unnecessary anxiety, legal violations, and expensive litigation.[15] Additionally, with a better understanding of the legal system, individuals become empowered to advocate for the changes that they would like to occur in schools.

Ultimately, increasing special education legal literacy should also lead to better outcomes for students with disabilities.

Who Benefits from Reading this Book

A diverse group of readers—including school leaders, teachers, special education instructors/professors, attorneys, parents, and others—will find the content of this book relevant.

School Leaders. School leaders of all levels—including special education directors, superintendents, technology directors, curriculum coordinators, assistant principals, deans, directors of human resources, and others—will be able to learn how to apply special education law to their daily practice. While principals and superintendents may receive some legal training in their preparation programs, other school leaders may not. Nonetheless, all leaders must understand and comply with the law. To illustrate, deans must understand manifestation determinations and other discipline procedures unique to students with disabilities; technology directors must be knowledgeable about assistive technology devices and accommodations that some students are entitled to receive; and special education directors must navigate the nuances of disability law to ensure the district remains legally compliant.

Teachers. Although often overlooked, current and future teachers will also benefit from reading this book. Teachers are on the front lines in schools where most legal dilemmas originate. Often, they are the ones who provide the first response when legal issues arise. For example, teachers will be the first ones to recognize that a student's Individualized Education Program (IEP) may require specific provisions to address a behavior that impedes learning. Teachers also must provide testing accommodations for eligible students. In addition to these child-specific issues, classroom teachers who understand special education law are better able to advocate for themselves in order to ensure they have adequate resources and training to serve these students.

Special Education Instructors/Professors. Importantly, instructors in special education departments who are responsible for preparing future teachers and leaders will also benefit from this book. Because it includes an up-to-date summary of the most critical special education issues, professors may opt to use *A Guide to Special Education Law* as a textbook in their Introduction to Special Education, Special Education Law, Leadership in Special Education, and other courses. Professors can also utilize this book as they conduct research. It includes a comprehensive summary and analysis of all the major special education court cases—including the fifteen edited U.S. Supreme Court cases in the appendix.

Attorneys. When attorneys need to answer a question about a specific topic, such as specific timelines required for due process complaints, they can review the corresponding chapter.[16] The book will quickly provide them with most recent and relevant cases, as well as an analysis of the case law. Similar to law review articles, the book chapters focus on particular topics; however, the chapters are shorter in length and more general in scope. Therefore, the book is especially useful for attorneys who are new to special education litigation, or who only handle these cases occasionally.

Parents and Others. In addition to leaders, teachers, instructors, and attorneys, many others—particularly parents of children with disabilities—will find the book useful. The book will give parents a comprehensive description of special education law in a reader-friendly format. The book also is a great resource for those working with special education advocacy organizations, or federal or state education government entities.

Therefore, no matter the specific role, this book will provide diverse groups with the opportunity to increase their special education legal literacy. When special education legal literacy is increased, disputes may be prevented which, in turn, will save time and resources.

How the Book is Organized

The following eleven chapters provide a comprehensive overview of special education law. Multiple chapters provide legal updates based on the recent developments in special education law. For example, various authors discuss how the Every Student Succeeds Act—the 2015 legislation that replaced the No Child Left Behind Act—impacts students with disabilities. Other chapters describe what schools must do in light of recent U.S. Supreme Court precedent, particularly the *Fry v. Napoleon Community Schools*[17] and *Endrew F. v. Douglas Co. School District,*[18] both of which were decided in 2017.

In addition, each chapter provides a comprehensive outline of the legal rules that pertain to a particular topic of special education law that derive from statutes, regulations, and relevant court decisions. Every chapter concludes with practical implications and recommendations.

An appendix provides readers with edited case summaries of fifteen landmark U.S. Supreme Court decisions, including the most recent decisions issued in 2017.

The book begins with a chapter about the American legal system in general, describing sources of law, the judiciary system, legal resources, and legal citations. Following that introductory chapter, the book proceeds as follows:

Chapter 3: *Fundamentals of Federal Disability Law.* This chapter outlines the major tenets of the three federal disability statutes: Section 504, ADA, and the IDEA. It serves as an introduction to the more detailed chapters that follow.

Chapter 4: *Discrimination under Section 504 of the Rehabilitation Act and Americans with Disabilities Act.* Next, the attention turns to the federal laws that generally prohibit discrimination against students with disabilities. Readers will learn about important anti-discrimination statutes that can provide substantial educational support to students with disabilities who, for various reasons, may not qualify for "special education services" under the IDEA. This chapter discusses the application of Section 504 and the ADA to students with disabilities, parents with disabilities, and school employees with disabilities. It describes how disability is defined under these laws, and what reasonable accommodations schools may need to provide.

Chapter 5: *Qualifying for Special Education Services under IDEA.* The fifth chapter begins the in-depth discussion of the various aspects of the most important piece of federal legislation that governs special education law, known as IDEA. This particular chapter focuses on the processes by which local school districts identify and evaluate students who may be eligible for special education services under IDEA. Related issues, such as Child Find and Response-to-Intervention (RtI), are detailed, as well as a review of parental involvement in the evaluation process.

Chapter 6: *IEPs, Least Restrictive Environment, and Placement.* The next chapter describes IDEA's guarantee of a free appropriate public education (FAPE) through an individualized education program (IEP) for each eligible student with a disability. The authors provide guidance about the extent of educational benefit that schools must provide students, which was most recently at issue in *Endrew F. v. Douglas Co. School District*, a 2017 decision of the U.S. Supreme Court.[19] The authors also summarize the rights of parents to participate in the IEP process and the legal issues related to the least restrictive environment (LRE) principle, which requires that students are taught in general education classes, to the maximum extent that is appropriate. In providing examples of the interplay among IEPs, LRE, and placement, the authors reference the most recent IDEA amendments, regulations, and case law.

Chapter 7: *Related Services under the IDEA.* This chapter addresses an important topic, namely the IDEA's requirement that school districts also provide "related services" to students with disabilities. The chapter covers the statutory definition of related services, as well as the judiciary's application of that definition to a variety of services ranging from transportation to psychological counseling. It outlines school districts' fiscal responsibilities, the nature and scope of related services, and IDEA's limits regarding a private right of action. The author describes how medical and nursing services are treated differently under IDEA. Finally, the timely and important topic of the use of service animals in school, which was discussed in U.S. Supreme Court's 2017 decision in *Fry v. Napoleon Community Schools*, is considered.[20]

Chapter 8: *Secondary School Transition Planning.* In this chapter, the focus shifts to IDEA's goal of ensuring an effective transition from childhood to adulthood for students with disabilities. In addition to defining transition services, the author outlines what schools must do in terms of transition planning once students reach age sixteen. The chapter describes the history and current status of federal legislation-related transition planning and employment of individuals with disabilities, including Congress' recent enactment of the Workforce Innovation and Opportunity Act (WIOA). The topic of transition services is critically important to fulfilling IDEA's goals of establishing "economic self-sufficiency" for individuals with disabilities to the greatest extent possible.[21]

Chapter 9: *Disciplining Students with Disabilities.* Next, the book explains IDEA's discipline requirements. It highlights key considerations regarding discipline of students with disabilities that flow from the pertinent regulations under IDEA and case law, with particular attention to the concept of "change in placement" that can be triggered in certain circumstances. The chapter then discusses the several categories of removal, including: short-term removals (less than ten day) removals, long-term removals (including change of placement), and interim alternative educational settings (IAES). The chapter also discusses the legal issues surrounding restraint and seclusion of students with disabilities.

Chapter 10: *Parental Rights.* The following chapter examines parental rights under the IDEA. School districts must adhere to a number of parental rights, including rights to be notified of school district actions; rights to give consent before school officials may take certain actions; rights to meaningful participation in decision making about the child; rights to seek independent evaluation; rights to access records; and rights to file complaints and to seek dispute resolution. The chapter provides a comprehensive review of these important procedural safeguards which, as recognized by the U.S. Supreme Court over thirty years ago, were of great importance to Congress when it first enacted special education legislation.[22]

Chapter 11: *Procedural Safeguards: Resolving Family-School Disputes.* The concept of dispute resolution is expanded upon in this chapter. The author explains how IDEA provides detailed procedures to resolve disputes between schools and parents. Specifically, resolution sessions, mediation, administrative due process hearings, judicial review, and state complaints are described.

Chapter 12: *Current Issues in Special Education.* The final chapter summarizes the major legal developments that have occurred in recent years. Every major special education court decision from 2016 is summarized. The decisions are organized into the following categories: entitlement to services, procedural safeguards, dispute resolution, placement, related services, assistive technology, transition services, discipline, remedies, and discrimination.

Of course *A Guide to Special Education Law* could be read from cover to cover, but, depending on the reader's need, it can be used in multiple ways, including:

- **Go-to Resource.** Whenever legal dilemmas arise, readers can use the book as a helpful reference.

  E.g., after receiving a report that a student with a disability will be suspended, a principal could read the chapter about discipline to determine which steps to take next.

- **Textbook.** Instructors could assign reading selections from the book in a variety of courses.

  E.g., an instructor of a special education law course could prepare the course syllabus by forming classes and reading assignments based on the topics of each chapter.

- **Training Tool.** Human resource directors and other school leaders could use the book when developing in-service training for school employees.

  E.g., after receiving parental complaints that teachers are failing to follow students' behavioral plans, a special education director could develop training based on the relevant chapters.

- **Professional Learning Community Resource.** Teachers and other school employees could collectively discuss and review portions the book to better understand how to handle current issues they are facing.

  E.g., if teachers are concerned about bullying of students with disabilities, then the teachers could review the chapter on Discrimination under Section 504 and ADA to analyze how they should respond.

- **Research Database.** Special education law researchers could use the book to identify legal trends.

  E.g., a professor researching transition planning could analyze the collective body of relevant court decisions by reviewing the pertinent chapter.

The Benefits of Increasing Special Education Legal Literacy

In sum, anyone who would like to increase their knowledge about current legal issues affecting students with disabilities should review *A Guide to Special Education Law*. Readers will not only increase their own special education legal literacy, but also will be able to apply the information to their practice, teaching, or research. Once armed with a greater understanding of special education law, readers will be better able to make more informed decisions, prevent legal violations, and advocate for positive changes. Ultimately, increasing special education legal literacy will lead to better outcomes for students with disabilities.

Endnotes

[1] Perry A. Zirkel & Brent L. Johnson, *The "Explosion" in Education Litigation: An Updated Analysis*, 265 EDUC. L. REP. 1 (2011).

[2] Janet R. Decker & Kevin P. Brady, *Increasing School Employees' Special Education Legal Literacy*, 36 J. SCH. PUB. RELS. 231, 231 (2016).

[3] Janet R. Decker, *Legal Literacy in Education: An Ideal Time to Increase Research, Advocacy, and Action*, 304 EDUC. L. REP. 679 (2014); Matthew Militello, David Schimmel & H. Jake Eberwein, *If They Knew, They Would Change: How Legal Knowledge Impacts Principals' Practice*, 93 NAT'L ASS'N SECONDARY SCH. PRINCIPALS BULL. 27 (2009); David Schimmel & Matthew Militello, *Legal Literacy for Teachers: A Neglected Responsibility*, 77 HARV. EDUC. REV. 257 (2007); DAVID M. SCHIMMEL, SUZANNE E. ECKES & MATTHEW C. MILITELLO, PRINCIPALS TEACHING THE LAW: 10 LEGAL LESSONS YOUR TEACHERS MUST KNOW (2010).

[4] Decker, *supra* note 3, at 680; *See also* David Schimmel, *The Risks of Legally Illiterate Teachers: The Findings, the Consequences and the Solutions*, 6 U. MASS. L. REV. 37 (2011); David Schimmel, Matthew Militello & Suzanne Eckes, *Principals: An Antidote to Educational Malpractice*, EDUC. WK., June 8, 2011; Barry L. Bull & Martha M. McCarthy, *Reflections on the Knowledge Base in Law and Ethics for Educational Leaders*, 31 EDUC. ADMIN. Q. 613 (1995).

[5] Schimmel & Militello, *supra* note 3, at 257–258.

[6] Decker, *supra* note 3, at 681.

[7] For example, Professor Shaver is the parent of a child with a disability, a son who was diagnosed with autism in 1999, when he was 15 months old. He first received special education services from a public school district in 2001. Professor Shaver anticipates that her son will receive services until September 2020, when he will have his 22nd birthday.

[8] The age requirements for eligibility are discussed in detail in Chapter 5.

[9] Disciplinary issues are discussed in Chapter 9. Related services, including transportation and some medical services, are discussed in Chapter 7. Transition services are discussed in Chapter 8.

[10] For a discussion of the importance of parental participation of in educational programming, *see* Elizabeth A. Shaver, *Should the States Ban the Use of Non-Positive Interventions in Special Education? Reexamining Positive Behavior Supports under IDEA*, 44 STETSON L. REV. 147, 177 (2014).

[11] Elizabeth A. Shaver, *Every Day Counts: Proposals to Reform IDEA's Due Process Structure*, 66 CASE WESTERN L. REV. 143, 164-65 (2015).

[12] Schimmel & Militello, *supra* note 3, at 262.

[13] *See e.g.,* Decker & Brady, *supra* note 2; Antonis Katsiyannis & Maria Herbst, *Minimize Litigation in Special Education*, 40 INTERVENTION SCH. & CLINIC 106 (2004); Jennifer Y. Wagner & Antonis Katsiyannis, *Special Education Litigation Update: Implications for School Administrators*, 94 NASSP BULL. 40 (2010).

[14] Barbara L. Pazey & Heather A. Cole, *The Role of Special Education Training in the Development of Socially Just Leaders: Building an Equity Consciousness in Educational Leadership Programs*, 49 EDUC. ADMIN. Q. 243 (2013); Donica N. Davidson & Bob Algozzine, *Administrators' Perceptions of Special Education Law*. 15 J. SPEC. EDUC. LEADERSHIP 43 (2002).

[15] *See* Regina Umpstead, *et al.,* HOW TO PREVENT SPECIAL EDUCATION LITIGATION: EIGHT LEGAL LESSON PLANS (2015).

[16] Due Process and State Complaints are discussed in Chapter 11.

[17] 137 S. Ct. 743 (2017).

[18] 137 S. Ct. 988 (2017).

[19] 137 S. Ct. 988 (2017).

[20] 137 S. Ct. 743 (2017).

[21] 20 U.S.C. § 1400(c)(1) (2012).

[22] Bd. of Educ. of Hendrick Hudson Cent. Sch. Dist. v. Rowley, 458 U.S. 176, 205 (1983) ("[W]e think that the importance Congress attached to these procedural safeguards cannot be gainsaid").

Chapter 2

The American Legal System

Charles J. Russo and Allan G. Osborne, Jr.

Introduction

Pursuant to the Tenth Amendment of the Federal Constitution, education in the United States is a function of the states.[1] Even so, before any discussion of legal issues arising in the context of public education can take place, it is important to understand the legal framework under which American schools operate, on both the federal and state levels. Accordingly, this introductory chapter examines the sources and types of laws in the American legal system. The chapter also reflects on how these various types of laws interact as they impact the daily operations of public schools.

Sources of Law

Generally

There are four sources of law in the United States: constitutions, statutes, regulations, and judicial decisions. These sources of law exist at both the federal and state levels.

A constitution is the fundamental law of a nation or state.[2] A statute, on the other hand, is an act of a legislative body, or a law enacted by Congress or a state legislature.[3] All statutes must be consistent with the controlling constitutions within their jurisdiction. Many statutes are accompanied by implementing regulations or guidelines written by officials in the agencies responsible for their execution and enforcement. Regulations are usually more specific than the statutes they are designed to implement, because they construe legislative intent as to how laws should work in practice.

The many judicial opinions interpreting constitutions, statutes, and regulations comprise a body of law known as case, judge-made, or common law. Relying heavily on the notion of binding precedent—that a ruling of the highest court in a jurisdiction is binding on lower courts in that jurisdiction—case law provides insight into how judges apply constitutions, statutes, and regulations to different factual situations. Cases from other jurisdictions, known as persuasive precedent, have no binding effect on courts outside their jurisdictions. In other words, decisions of courts in one jurisdiction are not binding on those in other jurisdictions, but may have some influence on how other courts may interpret the law, as judges may look to see how other jurists have dealt with the same or similar issues. As an applied example, this means that decisions of the United States Supreme Court are binding on all American courts, while orders of the Supreme Court of Ohio are binding only in Ohio and are persuasive in all other jurisdictions.

Constitutions

Simply put, the Constitution of the United States is the law of the land. Consequently, all federal statutes and regulations, state constitutions, state laws and regulations, and ordinances of local governmental bodies, including school board policies, are subject to the Constitution as interpreted by the United States Supreme Court and other courts. Only a limited number of sections of the Federal Constitution are implicated in school-related cases. For the most part, the amendments protecting individual rights, such as the First, Fourth, Fifth, and Fourteenth amendments, are the sections of the Constitution impacting the operation of the schools most dramatically.

The Federal Constitution specifies the four duties of the federal and state governments. Article I, Section 8, identifies the first, or enumerated, powers, those exclusively within the purview of the federal government. These include the duty "to provide for the common Defence [sic] and general welfare of the United States ... [t]o regulate Commerce with foreign Nations, and among the several States ... [t]o coin Money, and regulate the value thereof ... [t]o promote Post Offices ..., [and] [t]o constitute Tribunals inferior to the Supreme Court."

The second set of powers are implied, meaning that they are reasonably necessary to carry out the express duties of the federal (or a state) government. For example, in providing for the national defense, the federal government has the implied authority to create the Department of Defense and subordinate offices necessary to carry out its duties, such as draft boards during times of war.

According to the Tenth Amendment, the third set of powers, reserved, are those not delegated to the federal government by the Constitution, or prohibited by it to the States or to the people. For the purposes of practitioners and students of education law, the most important reserved power is education. This is because, despite its coverage of a wide area of powers, duties, and limitations, the Constitution is silent with regard to education, thereby rendering it a responsibility of individual states. An example of the final power, concurrent—meaning that it is shared by both the federal and state governments—is taxation.

Along the same line, state constitutions are the supreme laws in their jurisdictions, with which all state statutes, regulations, and ordinances must conform. State constitutions typically deal with many of the same matters as their federal counterpart, but often provide greater detail when addressing education. In operation, insofar as state constitutions can grant their citizens greater, but not fewer, rights than the Federal Constitution, they are supreme within their boundaries.

Statutes and Regulations

As noted, under the Tenth Amendment to the Constitution, education is reserved to the states.[4] Yet, Congress has the authority to enact laws under the General Welfare Clause of Article I, Section 8, by offering funds for purposes it believes will serve the public good. For example, Congress enacted a series of statutes that forever altered the landscape of public education, starting with the Civil Rights Act of 1964,[5] which subjects public school systems to its anti-discrimination in employment provisions.

Federal statutes often make funds available to state and local governments conditioned on their acceptance of specific requirements for the use of the money. As discussed below, when states accept federal funds, educational officials are bound by whatever conditions Congress has attached to the legislation. If challenged, federal courts must be satisfied that the conditions pass constitutional muster.

In 1987, Congress expanded its authority by defining a "program or activity" as encompassing "all of the operations of [an entity] any part of which is extended Federal financial assistance."[6] This broad general prohibition covers "race, color or national origin,"[7] "sex,"[8] and "otherwise qualified handicapped individuals,"[9] categories that have become increasingly important in school settings. For instance, in order to receive funding for students who receive special education under the Individuals with Disabilities Education Act (IDEA)[10]—originally enacted in 1975 as the Education for All Handicapped Children Act—states, often through their local educational agencies or school boards, must develop detailed procedures to identify and assess children with disabilities before serving them by offering each qualified student a free appropriate public education in the least restrictive environment.

Another key example of federal involvement in education occurred when Congress superseded its most recent reauthorization of the Elementary and Secondary Education Act of 1965, as the controversial No Child Left Behind Act in 2002,[11] by enacting the Every Student Succeeds Act (ESSA) in late 2015.[12] The ESSA keeps many parts of the NCLB, but eliminates some of its more controversial elements, such as adequate yearly progress standards, while returning additional power to states.

Regulations promulgated by the Federal Department of Education and other administrative agencies grant the executive branch the means to implement statutes by carrying out their full effect. In other words, while statutes set broad legislative parameters, regulations allow administrative agencies to provide details to satisfy the requirements of the law. Regulations, which are presumptively valid, generally carry the full force of the law unless courts interpret them as conflicting with the legislation.

Most of the laws impacting public schools are statutes enacted by state legislatures. Although, as indicated, state legislatures are subject to the limitations of federal law and of state constitutions, they are relatively free to establish their own systems of education. The law is well settled that state and local boards of education, administrators, and teachers have the authority to adopt and enforce reasonable rules and regulations to ensure the smooth operation and management of schools. State and local rules and regulations are thus subject to the same constitutional limitations as statutes passed by legislative bodies. Accordingly, if it is unconstitutional for Congress or state legislatures to enact laws violating the free speech rights of students, it is impermissible for teachers to do so by creating rules that apply only in their classrooms. It is also important to note that legislation or rule-making on any level, whether federal or state, cannot conflict with higher authorities such as constitutions.

Common Law

The duty of the courts is to interpret the law. When there is no codified law, or if statutes or regulations are unclear, courts apply common law. Common law is basically judge-made law, meaning that the courts may interpret the law in light of new or changing circumstances. The collective decisions of the courts make up the body of common law. When disputes involve legislation, the duty of the courts is to uncover, as best they can, the intent of the legislative bodies that enacted statutes.

To the degree that judicial decrees establish precedent, judges provide a measure of certainty and predictability because in basing their judgments on the collected wisdom of earlier litigation, they do not have to "start from scratch" whenever new, or seemingly new, legal issues arise. In other words, as noted briefly above, when judges consider a novel point of law, they often look to see how other jurists have addressed the same or similar issues in other jurisdictions, but are not obligated to follow those judgments. In this way, judges have considerable weight in terms of providing guidance on how statutes and regulations are to be applied to everyday situations.

Judicial Systems

The federal court system and most state judicial systems have three levels. The lowest level in the federal system consists of trial courts known as district courts. Each state has at least one federal district court, while larger states, such as California and New York, may have as many as four. Federal district courts are the basic triers of fact in legal disputes; they review evidence and render decisions based on the evidence presented by the parties to disputes. Depending on the situations, trial courts may review the records of administrative hearings that have been conducted, hear additional evidence, and/or hear the testimony of witnesses.

Parties not satisfied with the judgment of a federal trial court case may appeal to the federal circuit court of appeals within which their state is located. For example, a decision handed down by a federal trial court in New York would be appealed to the Second Circuit, which, in addition to New York, includes the states of Connecticut and Vermont. There are thirteen federal judicial circuits in the United States, eleven of which are numbered and two of which are housed in Washington, D.C.

Parties displeased with the orders of circuit courts may seek further review from the United States Supreme Court. Due to the sheer volume of cases appealed each year, the Supreme Court accepts less than one percent of the disputes in which parties seek further review. Cases typically reach the Supreme Court in requests for a writ of *certiorari*, which literally means "to be informed of."

When the Supreme Court agrees to hear an appeal, it grants a writ of *certiorari*. At least four of the nine Justices must vote to grant certiorari in order for a case to be heard.[13] Denying a writ of *certiorari* has the effect of leaving a lower court's decision unchanged,[14] but is of no precedential value beyond the parties to the litigation.

Each of the fifty states and various territories has a similar arrangement to the federal scheme, except that the names of the courts vary. In most states, there are also three levels of courts: trial courts, intermediate appellate courts, and courts of last resort. It is important to take great care with the names of state courts. For instance, the highest court in most states is named the supreme court. Yet, in New York, the trial court is known as the Supreme Court, while the state's highest court is called the Court of Appeals, typically the name of intermediate appellate court in most other jurisdictions.

When courts render their judgments, their opinions are binding precedent only within their jurisdictions and are persuasive elsewhere. It should be kept in mind that the term jurisdiction can refer to either the types of cases that courts can hear—such as appeals generally or in specific areas of the law, such as a family or juvenile matters—or the geographic areas over which they have authority. However, in this situation, reference is made to the geographic area. More specifically, this means that a judgment of the federal district court for Massachusetts is binding only in Massachusetts. The federal district court in Rhode Island might find a decision of the Massachusetts court persuasive, but it is not bound by its order. Nonetheless, a ruling of the First Circuit Court of Appeals is binding on all states within its jurisdiction, and lower courts in those states must rule consistently. A decision by the Supreme Court of the United States is, of course, enforceable as binding precedent in all fifty states and American territories.

As indicated, the complex American judiciary operates at both the federal and state levels. The most common feature of these systems is a three-tiered system with trial courts, intermediate appellate panels, and courts of last resort, most commonly named supreme courts.

Trial courts have general jurisdiction, meaning that there are typically few limits on the types of cases that they may hear. Trial courts rely on the case specifics, apply the law to the circumstances, and are generally presided over by a single judge or justice.

Intermediate state appellate courts, often known as courts of appeal, review cases when one or both parties to disputes are dissatisfied with the judgments of the lower courts. Appellate courts are ordinarily not triers of fact; rather, these judicial panels review the lower courts' applications of the law. In rare cases, appellate panels may reject the factual findings of lower courts if they are convinced that they were clearly erroneous. Appellate courts usually consist of a panel of judges. By way of illustration, at the federal level, appeals are usually heard by panels of three judges. In unusual circumstances, a party in a federal court can petition a circuit court for an *en banc* appeal— literally, "in the bench"—meaning that all justices in the circuit participate in the oral arguments and decision.

Finally, disputes may be appealed to courts of last resort. At the federal level, this is the Supreme Court. The Supreme Court has discretion to review rulings of lower federal courts and state high courts involving federal constitutional, statutory, or regulatory issues.

Insofar as education is a state function and federal courts exist for federal matters, state courts resolve most educational disputes. Unless there are substantial federal questions, disagreements must be tried in state courts. If substantial federal questions are involved with matters of state law, disputes may be litigated in either state or federal courts. When federal courts examine cases involving both state and federal law, they must follow interpretations of state law made by the state courts within the jurisdictions in which they are seated because there is no such thing as federal common law.

Legal Resources

The written opinions of most courts are generally available in a variety of published formats. The official version of Supreme Court opinions are in the United States Reports, abbreviated U.S. The same opinions, with additional research aids that make it easier to locate specific points of law in the opinions, are published in the Supreme Court Reporter (S. Ct.) and the Lawyer's Edition, now in its second series (L. Ed. 2d).

Opinions of federal circuit courts of appeal are published in the Federal Reporter, now in its third series (F.3d); cases that are not selected for publication in F.3d appear in the Federal Appendix (cited as Fed. Appx. or Fed. App'x), but are of limited precedential value. Federal district court cases are published in the Federal Supplement, now in its third series (F. Supp. 3d).

State court cases are published in a variety of publications, most notably West's National Reporter system, which divides the country up into seven regions: Atlantic, North Eastern, North Western, Pacific, South Eastern, South Western, and Southern. Most education-related cases are also republished in West's *Education Law Reporter*, a specialized series that ordinarily includes peer-reviewed articles on point.

Before being published in hard-bound volumes, most judgments are released in what are known as slip opinions, a variety of loose-leaf services, and electronic sources. Many commercial services also publish decisions in specialized areas. For example, special education court cases, as well as the outcomes of due process hearings, are reproduced in a loose-leaf format in the *Individuals with Disabilities Education Law Reporter* (IDELR), published by LRP Publications.

Statutes and regulations are also accessible in a variety of similar formats. Federal statutes are published in the United States Code (U.S.C.), the official version, or the United States Code Annotated (U.S.C.A.), published by West Publishing Company. Agency regulations of the United States appear in the Code of Federal Regulations (C.F.R.). Copies of education statutes and regulations can be downloaded via links on the U.S. Department of Education's website. Legal materials are also available online from a variety of sources, most notably WestLaw and LexisNexis. State laws and regulations are commonly available online from the websites of their states.

Reading Legal Citations

Legal citations are fairly easy to read. The first number indicates the volume number where the case, statute, or regulation is located, followed by the abbreviation of the book or series in which the material may be published. The second number indicates the page on which a case begins or the section number of a statute or regulation; if a second number is present, it refers to the page on which a quote is published.

Other than the Supreme Court, which specifies just the year, the last parts of citations identify the names of the courts and the years in which the disputes were resolved. For example, *Board of Education of the Hendrick Hudson Central School District v. Rowley,* the Supreme Court's first case interpreting what is now known as the IDEA, was originally decided by the federal trial court for the Southern District of New York, 483 F. Supp. 528 (S.D.N.Y., 1980), affirmed by the Second Circuit, 632 F.2d 945, (2d Cir. 1980), but reversed by the Supreme Court, 458 U.S. 176, 102 S. Ct. 3034, 73 L.Ed.2d 690 [5 Educ. L. Rep. 34] (1982). This means that the official version of the Court's opinion, rendered in 1982, can be found in volume 458 of the United States Report, starting on page 176; the other citations read similarly.

The IDEA, 20 U.S.C. §§ 1400 *et seq.* (2005) can be found in Title 20 of the United States Code beginning with section 1400. The IDEA's regulations, 34 C.F.R. §§ 300.1 can be found at Title 34 of the Code of Federal Regulations, starting with section 300.1.

Endnotes

[1] *San Antonio Indep. Sch. Dist. v. Rodriguez,* 411 U.S. 1, 35, 93 S. Ct. 1278, 36 L.Ed.2d 16 (1975), wherein the Justices refused to intervene in a school finance dispute from Texas, the majority ruled that "[e]ducation, of course, is not among the rights afforded explicit protection under our Federal Constitution. Nor do we find any basis for saying it is implicitly so protected."

2   B. A. GARNER, BLACK'S LAW DICTIONARY (8th ed.) (2004).

3   *Id.*

4   *See* Epperson v. State of Ark., 393 U.S. 97, 104, 89 S. Ct. 266, 21 L.Ed.2d 228 (1968).

5   42 U.S.C.A. § 2000e–2a.

6   Civil Rights Restoration Act, 20 U.S.C.A. § 1687.

7   42 U.S.C.A. § 2000d.

8   20 U.S.C.A. § 1681.

9   29 U.S.C.A. § 794.

10   20 U.S.C.A. §§ 1400 *et seq.*

11   20 U.S.C.A. §§ 6301 *et seq.*

12   P.L. 114-95, Dec. 10, 2015, 129 Stat. 1814.

13   The so-called "Rule of Four" is a long-standing judicial creation despite the fact that Congress may have been mindful of it in enacting the Judiciary Act of 1925. Earlier, Congress created *certiorari*, or discretionary review, in 1890 in 26 Stat. 826, Sections 4–6.

14   GARNER, *supra* n. 2.

Chapter 3

Fundamentals of Federal Disability Law

Julie F. Mead

Introduction

Today's school leaders, teachers, and parents must have a working knowledge of federal disability law. That knowledge is essential to attend to the needs of a diverse student body and workforce, and to realize equity in all workings of a school.[1] The precepts of Section 504 of the Rehabilitation Act of 1973,[2] the Individuals with Disabilities Education Act,[3] and the Americans with Disabilities Act[4] affect classroom instruction, student discipline, hiring and supervision of staff, and school-family relationships. All three acts are premised on the notion that in order for individuals with disabilities to enjoy equal educational or employment opportunities, sometimes difference of treatment must be applied. For example, equity requires that some deaf children be furnished with a sign language interpreter in order to access the learning of the classroom. Likewise, equity may necessitate that a worker who uses a wheelchair for mobility be allowed to rearrange his office space in order to allow for better accessibility to the files and equipment necessary to do his job. Understanding the boundaries formed by these three federal disability statutes empowers leaders both by specifying what is required and by elucidating the degrees of freedom available for creative use of building and district resources. This chapter is designed to explore the major tenets of these important laws and to serve as an introduction to the more detailed chapters that follow.

Section 504 of the Rehabilitation Act of 1973

Of the three laws under focus here, Section 504 of the Rehabilitation Act of 1973 (Section 504) is the oldest and, in some ways, the simplest. As a civil rights statute, its purpose is straightforward: it bars discrimination on the basis of disability by any recipient of federal funds.[5] As such, it applies to all public schools in the United States and any private schools that also receive federal monies. Accordingly, schools and school districts must ensure that all the programs offered are accessible to persons with disabilities. As an anti-discrimination statute, its coverage extends from birth to death. Therefore, it

17

has implications for students, employees, parents, and members of the general public who wish to access the benefits created by a school.

School employees and parents are probably most familiar with Section 504's application to students. Those students who have a "physical or mental impairment which substantially limits one or more of such person's major life activities"[6] must receive an education comparable to that of their nondisabled peers.[7] Major life activities include, among others, walking, talking, hearing, seeing, breathing, and learning.[8] The disability may be permanent (e.g., a visual impairment, cerebral palsy, or attention deficit disorder) or temporary.[9] In the case of temporary disabilities, the issue is whether the disability substantially affects the person for a sufficient period of time. As the Office for Civil Rights (OCR) explained: "[t]he issue of whether a temporary impairment is substantial enough to be a disability must be resolved on a case-by-case basis, taking into consideration both the duration (or expected duration) of the impairment and the extent to which it actually limits a major life activity of the affected individual."[10] It should be noted, however, that Congress amended the definition of "disability" in 2008, clarifying that "transitory" disabilities with an actual or expected duration of less than six months are excluded from the definition of a person with a disability.[11] In addition, care must be taken so that personnel do not discriminate against a person based on a perceived disability where one does not exist,[12] because Section 504 also prohibits discrimination against a person who "has a history" of a disability[13] or "is regarded as having" a disability.[14] Even though persons in these categories do not have a disability that impairs function, the law's protections recognize that discrimination is no less abhorrent simply because the person or persons discriminating jumped to an erroneous conclusion. Whether or not the disability actually exists, Section 504 protects individuals from discriminatory treatment based on the status characteristic of disability.

Once a child with a disability is identified, Section 504 requires that he or she receives meaningful access to the educational program provided by a school. Providing an education comparable to that of nondisabled peers means that school personnel may be required to make reasonable accommodations in order that the student's disability does not serve as a barrier to how the child can access information or demonstrate learning.[15] Reasonable accommodations may be physical (e.g., Braille, preferential seating, a notetaker, assistance with carrying supplies) or instructional (e.g., a sign language interpreter, extended time on a test, vocabulary assistance) and may include special education and related services.[16] Accommodations are determined by staff members in consultation with the parents[17] and are outlined on an accommodation plan. Although technically the regulations do not require it,[18] most schools prudently use written accommodation plans.[19]

Ensuring nondiscriminatory access to children with disabilities also requires attention to issues of harassment and bullying.[20] As such, schools must investigate any complaint of disability harassment in a timely fashion and then take appropriate action. As OCR explained in 2014 guidance:

If a school's investigation reveals that bullying based on disability created a hostile environment—i.e., the conduct was sufficiently serious to interfere with or limit a student's ability to participate in or benefit from the services, activities, or opportunities offered by a school—the school must take prompt and effective steps reasonably calculated to end the bullying, eliminate the hostile environment, prevent it from recurring, and, as appropriate, remedy its effects. Therefore, OCR would find a disability-based harassment violation under Section 504 and Title II [of the ADA] when: (1) a student is bullied based on a disability; (2) the bullying is sufficiently serious to create a hostile environment; (3) school officials know or should know about the bullying; and (4) the school does not respond appropriately.[21]

Section 504 also has implications for hiring and working with staff. Again, the Act protects those individuals who have mental or physical impairments that substantially limit them, or have a history of such impairments, or are regarded as having such.[22] Just as students must be reasonably accommodated in order to access educational opportunities, employees' disabilities must be reasonably accommodated in order to access employment opportunities.[23] Reasonableness has its bounds, however, and employers are not required to substantially alter the qualifications or essential requirements of a job in order to accommodate a worker's disability.[24] In addition, the employer is not expected to bear undue administrative or financial burdens when considering accommodations.[25]

Parents with disabilities also enjoy protection under Section 504. Schools must ensure that parents with disabilities, through reasonable accommodations when necessary, have access to parent-teacher conferences and any meetings concerning the child's progress and behavior in school.[26] For example, a teacher planning to meet with a parent who utilizes a wheelchair for mobility would have to be sure the meeting place was accessible to the parent.

Chapter 4 provides a detailed discussion of Section 504 and the obligations it places on schools.

Americans with Disabilities Act

Using its Constitutional power to regulate interstate commerce,[27] Congress enacted the Americans with Disabilities Act (ADA) in 1990.[28] The ADA extends the nondiscrimination protections of Section 504 beyond recipients of federal financial support to private employers and commercial establishments.[29] The law is divided into five titles, as follows:

- Title I – prohibits employment discrimination.[30]

- Title II – applies to all subdivisions of state and local government, regardless of whether they receive federal financial assistance.[31] Students in public schools are protected under this title.[32]

- Title III – prohibits discrimination by businesses that serve the public (e.g., stores, restaurants, hotels and motels, etc.).[33] Title III's provisions also apply to non-sectarian private schools, although private schools are not held to the same programmatic accessibility standards as are public schools. Private schools need only accommodate those children with disabilities that can be served with minor adjustments to the academic program.[34]

- Title IV – applies to telecommunications services such as telephone and television companies.[35]

- Title V – contains several miscellaneous but important provisions, including a statement that the ADA should not be read to require lesser standards than those of Section 504;[36] that a state's immunity from suit under the Eleventh Amendment is abrogated by the ADA;[37] that ADA's provisions apply to Congress and all agencies of the legislative branch;[38] that the term "individual with a disability" does not include active drug users[39] or transvestites;[40] and that homosexuality and bisexuality are not "impairments" under the ADA, and that various other "conditions" are not included under the term "disability."[41]

Congress amended the ADA in 2008[42] in order to correct what legislators considered inappropriate interpretations of the act by the U.S. Supreme Court.[43] The revisions clarify the definition of "major life activities"[44] and direct that "[a]n impairment that substantially limits one major life activity need not limit other major life activities in order to be considered a disability."[45] Moreover, the consideration of whether a disability substantially limits a person "shall be made without regard to the ameliorative effects of mitigating measures."[46] Finally, the revisions direct that reviewing courts should construe the definition of a disability "in favor of broad coverage of individuals under this Act."[47]

Even with these clarifications, Title II of the ADA largely mirrors the requirements of Section 504 with respect to the protections for students in the public school classroom and, accordingly, the requirements of both acts are often jointly referred to as "Section 504/ADA."[48] For public schools, then, additional ADA requirements often relate to construction and renovation requirements associated with physical accessibility.

Individuals with Disabilities Education Act

The Individuals with Disabilities Education Act (IDEA) is without doubt the most prescriptive of the three acts with regard to the educational experience of children with disabilities. First enacted in 1975 under the title, the Education for All Handicapped Children's Act (EAHCA),[49] Congress renamed the statute the Individuals with Disabilities Education Act (IDEA) in 1990, at the same time it enacted the ADA. Unlike Section 504 and the ADA, the IDEA is a funding statute, rather than a civil rights statute.[50] It provides funds to assist states to meet the needs of students whose disabilities "adversely affect a child's educational performance"[51] such that special education and related services are needed.[52] This piece of child welfare legislation serves as a complement to Section 504. You might say that Section 504 is the "stick" (punishing those who violate it by termination of federal funds), while the IDEA is the "carrot" (providing financial incentives for the appropriate delivery of special education[53] and related services[54]).

Therefore, a student with disabilities who is protected against discrimination under Section 504/ADA may not meet the more narrow definitions of disability to be able to qualify for services under the IDEA. To be eligible under IDEA, the student's profile of needs and abilities must match the definition of one or more disability categories specified by the IDEA.[55] These disability categories are "intellectual disabilities, hearing impairments (including deafness), speech or language impairments, visual impairments (including blindness), serious emotional disturbance . . ., orthopedic impairments, autism, traumatic brain injury, other health impairments, or specific learning disabilities."[56] Thus, those served under the IDEA are a subset of those protected under Section 504/ADA. For example, a child with a life-threatening food allergy would be protected from discrimination under Section 504 and the ADA, but may not qualify as a "child with a disability" under the IDEA. In addition, a child could have an impairment (e.g., a visual impairment or health-related issue) that is not severe enough to "adversely affect[] ...educational performance" as required by the regulations to qualify for services under the IDEA.[57] However, that child may still be entitled to accommodations under Section 504/ADA in order to receive an education comparable to students who are not disabled.

The IDEA is an extremely detailed law that requires school districts to document and justify the services provided to eligible children with disabilities. The IDEA creates a federal statutory right, or an entitlement, for each student with a disability. That entitlement is known as the right to a free appropriate public education (FAPE), which consists of special education and related services designed to address the unique needs of the individual child.[58] The law creates an affirmative obligation on the part of the state and its local school districts to identify and serve all eligible students with disabilities within their geographic boundaries.[59] This obligation to identify, locate, and serve children with disabilities also extends to those children whose parents have chosen to enroll them in private schools.[60] Students may be referred for evaluation by any school personnel or by parents. Once referred, the school district must review the child's records and design a series of assessments in order to determine whether the suspicions of a disability are founded.[61] Parents must be provided notice of their rights under the law, and must consent in writing to an evaluation before any testing may commence.[62] Once the evaluation is complete, the school personnel meet with the parents as an "IEP team" to determine eligibility together.[63] As mentioned before, the mere presence of a disability does not qualify a child for services under the IDEA.[64] Rather, eligibility is dependent on whether the disability adversely affects educational performance such that special education is needed, the degree to which may be further specified in the state's plan of service.[65] Chapter 5 describes the particulars of the IDEA evaluation and eligibility process.

Once eligibility is determined, the IEP team, which includes the parents, collaborates to produce an individualized education program (IEP).[66] The IEP is a document that delineates measurable annual goals for the child and specifies the kind and nature of services to be provided to or on behalf of the child.[67] As such, the IEP is the document by which FAPE is defined for an individual child—an individualized equity plan, if you will. Note that FAPE does not have a unitary definition under the law;[68] that is, what constitutes FAPE for one child may not provide FAPE for another. A child's unique needs dictate the goals, objectives, and services defined by the IEP. This fact reveals a foundational characteristic of the IDEA. All decisions must be based on individualized determinations of need, as opposed to considerations of group instruction or programmatic design. You might say the "I" looms large in the IDEA.

In 1982, the Supreme Court provided further explanation of FAPE and what it requires, with particular focus on the meaning of the word "appropriate." The Court explained that FAPE does not require that a child's potential be maximized, but rather that the IEP be "reasonably calculated to enable the child to receive educational benefits."[69] FAPE is a "basic floor of opportunity,"[70] a minimum level of service below which a district may not go.[71] Recently, the Supreme Court clarified the standard for FAPE, declaring that "[t]o meet its substantive obligation under the IDEA, a school must offer an IEP reasonably calculated to enable a child to make progress appropriate in light of the child's circumstances."[72]

Once the IEP team determines the child's IEP goals and objectives, the team must determine the issue of placement.[73] The IDEA requires that children with disabilities be educated in the least restrictive environment (LRE), another central principle of the IDEA. LRE requires that children be educated with their nondisabled peers to the "maximum extent appropriate."[74] The LRE principle was codified in the original EAHCA, and amendments made to the IDEA in 1997 and 2004 strengthened this principle by creating a strong presumption in favor of educating children with disabilities in traditional classroom settings.[75] The IEP team must first consider how the child's needs can be met in the regular class environment. This consideration must include a discussion of the curricular adaptations and supports, supplemental aids, and services that may make it possible to deliver the child's IEP in the general classroom.[76] However, even given that strong presumption of regular class placement with support, the LRE for some students may require placement in other than the regular classroom for part or all of the school day.[77] It is incumbent upon school personnel to show why, given the "nature and severity of the [child's] disability,"[78] and even with the addition of supplementary aids and services, as well as curricular adaptations and supportive services, FAPE cannot be achieved in the regular class setting for part or all of the child's school day. To that end, the law requires that school districts make available a "continuum of alternative placements" (e.g., resource rooms, special classes, special schools),[79] but that these other placements only be used when equity demands such a difference.

If a child's poor performance in the regular class motivates the IEP team to reexamine the appropriateness of a placement, it is helpful to note that the provisions of the IDEA essentially offer two explanations for such a problem: either the child is inadequately supported in the traditional classroom, or the child is inappropriately placed in that setting. The law requires that the IEP team carefully examine the first question before considering the second.

It is also important for all staff to comprehend that LRE is related to, but is not synonymous with, "inclusion." Inclusion is an educational philosophy defined as "providing all students within the mainstream appropriate educational programs which are challenging and yet geared to their capabilities and needs as well as any support and assistance they and/or their teachers may need to be successful in the mainstream."[80] Some even argue that all students with disabilities should be included at all times, regardless of the nature and severity of their disabilities. This stance, often referred to as "full inclusion," is inconsistent with the IDEA. The IDEA does not require that students with disabilities be included as much as *possible*—it requires that students with disabilities be included as much as *appropriate*.[81] The IDEA is predicated on the principle that sometimes appropriateness (that is, equity) requires something other than what is traditional to meet the unique needs of an individual child. However, it is certainly true that for most students with disabilities, an individualized examination of the needs of the child and the appropriate settings to address those needs will result in an "included" placement for all or part of the school day. Chapter 6 addresses provisions in the law regarding IEPs, least restrictive environment, and placement. Chapter 7 discusses the requirement to provide "related services" under the IDEA. Chapter 8 details requirements for transition services, which are those services that will enable a child to transition from school to work or college.

The final core component of the IDEA is procedural protections.[82] In order to protect the child's entitlement and to ensure that all decision making occurs in the proper context, the IDEA mandates detailed procedural requirements and safeguards. If parents believe that the school is not providing at least an appropriate education for their child, they can challenge the district through a "due process" hearing.[83] This hearing is presided over by an impartial hearing officer supplied by the state. The hearing officer makes findings of fact, and then applies the law to the facts of the situation.[84] Parents may challenge any decision relative to the process (e.g., evaluation, eligibility, appropriateness, placement). Likewise, if the district believes that parents are obstructing the school's ability to meet its obligation of FAPE for the child by refusing to consent to an evaluation, the district may request a due process hearing to settle the dispute.[85] Hearing decisions may be appealed in state or federal court.[86] Provisions also require school districts to make available mediation as a mechanism for resolving any dispute with parents and avoiding the more adversarial hearing process.[87] Chapters 10 and 11 describe parental rights and the dispute resolution process in detail.

Another major addition to the law in 1997, and revised in 2004, includes the creation of provisions detailing procedural safeguards for children with disabilities facing disciplinary sanctions.[88] These provisions essentially codify earlier case law and require disciplinarians to ensure that children with disabilities are treated equitably by the process.[89] The particulars of the discipline provisions are detailed in Chapter 9.

Finally, case law has established that parents who prevail at the hearing or in court may be entitled to remedies under the court's broad authority to fashion "such relief as the court determines is appropriate."[90] These remedies include recovery of attorney fees;[91] reimbursement of costs, including tuition costs borne by the parent;[92] and compensatory education.[93]

Recommendations for Practice

This chapter has provided an overview of federal disability law as it applies to public schools today. Subsequent chapters will further elaborate on these themes. They include the following:

- Chapter 4: Discrimination under Section 504 of the Rehabilitation Act and Americans with Disabilities Act
- Chapter 5: Qualifying for Special Education Services under IDEA
- Chapter 6: IEPs, Least Restrictive Environment, and Placement
- Chapter 7: Related Services under the IDEA
- Chapter 8: Secondary School Transition Planning
- Chapter 9: Disciplining Students with Disabilities
- Chapter 10: Parental Rights
- Chapter 11: Procedural Safeguards: Resolving Family-School Disputes

Considering the issues related to this topic, those with an interest in the application of federal disability law to public schools should consider the following recommendations for practice:

1. Develop a full understanding of federal disability law and its application to schools.

2. Develop a firm grasp of state laws and regulations that complement these federal laws. Particular attention should be paid to provisions that heighten the standards or requirements set by federal law.

3. Fully examine local policies and procedures that have been created to fulfill the obligations created by these laws.

4. Periodically review local policies to be certain they are current and accurately reflect the federal and state laws upon which they are founded.

5. Determine who can serve as a network of support within the school, the district, and the community to help all staff and family members understand these laws and to help keep abreast of changes in the law.

6. Provide staff development opportunities so that all staff members understand their responsibilities under the law.

7. Cultivate relationships to leverage the expertise of various entities with a mutual interest in the topic, including schools, school districts, professional organizations, disability advocacy groups, and parent groups. Doing so allows the school and school district to establish the kind of cooperative relationships envisioned between parents and school personnel in the IDEA.

8. Find a mechanism for remaining current with the developments in this rapidly evolving area of school law. Numerous organizational and commercial newsletters, including updates through email or social media, serve this function. In addition, school districts and parents may utilize a law firm that provides such updates on either a regular or as-needed basis. School personnel should be sure to be on the "routing list" for any such publications received by the school district.

Endnotes

* Judith I. Risch contributed to earlier versions of this chapter.
1 This chapter builds, in part, on sections of Julie Mead, *"The Legal Foundations of Equity: Protecting Access to Education,"* in FOUNDATIONS OF DEMOCRATIC EDUCATION, (M.J. O'Hair, *et. al.*, eds. 2000).
2 29 U.S.C. § 794 (2012): 34 C.F.R. § 104.1 *et seq.* (2016).
3 20 U.S.C. § 1400 *et seq.* (2012); 34 C.F.R. § 300.1 *et seq.* (2016).
4 42 U.S.C. § 12101 *et seq.* (2012).
5 29 U.S.C. § 794 (2012).
6 34 C.F.R. § 104.3(j)(1)(i) (2016).
7 34 C.F.R. § 104.3(k)(2) (2016).
8 34 C.F.R. § 104.3(j)(2)(ii) (2016).
9 *See, e.g.,* In re Castillo v. Schriro, 15 N.Y.S.3d 645 (N.Y. Sup. Ct. 2015); Antone v. Nobel Learning Communities, Inc., No. 11-3717 2012 WL 174960 (D.N.J. Jan. 19, 2012); Davis (CA) Joint Unified Sch. Dist. 31 IDELR 186 (OCR 1999).
10 *Protecting Students with Disabilities: Frequently Asked Questions about Section 504 and the Education of Children with Disabilities,* U.S. DEP'T. OF EDUC., http://www2.ed.gov/about/offices/list/ocr/504faq.html (last visited Sept. 12, 2016).
11 42 U.S.C. § 12102(3)(B) (2012). The revisions were made as part of the 2008 Amendments Act to the ADA, which included a conforming provision that likewise revises the meaning of "disability" under Section 504. *See* Pub. L. No. 110-325, § 7, 122 Stat. 3553 (2008).

[12] 34 C.F.R. § 104.3(j)(2) (2016).

[13] 34 C.F.R. § 104.3(j)(1)(ii) (2016).

[14] 34 C.F.R. § 104.3(j)(1)(iii) (2016).

[15] 34 C.F.R. § 104.34(a) (2016).

[16] 34 C.F.R. § 104.33(b) (2016).

[17] 34 C.F.R. § 104.35(c) (2016).

[18] 34 C.F.R. §§104.31 – 104.39 (2016).

[19] *See, e.g., A Parent and Teacher Guide to Section 504: Frequently Asked Questions*, FLA. DEP'T. OF EDUC., http://www.fldoe.org/core/fileparse.php/7690/urlt/0070055-504bro.pdf.

[20] Catherine Lhamon, Dear Colleague Letter, U.S. DEP'T. OF EDUC., (Oct., 21, 2014), https://www2.ed.gov/about/offices/list/ocr/letters/colleague-bullying-201410.pdf.

[21] *Id.* at 4.

[22] 34 C.F.R. § 104.3 (2016).

[23] 34 C.F.R. § 104.11(a)(1) (2016).

[24] 34 C.F.R. § 104.12(a) (2016).

[25] Southeastern Cmty. Coll. v. Davis, 442 U.S.397 (1979).

[26] Rothschild v. Grottenthaler, 907 F.2d. 286 (2d Cir. 1990).

[27] United States Constitution, Article 1, Section 8, Clause 3 ("Congress shall have Power... to regulate Commerce with foreign Nation, and among the several States...").

[28] Pub. L. No. 101-336, 104 Stat. 327 (1990).

[29] 42 U.S.C. § 12101 (2012).

[30] 42 U.S.C. §§ 12111-12117 (2012).

[31] 42 U.S.C. §§ 12131-12165 (2012).

[32] *Questions and Answers on the ADA Amendments of 2008 for Students with Disabilities Attending Public Elementary and Secondary Schools*, U.S. DEP'T. OF EDUC., http://www2.ed.gov/about/offices/list/ocr/docs/dcl-504faq-201109.html (last visited Sept. 20, 2016).

[33] 42 U.S.C §§ 12181-12189 (2012).

[34] *See, e.g.*, U.S. Department of Justice, Civil Rights Division, *Justice Department Settles with Private Montessori School to Prevent Disability Discrimination* (Sept. 29, 2014), https://www.justice.gov/opa/pr/justice-department-settles-private-montessori-school-prevent-disability-discrimination (last visited Sept. 12, 2016).

[35] 47 U.S.C. § 225 (2012).

[36] 42 U.S.C. §§ 12201-12213 (2012).

[37] 42 U.S.C. § 12202 (2012).

[38] 42 U.S.C. § 12209 (2012).

[39] 42 U.S.C. § 12210 (2012).

[40] 42 U.S.C. § 12208 (2012).

[41] 42 U.S.C. § 12211(a) and b) (2012) (conditions enumerated include, among others, pedophilia, exhibitionism, voyeurism, compulsive gambling, kleptomania, and pyromania).

[42] *See* Pub. L. No. 110-325, 122 Stat. 3553 (2008).

[43] *Id.* at § 2, citing Sutton v. United Air Lines, Inc., 527 U.S. 471 (1999) and Toyota Motor Mfg., Ky., Inc. v. Williams, 534 U.S. 184 (2002).

[44] 42 U.S.C. § 12102(2)(A) (2012) ("major life activities include, but are not limited to, caring for oneself, performing manual tasks, seeing, hearing, eating, sleeping, walking, standing, lifting, bending, speaking, breathing, learning, reading, concentrating, thinking, communicating, and working.").

[45] 42 U.S.C. § 12102(4)(C) (2012).

[46] 42 U.S.C. § 12102(4)(E)(i) (2012). Mitigating measures include "medication, medical supplies, equipment, or appliances, low-vision devices (which do not include ordinary eyeglasses or contact lenses), prosthetics including limbs and devices, hearing aids and cochlear implants or other implantable hearing devices, mobility devices, or oxygen therapy equipment and supplies." 42 U.S.C. § 12102(4)(E)(i)(I) (2012).

[47] 42 U.S.C. § 12102(4)(A) (2012).

[48] *See, e.g.,* Perry A. Zirkel, *A National Update of Case Law 1998 to the Present under the IDEA and Section 504/A.D.A.,* NAT'L. ASS'N. OF STATE DIRECTORS OF SPECIAL EDUC., http://www.nasdse.org/LinkClick.aspx?fileticket=gDUBs9sKzRw%3d&tabid=578 (last visited Sept. 20, 2016).

[49] Pub. L. No. 94-142, 89 Stat. 773 (1975).

[50] 20 U.S.C. § 1400(d)(1) (2012).

[51] 34 C.F.R. § 300.8 (2016).

[52] 20 U.S.C. § 1401(3)(A)(ii) (2012).

[53] 20 U.S.C. § 1401(29) (2012), ("The term 'special education' means specially designed instruction, at no cost to parents, to meet the unique needs of a child with a disability, including--(A) instruction conducted in the classroom, in the home, in hospitals and institutions, and in other settings; and (B) instruction in physical education.")

[54] 20 U.S.C. § 1401(26) (2012) ("The term 'related services' means transportation, and such developmental, corrective, and other supportive services (including speech-language pathology and audiology services, interpreting services, psychological services, physical and occupational therapy, recreation, including therapeutic recreation, social work services, school nurse services designed to enable a child with a disability to receive a free appropriate public education as described in the individualized education program of the child, counseling services, including rehabilitation counseling, orientation and mobility services, and medical services, except that such medical services shall be for diagnostic and evaluation purposes only) as may be required to assist a child with a disability to benefit from special education, and includes the early identification and assessment of disabling conditions in children.").

[55] 20 U.S.C. § 1401(3) (2012); 34 C.F.R. § 300.8 (2016).

[56] 20 U.S.C. § 1401(3) (2012).

[57] 34 C.F.R. § 300.8 (2016).

[58] 20 U.S.C. § 1401(9) (2012).

[59] 20 U.S.C. § 1412(a)(3). IDEA uses the terms state education agency (SEA), 20 U.S.C. § 1401(32) (2012), and local education agency (LEA). 20 U.S.C. § 1401(19) (2012). It should be noted that some charter schools may be LEAs for the purposes of IDEA. 20 U.S.C. § 1413(e)(1)(B) (2012).

[60] 20 U.S.C. § 1412 (a)(3)(A) (2012); 34 C.F.R. § 300.111 (2016). The rights afforded children enrolled by their parents in private settings are not coextensive with those of children in the public setting. These students enjoy only a group entitlement as opposed to an individual one and must be served "consistent with [their] number and location." 20 U.S.C. § 1412 (a)(10)(A) (2012); 34 C.F.R. § 300.132 (2016). In addition, IDEA only requires LEAs to expend federal dollars on those children in private schools and makes no requirements for the expenditure of state or local funds, 20 U.S.C. § 1412 (a)(10)(A)(i)(I) (2012); 34 C.F.R. § 300.133(c) (2016). Of course, states may impose additional requirements through state statutes.

[61] 20 U.S.C. § 1414 (b)(2) (2012).

[62] 20 U.S.C. § 1414 (a)(1)(D) (2012).

[63] IEP refers to the Individualized Education Program. 20 U.S.C. § 1401(14) (2012). Chapter 5 details the required composition of IEP teams and the processes used in determining eligibility of a child under the IDEA. Chapter 6 details the required elements of an IEP and factors related to its implementation.

[64] Although mere presence of a disability does qualify a child for *protection from discrimination* and an education comparable to that of non-disabled peers under Section 504/ADA. *See* Discussion of Section 504, *supra,* and Chapter 4.

[65] 34 C.F.R. § 300.100 (2016).

[66] 20 U.S.C. § 1414(d) (2012).

[67] The IEP should also specify any curricular adaptations, supports, supplementary aids, and services. 20 U.S.C. § 1414 (d)(1)(A)(i)(IV) (2012); 34 C.F.R. § 300.320(a)(3) (2016).

[68] Board of Educ. of Hendrick Hudson Cent. Sch. Dist. v. Rowley, 458 U.S. 176, 202 (1982) (declining to establish a single test to determine whether FAPE has been provided).

[69] *Id.* at 207.   However, state law may place requirements for a higher level of service on its LEAs.

[70] *Id.* at 201.

[71] *Id.* at 200 (citations omitted).

[72] Endrew F. v. Douglas Cty. Sch. Dist., 137 S.Ct. 988 (2017).

[73] 20 U.S.C. § 1414(e) (2012); 34 C.F.R. § 300.327 (2016).

[74] 20 U.S.C. § 1412(a)(5) (2012).

[75] S. Rep. No. 105-17, (1997), *available at* 1997 WL 244967; *see also* Julie F. Mead, *Expressions of Congressional Intent: Examining the 1997 Amendments to the IDEA*, 127 West Educ. L. Rep. 511(1998).

[76] 20 U.S.C. § 1414(d)(1)(A)(i)(V) (2012); 34 C.F.R. § 320(a)(5) (2016).

[77] *See, e.g.*, Baquerizo v. Garden Grove Unified Sch. Dist., 826 F.3d 1179 (9th Cir. 2016); T.M. v. Cornwall Cent. Sch. Dist., 752 F.3d 145 (2nd Cir. 2014); Houston Indep. Sch. Dist. v. V.P. *ex rel.* Juan P., 582 F.3d 576 (5th Cir. 2009).

[78] 20 U.S.C. § 1412(a)(5) (2012).

[79] 34 C.F.R. § 300.115 (2016).

[80] William Stainback, Support Networks for Inclusive Schooling: Interdependent Integrated Education, 3 (1990).

[81] 20 U.S.C. § 1412(a)(5) (2012).

[82] 20 U.S.C. § 1415 *et.seq.* (2012).

[83] 20 U.S.C. § 1415(f) (2012).

[84] 20 U.S.C. § 1415(h) (2012).

[85] 20 U.S.C. § 1414(a)(1)(D)(ii)(I) (2012).

[86] 20 U.S.C. § 1415(i)(2) (2012).

[87] 20 U.S.C. § 1415(e) (2012).

[88] 20 U.S.C. § 1415(k) (2012).

[89] *See also* Mead, *supra* note 74, at 524 ("Essentially these provisions, like the judicial interpretations from which they stem, demonstrate that when school officials consider the discipline of students with disabilities they must ask three critical questions to ensure that the disciplinary sanction does not result in discrimination on the basis of disability and to ensure equity: (1) Is the behavior a manifestation of the disability? (2) Does the disciplinary consequence result in a change of placement thereby invoking the procedures of IDEA? and (3) Was the child receiving an appropriate programming [sic] at the time the misbehavior occurred?").

[90] 20 U.S.C. § 1415(i)(2)(C) (2012).

[91] 20 U.S.C. § 1415(i)(3) (2012).

[92] School Comm. of Town of Burlington v. Dep't of Educ. of Mass., 471 U.S. 359 (1985); Florence Cty. Sch. Dist. Four v. Carter, 510 U.S. 7 (1993).

[93] *See, e.g.*, B.D. v. District of Columbia, 817 F.3d 792 (D.C. Cir. 2016); Doe v. East Lyme Bd. of Educ., 790 F.3d 440 (2nd Cir. 2015); Ferren C. v. Sch. Dist. of Phila., 612 F.3d 712 (3d Cir. 2010). For a general discussion of remedies under the IDEA, *see* Dixie Snow Huefner and Cynthia M. Herr, Navigating Special Education Law and Policy, 61-274 (2012).

Chapter 4

Discrimination under Section 504 of the Rehabilitation Act and Americans with Disabilities Act

Allan G. Osborne, Jr.

Introduction

Two civil rights statutes, Section 504 of the Rehabilitation Act of 1973 (Section 504)[1] and the Americans with Disabilities Act (ADA),[2] as amended, prohibit discrimination against individuals with disabilities. Section 504, which applies only to recipients of federal funds, prohibits such recipients from discriminating against individuals with disabilities in the provision of services or employment. Section 504 applies to any agency that receives federal funds; thus, it applies to all public schools and many private schools. The ADA extends Section 504's coverage to the private sector. To the extent that the two statutes are similar, lawsuits alleging discrimination in the context of public schools are usually filed under both acts and their disposition is often identical.

Individuals are considered to have disabilities under Section 504 and the ADA if they have physical or mental impairments that substantially limit one or more of their major life activities, have a record of such impairments, or are regarded as having such impairments.[3] Major life activities are "functions such as caring for oneself, performing manual tasks, walking, seeing, hearing, speaking, breathing, learning, and working."[4] The ADA Amendments Act of 2008 expanded upon this list by adding the following major life activities: "eating, sleeping, walking, standing, lifting, bending, speaking, breathing, learning, reading , concentrating, thinking, communicating," and the operation of major bodily functions.[5] It is important to note that this list is not exhaustive.[6] According to a Dear Colleague Letter issued by the U.S. Department of Education's Office for Civil Rights in 2012, "Congress intended to ensure a broad scope of protection…and to convey that the question of whether an individual's impairment is a disability under the ADA and Section 504 should not demand extensive analysis."[7] This expansion upon the definition of a disability was an effort to return to the original intent of the law, which Congress believed had been inaccurately narrowed through the Supreme Court's interpretation as evidenced in case law.[8] In general, individuals are otherwise qualified for purposes of Section 504 and the ADA if they are capable of meeting all of a program's requirements in spite of their disability.[9] If individuals are otherwise qualified, recipients of federal funds are expected to make reasonable accommodations for their disabilities, unless doing so would create an undue hardship.[10]

Individuals are not considered to have disabilities for purposes of Section 504 and the ADA if their major life activities are not substantially limited by the condition.[11] Although prior case law found that short-term conditions,[12] or those that can be mitigated, were not considered to be impairments under Section 504,[13] the ADA Amendments Act of 2008 clarified that the term *substantially limits* should be broadly interpreted and the determination made "without regard to the ameliorative effects of mitigating measures."[14] The only exceptions are eyeglasses and contact lenses. It remains to be decided on a case-by-case basis whether particular temporary impairments constitute disabilities. For example, impairments that are episodic or in remission may be considered to be disabilities if they substantially limit major life activities when active.[15] However, Congress determined that an individual is not regarded as having a disability if the impairment is minor, or lasts six months or less.[16]

This chapter discusses the application of Section 504 and the ADA to three distinct groups of individuals present in the educational setting. Students with disabilities at the elementary and secondary level are protected by and have rights under Section 504 and the ADA, as well as the Individuals with Disabilities Education Act (IDEA).[17] Although there are exceptions, for the most part, any student covered by the IDEA would also be covered under Section 504 and the ADA;[18] however, the reverse is not always true. Many students who are not eligible under the IDEA are still entitled to the anti-discrimination protections of Section 504 and the ADA. For example, a student with physical challenges who does not require special education and related services would not be entitled to the provisions of the IDEA, but would be entitled to accommodations under Section 504 and the ADA.

Under Section 504 and the ADA, schools may not discriminate against parents who are disabled. Thus, schools must provide accommodations to parents with disabilities to allow them to participate in activities that are essential to the education of their children. For example, schools must provide reasonable accommodations to allow parents with disabilities to participate in parent-teacher conferences and attend school functions.

School employees are entitled to the protections of Section 504 and the ADA. Employers are required to provide reasonable accommodations to otherwise qualified employees who have disabilities. However, as will be discussed later in this chapter, there are limits as to how far employers must go to provide reasonable accommodations.

Legal Issues

Students

As stated above, students with disabilities are entitled to the protections of Section 504 and the ADA, as well as the IDEA. Section 504 and the IDEA specifically entitle students to a free appropriate public education (FAPE). Like the IDEA, Section 504 does not require a school board to provide students with disabilities with an education that maximizes potential; it only requires reasonable accommodations that will give a student with disabilities the same access to the benefits of a public education that is provided to all students.[19] Usually compliance with the IDEA will translate into compliance with Section 504. Thus, if a school district provides a FAPE under the provisions of the IDEA, the school district also will meet its obligations under Section 504.[20] In fact, the same process may be used to determine if a student is eligible to receive services under either statute.[21] When a student with disabilities is not entitled to services under the IDEA, a school board still may be required to provide educational services under Section 504 so that the student's needs can be met as adequately as the needs of students who do not have disabilities.[22]

Services are typically provided under what is commonly known as a Section 504 service plan. Section 504 does not spell out what should be contained in such a plan, nor even that it has to be written. Even so, it is best to develop written service plans that include demographic information about the students, along with detailed information about the students' impairments and the accommodations or services that will be provided.[23]

Schools cannot exclude students from any of their programs simply because the students have disabilities. For example, courts have ruled that schools cannot exclude a student who has AIDS absent evidence that the student poses a health risk to his classmates or teachers.[24] Similarly, schools may not exclude students who have other health impairments[25] or other disabilities, such as mental retardation,[26] learning disabilities,[27] or attention deficit hyperactivity disorder (ADHD).[28] Public schools may not exclude students with disabilities for behavior that is a manifestation of their disabilities; however, disruptive or dangerous students may be moved to more restrictive environments.[29]

Students with disabilities may not be subjected to differential treatment because of their disabilities or because of the accommodations they receive. In one high-profile case, a court issued an injunction to prevent a school board from adopting a new policy that would allow for multiple valedictorians.[30] The court found that the proposed policy was intended and designed to have a particular exclusionary effect on a student with disabilities who earned the valedictorian honor under the former policy. In the court's view, the new policy was being implemented solely because the student had received accommodations due to her disability.[31]

Schools must provide reasonable accommodations so that students with disabilities may access its programs. This may involve alterations to the physical facilities, such as building wheelchair ramps, removing architectural barriers, or allowing use of elevators so that students may physically enter and get around the school buildings and grounds.[32] In some situations schools also must allow students to bring service animals into their classrooms as an accommodation, particularly if use of the service animal is necessary for the students to have a degree of independence.[33] Schools may even be required to provide a handler for the service animal.[34] If the students are quite independent, or if the presence of service animals could present health risks to others, the school may not be required to allow the students to be accompanied by the animal.[35]

The ADA and its implementing regulations require public entities to take steps to make existing services equally accessible to individuals with communication disabilities, as long as doing so does not pose an undue burden or require a fundamental change to their programs.[36] The IDEA's FAPE requirements and the ADA's communication requirements are significantly different. Thus, in some, but not all, situations schools may be required to provide services under the ADA to deaf or hearing-impaired students that are different from those required under the IDEA.[37] In providing auxiliary aids and services, the ADA requires public entities to give primary consideration to the requests of the individual with disabilities.[38] Also, the ADA requires public schools to communicate as effectively with students with disabilities as with other students by providing auxiliary aids that will afford them an equal opportunity to participate in, and enjoy the benefits of, the schools' programs.[39]

Schools are not required to provide accommodations that go beyond what would be considered to be reasonable. Accommodations that are excessively expensive, expose the school personnel to excessive risk, or require schools to substantially modify the mission or purpose of their programs, are not mandated.[40] In this regard, school boards are not necessarily required to make alterations to or provide accommodations in the student's home schools. School officials may enroll students with disabilities in other schools that are accessible, or that have the appropriate accommodations available. In the interests of economy, school boards may centralize programs rather than offer duplicative programs in each of its schools.[41] However, school boards must provide students with disabilities with facilities that are comparable to those provided to students who do not have disabilities.[42]

School boards are not required to fundamentally alter programs to allow participation by students with disabilities who are not otherwise qualified for the programs. For example, if a student with disabilities does not meet the basic requirements for participation in an academic program, school officials are not required to accept the student into the program just because he or she has a disability. As long as the school's participation requirements are neutral and are not specifically designed to exclude students with disabilities, a student's exclusion from the program due to failure to meet entrance requirements is not discriminatory.[43]

Many school districts currently have a school choice policy whereby parents may elect to send their children to a school other than the neighborhood school. Although these policies cannot be used to exclude a student with disabilities solely because of the disability, students with disabilities may be excluded due to other considerations. For example, the Sixth Circuit Court of Appeals found that a student with disabilities whose application for school choice was denied was not subject to discrimination because the denial was a function of his residence and the funds associated with his education, and not solely because of his disability.[44] Most school choice policies require the parents to provide their own transportation if they elect to send their children to a distant school. If the child has a disability, a school board is not required to provide that student with special transportation to the school of choice, as long as the board has offered an appropriate program at the student's home school.[45] Even so, if, under the school choice policy, the board provides transportation to students without disabilities, it is also required to provide transportation to students with disabilities.

Health-related services are among the most common accommodations schools provide to students with disabilities. Under Section 504 and the ADA schools are required to provide students with disabilities with basic health services such as catheterization[46] and administration of medication. However, a school nurse is not required to administer medication if the prescription exceeds the normal recommended dosage.[47]

The requirements for testing accommodations have received much interest among school administrators, as many states now require students to pass examinations to graduate from high school and earn a diploma.[48] Again, Section 504 and the ADA require accommodations that would allow students with disabilities to take tests on an equal footing with peers who are not disabled, but would not require a fundamental alteration in the content of the tests themselves. In other words, school boards may be required to modify how tests are administered, but are not required to modify the actual content of the tests. Thus, Section 504 and the ADA would require schools to give Braille versions of the test to students with visual impairments, or provide assistance in recording answers to physically challenged students, but would not require that easier test items be administered to students with learning disabilities. Basically, school officials are required to provide modifications that will allow the students to take the tests, but do not need to modify the item content or compromise the validity of the tests.[49]

Many questions have arisen regarding the participation of students with disabilities in extracurricular or athletic programs. Just as students are entitled to accommodations so that they can participate in schools' academic programs, they also may be entitled to accommodations to allow them to participate in schools' extracurricular programs.[50] One court wrote that a hearing-impaired student was entitled to the services of a sign-language interpreter so that she could understand the directions of her basketball coach.[51]

Some students, due to their disabilities, do not meet the usual requirements for participation. In many cases, school boards and athletic associations
are required to waive the normal requirements for participation unless doing
so would fundamentally alter the programs or impose excessive burdens
on the agencies. Thus, schools or athletic associations may be required to
waive grade-point-average requirements, but may not be required to waive
age-limitation[52] or eight-semester rules.[53] This issue is very controversial,
however, and the outcome of a lawsuit frequently depends on the particular
circumstances. When students transfer from one school to another in order to
receive special education services, the schools may be required to waive any
rules requiring the students to sit out a period of time before being eligible
for athletics.[54] Nevertheless, school boards may not be required to waive their
requirements that student-athletes adhere to specific codes of conduct to participate in sports.[55] Also, school officials may justifiably exclude students if
there is evidence that the students are at an increased risk of serious injury,
or could put others at risk, due to their disabilities.[56] In such instances, school
administrators may seek medical direction and clearance for physical activities from the student's doctors.[57]

School administrators need to pay particular attention to situations
where students may be bullied or harassed because of their disabilities.[58]
When students with disabilities or their parents raise allegations of bullying
or harassment, school officials must take action to curb the activity. Even if
the steps school officials take to stop the bullying and harassment are unsuccessful, they generally will be exonerated as long as they investigated and
responded reasonably to all alleged incidents.[59] Conversely, courts will allow
allegations of disability discrimination to proceed in the face of evidence that
school officials failed to address incidents of bullying.[60] Similarly, school
administrators need to investigate and take appropriate action regarding any
incidents of teacher misconduct toward students with disabilities.[61]

When courts determine that school boards have violated students' rights
under Section 504 or the ADA, the usual remedy is prospective relief in the
form of orders to take corrective action. In some situations, school boards
may be ordered to provide compensatory services to make up for any losses
students suffered due to the denial of their rights. Generally, boards are not
held liable for violations of Section 504 or the ADA unless the plaintiffs can
show that officials acted in bad faith, showed gross misjudgment, or acted
with deliberate indifference. Courts will not uphold allegations of Section
504 or ADA violations in situations where school officials made good faith
efforts to provide accommodations even if their efforts fell short.[62] Even when
it can be shown that school boards failed to provide a FAPE as mandated by
the IDEA, courts will not enter a finding of intentional discrimination in the
absence of bad faith, gross misjudgment, or deliberate indifference.[63] On the
other hand, courts have determined that school boards violated Section 504 or
the ADA when school officials have egregiously disregarded students' needs.[64]

Parents

School districts also are required to supply reasonable accommodations so that parents who have disabilities are able to participate in activities essential to their child's education. One court required a school to provide a sign-language interpreter so that parents who were hearing impaired could participate in school-initiated conferences regarding the academic and disciplinary aspects of their child's educational program.[65] Under this ruling, school boards would not be required to provide accommodations for other school functions in which parental participation is not necessary, such as school plays or even graduation ceremonies. The school would, however, be required to allow parents to provide their own accommodations. For example, the school could not prevent parents from bringing their own sign-language interpreter to a graduation ceremony.

School facilities also must be accessible so that parents can attend school functions. This does not mean that school boards must provide the exact accommodations a parent desires. In one case, a parent who used a wheelchair filed suit because the school's stadium did not have accessible seating in its bleachers, requiring her to watch the game from a concrete walkway in front of the bleachers. The trial court ascertained that the stadium as a whole was accessible to individuals in wheelchairs, and the fact that the arrangements were not satisfactory to the complaining parent did not contradict the testimony of other wheelchair users, who stated that the arrangements were satisfactory.[66] The Ninth Circuit agreed that the parent's subjective complaint that her experience was unsatisfactory was not sufficient to establish disability discrimination. The court pointed out that a public entity is not required to make existing facilities comply with the ADA, but only required to provide program access. Thus, the court affirmed that the district had complied with federal law, since football games in a school district's stadium were accessible to individuals who used wheelchairs, even though the bleachers were not.[67] On the other hand, a federal trial court in California held that a father who alleged that he could not watch his daughter's golf game because of barriers to access in the parking lot, bathroom, and the course itself had stated a prima facie claim of discrimination under Section 504 and the ADA.[68]

Employees

School districts may not refuse to hire an applicant who has a disability, or in any way discriminate against an employee with a disability, as long as the applicant or employee is otherwise qualified for the position. An employer must, however, provide reasonable accommodations that will allow the employee or prospective employee to perform the job in question.

Discrimination Claims

Generally, in order to maintain discrimination claims under Section 504 or the ADA, employees must show that they were treated differently than employees without disabilities, or that the employer made an adverse employment decision because of the individual's disability. For example, a part-time worker with a disability could not maintain a discrimination claim when he was laid off after he had worked the maximum number of hours allowed for part-time workers, since part-time employees who were not disabled had been laid off for the same reason.[69]

In another lawsuit, a former high school principal who was a recovering alcoholic was unable to show that a school district discriminated against him when it abolished his position and did not appoint him to the newly created position of combined elementary and high school principal.[70] For economic reasons, the school district had combined the two positions, but offered the new job to the former elementary principal because he was certified for grades K-12, whereas the former high school principal was not.

Employees with disabilities cannot maintain discrimination claims if they do not have the skills to satisfactorily perform the job in question, even when provided with accommodations. Courts will dismiss discrimination claims if the school districts can show that adverse employment decisions were made for nondiscriminatory reasons. For example, one court held that an employee with a disability was not discriminated against when the employer was able to show that the employee had not been promoted because his work performance was not up to standards, and it had not improved even after he was provided with accommodations.[71] Another court agreed that evidence showed a school board's decision to terminate a teacher was based on nondiscriminatory reasons, specifically failing two fitness-for-duty examinations, as well as her inability to control her classroom, her failure to properly implement the reading curriculum, her failure to accurately enter grades, and her excessive absences.[72]

Employees also cannot maintain discrimination claims if their alleged disabilities are not covered by Section 504 or the ADA. One court held that the term "individual with disabilities" does not include an individual with sexual behavior disorders.[73] In that case, an instructor had been fired for violating the school's sexual harassment policy, but alleged that he was wrongfully terminated because he had a sexual addiction that was a mental disability under Section 504. Similarly, a federal trial court found that an administrator who had a knee injury was not covered by the ADA because she failed to show that the injury was a permanent, long-term disability that substantially limited a major life activity.[74] The court noted that although the effects of the injury included difficulty standing, walking, and sitting for long periods, it did not rise to the level of a substantial limitation.

Employers are permitted to take appropriate disciplinary action against employees who commit egregious or criminal acts of misconduct, regardless of whether the employees are disabled. One court upheld the termination of a coach who had been arrested for driving under the influence of alcohol and public intoxication.[75] The court posited that the employer could hold an alcoholic employee to the same performance and behavior standards as other employees, even if the unsatisfactory performance was due to the employee's alcoholism. Another court found that a teacher's dismissal for egregious behavior and unprofessional interactions with students was legitimate and nondiscriminatory.[76] The court commented that the ADA does not require employers to excuse employees' misconduct, even when precipitated by disabilities. Similarly, employees can be terminated for excessive absenteeism, even if the absences are related to disabilities, since being present is considered to be an essential requirement of any job.[77]

Otherwise Qualified Individual with a Disability

The Supreme Court has indicated that an individual with a disability is otherwise qualified if that person can perform all essential requirements of the position in question in spite of the disability.[78] Thus, if the individual cannot perform essential functions of the position, even with reasonable accommodations, the individual is not otherwise qualified.

An essential requirement of most positions, especially those in school systems, is regular attendance. Employees who are unable to attend the workplace in a reliable and predictable manner are not otherwise qualified.[79] Section 504 and the ADA do not protect excessive absenteeism, even when it is caused by disabilities.[80] By the same token, school districts are not required to grant indefinite leaves of absence to allow employees to care for others who are ill.[81]

Classroom teachers are expected to be able to be physically present in classrooms and interact with students. Teachers who, due to disabilities, are unable to interact with students may not be entitled to assignments that do not involve sustained contact with large groups of students. Classroom teaching and disciplining students would generally be considered essential functions of teachers' jobs, and the inability to teach in classrooms or discipline students in most situations would mean that the individuals could not meet all requirements of their teaching positions in spite of their disabilities.[82] However, if non-classroom positions are available, the teachers may be entitled to reassignment to one of those open positions.[83]

Failure to meet teacher certification requirements may disqualify individuals, even if the failure is allegedly due to disabilities. A teacher who claimed to be learning disabled, and had not passed the communications portion of the National Teachers Examination after numerous attempts, was not considered to be otherwise qualified for teacher certification.[84] The court found that the skills measured by the communications portion of the examination were necessary for competent performance as a classroom teacher. Thus, the court said that the teacher was not otherwise qualified because she could not perform the essential functions of the position.

Similarly, employers can expect individuals to be able to perform their duties in a safe manner.[85] For example, bus drivers who have poorly controlled diabetes are not otherwise qualified, since they pose an unpredictable risk of developing hypoglycemia or the complications of hypoglycemia[86] that may include a sudden loss of vision or consciousness. On the other hand, if the diabetes can be controlled and the bus driver's fitness to operate the vehicle easily monitored, the driver would be considered otherwise qualified.[87] The same would be true for drivers who have other medical conditions such as a seizure disorder[88] or a heart condition. The employee in question must be individually assessed for fitness to perform the duties of the job. Before refusing to hire an individual with a disability due to perceived risk, an employer must determine the nature, duration, and severity of the risk; the probability that the potential injury will actually occur; and the possibility that reasonable modifications of policies, practices, or procedures will mitigate the risk.[89]

Section 504 and the ADA also do not protect misconduct, even when it can be attributed to disabilities.[90] One court upheld the dismissal of an alcoholic employee who had repeatedly reported to work intoxicated and unable to perform his duties.[91] The court found that the employee was dismissed because of his misconduct, not his alcoholism, and that relief was not available under Section 504 for misconduct. Similarly, another court upheld the dismissal of a teacher who had been arrested and charged with possession of cocaine.[92] The court declared that his criminal conduct undermined his ability to work as a teacher.

Reasonable Accommodations

Under Section 504 and the ADA, employers must provide reasonable accommodations so that otherwise qualified employees with disabilities can work and compete with their colleagues who do not have disabilities.[93] The purpose of providing accommodations is so that employees with disabilities can lead normal lives.[94] Accommodations may include alterations to the physical environment, adjustments to employees' schedules, or minor changes in the employees' job responsibilities. What is, and is not, a reasonable accommodation has been the subject of much litigation.

Employers are not required to supply accommodations if doing so places undue burdens on the employers. Minor accommodations, however, are generally not held to be excessively burdensome. For example, one court held that monitoring a diabetic's ability to operate a school bus on a daily basis would not place an undue burden on the school system.[95] Generally, it is the school board's responsibility to show that requested accommodations would create an undue financial or administrative burden.[96]

Employers also are not required to make accommodations that would essentially change the nature of the positions. However, employers may be required to reassign employees with disabilities to other positions. This may be required when employees are unable to perform the essential functions of their current jobs even with reasonable accommodations, and there are, or soon will be, vacant positions that the employees are able to perform.[97] In the case of classroom teachers, reassignment to non-teaching positions could be required if such positions exist in the districts.[98] Reassignment is not required, however, when there are no other positions available for which the employees are qualified.[99] Employers are not required to create new positions, or accommodate employees with disabilities by eliminating essential aspects of their current positions.[100] For example, the Eleventh Circuit Court of Appeals affirmed that the ADA did not require a school district to create a part-time teaching position to accommodate a teacher who was unable to work full time.[101]

As indicated in the previous section, regular attendance is considered to be an essential requirement of most jobs. Employers are not required to let employees with disabilities work only when their conditions allow.[102] For example, one court held that a requested accommodation of being allowed to work only when the employee's illness permitted would result in an undue hardship to the employer.[103] An employee who cannot report to work on a consistent basis may not be considered to be otherwise qualified.[104] One court stated that allowing intermittent absences was not a reasonable accommodation contemplated by the ADA.[105] On the other hand, in another situation, a court determined that a school board had adequately accommodated a teacher whose illness caused frequent absences when it hired a long-term substitute to work alongside the teacher.[106]

State Immunity under Section 504

The issue of whether a state is immune from a lawsuit under Section 504 or the ADA has resulted in mixed opinions from the courts, even though Congress has amended Title VI of the Civil Rights Act to affirm that states are not immune to lawsuits filed in federal courts under a variety of civil rights statutes including Section 504.[107] Most courts reviewing the question have been determined that states do not enjoy Eleventh Amendment immunity from lawsuits brought under Section 504. The First,[108] Third,[109] Fifth,[110] Sixth,[111] Eighth,[112] and Tenth[113] Circuits have ruled that Puerto Rico, New Jersey, Louisiana, Texas, Ohio, Arkansas, and Kansas, respectively, have waived their immunity under Section 504 by accepting federal funds.[114] Conversely, the Eleventh Circuit has ruled that suits in federal court by state employees to recover money damages under Section 504 are barred by the Eleventh Amendment.[115]

The ADA includes a provision that states are not immune to suit for violations of the statute.[116] The Eleventh Circuit, on remand from the Supreme Court, has held that suits in federal court by state employees to recover money damages by reason of the state's failure to comply with the ADA or Section 504 are barred by the Eleventh Amendment .[117] Whether individuals who are denied access to programs and services can bring suit against states for damages depends on the specific facts of the case.[118] Individuals with disabilities may bring suit for injunctive relief.

Damages

Individuals may be entitled to damages if they are able to show that their rights under Section 504 or the ADA were egregiously disregarded. To be entitled to compensatory damages under Section 504 and the ADA, a plaintiff must prove that the defendant intentionally discriminated against her on the basis of her disability.[119] A New York court also stated that allegations that school officials failed to provide special education services, if proven, could constitute a deliberate indifference to the fact that a student's rights were being violated and could entitle the student to damages.[120] However, a school board will not generally be held liable as long as a good faith effort was made to address the student's or employee's disabilities.[121]

Individual school officials may be held personally liable for their actions under Section 504 and the ADA if a plaintiff can show that they acted with bad faith or gross misjudgment.[122] An individual teacher could be held liable for flagrant failure to abide by the terms of a student's IEP or Section 504 service plan.[123] A federal trial court in Pennsylvania saw no difficulty in holding individuals liable for violations of Section 504 and the ADA.[124]

Recommendations for Practice

1. Students with disabilities may not be excluded from public schools or denied services solely on the basis of their disabilities.

2. Students with disabilities may not be subjected to differential treatment because of their disabilities, or because they receive accommodations for their disabilities.

3. If students with disabilities do not qualify for special education and related services under the IDEA, school officials should determine if they require reasonable accommodations under Section 504 and the ADA.

4. School authorities should make individualized determinations regarding waivers of participation requirements for student-athletes who may not meet the usual requirements of their disabilities.

5. School administrators may request medical clearance before allowing students with disabilities to participate in sports, if they have reason to believe that the students have increased risks of injury.

6. School administrators must be diligent in responding immediately to allegations that students with disabilities were bullied or harassed by other students, or were subjected to abuse by staff. Such allegations must be thoroughly investigated and appropriate action must be taken against perpetrators.

7. Accommodations must be provided to parents with disabilities so that they can participate in school functions essential to their children's education, such as parent-teacher conferences.

8. To maintain discrimination claims under Section 504 or the ADA, employees must show that their disabilities are covered under Section

504 and the ADA, that adverse employment decisions were made because of their disabilities, and that the employees have the skills to perform the jobs in question.

9. Employees are not otherwise qualified if they cannot perform the essential functions of the positions, even with reasonable accommodations.

10. Employees must be individually assessed for fitness to perform the jobs in question.

11. Employers are not required to provide accommodations if doing so would create undue financial or administrative burdens.

12. If employees with disabilities are no longer able to perform the essential functions of their jobs, employers must transfer the employees to other vacant positions if they exist and the employees are qualified for the positions; however, employers are not required to create new positions for employees with disabilities.

13. In most jurisdictions, sovereign immunity cannot be used as a defense in a lawsuit under Section 504.

14. School employees can be held personally liable for damages for acts of discrimination that are egregious and intentional.

Endnotes

[1]   29 U.S.C. § 794 (2012).

[2]   42 U.S.C. §§ 12101-12213 (2012).

[3]   29 U.S.C. § 705(20)(B); 42 U.S.C. § 12102(1) (2012).

[4]   34 C.F.R. § 104.3(j)(2)(ii) (2016); 42 U.S.C. § 12102(2) (2012).

[5]   42 U.S.C. §§ 12102(2)(A)-(B) (2012).

[6]   42 U.S.C. § 12102(2)(A) (2012).

[7]   Russlynn Ali, Dear Colleague Letter, U.S. Dep't. of Educ. (Jan. 19, 2012), http://www2. ed.gov/about/offices/list/ocr/letters/colleague-201109.html) (last visited Nov. 28, 2016); 42 U.S.C. § 12102(4)(A) (2012).

[8]   Sutton v. United Air Lines, Inc., 527 U.S. 471, 487-89 (1999) (severely myopic individuals whose vision impairments are remedied by corrective lenses are not disabled within the meaning of the ADA); Toyota Motor Mfg. Ky., Inc. v. Williams, 534 U.S.184, 196-98 (2002) (individual diagnosed with carpal tunnel syndrome not disabled within the meaning of the ADA because she failed to present evidence of a permanent or long-term inability to engage in activities that are central to most people's daily lives).

[9]   Sch. Bd. of Nassau Cnty. v. Arline, 480 U.S. 273 (1987); Southeastern Cmty. Coll. v. Davis, 442 U.S. 397 (1979).

[10] 34 C.F.R. § 104.12(a) (2016).

[11] Welsh v. City of Tulsa, 977 F.2d 1415 (10th Cir. 1992); Mackie v. Runyon, 804 F. Supp. 1508 (M.D. Fla. 1992).

[12] Paegle v. Dep't of the Interior, 813 F. Supp. 61 (D.D.C. 1993).

[13] Sutton v. United Air Lines, 527 U.S. 471 (1999); Murphy v. United Parcel Serv., 527 U.S. 516 (1999); Albertson's, Inc. v. Kirkingburg, 527 U.S. 555 (1999). Although these cases were decided according to the Americans with Disabilities Act, they are relevant to the discussion

of Section 504 due to the similarities in both statutes' definitions of an individual with a disability.

[14] 42 U.S.C. § 12102(4)(E)(i)(I)-(IV) (2012).

[15] 42 U.S.C. § 12102 (4)(D) (2012).

[16] 42 U.S.C. § 12102(3)(B) (2012).

[17] 20 U.S.C. § 1400 *et seq* (2012).

[18] For an exception, *see* Ellenberg v. N.M. Military Inst., 572 F.3d 815 (10th Cir. 2009), where the court affirmed that eligibility for services under the IDEA did not automatically establish that a child was disabled under Section 504. The court reasoned that eligibility for special education under the IDEA demonstrates a child's disability, but that disability is not necessarily one that substantially limits the major life activity of learning.

[19] J.D. v. Pawlet Sch. Dist., 224 F.3d 60 (2d Cir. 2000).

[20] *See, e.g.,* Wenger v. Canastota Cent. Sch. Dist., 961 F. Supp. 416 (N.D.N.Y. 1997), *aff'd in part, vacated in part on other grounds*, 146 F.3d 123 (2d Cir. 1998); McGraw v. Bd. of Educ. of Montgomery Cnty., 952 F. Supp. 248 (D. Md. 1997); D.F. v. W. Sch. Corp., 921 F. Supp. 559 (S.D. Ind. 1996); Cordrey v. Euckert, 917 F.2d 1460 (6th Cir. 1990); Puffer v. Raynolds, 761 F. Supp. 838 (D. Mass. 1988).

[21] N.L. *ex rel.* Ms. C. v. Knox Cnty. Sch., 315 F.3d 688 (6th Cir. 2003).

[22] Lyons v. Smith, 829 F. Supp. 414 (D.D.C. 1993).

[23] For more detailed information about Section 504 service plans, *see* Charles J. Russo & Allan G. Osborne, SECTION 504 AND THE ADA (Corwin Press).

[24] Doe v. Dolton Elem. Sch. Dist. No. 148, 694 F. Supp. 440 (N.D. Ill. 1988); Thomas v. Atascadero Unified Sch. Dist., 662 F. Supp. 376 (C.D. Cal. 1987).

[25] Thomas v. Davidson Acad., 846 F. Supp. 611 (M.D. Tenn. 1994); Jeffrey S. v. State Bd. of Educ. of Ga., 896 F.2d 507 (11th Cir. 1990).

[26] Oberti v. Bd. of Educ. of the Borough of Clementon Sch. Dist., 801 F. Supp. 1392 (D.N.J. 1992), *aff'd*, 995 F.2d 1204 (3d Cir. 1992).

[27] I.D. v. Westmoreland Sch. Dist., 788 F. Supp. 634 (D.N.H. 1992).

[28] *See, e.g.,* Bercovitch v. Baldwin Sch., 964 F. Supp. 597 (D.P.R. 1997) *) rev'd on other grounds*, 133 F.3d 141 (1st Cir. 1998)..

[29] *See, e.g.,* S-1 v. Turlington, 635 F.2d 342 (5th Cir. 1981); Sherry v. N.Y. State Educ. Dep't, 479 F. Supp. 1328 (W.D.N.Y. 1979).

[30] Hornstine v. Twp. of Moorestown, 263 F. Supp. 2d 887 (D.N.J. 2003).

[31] *See* Weixel v. Bd. of Educ. of the City of N.Y., 287 F.3d 138 (2d Cir. 2002), where the court found that school officials failed to make reasonable accommodations for a student who could not attend school due to documented illness resulting in her receiving educational services for most of one school year.

[32] *See, e.g.,* Celeste v. E. Meadow Union Free Sch. Dist., 373 F. App'x 85 (2d Cir. 2010); D.R. *ex rel.* Courtney R. v. Antelope Valley Union High Sch. Dist., 746 F. Supp. 2d 1132 (C.D. Cal. 2010); Begay v. Hodel, 730 F. Supp. 1001 (D. Ariz. 1990).

[33] Sullivan v. Vallejo City Unified Sch. Dist., 731 F. Supp. 947 (E.D. Cal. 1990). The ADA's regulations pertinent to service animals can be found at 28 C.F.R. § 35.136 (2016).

[34] *See, e.g.,* Alboniga v. Sch. Bd. of Broward Cnty., 87 F. Supp. 3d 1319 (S.D. Fla. 2015).

[35] *See, e.g.,* Cave v. E. Meadow Union Free Sch. Dist., 480 F. Supp. 2d 610 (E.D.N.Y. 2007).

[36] 28 C.F.R. § 35.160 (2016).

[37] *See, e.g.,* K.M. *ex rel.* Bright v. Tustin Unified Sch. Dist., 725 F.3d 1088 (9th Cir. 2013), *cert. den'd* 134 S. Ct. 1493 (2014).

[38] 28 C.F.R. § 35.160(b)(2) (2016).

[39] 28 C.F.R. § 35.160(a)(1) (2016). *See also* Vanita Gupta, Michael Yudin, & Catherine Lhamon, *Dear Colleague Letter*, U.S. DEP'T OF JUSTICE & U.S. DEP'T OF EDUC. (Nov. 12, 2014). http://www2.ed.gov/about/offices/list/ocr/letters/colleague-effective-communication-201411.pdf.

[40] Eva N. v. Brock, 741 F. Supp. 626 (E.D. Ky. 1990); Kohl v. Woodhaven Learning Ctr., 865 F.2d 930 (8th Cir. 1989).

[41] *See, e.g.,* Barnett v. Fairfax Cnty. Sch. Bd., 927 F.2d 146 (4th Cir. 1991).

[42]   Hendricks v. Gilhool, 709 F. Supp. 1362 (E.D. Pa. 1989).

[43]   St. Johnsbury Acad. v. D.H., 240 F.3d 163 (2d Cir. 2001).

[44]   Clark v. Banks, 193 F. App'x 510 (6th Cir. 2006); *see also* Dutkevitch v. PA Cyber Charter Sch., 439 F. App'x 177 (3d Cir. 2011) (affirming that a student with disabilities was not discriminated against when his application for admission to an out-of-district charter school was denied, since the denial was based on the school's admission policies which applied equally to all out-of-district students.)

[45]   Timothy H. v. Cedar Rapids Cmty. Sch. Dist., 178 F.3d 968 (8th Cir. 1999).

[46]   Irving Indep. Sch. Dist. v. Tatro, 468 U.S. 883, 104 S. Ct. 3371, 82 L. Ed. 2d 664 (1984).

[47]   DeBord v. Ferguson-Florissant Sch. Dist., 126 F.3d 1102 (8th Cir. 1997); Davis v. Francis Howell Sch. Dist., 104 F.3d 204 (8th Cir. 1997).

[48]   In fact, the IDEA requires the participation of students with disabilities in state testing programs. 20 U.S.C. § 1412(a)(17) (2012); 34 C.F.R. § 300.138 (2016).

[49]   Brookhart v. Ill. State Bd. of Educ., 697 F.2d 179 (7th Cir. 1983). Many of the lawsuits concerning testing accommodations are at the collegiate level under the Americans with Disabilities Act, but can be instructive. *See, e.g.,* Rush v. Nat'l Bd. of Med. Examiners, 268 F. Supp. 2d 673 (N.D. Tex. 2003) (learning disabled student given additional time to take medical exam); Stern v. Univ. of Osteopathic Med. and Health Scis., 220 F.3d 906 (8th Cir. 2000) (student failed to show that requested accommodations were related to his dyslexia); Biank v. Nat'l Bd. of Med. Examiners, 130 F. Supp. 2d 986 (N.D. Ill. 2000) (medical student failed to show that his dyslexia would significantly limit his ability to pass an exam unless given additional time); D'Amico v. N.Y. State Bd. of Law Examiners, 813 F. Supp. 217 (W.D.N.Y. 1993) (additional time granted to a visually impaired student to take state bar exam).

[50]   *See* Seth Galanter, *Dear Colleague Letter*, U.S. Dep't of Educ. (Jan. 25, 2013), http://www2. ed.gov/about/offices/list/ocr/letters/colleague-201301-504.pdf.

[51]   State *ex rel.* Lambert by Lambert v. W. Va. State Bd. of Educ., 447 S.E.2d 901 (W.Va. Ct. App. 1994).

[52]   M.H. v. Mont. High Sch. Ass'n, 929 P.2d 239 (Mont. 1996); Sandison v. Mich. High Sch. Athletic Ass'n, 64 F.3d 1026 (6th Cir. 1995); Pottgen v. Mo. State High Sch. Activities Ass'n, 40 F.3d 926 (8th Cir. 1994); Starego v. N.J. State Interscholastic Athletic Ass'n, 970 F. Supp. 2d 303 (D.N.J. 2013); *but see* Dennin v. Conn. Interscholastic Athletic Conference, 913 F. Supp. 663 (D. Conn. 1996), *dismissed as moot* 94 F.3d 96 (2d Cir. 1996); Johnson v. Fla. High Sch. Activities Ass'n, 899 F. Supp. 579 (M.D. Fla. 1995), *vac'd and rem'd with instructions to dismiss as moot* 102 F.3d 1172 (11th Cir. 1997); Univ. Interscholastic League v. Buchanan, 848 S.W.2d 298 (Tex. Ct. App. 1993).

[53]   McPherson v. Mich. High Sch. Athletic Ass'n, 119 F.3d 453 (6th Cir. 1997); Starego v. N.J. State Interscholastic Athletic Ass'n, 970 F. Supp. 2d 303 (D.N.J. 2013); Rhodes v. Ohio High Sch. Athletic Ass'n, 939 F. Supp. 584 (N.D. Ohio 1996).

[54]   Crocker v. Tenn. Secondary Sch. Athletic Ass'n, 735 F. Supp. 753 (M.D. Tenn. 1990), *aff'd sub nom.* Metropolitan Gov't of Nashville and Davidson Cnty. v. Crocker, 908 F.2d 973 (6th Cir. 1990) (mem.).

[55]   Long v. Bd. of Educ., Dist. 128, 167 F. Supp. 2d 988 (N.D. Ill. 2001) (stating that a waiver of the application of the code of conduct would be unreasonable as it would send the message to others that a challenge in federal court could thwart the enforcement of rules).

[56]   Pahulu v. Univ. of Kan., 897 F. Supp. 1387 (D. Kan. 1995); Kampmeier v. Nyquist, 553 F.2d 296 (2d Cir. 1977); *but see* Pace v. Dryden Cent. Sch. Dist., 574 N.Y.S.2d 142 (N.Y. Sup. Ct. 1991) (order issued on the basis of state law); Grube v. Bethlehem Area Sch. Dist., 550 F. Supp. 418 (E.D. Pa. 1982); Wright v. Columbia Univ., 520 F. Supp. 789 (E.D. Pa. 1981).

[57]   Doe v. Woodford Cnty. Bd. of Educ., 213 F.3d 921 (6th Cir. 2000); Ripple v. Marble Falls Indep. Sch. Dist., 99 F. Supp. 3d 662 (W.D. Tex. 2015) (finding that school officials did not act with bad faith or gross professional misjudgment with regard to a student's safety where his doctors cleared him to play).

[58]   *See* Catherine Lhamon, *Dear Colleague Letter*, U.S. Dep't of Educ. (Oct. 21, 2014), http://www2.ed.gov/about/offices/list/ocr/letters/colleague-bullying-201410.pdf).

[59] Nevills v. Mart Indep. Sch. Dist., 608 F. App'x 217 (5th Cir. 2015); Estate of Lance v. Lewisville Indep. Sch. Dist., 743 F.3d 982 (5th Cir. 2014); Long v. Murray Cnty. Sch. Dist., 522 F. App'x 576 (11th Cir. 2013).

[60] Estate of Barnwell v. Watson, 44 F. Supp. 3d 859 (E.D. Ark. 2014).

[61] Shadie v. Hazleton Area Sch. Dist., 580 F. App'x 67 (3d Cir. 2014); J.S. III v Houston Cnty. Bd. of Educ., 120 F. Supp. 3d 1287 (M.D. Ala. 2015); Doe v. Darien Bd. of Educ., 110 F. Supp. 3d 386 (D. Conn. 2015); Rideau v. Keller Indep. Sch. Dist., 978 F. Supp. 2d 678 (N.D. Tex. 2013).

[62] *See, e.g.,* D.A. *ex rel.* D.A. v. Houston Indep. Sch. Dist., 629 F.3d 450 (5th Cir. 2010) (ruling that a school board's decision to delay an evaluation did not demonstrate bad faith or gross misjudgment); Zachary M. v. Bd. of Educ. of Evanston Twp. High Sch. Dist. No. 202, 829 F. Supp. 2d 649 (N.D. Ill. 2011) (finding that a school board was not deliberately indifferent to a claim that a student was disabled and needed accommodations after determining that school officials had conducted a careful review of the student's circumstances); Williams v. Dist. of Columbia, 771 F. Supp. 2d 29 (D.D.C. 2011) (holding that a school board's failure to timely evaluate a student did not rise to the level of a Section 504 violation in the absence of any inference of bad faith or gross misjudgment).

[63] *See, e.g.,* T.M. v. Dist. of Columbia, 961 F. Supp. 2d 169 (D.D.C. 2013); Alston v. Dist. of Columbia, 770 F. Supp. 2d 289 (D.D.C. 2011); Taylor v. Dist. of Columbia, 683 F. Supp. 2d 20 (D.D.C. 2010); Lucas v. Dist. of Columbia, 683 F. Supp. 2d 16 (D.D.C. 2010); Torrence v. Dist. of Columbia, 669 F. Supp. 2d 68 (D.D.C. 2009).

[64] *See, e.g.,* Stewart v. Waco Indep. Sch. Dist., 711 F.3d 513 (5th Cir. 2013), *vacated in part on rehearing en banc,* 599 F. App'x 534 (5th Cir. 2013) (concluding that parent stated a plausible claim of gross misjudgment when school officials failed to alter a student's IEP to prevent sexual abuse); K.D. *ex rel.* J.D. v. Starr, 55 F. Supp. 3d 782 (D. Md. 2014) (finding that teachers' consistent failure to provide agreed-upon accommodations supported allegations of bad faith and gross misjudgment); A. *ex rel.* Mr. A. v. Hartford Bd. of Educ., 976 F. Supp. 2d 164 (D. Conn. 2013) (holding that school officials' failure to implement a hearing officer's order to provide a FAPE was motivated by discrimination resulting from deliberate indifference, bad faith, and gross misjudgment); Rideau v. Keller Indep. Sch. Dist., 978 F. Supp. 2d 678 (N.D. Tex. 2013) (finding that a dispute of material fact existed concerning whether school officials exercised gross misjudgment by allowing a teacher to continue after allegations that he had physically abused students); A.B. *ex rel.* B.S. v. Adams-Arapahoe 28J Sch. Dist., 831 F. Supp. 2d 1226 (D. Colo. 2011) (concluding that a special education teacher's supervisors' failure to take any action concerning allegations that the teacher had used a restraint chair in a manner that denied a child the right to participate in her education was evidence that the school board was deliberately indifferent); S.L.-M. *ex rel.* Liedtke v. Dieringer Sch. Dist. No. 343, 614 F. Supp. 2d 1152 (W.D. Wash. 2008) (finding that a reasonable jury might conclude that several instances in the record where school personnel ignored requests for accommodations amounted to deliberate indifference); James S. *ex rel.* Thelma S. v. Sch. Dist. of Phila., 559 F. Supp. 2d 600 (E.D. Pa. 2008) (holding that a parent's allegations of a school board's pattern of dereliction spanning several years despite requests for intervention, if proven, were sufficient to survive a motion to dismiss).

[65] Rothschild v. Grottenthaler, 725 F. Supp. 776 (S.D.N.Y. 1989), *aff'd in part, vac'd and rem'd in part,* 907 F.2d 286 (2d Cir. 1990).

[66] Greer v. Richardson Indep. Sch. Dist., 752 F. Supp. 2d 746 (N.D. Tex. 2010), *aff'd,* 472 F. App'x 287 (5th Cir. 2012).

[67] Daubert v. Lindsay Unified Sch. Dist., 760 F.3d 982 (9th Cir. 2014).

[68] Miller v. Ceres Unified Sch. Dist. 141 F. Supp. 3d 1038 (E.D. Cal. 2015).

[69] Spells v. Cuyahoga Cmty. Coll., 889 F. Supp. 1023 (N.D. Ohio 1994).

[70] Pierce v. Engle, 726 F. Supp. 1231 (D. Kan. 1989).

[71] Adrain v. Alexander, 792 F. Supp. 124 (D.D.C. 1992).

[72] Belasco v. Warrensville Heights City Sch. Dist., 86 F. Supp. 3d 748 (N.D. Ohio 2015).

[73] Winston v. Me. Technical Coll. Sys., 631 A.2d 70 (Me. 1993).

[74] Sampson v. Methacton Sch. Dist., 88 F. Supp. 3d 422 (E.D. Pa. 2015); *see also* Harris v. Adams, 873 F.2d 929 (6th Cir. 1989); (finding that an applicant was unable to show that his asthma substantially limited a major life activity); Johnson v. Beach Park Sch. Dist., 103 F. Supp. 3d 931 (N.D. Ill. 2015) (holding that an applicant's vague assertions that she couldn't stand all day or walk for miles were not sufficient to conclude that any major life activities were substantially limited).

[75] Maddox v. Univ. of Tenn., 62 F.3d 843 (6th Cir. 1995).

[76] Willis v. Norristown Area Sch. Dist., 2 F. Supp. 3d 597 (E.D. Pa. 2014).

[77] Walders v. Garrett, 765 F. Supp. 303 (E.D. Va. 1991); Linares v. City of White Plains, 773 F. Supp. 559 (S.D.N.Y. 1991).

[78] *See* School Bd. of Nassau County v. Arline, 480 U.S. 273 (1987); Southeastern Cmty. Coll. v. Davis, 442 U.S. 397 (1979).

[79] Gardner v. Sch. Dist. of Phila., 636 F. App'x 79 (3d Cir. 2015); Santiago v. Temple Univ., 739 F. Supp. 974 (E.D. Pa. 1990).

[80] Carr v. Reno, 23 F.3d 525 (D.C. Cir. 1994); Jackson v. Veterans Admin., 22 F.3d 277 (11th Cir. 1994); Linares v. City of White Plains, 773 F. Supp. 559 (S.D.N.Y. 1991).

[81] Bimberg v. Elkton-Pigeon-Bay Port Laker Schs., 860 F. Supp. 2d 396 (E.D. Mich. 2012), *aff'd*, 512 F. App'x 462 (6th Cir. 2013).

[82] Siudock v. Volusia Cnty. Sch. Bd. 568 F. App'x 659 (11th Cir. 2014).

[83] Mustafa v. Clark Cnty. Sch. Dist., 876 F. Supp. 1177 (D. Nev. 1995), *aff'd in part, rev'd in part and rem'd,* 157 F.3d 1169 (9th Cir. 1998).

[84] Pandazides v. Va. Bd. of Educ., 804 F. Supp. 794 (E.D. Va. 1992), *rev'd on other grounds* 13 F.3d 823 (4th Cir. 1994); *see also* Johnson v. Bd. of Trs. of Boundary Cnty. Sch. Dist. No. 101, 666 F.3d 561 (9th Cir. 2011) (affirming that a teacher who failed to complete requirements to renew her certification was not qualified within the meaning of Section 504); Falchenberg v. N.Y. State Dep't of Educ., 338 F. App'x 11 (2d Cir. 2009) (affirming that a teacher's request to take a portion of the licensure test orally and not be required to indicate spelling, punctuation, capitalization, and paragraphing was the type of fundamental alteration to the test that did not need to be made).

[85] Chiari v. City of League City, 920 F.2d 311 (5th Cir. 1991).

[86] Wood v. Omaha Sch. Dist., 25 F.3d 667 (8th Cir. 1994).

[87] *See, e.g.* Commonwealth, Dep't of Transp., Bureau of Driver Licensing v. Tinsley, 564 A.2d 286 (Pa. Commw. Ct. 1989).

[88] Commonwealth, Dep't of Transp., Bureau of Driver Licensing v. Chalfant, 565 A.2d 1252 (Pa. Commw. Ct. 1989).

[89] Bombrys v. City of Toledo, 849 F. Supp. 1210 (N.D. Ohio 1993).

[90] Wilber v. Brady, 780 F. Supp. 837 (D.D.C. 1992).

[91] Gonzalez v. Cal. State Pers. Bd., 39 Cal. Rptr. 2d 282 (Cal. Ct. App. 1995); *see also* Baptista v. Hartford Bd. of Educ., 427 F. App'x 39 (2d Cir. 2011) (affirming that the dismissal of an employee whom the employer alleged had been drunk on the job did not constitute disability discrimination).

[92] Gedney v. Bd. of Educ. of Groton, 703 A.2d 804 (Conn. Ct. App. 1997).

[93] Fink v. N.Y. City Dep't of Pers., 855 F. Supp. 68 (S.D.N.Y. 1994).

[94] McWright v. Alexander, 982 F.2d 222 (7th Cir. 1992).

[95] Commonwealth of Pa. v. Tinsley, 564 A.2d 286 (Pa. Commw. Ct. 1989).

[96] Byrne v. Bd. of Educ., Sch. Dist. of W. Allis - W. Milwaukee, 741 F. Supp. 167 (E.D. Wis. 1990).

[97] Ransom v. State of Ariz. Bd. of Regents, 983 F. Supp. 895 (D. Ariz. 1997).

[98] Mustafa v. Clark Cnty. Sch. Dist., 157 F.3d 1169 (9th Cir. 1998).

[99] Black v. Frank, 730 F. Supp. 1087 (S.D. Ala. 1990).

[100] Alexander v. Frank, 777 F. Supp. 516 (N.D. Tex. 1991).

[101] Rabb v. Sch. Bd. of Orange Cnty., 590 F. App'x 849 (11th Cir. 2014). *See also* Waltherr-Willard v. Mariemont City Schs., 601 F. App'x 385 (6th Cir. 2015) (affirming that a school board

was not required to create a new position of displace an existing teacher at a high school to accommodate an elementary teacher who had a fear of young children).

[102] Huber v. Howard Cnty., 849 F. Supp. 407 (D. Md. 1994).

[103] Walders v. Garrett, 765 F. Supp. 303 (E.D. Va. 1991). *Also see* Kurek v. N. Allegheny Sch. Dist., 233 F. App'x 154 (3d Cir. 2007) (affirming that allowing a teacher to leave school early was not a reasonable accommodation where it would effectively increase other teachers' workloads).

[104] Ramirez v. N.Y. City Bd. of Educ., 481 F. Supp. 2d 209 (E.D.N.Y. 2007).

[105] Preddie v. Bartholomew Cnty. Consol. Sch. Dist., 44 F. Supp. 3d 800 (S.D. Ind. 2014), *aff'd in part, rev'd in part and remanded, sub. nom.,* Preddie v. Bartholomew Cty. Cons. Sch. Corp., 799 F.3d 806 (7th Cir. 2015).

[106] Nichols v. Harford Cnty. Bd. of Educ., 189 F. Supp. 2d 325 (D. Md. 2002).

[107] 42 U.S.C. § 2000d-7 (2012).

[108] Nieves-Marquez v. Commonwealth of P.R., 353 F.3d 108 (1st Cir. 2003).

[109] A.W. v. Jersey City Pub. Sch., 341 F.3d 234 (3d Cir. 2003).

[110] Bennett-Nelson v. La. Bd. of Regents, 431 F.3d 448 (5th Cir. 2005); Miller v. Tex. Tech Univ. Health Scis. Ctr., 421 F.3d 342 (5th Cir. 2005); Pace v. Bogalusa City Sch. Bd., 403 F.3d 272 (5th Cir. 2005).

[111] Carten v. Kent State Univ., 282 F.3d 391 (6th Cir. 2002).

[112] Jim C. v. United States, 235 F.3d 1079 (8th Cir. 2000).

[113] Robinson v. Kansas, 295 F.3d 1183 (10th Cir. 2002).

[114] *See also* Shepard v. Irving, 204 F. Supp. 2d 902 (E.D. Va. 2002)), *aff'd in part, rev'd in part and remanded,* 77 F. App'x 615, 616 (4th Cir. 2003); Patricia N. v. LeMahieu, 141 F. Supp. 2d (D. Haw. 2001); Patrick and Kathy W. v. LeMahieu, 165 F. Supp. 2d 1144 (D. Haw. 2001); Werner v. Colo. State Univ., 135 F. Supp. 2d 1137 (D. Colo. 2000).

[115] Garrett v. Univ. of Ala. at Birmingham, 261 F.3d 1242 (11th Cir. 2001), *on remand sub nom. from* Bd. of Trs. of the Univ. of Ala. v. Garrett, 531 U.S. 356 (2001); *see also* Biggs v. Bd. of Educ. of Cecil Cnty., 229 F. Supp. 2d 437 (D. Md. 2002).

[116] 42 U.S.C. § 12202 (2012).

[117] Garrett v. Univ. of Alabama at Birmingham, 261 F.3d 1242 (11th Cir. 2001), *on remand sub nom. from* Bd. of Trs. of the Univ. of Alabama v. Garrett, 531 U.S. 356 (2001).

[118] *See* Tenn. v. Lane, 541 U.S. 509 (2004) (holding that sovereign immunity was waived under the ADA in regards to access to courts).

[119] Swenson v. Lincoln County Sch. Dist. No. 2, 260 F. Supp. 2d 1136 (D. Wyo. 2003).

[120] Butler v. S. Glens Falls Cent. Sch. Dist., 106 F. Supp. 2d 414 (N.D.N.Y. 2000). *See also* Chambers v. Sch. Dist. of Phila. Bd. of Educ., 827 F. Supp. 2d 409 (E.D. Pa. 2011)(holding that a plaintiff must prove intentional discrimination to be entitled to damages), *aff'd in part, rev'd in part and remanded,* 537 F. App'x. 90 (3d Cir. 2013) (reversing and remanding because there was a genuine dispute of material fact as to whether the school district was intentionally indifferent sufficient to establish discrimination).

[121] *See, e.g.,* Finn *ex rel.* Steven P. v. Harrison Cent. Sch. Dist., 473 F. Supp. 2d 477 (S.D.N.Y. 2007); Sellers v. Sch. Bd. of Mannassas, 141 F.3d 524 (4th Cir. 1998).

[122] Bradley v. Ark. Dep't of Educ., 301 F.3d 952 (8th Cir. 2002); Alston v. Dist. of Columbia, 561 F. Supp. 2d 29 (D.D.C. 2008).

[123] Doe v. Withers, Civ. No. 92-C-92, 20 IDELR 422 (W.Va. Cir. Ct. 1993).

[124] McCachren v. Blacklick Valley Sch. Dist., 217 F. Supp. 2d 594 (W.D. Pa. 2002).

Chapter 5

Qualifying for Special Education and Related Services under IDEA

Elizabeth A. Shaver

Introduction

Special education services for students with disabilities first became widely available after Congress passed the Education for All Handicapped Children's Act (EAHCA) in 1975.[1] The EAHCA provided that, in exchange for federal education funding, the states were required to develop a statewide plan under which each child with disability would receive a "free appropriate public education," or FAPE.[2] In 1990, Congress reauthorized the EAHCA, along with several substantive amendments, including renaming the statute the Individuals with Disabilities Education Act (IDEA).[3] IDEA was again reauthorized and amended in both 1997 and 2004.[4]

As a funding statute, IDEA conditions a state's ability to access federal education funds upon the development of a "plan" (statewide laws and regulations) that complies with all of IDEA's very detailed requirements.[5] The state also must monitor local school districts' compliance with both IDEA and all state laws and regulations.[6] Although IDEA is a highly detailed federal statute, its basic working premise is that each state must develop its own plan to comply with IDEA. Indeed, as to many items, IDEA allows the states discretion in developing policies or procedures, leading to some variation in IDEA implementation from state to state.[7] Thus, to fully comply with IDEA, local school districts must follow both federal and state law, including regulations issued by the U.S. Department of Education and the state educational agency.[8] Principals are encouraged to be familiar with both state and federal regulations and to use the resources of their state educational agency whenever issues regarding IDEA compliance arise.

This chapter focuses on the processes by which local school districts identify and evaluate students who may be eligible for special education services under IDEA. It is important to understand that IDEA imposes an affirmative obligation upon local school districts to identify children who may be in need of special education services ("child find") and to conduct a thorough evaluation using scientifically sound, research-based methods. The failure to identify and evaluate a child who is in need of special education services can result in an adverse judicial ruling that the district failed to provide the child with a FAPE. In particular, as discussed in more detail below, "Response to Intervention" (RtI) is not a substitute for special education services under

IDEA. If a school district does not provide special education services to an eligible child and the child's parents obtain services elsewhere at their own expense, the district could be required to reimburse parents for their expenses, including tuition reimbursement for expensive private school tuition.[9]

This chapter also reviews parental involvement in the evaluation process, including the requirement that parents must consent to any evaluation of their child, and the right of parents to seek an independent evaluation of their child by non-school personnel.

Eligibility to Receive Special Education and Related Services

In order to be eligible to receive special education services, a student must be of (a) an appropriate age, (b) meet IDEA's definition of a "child with a disability," and (c) due to that disability, need special education and related services.[10]

Age Requirement

Children between the ages of 3 and 21 are eligible to receive special education services, although Part B of IDEA does provide that a state is not required to provide special education services to children between ages 3-5 or 18-21 if doing so would be "inconsistent with state law or practice."[11] In essence, a state may choose to implement its own age requirements for public school education; however, the state may not follow a practice that employs different age requirements for students with disabilities as compared to students without disabilities.[12]

The maximum age limit of public school enrollment does differ by state and, in some states, the determination of a maximum age limit is within the discretion of a local school board.[13] For example, Montana law provides that a public school pupil includes children only up to age 19.[14] In contrast, Michigan law provides that a student with a disability includes students up to age 26.[15]

In addition, either the state or the local school board may have its own practice with regard to the cessation of special education services for a student who exceeds the maximum age limit during the school year.[16] Principals should be aware of any state statutes or regulations that dictate either a minimum or maximum age for public school education, as well as local policies regarding cessation of services for students with disabilities who reach the maximum age limit during the school year. It is important that policies be applied uniformly so as to avoid the appearance of any improprieties. Parents are advised to ask their school personnel what the district's policy is regarding students who reach the maximum age during the school year, in order to ensure that their child is being treated as fairly as other students with disabilities.

There is no requirement that a school district provide a child with special education services after high school graduation. However, this only applies to students who have been awarded a "regular high school diploma," not an alternative degree that is not fully aligned with the state's academic standards, such as a certificate or GED.[17] Thus, students with disabilities who receive a regular high school diploma will matriculate out of public school education consistent with their typically developing peers. Students with disabilities who receive a social graduation—that is, those who do not receive a regular high school diploma—should continue to receive special education services as part of the transition planning contained within each student's IEP. Chapter 8 discusses transition planning in more detail.

Disability Categories

In addition to the age requirement, a student must be considered a "child with a disability" as defined by IDEA; that is, a child whose characteristics fall within one of thirteen disability categories identified by IDEA.[18] These categories are: autism, deaf-blindness, deafness, emotional disturbance, hearing impairment, intellectual disability,[19] multiple disabilities, orthopedic impairments, other health impairment, specific learning disability, speech or language impairment, traumatic brain injury, and visual impairment, including blindness.[20] For children between the ages of 3 and 9 (or any subset of that age range), the state and its local school districts may, in their discretion, use the term "developmental delay" to identify a child as a child with a disability who is entitled to special education services.[21] This category of developmental delay allows a school district to begin offering services to a younger child for whom a definitive diagnosis cannot be made.

Even with regard to the thirteen enumerated categories, IDEA provides that the statute does not "require that children be classified by their disability,"[22] so long as the child is appropriately deemed eligible under IDEA and offered special education services that would provide a FAPE.[23] In other words, IDEA "charges a school with the responsibility of developing an appropriate education, not with coming up with a proper label."[24] Some children may not be easily classified into only of the one of the enumerated disability categories.[25] In that case, the parents and the school district should not be involved in a "code war" regarding labels.[26] As long as the disability category identified by the school district is a reasonable one, a parent cannot establish a violation of IDEA merely by arguing that a different category should have been chosen. For example, if a school district classifies a child's disability as "emotional disturbance," the parent's argument that the child was denied a FAPE because the appropriate classification was "Asperger syndrome" will not prevail so long as the district offered special education services that were sufficient to provide a FAPE.[27]

In addition, IDEA does not set forth the diagnostic criteria or assessment tools to be used in evaluating whether a child falls within a particular diagnostic category.[28] As a general matter, certain IDEA categories—such as deaf-blindness, deafness, hearing impairment, orthopedic impairments, speech or language impairment, or visual impairment—involve disabilities that typically are readily observable outside of the school context and are first diagnosed by medical professionals even before the child enters kindergarten.[29] Other categories, particularly the categories of emotional disturbance, intellectual disability, specific learning disability, and other health impairment, more often can be recognized first in the school context and generally involve much more subjective or judgmental diagnostic criteria, rather than a known medical cause.[30]

The category of "emotional disturbance," for example, has a complicated definition, as follows:

> Emotional disturbance means a condition exhibiting one or more of the following characteristics over a long period of time and to a marked degree that adversely affects a child's educational performance:
>
> (A) An inability to learn that cannot be explained by intellectual, sensory, or health factors.
>
> (B) An inability to build or maintain satisfactory interpersonal relationships with peers and teachers.
>
> (C) Inappropriate types of behavior or feelings under normal circumstances.
>
> (D) A general pervasive mood of unhappiness or depression.
>
> (E) A tendency to develop physical symptoms or fears associated with personal or school problems.[31]

"Other health impairment" is defined as a condition "having limited strength, vitality, or alertness, including a heightened alertness to environmental stimuli, that results in limited alertness with respect to the educational environment, that is due to chronic or acute health problems such as asthma, attention deficit disorder or attention deficit hyperactivity disorder, diabetes, epilepsy, a heart condition, hemophilia, lead poisoning, leukemia, nephritis, rheumatic fever, sickle cell anemia, and Tourette syndrome."[32] "Intellectual disability" is defined as a condition manifested by "significantly subaverage general intellectual functioning, existing concurrently with deficits in adaptive behavior and manifested during the developmental period."[33]

The evaluation process, which is described in more detail below, will involve a large group of school personnel and input from parents. However, principals should be aware that racial minority students historically have been disproportionately identified as requiring special education services.[34] Data over more than two decades reveals that the percentage of minority students who receive special education services is greater than their percentage of the total school-age population.[35] In addition, minority students statistically are disproportionately identified into particular disability categories, namely the subjective or "judgmental categories" of emotional disturbance and intellectual disability.[36]

In amending and reauthorizing IDEA in 2004, Congress took steps to address the issue of disproportionality. Specifically, Congress required the states to develop policies and procedures "designed to prevent the inappropriate overidentification or disproportionate representation by race and ethnicity of children as children with disabilities."[37] To help identify districts where disproportionality may be occurring, Congress required the states and local school districts to supply the U.S. Department of Education with annual data that shows, among other things, the number of children identified by race and ethnicity who are found to be within each disability category.[38] State educational agencies are obligated to monitor data to consider whether disproportionate representation of minority students may be occurring; depending on the outcome of a state review, the state may require a local school district to revise its policies or procedures.[39] Depending on the racial and ethnic composition of any one school district, school administrators may be particularly mindful of overrepresentation in special education, or disproportionality between disability categories.

An Adverse Effect on Educational Performance

IDEA's definition of a child with a disability also requires that, due to the identified disability, the child "needs special education and related services"[40] in order to access the curriculum. The federal regulations issued by the U.S. Department of Education further clarify that such a need for special education services arises when the student's disability "adversely affect[s]" the student's educational performance.[41] While federal law does not define either "adverse effect" or "educational performance," according to the Office of Special Education and Rehabilitative Services (OSERS, formerly known as the Office of Special Education Programs, or OSEP), the term "educational performance" is to be more broadly interpreted than "academic performance."[42] A student who is considered bright and can perform well on standardized tests nonetheless may be eligible under IDEA as a child with a disability if the student's disability adversely affects his or her social, health, emotional, communicative, physical or vocational needs.[43] This broad definition of adverse effect comports with IDEA's goal to prepare students with disabilities for employment and independent living.[44]

In addition, some states have issued laws or regulations that define an adverse effect on educational performance. For example, West Virginia law specifies that an "adverse effect" on educational performance is a "harmful or unfavorable influence" of the disability on the child's performance.[45] West Virginia also specifies that the phrase "educational performance" means both academic areas and nonacademic areas such as daily life activities, mobility, pre-vocational and vocational skills, social adaptation, and self-help skills.[46] In other states, the term is not defined at all. Principals are advised to become familiar with their particular state's interpretation of the term "adverse effect," as well as any guidance concerning the scope of the phrase "educational performance." It is the presence of this adverse effect on educational performance that will demonstrate the child's need for special education and related services.

The "Child Find" Requirement

Locating and Identifying Students Who May Be Eligible For Special Education

IDEA is quite clear that school districts have an affirmative obligation to locate, identify and evaluate children who may be suspected of having an IDEA-eligible disability.[47] In IDEA parlance, this is called the "child find" requirement.[48] While, the states are left to develop their own identification procedures, IDEA requires that the states have policies and procedures to "ensure" that all children in need of special education services are found.[49] The child find requirement extends not just to children already enrolled in public schools, but extends to all children who may be entitled to special education services from the district, even if they are not currently enrolled in school. Thus, child find extends to infants and toddlers located within the district, to homeless and homeschooled children within the district, and to children who have been enrolled in private schools at the election of their parents for any reason, including a desire to obtain a religiously based education.[50] In fact, under IDEA, school districts have the obligation to evaluate a child not enrolled in public school if the child is either a resident of the school district (and thus, could attend public school within the district) or is enrolled in a private school that is physically located with the boundaries of the school district.[51]

As to children not yet attending school, comprehensive child find efforts can include posting notices in the local paper, making information available on a website, sending residents the information in their tax bills, and placing targeted posters and pamphlets in private schools.[52]

As to children already enrolled, school districts most commonly will "locate" a child who requires an evaluation when the child's parents request that an evaluation be done. While a parent's request to have the child evaluated must be taken very seriously, a parent's request alone does not trigger the requirement to conduct an evaluation.[53] Rather, that obligation arises when that the district "suspects" that the child may have an IDEA-eligible disability, even if the child is advancing from grade to grade.[54] "School districts may not ignore disabled students' needs, nor may they await parental demands before providing special instruction."[55] The threshold for "suspicion" is relatively low, and the inquiry is not whether the child actually qualifies for services, but whether the child should be evaluated.[56] While the failure to initiate an evaluation can violate the child's rights under IDEA, to establish such a violation, school officials must have "overlooked clear signs of disability," been "negligent in failing to order testing," or have had "no rational justification for not deciding to evaluate."[57] In addition, where the district has conducted prior evaluations of a child, it appropriately may deny a parent's request for additional evaluations if the district does not suspect that the child is a child with a disability.[58] School officials cannot, however, exclude students whom they suspect of having disabilities due to the anticipated expense of services or the severity of disability.[59]

The first time a district may become aware of the need to conduct an evaluation is when the child becomes the subject of disciplinary proceedings. A student who previously had not received special education services may be protected under IDEA from disciplinary action if the school district had "knowledge" that the child was a child with a disability.[60] A school district is deemed to have knowledge if the child's parent expressed concern in writing (to supervisors, administrators or a teacher) that the child needs special education and related services;[61] if the parents had requested an evaluation of the child;[62] or if a teacher or other school personnel had "expressed specific concerns about a pattern of behavior demonstrated by the child directly" to the district's special education director or other district supervisors.[63] If the child had not been evaluated previously, but the district has the requisite "knowledge" that the child may be a child with a disability, then the child is entitled to assert protections under IDEA, which requires the district to conduct an evaluation and, if necessary, provide the child with special education services.[64] A school might have knowledge that a student might be a child with a disability when the student has failed all of her classes, school personnel are aware that the student takes medication for attention deficit disorder, and school personnel have discussed whether the student might benefit from special education services.[65]

In addition, if the child's parent requests an evaluation after the initiation of disciplinary proceedings, even if the district did not have any prior knowledge that the child was a child with a disability, an expedited evaluation should be conducted and eligibility determined.[66]

If a parent has requested an evaluation, but the district determines not to conduct the evaluation on the grounds that it has no reason to suspect that a child has a disability, the district should supply the parents with written notice indicating all the reasons why the district will not be conducting an evaluation.[67] The district also must provide the parents with a copy of their "procedural safeguards," which is a document that details all of the parental rights available under IDEA. Among those is the right of a parent to initiate a due process hearing to contest, among other things, the district's decision not to evaluate a child. Because the district's decision not to evaluate the child obviously means that the child will not receive special education services under IDEA, it is highly recommended that the district absolutely ensure the parents are made aware of their right to contest that decision. IDEA contains time limitations on the filing of due process hearings to contest determinations but, if the parents are not given sufficient notice of their rights, those time limitations will not apply.[68]

Requests For and Consent to Evaluation

An initial evaluation of a child can be requested by the child's parent; the school district itself; the state educational agency; or another state agency, most likely a child welfare agency, if the child is in foster care or otherwise is a ward of the state.[69] In the case of a child who is a ward of the state, the district nonetheless must seek to obtain the consent of the child's parent, unless the parent cannot be located (despite reasonable efforts to do so), parental rights have been terminated under state law, or the right of the parent to make educational decisions has been subrogated by a judge in accordance with state law.[70]

IDEA provides that, before conducting any initial evaluation of a child, the district must obtain the informed consent of a parent.[71] In seeking the parent's informed consent, the school district is obligated to provide the child's parents with written notice of the district's proposal to evaluate the child and to obtain the parent's written consent to proceed with an evaluation.[72] That written notice must make the parent aware of the particular forms of assessments or testing that the district proposes to use in evaluating the child, so that parents are aware not just that an evaluation is taking place, but specifically what the evaluation process will entail.[73] Valid consent is given only when the parent has received all pertinent information relative to the district's proposal to evaluate the child—if necessary in the parent's native language or some other form of communication—and that the written consent obtained from the parent describes the evaluation process and lists any records that might be released, and to whom.[74]

Sometimes parents may not respond to a district's request to conduct an initial evaluation of a child. Federal law requires that the district undertake "reasonable efforts" to obtain informed consent from the child's parents.[75] Those reasonable efforts include telephone contacts, correspondence to the parents, and home and workplace visits.[76] The district must maintain detailed records of these efforts to obtain parental consent.[77]

A school district may not conduct an initial evaluation of a child without either valid parental consent, or the order of a due process hearing officer that such an evaluation should take place. If the parent does not provide consent to an initial evaluation, either by denying the district's request or simply not responding to the district's request, the district cannot proceed to evaluate the child. However, the district may file an administrative due process proceeding in order to obtain a decision allowing the evaluation to be conducted.[78]

Parental consent for periodic (usually three-year) evaluations differs only slightly from the procedures to obtain parental consent for an initial evaluation. IDEA provides that, if the district has undertaken reasonable efforts to obtain the parent's consent, but the parent has not responded to those requests, the district may conduct a reevaluation of the child.[79]

A parent's consent to conduct an evaluation cannot be construed as consent for placement or the initiation of special education services.[80] In addition, parental consent to an evaluation can be revoked at any time.[81] In that case, the evaluation must cease and the district is not at any risk of a claim that it failed to comply with the provisions of IDEA. However, while the district is not required to do so, best practice would suggest that school personnel contact the child's parents to determine the reasons why they decided to revoke their consent, and to reach some agreement that will allow the evaluation to be completed. The district also could offer the parents the opportunity to participate, at no cost, in a mediation conducted by an impartial third party who is not an employee of the district.[82] Mediation might be an appropriate venue for parents to discuss any concerns they might have about the evaluation process.

Sometimes the question of who exactly is the child's "parent" for IDEA purposes is a thorny one, particularly in cases where the child's parents are divorced or the child is in foster care. IDEA defines the parent of a child as the child's natural or adoptive parent; a foster parent, if allowed under state law; a guardian; an individual acting in the place of a parent with whom the child resides; an individual who is legally responsible for the child's welfare; or an appointed "surrogate" parent, if allowed under state law.[83] This issue of who may act as a parent and the rights of both parents to participate in IDEA decision making in the event of a divorce is largely a matter of state law. Traditionally, issues relating to parental rights in the event of a divorce have been part of state family law and the express terms of child custody agreements,[84] and IDEA expressly allows each state to determine the rights of foster or surrogate parents to act as a parent for IDEA purposes. Thus, principals are advised to seek state-specific information whenever there is a question as to an individual's ability to act as a parent. Parents who may be involved in divorce proceedings are strongly advised to consult with a family law attorney who is familiar with state law regarding child custody and educational decisions for children with disabilities.

The Evaluation Process

Once identified as a child who may be eligible under IDEA, the district is required to conduct a "full and individual" initial evaluation of the child.[85] The evaluation must employ proper techniques and methods. Specifically, the district must use "a variety of assessment tools and strategies," including information provided by the child's parent.[86] The district must consider just not academic performance, but also functional and developmental information regarding the child.[87] IDEA specifically prohibits the use of any "single measure or assessment as the sole criterion for determining" eligibility under IDEA.[88] The district must ensure that the assessment measures and materials are selected and administered in ways that will not discriminate by race or culture.[89] Any assessments must be administered in the most appropriate language that will provide the best results regarding the child.[90] All assessments must administered by "trained and knowledgeable personnel."[91]

Importantly, the district also must ensure that the child is evaluated "in all areas of suspected disability" and not just as to one of the disability categories.[92] Any assessments conducted by school personnel to determine "appropriate instructional strategies for curriculum implementation" are not an evaluation under IDEA.[93] Thus, general assessments or screening of the student population cannot serve as an IDEA evaluation.

During the evaluation process, parents can provide important information. Parents should be forthcoming in supplying school personnel with any privately obtained evaluations or data that they believe would help the district in assessing the child, and should timely complete any assessments provided by the district. Good cooperation between school personnel and parents will produce an accurate and complete assessment of the child.

For children who previously have been deemed eligible for special education services, a reevaluation must be conducted at least every three years.[94] Reevaluations may be conducted more frequently than that, and a reevaluation must be conducted if either the child's parent or teacher requests one;[95] however, the district is not required to conduct a reevaluation more than once a year if it does not wish to do so.[96] The general practice is for reevaluations to occur every three years.

The evaluation is to determine whether the child is a child with a disability under IDEA and to determine the educational needs of the child.[97] Thus, the evaluation report must address not only eligibility under IDEA, but also provide information about the child's educational needs. In that manner, the evaluation report provides the underlying information that is necessary to allow the district, along with parents, to develop the child's individualized education program (IEP). The process of developing an IEP is discussed in detail in Chapter 6.

Once the district has completed its assessments, it must supply a copy of the evaluation report to the child's parents and the documentation of the eligibility determination.[98] Federal law does not specifically require a face-to-face meeting with parents to discuss the evaluation report, but some states may require such a meeting.

Response to Intervention (RtI)

When IDEA was amended in 2004, Congress inserted a provision regarding the evaluation procedures for one of the thirteen disability categories, the category of specific learning disability. As to this category, which includes learning disorders that affect a child's abilities or skills in reading, writing, or mathematics (dyslexia, dysgraphia, dyscalcula), Congress provided that a district could, as part of the evaluation process, determine if the child "responds to scientific, research-based intervention."[99] The use of such a scientific, research-based intervention as a means to evaluate whether a child has a specific learning disability under IDEA is known as a "Response to Intervention" (RtI) approach.[100] Prior to the use of RtI, one principal evaluative method to determine whether a child met IDEA's definition of a specific learning disability was the use of a "severe discrepancy" (IQ) form of testing.[101] Many professionals long had considered the use of the severe discrepancy model as a flawed means to evaluate learning disabilities, and RtI was developed in order to provide an alternative process by which a child could simultaneously be evaluated for eligibility under IDEA and also receive early intervention.[102]

RtI uses a multi-tiered system of support, under which children who are struggling with certain academic skills receive increasing levels of interventions along with periodic assessments to determine the need for additional instruction or more intensive instructions.[103] Typically, an RtI model will involve three tiers of interventions, which increase in both intensity and duration as a child moves through the various tiers.[104] A child who shows little improvement even after the implementation of the highest (Tier 3) level of interventions likely will be referred for a comprehensive evaluation under IDEA and consideration of eligibility to receive special education services.[105]

While RtI can be a very effective tool to provide early intervention to struggling students, concerns have been expressed that the use of RtI and its multi-tiered forms of intervention can unnecessarily delay the process by which a child is evaluated under IDEA. In response to that concern, the federal Office of Special Education and Rehabilitation Services (OSERS) issued a Memorandum to the States reiterating that "the use of RtI strategies cannot be used to delay or deny the provision of a full and individual evaluation" under IDEA.[106] Importantly, when parents request that an evaluation be conducted of a child who has received interventions under an RtI model, the district cannot simply rely on the RtI data as a means to assert that the child is making sufficient progress and thus is not eligible under IDEA.[107] The RtI model and the data collected using RtI does not obviate the need for a full evaluation using a variety of assessment tools and, importantly, input from the child's parents.

Thus, principals should be aware that, while RtI can be a valuable tool to provide early intervention for struggling students, it can never serve as a substitute for either a comprehensive evaluation or the provision of special education services. Parents should accept a district's offer to have their child participate in RtI and give the RtI strategies sufficient time for data collection and analysis, while also being mindful that RtI is not the equivalent of special education services. After sufficient time has elapsed, if parents believe that RtI strategies have not meaningfully addressed their child's issues, they should inquire about the propriety of conducting an evaluation of the child under IDEA.

Timeframe to Conduct Evaluation

IDEA provides that the initial evaluation of a child must be completed within sixty days or consistent with a timeframe established by the state.[108] Timeframes can vary greatly by state. Many states have adopted IDEA's sixty-day deadline, which requires that the evaluation be completed within sixty days after receipt of the parent's consent.[109] The state of Delaware requires that the evaluation be completed within either forty-five school days or ninety calendar days from receipt of parental consent.[110] Up through July 1, 2017, the District of Columbia's timeline to complete an evaluation is 120 days; after July 1, 2017, the applicable timeline is sixty days.[111] Indiana regulations require that an evaluation be completed within fifty "instructional days," except that Indiana regulations also provide that, if the child previously received RtI, the time to complete the evaluation is reduced to twenty instructional days.[112]

Compliance with the specific timeline for completing an evaluation under IDEA is critical, so school personnel are advised to be well aware of their specific state requirements.

Parents' Rights to a Private Independent Educational Evaluation (IEE)

Parents who disagree with an evaluation conducted by their school district have the right to request that the school district pay for an "independent educational evaluation" (IEE) to be conducted by a qualified examiner who is not an employee of the district.[113] In those circumstances, the district has the option to either pay for the IEE or initiate a due process hearing to demonstrate the appropriateness of its evaluation.[114] While a district theoretically can choose between paying for an IEE or litigating the issue in a due process hearing, in practice the district almost certainly will agree to pay for the IEE, simply because the cost of the IEE will be significantly less than the cost associated with a due process hearing. Parents may seek a district-funded IEE for each evaluation that is mandated under IDEA, including both the initial evaluation and any periodic reevaluation.[115]

If the parents request information about private examiners, the district must provide information about where an IEE may be obtained, including a list of qualified examiners, although the LEA cannot limit the parents' choice to particular examiners.[116] The district may ask the parents to identify the reasons why they disagree with the district's evaluation, but the parents are not required to provide any information as a precondition to an IEE paid for by the district.[117] Any evaluator who conducts an IEE that is paid for at public expense must follow the criteria for evaluations under federal and state law.[118] In addition, a hearing officer in any due process hearing that addresses any issue involving a child's right to special education under IDEA may order that an IEE be conducted at district expense.[119] If an IEE is conducted at district expense, the results of such an evaluation must be shared with the school district.[120]

Of course, parents are able to have their child evaluated at their own expense at any time. If parents do obtain an IEE at their own expense, and share the results of the privately funded IEE with the school district, the district is required to consider the results of that evaluation in making decisions under IDEA with regard to the child.

Recommendations for Practice

The process by which a child who may require special education services is located, identified, and evaluated is a thorough one that requires strict adherence to both technical requirements (e.g., timelines) and substantive standards (e.g., adverse effect on educational performance). The evaluation process itself will involve a variety of school personnel with various areas of expertise and, importantly, must include input from the child's parents. Stakeholders are advised to pay particular attention to the following issues:

1. Become familiar with federal and state regulations regarding the identification, location and evaluation of child under IDEA and/or the resources by which information can be located (e.g., the website of the state educational agency).

2. Understand the state age limitations for enrollment in public school and how those limitations apply to students served under IDEA. The local district's policies and practices regarding the cessation of special education services for students who reach the maximum age limit during a school year also must be made clear and applied uniformly.

3. School leaders are advised to review and consider data regarding the total number of students, disaggregated by race and ethnicity, served under IDEA as a percentage of the school-age population in general. Also consider the data regarding the distribution of students with disabilities among the various disability categories set forth in IDEA.

4. Understand the state definition and local policies and practices regarding the determination of an "adverse effect on educational performance." Parents should be particularly aware of this definition when they seek special education services for nonacademic educational programming, such as social interactions, etc.

5. Parents should be meticulous in documenting parental requests to have an evaluation conducted, and the district's strict adherence to the requirements of valid written consent obtained after the parent receives both a detailed written notice of the proposed evaluation and a copy of the procedural safeguards.

6. Ensure that, as to all aspects of the process, the parents are provided information in their native language, if that is necessary to ensure that parents are informed of and understand their rights. Parents should be comfortable that they understand the evaluation process and that the district will conduct a variety of assessments in order to obtain the best data regarding any suspected disabilities.

7. School leaders should undertake reasonable efforts to obtain parental consent whenever the district seeks to evaluate a child. Document those efforts and maintain detailed records.

8. Educators also should understand and follow state policies and procedures regarding the means by which the parents are informed of the results of an evaluation including, at a minimum that the parents are supplied with a copy of the report and testing results. If state law requires a meeting with parents, hold the meeting.

9. School personnel should ensure that evaluations use various forms of assessment or testing materials that are appropriate for the areas of suspected disability; that any assessments or tests are administered by knowledgeable personnel; that parental input is obtained as part of the evaluation process; that assessments do not have any racial or cultural bias; and that, if necessary, assessments are conducted in a language other than English so as to ensure that the most valid assessments of the child's abilities are obtained. Parents should provide any additional evaluations or data that they believe would help the district in assessing the child, and should timely complete any assessments provided by the district.

10. In a district that employs RtI, be mindful that RtI cannot be used to delay or deny a child's right to a thorough evaluation. Parents should agree to RtI strategies, as they are effective for many children. Yet, both parents and school personnel should review RtI data often to determine whether, in the case of a particular child, an IDEA evaluation should be conducted.

11. School personnel should comply with IDEA's requirements when a parent requests an IEE, including paying for the IEE.

12. School personnel should comply with the state's timeframes for obtaining parental consent and completing an evaluation.

Endnotes

[1] Pub. L. No. 94-142, 89 Stat. 773 (1975).

[2] Pub. L. No. 94-142, § 612(1) 89 Stat. 773.

[3] Pub. L. No. 101-476, 104 Stat. 1103 (1990).

[4] Pub. L. No. 105-17, 111 Stat. 37 (1997); Pub. L. No. 108-446, 118 Stat. 2467 (2004).

[5] *See* 20 U.S.C. § 1412 *et. seq.* (2012) (outlining state eligibility requirements).

[6] *Id.*

[7] Examples include such choices as to whether a foster parent may act as a parent for IDEA purposes, or whether the state will implement a single-tier or two-tiered administrative process to resolve disputes. *See* 20 U.S.C. § 1401(23) (2012) (defining foster parent); 20 U.S.C. § 1415(f)(1)(A) (2012) (due process procedures).

[8] IDEA is full of acronyms. Note, for example, that IDEA labels a state department of education is known as the "state educational agency," or "SEA." 20 U.S.C. § 1401(19) (2012).

Local school districts are referred to as "local educational agencies," or "LEAs." 20 U.S.C. § 1401(32) (2012).

9   Forest Grove Sch. Dist. v. T.A., 557 U.S. 230 (2009).

10 20 U.S.C. § 1401(3) (2012).

11 20 U.S.C. § 1412(a)(1)(A) (2012) (identifying children between ages 3-21 as eligible); 20 U.S.C. § 1412(a)(1)(B) (2012) (providing limitations for ages 3-5 and 18-21 if inconsistent with state practice). Part C of IDEA governs the provision of early intervention services to eligible children between birth and age 3. *See* 20 U.S.C. § 1431 *et. seq.* (2012).

12 B.T. v. Hawaii Dep't. of Ed., 637 F. Supp. 3d 856 (D. Haw. 2009).

13 Margo Mikulecky, "*School Attendance Age Limits*," EDUCATION COMM'N OF THE STATES (April 2013), http://www.ecs.org/clearinghouse/01/07/04/10704.pdf.

14 MONT. CODE ANN. § 20-1-101(16) (West. 2017). There have been efforts to raise the age limit in Montana but, as of date of publication, they have not been successful. *See* Chelsea Davis *"Funding Limit that Caps Montana High School Graduation Age a "Travesty,"Legislators Say,"* MISSOULIAN (Jul. 1, 2016), available at http://missoulian.com/news/local/funding-limit-that-caps-montana-high-school-graduation-age-a/article_f1faba5b-7284-5f6b-a968-4426635bbb87.html (last visited Jan. 24, 2017).

15 MICH. ADMIN. CODE R. 340.1702 (West. 2017).

16 *Id.* (providing that a child who reaches age 26 during the school year may continue to receive special education services through the end of the school year).

17 34 C.F.R. § 300.102(a)(3) (2016).

18 20 U.S.C. § 1401(3)(A) (2012); 34 C.F.R. § 300.8 (2016).

19 IDEA has been amended to change the category from "mental retardation" to "intellectual disability" in order to comply with Congressional action to remove the phrase "mental retardation" from all federal statutes. *See* 20 U.S.C. § 1401(3)(A)(i) (2012) (identifying the category as one of intellectual disability). However, the federal regulations, which are compiled in the Code of Federal Regulations, have not been similarly amended. For this reason, the federal regulations still refer to this disability category as "mental retardation." *See* 34 C.F.R. § 300.8(c)(6) (2016).

20 *Id.*

21 20 U.S.C. § 1401(3)(B) (2012).

22 20 U.S.C. § 1412(a)(3)(B) (2012).

23 *Id.*

24 Heather S. v. Wisconsin, 125 F.3d 1045, 1055 (7th Cir. 1997).

25 Pohorcki v. Anthony Wayne Local Sch. Dist., 637 F. Supp. 2d 547 (N.D. Ohio 2009).

26 J.W. v. Contoocook Valley Sch. Dist., 154 F. Supp. 2d 217, 227-28 (D.N.H. 2001).

27 *Pohorcki*, 637 F. Supp. 2d at 556-57.

28 Rebecca Vallas, *"The Disproportionality Problem: The Overrepresentation of Black Students in Special Education and Recommendations for Reform,"* 17 VA. J. SOC. POL'Y & L. 181, 183 (2009).

29 Sarah E. Redfield & Theresa Kraft, *"What Color Is Special Education?"* 41 J. L. & EDUC. 129, 164 (2012).

30 *Id.*

31 34 C.F.R. § 300.8(c)(4)(i) (2016). The definition also provides that this category does not cover children who are "socially maladjusted," although that phrase is not separately defined. 34 C.F.R. § 300.8(c)(4)(ii) (2016).

32 34 C.F.R. § 300.8(c)(9) (2016).

33 34 C.F.R. § 300.8(c)(6) (2016).

34 20 U.S.C. § 1400(c)(12)(B) (2012).

35 *See* U.S. COMM'N ON CIVIL RIGHTS *"Minorities in Special Education"* (April 2009), http://www.usccr.gov/pubs/MinoritiesinSpecialEducation.pdf.

36 20 U.S.C. § 1400(c)(12)(C) (2012).

37 20 U.S.C. § 1412(a)(24) (2012).

38 20 U.S.C. § 1418(a) (2012).

[39] *See* Letter from Alexa Posny to State Directors of Education, U.S. Dep't. of Educ. (Apr. 24, 2007), http://www2.ed.gov/policy/speced/guid/idea/letters/2007-2/osep0709disproportion-ality2q2007.pdf.

[40] 20 U.S.C. § 1401(3) (2012).

[41] 34 C.F.R. § 300.8 (2016) (defining a "child with a disability").

[42] *See* Letter from Alexa Posny to Catherine D. Clarke, U.S. Dep't. of Educ., (Mar. 8, 2007), https://www2.ed.gov/policy/speced/guid/idea/letters/2007-1/clarke030807disability1q2007.pdf.

[43] Seattle Sch. Dist. No. 1 v. B.S., 82 F.3d 1493, 1500 (9th Cir. 1996), quoting H.R. Rep. No. 410, 1983 U.S.C.C.A.N. 2088, 2106.

[44] 20 U.S.C. § 1400(d)(1)(A) (2012).

[45] *See., e.g.,* Wa. Va. Code R. § 126-16-5 (2016).

[46] *Id.*

[47] 20 U.S.C. § 1412(a)(3) (2012).

[48] *Id.*

[49] 20 U.S.C. §§ 1401(3) & 1412(a)(3) (2012); 34 C.F.R. § 300.111 (2016).

[50] *Id.*

[51] 20 U.S.C. § 1412(a)(10)(A)(ii) (2012) (extending child find to children enrolled in private schools at the election of their parents).

[52] P.P. v. West Chester Area Sch. Dist., 585 F.3d 727 (3d Cir. 2009).

[53] Hoffman v. East Troy Comm. Sch. Dist., 38 F. Supp. 2d 750 (E.D. Wis. 1999).

[54] 34 C.F.R. § 300.111(c)(1) (2016).

[55] Reid *ex rel.* Reid v. Dist. of Columbia, 401 F.3d 516, 518 (D.C. Cir. 2005).

[56] Dep't of Ed., State of Hawaii v. Cari Rae, 158 F. Supp. 2d 1190, 1195 (D. Haw. 2001).

[57] Bd. of Educ. v. L.M., 478 F.3d 307, 313 (6th Cir.2007).

[58] Krista P. v. Manhattan Sch. Dist., 255 F. Supp. 2d 873 (N.D. Ill. 2003).

[59] Timothy W. v. Rochester N.H. Sch. Dist., 875 F.2d 954 (1st Cir. 1989).

[60] 20 U.S.C. § 1415(k)(5)(A) (2012).

[61] 20 U.S.C. § 1415(k)(5)(B)(i) (2012).

[62] 20 U.S.C. § 1415(k)(5)(B)(ii) (2012).

[63] 20 U.S.C. § 1415(k)(5)(B)(iii) (2012).

[64] 20 U.S.C. § 1415(k)(5)(A) (2012).

[65] S.W. v. Holbrook Pub. Sch., 221 F. Supp. 2d 222, 226 (D. Mass. 2002).

[66] 20 U.S.C. § 1415(k)(5)(D)(ii) (2012).

[67] 20 U.S.C. § 1415(b)(3)(B) (2012).

[68] 20 U.S.C. § 1415(b)(6)(B) (2012); 20 U.S.C. § 1415(f)(3)(D) (2012).

[69] 20 U.S.C. § 1414(a)(1)(B) (2012).

[70] 20 U.S.C. § 1414(a)(1)(D)(3) (2012).

[71] 20 U.S.C. § 1414(a)(1)(D)(i)(I) (2012).

[72] 20 U.S.C. § 1415(b)(3) (2012).

[73] 20 U.S.C. § 1415(c)(1) (2012).

[74] 34 C.F.R. § 300.9 (2016).

[75] 34 C.F.R. § 300.300(a)(iii) (2016).

[76] 34 C.F.R. § 300.300(d)(5) (2016); 34 C.F.R. § 300.322(d) (2016).

[77] *Id.*

[78] 20 U.S.C. § 1414(a)(1)(D)(ii)(I) (2012).

[79] 20 U.S.C. § 1414(c)(3) (2012).

[80] *Id.*

[81] 34 C.F.R. § 300.9 (2016).

[82] 34 C.F.R. § 300.506 (2016).

[83] 20 U.S.C. § 1401(23) (2012).

[84] Navin v. Park Ridge Sch. Dist., 270 F.3d 1146, 1148 (7th Cir. 2001).

[85] 20 U.S.C. § 1414(a) (2012).

[86] 20 U.S.C. § 1414(b)(2)(A) (2012).

[87] *Id.*

[88] 20 U.S.C. § 1414(b)(2)(B) (2012).

[89] 20 U.S.C. § 1414(b)(3)(A)(i) (2012).

[90] 20 U.S.C. § 1414(b)(3)(A)(ii) (2012).

[91] 20 U.S.C. § 1414(b)(3)(A)(iv) (2012).

[92] 20 U.S.C. § 1414(b)(3)(B) (2012).

[93] 20 U.S.C. § 1414(a)(1)(E) (2012).

[94] 20 U.S.C. § 1414(a)(2)(B) (2012).

[95] 20 U.S.C. § 1414(a)(2)(A) (2012).

[96] 20 U.S.C. § 1414(a)(2)(B) (2012).

[97] 34 C.F.R. § 300.301(c)(2) (2016).

[98] 20 U.S.C. § 1414(b)(4)(B) (2012).

[99] 20 U.S.C. § 1414(a)(6)(B) (2012).

[100] Ruth Colker, *"Politics Trumps Science: The Collision Between No Child Left Behind and the Individuals With Disabilities Education Act,"* 42 J. L. & EDUC. 585, 589 (2013).

[101] *Id.* at 592-93.

[102] Amanda M. Vanderheyden, et. al., *"Scientifically Supported Identification of SLD using RtI: A Response to Colker."* 42 J. L. & EDUC. 229, 230-32 (2013); Orhan Cakiroglu, *"Response to Intervention: Early Identification of Students with Learning Disabilities,"* 7 INT'L. J. OF EARLY CHILDHOOD SPECIAL EDUCATION 170-182 (2015).

[103] *See* http://www.rtinetwork.org/learn/what/whatisrti (website of the National Center for Learning Disabilities); Cakiroglu, *supra* note 102, at 172-73 (describing tiered levels of intervention); Vanderheyden, *supra* note 102, at 248.

[104] Cakiroglu, *supra* note 102, at 172-73.

[105] *Id.*; Vanderheyden, *supra* note 102, at 248.

[106] *See* Michael K. Yudin & Melody Musgrove, Dear Colleague Letter, U.S. DEP'T. OF EDUC. 4 (Nov. 17, 2015), https://www2.ed.gov/policy/speced/guid/idea/memosdcltrs/guidance-on-fape-11-17-2015.pdf.

[107] Greenwich Bd. of Educ. v. G.M., 2016 WL 3512120 (D. Conn., June 21, 2016).

[108] 20 U.S.C. § 1414(a)(1)(C) (2012); 34 C.F.R. § 300.301(c)(i)(ii) (2016).

[109] *See, e.g.,* FLA. ADMIN. CODE R. 6A-6.0331(2016); GA. COMP. R & REGS. 160-4-7-.04(b)1 (2016); HAW. CODE R. §8-60-33(c)(1) (2016); LA. ADMIN. CODE tit. 28, pt. XLIII §302.A. (2016); 05-071-101 ME. CODE R. §V3(a)(3)(A) (2016); OHIO ADMIN. CODE §3301-51-06(B)(4) (2016); 21-2 R.I. CODE R. §54:D (2016).

[110] 14 DEL. ADMIN. CODE § 925 (2016).

[111] D.C. MUN. REG. tit. 5, subtitle 5E §3005.2 (2016).

[112] 511 IND. ADMIN. CODE 7-40-5(d) (2016).

[113] 34 C.F.R. § 300.502(b) (2016).

[114] 34 C.F.R. § 300.502(b) (2016).

[115] 34 C.F.R. § 300.502(b) (5) (2016).

[116] 34 C.F.R. § 300.502(a)(2) (2016).

[117] 34 C.F.R. § 300.502(b)(4) (2016).

[118] 34 C.F.R. § 300.502(e)(1) (2016).

[119] 34 C.F.R. § 300.502(d) (2016).

[120] 34 C.F.R. § 300.502(c)(1) (2016).

Chapter 6

IEPs, Least Restrictive Environment, and Placement

Jean B. Crockett and Mitchell L. Yell

Introduction

The Individuals with Disabilities Education Act (IDEA),[1] which originally became law as The Education for All Handicapped Children Act (EAHCA) in 1975,[2] sought to remedy the exclusion of millions of children from public instruction based solely upon their disabilities. The IDEA affirms the guarantee of a free appropriate public education (FAPE) through an individualized education program (IEP) for each eligible student with a disability.[3] From its enactment to its most recent reauthorization, the law has required that decisions about special education programming and placements be team-based and child-centered. The least restrictive environment (LRE) principle guides placement decisions so that students can be taught in regular classes, to the maximum extent appropriate to their individual needs, and in alternative settings when teams of parents and professionals determine that they cannot make satisfactory progress in regular classes, even with specialized supports.[4]

Although legal procedures guide its delivery, special education is not about law; it is about educating students with disabilities in specialized ways that build upon their strengths and strengthen their weaknesses. Special education is not about *where* students are educated, but about *how* young people are prepared for their futures through far-sighted programming and personalized supports. If students with disabilities were just like everyone else, there would be no need for special education. If schools were not accountable for the learning of every student, there would be less urgency to treat some students differently in order to ensure their success. Special education continues to rely on law because justice has not been blind to students whose learning needs are exceptional, or to the extraordinary efforts required by school systems in providing their education.[5]

In this chapter, the interplay among IEPs, the LRE, and placements is explained and illustrated, with examples drawn from the IDEA Amendments of 2004,[6] the 2006 Federal Regulations,[7] and relevant case law. References are made to guidance from the U.S. Supreme Court addressing IEP disputes, and the shared responsibility of school officials and parents to improve outcomes for students with disabilities.

Legal Issues

School administrators are critical to ensuring effective special education in schools. Moreover, principals are challenged to provide all students with a high-quality education in accordance with their state's academic content standards, as required by the Every Student Succeeds Act (ESSA).[8] Additionally, according to the ESSA, most students with disabilities are to be taught the same challenging academic content as nondisabled students.[9] The IDEA 2004, although aligned with ESSA, expects educators to teach special education students differently, and sometimes to teach them different things, using teaching methods that specifically address each student's needs, all of which is outlined in a personalized IEP. Some educators and members of society prefer that students with disabilities perform in the same way as typically developing students, even though allowing students with disabilities to do things differently could lead to more efficient performance.[10] Special education, in contrast, addresses the individual differences of students with disabilities head-on, providing students who learn differently with more intensive and specialized instruction so they can learn appropriately and participate in their communities.

Defining Special Education and the Purpose of the IDEA

According to the statute, the purpose of the IDEA is clear: "to ensure that all children with disabilities have available to them a free appropriate public education that emphasizes special education and related services designed to meet their unique needs, and prepare them for further education, employment and independent living."[11] All children with disabilities ages 3-21 who need special education have the right to FAPE, including children with disabilities who have been suspended or expelled from school, as well as children who are advancing from grade to grade or who have not failed or been retained in a course or grade.[12]

The provision of FAPE, in the wording of the purpose statement, emphasizes special education and related services. As defined in the statute, special education has an instructional mission, having been defined as "specially designed *instruction,* at no cost to parents, to meet the unique needs of a child with a disability, including ... instruction conducted in the classroom, in the home, in hospitals and institutions, and in other settings...."[13] *Specially designed instruction* refers to more than academic instruction and extends to meeting students' social, emotional, behavioral, physical, and vocational needs.[14] The term was defined for the first time in the 1999 regulations to the IDEA Amendments of 1997.[15] The current regulations defined "specially designed instruction" as follows:

> Specially-designed instruction means adapting, as appropriate to the needs of an eligible child under this part, the content, methodology, or delivery of instruction-

i. To address the unique needs of the child that result from the child's disability; and

ii. To ensure access of the child to the general curriculum, so that he or she can meet the educational standards within the jurisdiction of the public agency that apply to all children.[16]

The sequence of these requirements indicates that ensuring genuine access to the general curriculum depends upon first addressing a student's unique needs. The primary imperative for school officials is to provide special education—specially designed instruction—that addresses the specific disability-related needs of each student. Special education, with its related services and specialized supports, is the vehicle through which the IDEA delivers the individualized interventions designed "to minimize the impact of disability and maximize the opportunities for children with disabilities to participate in general education in their natural community."[17] When appropriate techniques are delivered effectively, the likelihood is increased that each student will benefit and be able to adjust to the demands of the schoolhouse.

The secondary imperative is to ensure that special education students have access to the general curriculum. School officials must ensure that all students have access to the same opportunities because, if appropriate special education is being provided to them, more students with disabilities should be able to learn challenging academic content successfully. This, in turn, should help them be better prepared to participate in and contribute to society, and live as independently and productively as they can.[18] However, it would be a serious mistake for educators, however, to misunderstand this imperative as somehow requiring that students with disabilities receive the *same* curriculum as do general education students. In fact, in a November 2015 "Dear Colleague" Letter, the Office of Special Education and Rehabilitative Services (OSERS) of the U.S. Department of Education warned that this imperative should guide "but not replace the individualized decision-making required in the IEP process."[19] Clearly, the IDEA's focus on the individual needs of each child with a disability remains the primary imperative. Thus, all stakeholders, particularly school administrators and parents, must keep focused on devising educational programming that best meets the child's unique needs.

It is also important to note that participation in the general curriculum does not mean the same thing as inclusion in general education classes. "Inclusion in a regular classroom concerns the setting where a student with a disability is educated. . . Participation in the general curriculum concerns what a student learns."[20] The IDEA has never required that students receive inclusive instruction, but the law expects that students for whom the LRE is not the general classroom will be taught the general curriculum to the maximum extent appropriate to their learning needs, wherever they receive instruction.

In providing students with FAPE, the IDEA requires school personnel to follow a proper sequence: finding a student eligible to receive special education, conducting an assessment to determine a student's unique educational needs, developing a student's IEP, and then determining the instructional placement that, for this particular student, constitutes the LRE.[21] In order to ensure educational benefit for individual students and to protect their educational rights in the process, decisions regarding IEPs and instructional placement must never be made by one individual—either a parent or a school official. Instead, programming and placement decisions are to be made by the consensus of a team comprising the child's parents and school personnel.

IDEA stipulates that IEP teams must include the following members: (1) the parents of the child; (2) at least one general education teacher (if the child is, or may be, participating in the general education environment); (3) at least one special education teacher of the child, or, if appropriate, at least one special education provider of the child; (4) a representative of the public agency who is qualified to provide, or supervise the provision of, specially designed instruction to meet the unique needs of children with disabilities, is knowledgeable about the general curriculum, and is knowledgeable about the availability of resources of the public agency; (5) an individual who can interpret the instructional implications of evaluation results, who may already be a member of the team; (6) at the discretion of the parent or the agency, other individuals who have knowledge or special expertise regarding the child, including related services personnel as appropriate; and (7) if appropriate, the child.[22]

IEPs: Prescribing an Appropriate Education

A FAPE remains the centerpiece of the IDEA, and the concept of FAPE is assured through the IEP process. A FAPE is defined as special education and related services that are provided at public expense, under public direction, and that meet the standards set by the state's department of education.[23] School officials must provide FAPE across the grade levels for school-aged youth in preschools, elementary schools, or secondary schools, and the special education and related services students receive must be provided in conformity with their IEPs.[24] In general, an IEP is a written document that describes a child's educational needs, details the special education and related services the district will provide to meet those needs, and stipulates the goals that will serve to assess whether the student's needs were, indeed, met.[25]

Failure to develop and implement an IEP correctly is a denial of FAPE and a violation of law.[26] Although formats will vary across school systems, each IEP must include the following information, for the following reasons:

1. *Performance Data.* The IDEA directs that an IEP must address the student's "present levels of academic achievement and functional performance."[27] This description must include how the disability affects the student's participation and progress in the general curriculum (or, for preschoolers, appropriate activities). This statement provides the starting point from which progress will be assessed, and it is recommended that performance data be stated measurably.

2. *Measurable Annual Goals.* Measurable annual goals are required in IEPs. The IDEA 2004 stipulates the inclusion of measurable academic and functional goals,[28] eliminating mandatory short-term objectives for most students. A description of benchmarks or short-term objectives must be included only for students with the most significant cognitive disabilities taking off-level assessments, or what the statute refers to as "alternate assessments aligned to alternate achievement standards."[29]

Traditionally, benchmarks or short-term objectives were included in IEPs so that personnel would know how to meet the student's disability-related needs and how to enable involvement and progress in the general curriculum. Measurable goals have always been required so that the effectiveness of the district services could be evaluated.[30] Goals should focus on what a student needs to learn both within and beyond the general education curriculum, because students with disabilities often need intensive instruction in curricular areas not addressed by the general education curriculum such as social skills, self-advocacy, cognitive strategies, and independent living.[31]

3. *A Means to Measure Progress.* A statement is required to show how the child's progress toward the annual goals will be measured. The IDEA 2004 allows school systems to use "quarterly or other periodic reports, concurrent with the issuance of report cards" that delineate the progress the child is making toward meeting the annual goals.[32] The parents of special education students should be informed about progress at least as often as parents of nondisabled children, so that they might evaluate the extent to which the progress is sufficient to enable their child to achieve the goals by the end of the IEP period.[33]

4. *Services and Modifications.* A statement must address the special education, related services, and supplementary aids and services that are to be provided to the student. The IDEA 2004 requires that these practices be "based on peer-reviewed research to the extent practicable."[34] The statement must also address specific program modifications or supports for personnel, so that the student can progress toward annual goals, progress in the general curriculum, and be educated and participate in extracurricular and nonacademic activities with other students, both those with disabilities and those without disabilities.[35] The regular education teacher on the IEP team is expected to help in determining the appropriate classroom services and modifications necessary for teaching the student appropriately.[36]

5. *Instructional Placement.* The IEP document must contain an explanation regarding the extent, if any, to which the student will not participate with nondisabled students in regular classes and in non-academic activities.[37] As a result, the percentage of time a student spends in special settings for special purposes can be linked

directly to the measurable goals, services, and modifications that the IEP team determined to be most appropriate for the student. This practice prevents teams from determining placements by disability category, or by administrative convenience, and promotes placements that foster the delivery of appropriate instruction.[38]

6. *Individually Appropriate Testing Accommodations.* The IDEA 2004 addresses test administration and accountability for results, requiring a statement of "any individual appropriate accommodations that are necessary to measure the academic achievement and functional performance of the child on State and district-wide assessments."[39] If the IEP team determines that the student will take an alternate assessment of achievement, a statement must address why he or she cannot participate in the regular assessment, and why the alternate assessment is individually appropriate.[40]

7. *Initiation Date and Service Delivery Details.* The IEP also must include the projected date for the beginning of the services and modifications prescribed for the student, as well as the anticipated frequency, location, and duration of those services and modifications.[41] No services are to be provided to a student prior to the initiation date of the IEP.[42]

8. *Transition Services.* The IDEA 2004 emphasizes accountability for transition services promoting post-school employment or education for students with disabilities. New provisions require that a statement of appropriate, measurable, postsecondary goals and transition services be formulated no later than the first IEP in effect when a student turns 16 years old, and then be updated annually.[43] Specific, measurable goals must be based upon age-appropriate transition assessments related to training, education, and employment, and, when appropriate, independent living skills. The transition services to be provided (including the prescribed courses of study) must be necessary to assist the student in reaching those goals.[44] At least one year before the student reaches the age of majority under state law, a statement must be included in the IEP signifying that the student has been informed of the rights that would transfer to him or her upon reaching the age of majority.[45]

In addition to the more specific requirements described above, the IDEA sets forth a number of additional considerations that a student's IEP team must consider.[46] Teams must consider the strengths of the student[47] and the parents' concerns for enhancing the education of their child.[48] Individualization is an essential component of transition services.[49] The IEP team also must consider the results of the initial or most recent evaluation of the student and, as appropriate, the results of the student's performance on any general state or district-wide assessment programs.[50] Finally, the team is required to consider both the academic and the functional needs of the child.[51]

In certain circumstances, special factors must be considered by the team and documented in the IEP.[52] In the case of a student whose behavior impedes his or her learning or that of others, IEP teams must consider, if appropriate, strategies to address that behavior, including positive behavioral interventions, strategies, and supports.[53] It is important to note that this requirement is not just for students with emotional disturbance. In the case of students with limited English proficiency, IEP teams must consider language needs as they relate to the IEP.[54] For students who are blind or visually impaired, IEP teams must provide for instruction in Braille and the use of Braille unless the team determines, after an evaluation of the student's reading and writing skills and needs, that instruction in Braille or the use of Braille is not individually appropriate.[55]

IEP teams must also consider the communication needs of students. In the case of a student who is deaf or hard of hearing, the team must consider language and communication needs; opportunities for direct communications with peers and professional personnel in the student's language and communication mode; academic level; and full range of needs, including opportunities for direct instruction in the student's language and communication mode.[56] IEP teams must consider whether students require assistive technology devices and services.[57] If, in considering any of these special factors, the team determines that a student needs a particular device or service (including an intervention, accommodation, or other program modification) in order to receive FAPE, the team must include a statement to that effect in the student's IEP.[58]

The IDEA 2004 included provisions designed to reduce the number of meetings and the amount of paperwork associated with IEPs. These provisions address attendance at meetings, changes to the IEP, and programming for transfer students. The IDEA now requires school systems to ensure FAPE to students with IEPs transferring from other states within the same academic year.[59] Services comparable to those in the IEP developed in the other state must be provided, in consultation with parents, until the school system conducts an evaluation and, if appropriate, develops a new IEP.[60] A student with an IEP who transfers within the same state within the same academic year are also to be provided with comparable services to the IEP developed by the prior district until the receiving school system either adopts the prior IEP or develops and implements a new one.[61]

IDEA 2004 modified the requirements for team members to attend IEP meetings. When parents agree in writing, members may be excused who have provided input into the IEP prior to the meeting, or whose areas of curriculum or related services are not being modified or discussed at the meeting.[62] The IDEA does require that school systems invite appropriate early intervention service providers to initial IEP meetings if requested by parents to smooth the transition from preschool.[63] Parents and professionals may also agree to meet using alternative means, such as telephone and video conferences.[64]

In reviewing the critical components and special factors to be included in developing IEPs, it becomes clear how the IEP document is intended to carry out the stated purpose of the IDEA. An IEP is not a simple plan of action; an IEP is a specific program designed to achieve results for a specific student. Educational programs of any kind are designed to address learning targets by setting measurable goals and developing ways to evaluate whether the services provided to the recipients were sufficient to meet the goals. Individualized education programs are no exception. To address the kinds of educational benefit a student might receive, the IEP process must rely on an analysis of performance data enhanced by the thoughtful consideration of the transition supports necessary to guide a special education student toward his or her future.

Determining the Extent of Educational Benefit

School officials might well ask the question, what is the proper measure of educational benefit for special education students in this era of standards-based reform?[65] The basic right to learn is the centerpiece of the accountability movement, and the proof of learning is now assumed to rest in positive results, not perfectly executed procedures. Program improvements and educational progress for typically developing students are being assessed against standard measures. However, assessing the progress of special education students is complicated by the nature of the disability and the type of assessments used by most states. Accommodations can conflict with the construct validity of tests, and research has yet to provide assurance that these assessments are accurately measuring what students really know and are able to do.[66] There are also major concerns with whether these assessments are broad enough to capture the various ways that special education students demonstrate their capabilities rather than their disabilities.[67]

A fixed standard of *appropriate* has never been set by Congress nor established by the courts.[68] In a landmark special education decision issued in 1982, known as *Board of Education of Hendrick Hudson Central School District v. Rowley*,[69] the U.S. Supreme Court determined that *appropriate* meant tailored to a child's individual needs, not to the needs of the school system; however the Court also found that a child's IEP provided an "appropriate" education so long as it was reasonably designed to enable the child to obtain educational benefit, and not a higher standard that would require the IEP to maximize a child's educational potential.[70] Since the *Rowley* decision, cases addressing a FAPE have hinged on the provision of an IEP that was reasonably calculated to address a student's unique educational needs and provide educational benefit. Educational benefit was not substantively defined by the Court as an opportunity equal to that of non-disabled children, nor did the justices establish a test that would determine the adequacy of the benefits special education students should receive.[71] However, the Court provided guidance in the form of a two-part inquiry to determine if the programming designed for a student was appropriate. First, has the program embodied in the IEP been developed by the school system in a manner procedurally consistent with the law, and second, is the IEP based on a student's unique educational needs and reasonably calculated to confer educational benefit? If this two-part analysis has been met, the school system has complied with the obligations imposed by Congress, and "the courts can require no more."[72]

Most states define an appropriate education according to the federal standard set by the Supreme Court and, in some cases, courts have used colorful language to illustrate its meaning. For example, the federal Sixth Circuit Court of Appeals used an automotive metaphor in noting that school systems are required to provide "the educational equivalent of a serviceable Chevrolet" to each student, rather than a Cadillac.[73] The court noted that "the Chevrolet offered to [the student] is in fact a much nicer model than that offered to the average student," suggesting that a customized model offers special value in driving students with special needs toward successful outcomes.[74] This last concept is important to note because the benefit conferred by an IEP must be more than de minimis, or trivial.[75] And yet the courts struggle to be more explicit in relating the concept of appropriateness to an individual student's needs, taking into consideration the child's capacity to learn.[76]

In recent years, the concept of *appropriate* has been linked to the contents of the IEP with empirical data about student outcomes.[77] Increased attention to academic performance, especially for students with learning disabilities, characterizes some decisions in which passing grades in regular classes were seen as indicators of FAPE for students pursuing a regular high school diploma.[78] Good grades may provide some evidence of compliance with the IDEA, but as a matter of law, they do not determine whether a school district provided FAPE.[79] In some cases, good report card grades were seen as encouragements rather than as achievements reflecting a student's progress.[80] In *Hall v. Vance County Board of Education,*[81] the Fourth Circuit Court of Appeals discounted grades and turned to standardized test scores and independent evaluations to determine that a student with severe learning disabilities had been denied FAPE, despite passing grades and promotion to the next grade level. The Supreme Court in *Florence County School District Four v. Carter*[82] referred to the *Rowley* decision in noting the appropriate amount of regular education progress depends upon the abilities of each individual special education student. In this case, the IEP goals for Shannon Carter, a student with specific learning disabilities, were determined to be insufficient considering her capability for achieving more than four months growth over one year's time. In other cases, some students, because of the extent of their disabilities, will not be able to perform at grade level or will take more time than typical to do so.

It is important to note that, if a student is denied FAPE, a school district may be required to reimburse parents for private school tuition. In the case of *Cypress-Fairbanks Independent School District v. Michael F.,*[83] the Fifth Circuit Court of Appeals determined that an appropriate IEP must provide educational benefits that are likely to produce meaningful progress for a student, rather than regression or minimal educational advancement. In finding that the school system's IEP provided an appropriate education to Michael, a student with attention deficit hyperactivity disorder (ADHD) and Tourette syndrome, the court considered four factors: (1) was the program individualized on the basis of the student's assessment and performance; (2) was the program administered in the least restrictive environment; (3) were the services provided in a coordinated and collaborative manner by the key stakeholders; and (4) were positive academic and nonacademic benefits demonstrated?[84]

The Fifth Circuit further determined that the Michael's IEP was specifically designed to address his individual needs, and that he had been placed in the least restrictive educational environment consistent with those needs.[85] The court relied on testimony provided by individuals who had direct and frequent contact with Michael, including personnel who coordinated his academic and behavioral services when he attended district schools.[86] Accordingly, Michael was achieving passing grades in classes, as well as managing his behavior well enough to eat lunch and travel through the building without a chaperone.[87] Using the four-point test, the court determined that the IEP "was reasonably calculated to, and in fact did, produce meaningful educational benefits both academically and behaviorally."[88] For these reasons, the court denied tuition reimbursement to Michael's parents for enrolling him in private school because the district had met its obligation to provide an appropriate IEP.[89] The court also ordered his parents to pay certain of the district's costs, but not attorney fees.[90]

The Fifth Circuit similarly defined *appropriate* as being demonstrated by student outcome data in the case of *Houston Independent School District v. Bobby R.*,[91] in which parents were also denied reimbursement for their son's private school tuition. In deciding whether the IEP for Caius, a student with dyslexia and attention deficit disorder, had conferred demonstrable academic and non-academic benefits, the court again applied the four factors outlined in the *Michael F.* case.[92] In this case, the court used grade-level test scores from the Woodcock-Johnson cognitive and achievement test batteries as objective evidence of Caius's progress. In explaining its decision, the court made several things clear:

1.   A student's academic and non-academic development should be measured against that individual student's prior performance and not by his relation to the rest of the class.[93]
2.   Declining percentile scores do not necessarily represent a lack of educational benefit, rather the student's inability to maintain the same level of academic progress achieved by his non-disabled peers in regular classes.[94]
3.   It is not necessary for the student to improve in every area in order to obtain educational benefits from the IEP.[95]
4.   The party challenging the IEP must show more than a trivial failure to implement all elements of the IEP, and instead must demonstrate

that the school system failed to implement substantial or significant provisions of the IEP.[96]

The Fifth Circuit referred to the Supreme Court's decision in *Rowley* in stating that the question whether the student might have received a greater benefit under different circumstances was not relevant because the IDEA does not require maximization of a disabled student's educational potential.[97] The court noted that, although school officials have some flexibility in implementing IEPs, they are held accountable for material failures and for providing a child with meaningful educational benefits.

After more than three decades since deciding *Rowley*, the Supreme Court again addressed the meaning of the word "appropriate" and, in particular, the means by which an "educational benefit" is measured. In 2015, the Tenth Circuit Court of Appeals decided a case, *Endrew F. v. Douglas City School District RE-1*,[98] in which it examined the means to determine whether a student's IEP was reasonably calculated to provide education benefit. The case involved an appeal of an administrative law judge's (ALJ) decision with regard to a due process complaint filed by the child's parents.[99] The student's parents contended that the school district had not provided a FAPE and sought tuition reimbursement because they had placed him in a private school.[100] The ALJ had ruled that the Douglas City School District had provided a FAPE, and thus denied reimbursement.[101] The student's parents then filed in federal district court and, after the district court affirmed the ALJ's decision, filed an appeal with the Tenth Circuit.[102]

The Tenth Circuit, in applying the first part of the *Rowley* test, found that the school district had not committed any procedural errors that would result in the denial of a FAPE.[103] The court then addressed the parents' contention that the IEP was substantively inadequate because it did not provide meaningful educational benefit. The Tenth Circuit court found that the school district's IEP had met the second part of the *Rowley* test because the IEP did provide "some educational benefit," even as the Tenth Circuit acknowledged that other federal appellate courts have applied a higher standard of "meaningful educational benefit."[104] According to the Tenth Circuit court to meet the test of providing FAPE, a school district only had to provide an education that conferred a little more than de minimis, or trivial, educational benefit to the student in question.

On December 22, 2015, the parents filed a petition for a writ of certiorari with the U.S. Supreme Court.[105] The parents' petition posed the following question for the Court's review: "What is the level of educational benefit that school districts must confer on children with disabilities to provide them with a free appropriate public education guaranteed by the Individuals with Disabilities Education Act?"[106] On August 18, 2016, the U.S. Solicitor General filed an amicus brief in which the government urged the Supreme Court to grant the petition.[107] On September 29, 2016, the Supreme Court granted the parents' petition, thus agreeing to hear the case.[108] Oral arguments in the case were heard on January 11, 2017 and on March 22, 2017, the High Court announced its decision in *Endrew*.[109]

Chief Justice John Roberts wrote the opinion for the unanimous Court. In the decision, Justice Roberts wrote for a school district "to meet its substantive obligation under the IDEA, a school must offer an IEP reasonably calculated to enable a child to make progress appropriate in light of the child's circumstances."[110] Justice Roberts also noted that the new standard that the justices developed was "markedly more demanding than the 'merely more than de minimis' test applied by the tenth circuit,"[111] and that "(a) substantive standard not focused on student progress would do little to remedy the pervasive and tragic academic stagnation that prompted Congress to act" in 1975.[112]

The Supreme Court's new educational benefit standard requires that schools offer an IEP reasonably calculated to enable a child to make appropriate progress in light of the child's circumstances. Justice Roberts noted that the new standard was not a formula and that although the new educational benefit standard was clearly higher than the de minimis educational benefit standard, it was not a prescription for hearing officers and judges to follow when determining if a school district has conferred educational benefit. Rather, the decision means that hearing officers and judges will need to focus on the appropriateness of an IEP on a case-by-case basis and judge the adequacy of the IEP vis a vis "the unique circumstances of the child for whom it was created."[113] As Justice Robert's wrote:

> A reviewing court may fairly expect (school officials) to be able to offer a cogent and responsive explanation for their decisions that shows the IEP is reasonably calculated to enable the child to make progress appropriate in light of his (or her) circumstances.[114]

Selection of Educational Methodologies for Particular Students

The *Rowley* and the *Endrew* courts clarified that, once an IEP has been determined to be appropriate, deference is to be extended to professionals, and courts are not to substitute their judgments for those of experts with regard to educational methodologies.[115] However, recent increases in litigation addressing private school tuition reimbursement, particularly cases involving students with autism, suggest that methodology is not escaping scrutiny as relevant to FAPE.[116] In *Nein v. Greater Clark County School Corporation*,[117] the federal district court determined that Lucas, an illiterate 12-year-old with severe learning disabilities and a full-scale IQ of 95, was making insufficient progress in the county's Milestones reading program.[118] Even though he was being promoted and making good grades, Lucas could not even read restroom signs.[119] The court drew on the Sixth Circuit's metaphor, finding that the county's insufficiently intensive reading instruction from grade 1-4 provided him "a Chevrolet without a transmission—even if the engine might run, no power ever reached the wheels."[120]

While school systems are entitled to deference in selecting educational methodologies, the school system nonetheless must evaluate a teaching method proposed by the child's parents and cannot "predetermine" to reject that proposed methodology. In *Deal v. Hamilton Board of Education*,[121] the Sixth Circuit held that the federal district court had erred in substituting his own judgment on teaching methodology for that of the administrative hearing officer, who had determined that the school district had violated IDEA by summarily rejecting the parents' proposed teaching methodology.[122] In so holding, the Sixth Circuit noted that, when different methodologies result in vastly different outcomes for the student, providing a lesser program could result in a denial of FAPE.[123] In its decision issued after the Sixth Circuit remanded the case, the federal district court determined that the school district's proposed IEP, together with its proposed teaching methodology, had provided a FAPE.[124] Quoting *J.P. v. West Clark Community Schools*,[125] the federal district court in *Deal* clarified that "whether an approach used in any particular case 'qualifies' as a sound educational practice is fact-specific."[126]

The *J.P.* case also involved a student with autism.[127] In the case, the court determined that, when confronted with a dispute involving competing educational approaches, the court must consider the following criteria: (a) whether school officials can explain the specific benefits of using the methods with the particular child; (b) whether local educators have the experience and expertise to use them successfully; and (c) whether qualified educational experts consider the methods to be at least adequate under the circumstances.[128] In the *J.P.* case, the court found that the district had provided sufficient answers to questions about methodology and that evidence, along with the judgment of the hearing officer, was sufficient for the court to determine that a FAPE had been provided.[129]

The validity of selected practices is a serious concern in providing FAPE.[130] Provisions in the IDEA 2004 require IEPs to include "a statement of the special education and related services and supplementary aids and services, based on peer-reviewed research to the extent practicable, to be provided to the child, or on behalf of the child" to enable appropriate advancement toward annual goals, and participation and progress in the general curriculum.[131] The requirement is intended to strengthen the effectiveness of methods used by school districts, increasing the probability that a given approach "works" and is reasonably calculated to result in educational benefit.[132] In science, researchers enhance their credibility when their work is reviewed by other experts and published in scholarly journals. In schools, educators enhance their effectiveness when they use validated methods in the ways they were intended and with the group of students for whom they were designed.

With regard to whether parents or school districts bear the burden of proving that an IEP provides an appropriate education (or FAPE), the IDEA is silent, but in *Schaffer v. Weast*,[133] the Supreme Court decided that the burden of persuasion rests with the party seeking relief. In effect, this means that parents who challenge an IEP must prove to a hearing officer that the district denied their child FAPE, unless state laws suggest otherwise.[134] In the pro-parent decision of *Winkelman v. Parma City School District*,[135] the Court held that the IDEA grants parents independent, enforceable rights, not limited to procedural and reimbursement-related matters, but extending to the substantive formulation of their child's educational program. Collectively, these Supreme Court decisions underscore the shared responsibility throughout the IEP process for professional diligence in meeting a child's individual needs, and parental vigilance in ensuring that those needs are met appropriately.

The IEP was referred to by the Supreme Court in *Rowley* as a "written record of reasonable expectations."[136] However, educators have too often focused IEPs on expectations for what a student will achieve, including lengthy lists of goals, instead of emphasizing expectations for what the school system will provide. From the perspective of distributed leadership, IEPs are tools that communicate to members across various professional communities what needs to be done, specifically and intensively, to help a child learn.[137] From the perspective of law, IEPs secure the right to an individually appropriate education, prompting one advocate to remark, "you can fight over placement all you want, but if you want to win, you need to control the content of the IEP."[138]

LRE: Utilizing the Principle of the Least Restrictive Environment

Not all cases determining the appropriateness of an IEP involve disputes over placement, but all disputes over placement are determined by the appropriateness of an IEP. The most contentious of these disputes have centered on issues of placement in the LRE. The LRE requirements of the IDEA set out the factors to consider in educating students with and without disabilities together to the maximum extent appropriate.[139] In the language of law, the LRE principle is considered to be a rebuttable presumption. In other words, the law presumes that the least restrictive placement for any student to receive appropriate instruction is the regular education classroom. Presumptive placement in the regular education classroom is rebutted by convincing evidence that a particular student would receive an appropriate education in an alternative placement. For this reason, school officials are legally required to make a full continuum of alternative learning environments available across the system that range from regular classes, special classes, separate schools, residential facilities, hospitals, to home settings.[140]

The IDEA's federal regulations set out the requirements that school officials must follow in order to prevent the troubling practice of placing special education students in general education classes without regard to their specific learning needs. The IDEA regulations set out fact-specific guidelines stipulating that placement decisions must be made by a group of people, including the student's parents and others who are knowledgeable about the child, the meaning of the evaluation data, and the placement options.[141] Placement decisions are also to be made in conformity with the LRE provisions.[142] Placement decisions must be made annually, must be based on the IEP, and must give consideration to any potential harmful effect on the child or to the quality of the required services.[143] Unless their IEPs require otherwise, students with disabilities are expected to attend a school as close to home as possible or the school they would attend if they were not disabled.[144] A special education student must not be removed from education in age-appropriate regular classrooms solely because of needed modifications in the general curriculum[145] Indeed, the IDEA expressly provides that, for some students with disabilities, the appropriate placement may be in a private school, with the tuition being paid for by the public school system.[146]

Under the IDEA, the LRE is not a specific location but the outcome of a procedural process in which, when determining placement, greater weight is given to the requirement of FAPE than to other factors, such as an interest in integrating students with disabilities across instructional settings. In making placement decisions, courts should carefully compare the FAPE requirement that the student obtain educational benefit with the statute's overall preference for placement in the regular classroom. Parents and professionals, less familiar with the law's presumptive language, often confuse the terms mainstreaming, inclusion, and LRE, but these terms do not have interchangeable meanings.[147] Mainstreaming implies that special education and general education students will be educated together as appropriate but not exclusively.[148] Full inclusion implies that students with disabilities have an absolute right to regular class placement.[149] The term LRE is not synonymous with inclusion, but rather requires that placement decisions for students be made on the basis of an appropriate IEP.[150] In other words, the LRE is the least restrictive (most inclusive) education setting in which the student can obtain the educational benefits sought by the student's IEP. The IDEA does not require the practices of mainstreaming and inclusion;[151] rather educators often see them as strategies that can be used to operationalize the LRE principle in schools. The concept of LRE means that, when school officials cannot provide a beneficial education to a student with disabilities in the same way they do for typically developing students, they must meet their obligation to provide FAPE using the *least* restrictive alternative to usual practices.[152]

In making LRE placement decisions, school officials should keep the issue of place in perspective by remembering that *where* a student receives instruction is only one component of an appropriate education. Some students may need instruction that cannot be provided in regular classes because they need to learn something different than general education students, such as Braille, American Sign Language, or specific technologies that are more efficiently taught in other settings. Some students may need to learn things differently, such as students with severe learning disabilities who need intensive reading instruction in more private learning environments, or students with cognitive disabilities whose job training and life skills curriculum requires them to spend time in community-based settings. The LRE requirement compels school systems to make a continuum of options possible so that IEP teams can make appropriate student-centered placement decisions across a range of viable alternatives.[153]

In making legally correct placement decisions, what might be *possible* for the system to provide should not be construed as synonymous with what would actually be *appropriate* for a particular student to receive because some possibilities can cause harm. For this reason, school officials need to tally the benefits of regular classes for each special education student, but also calculate the risks. Educational harm can result when decisions about students are based on stereotypes instead of individual strengths; when students are misplaced and left in separate settings that do not match their needs; or when they are included in regular classes without receiving services that comport with their IEPs. The word *harm* is mentioned only once in the IDEA, and that is in the LRE requirements of the federal regulations.[154]

Placement: Determining Appropriate Educational Settings

Currently, there is no national framework employed by courts in making placement decisions. The Supreme Court has not decided any cases involving placement, so each federal appellate circuit court uses its preferred framework to resolve cases related to LRE.[155] Several circuit courts have devised judicial tests, or analytic frameworks, to evaluate whether a school system has complied with the LRE requirement such that the student with disabilities who is in a regular class placement is achieving satisfactory educational benefit.[156] Circuits not relying on analytic frameworks balance the benefit of special education and general education in determining if a student can be educated satisfactorily in regular classes. These judicial tests illustrate critical components to consider in making placement decisions.

One such framework was developed by the Sixth Circuit Court of Appeals in its 1983 decision in *Roncker v. Walter*,[157] in which the court addressed the fundamental question whether a student should be educated in a general education setting as opposed to a segregated setting. This framework uses a feasibility test, or a portability test, to determine whether services that make a specialized or segregated placement superior could be feasibly provided in a regular education setting.[158] Feasibility is defined by whether any marginal benefits of typical settings are outweighed by the benefits of the special setting; whether the student is disruptive in a typical setting; and whether the costs of serving one student in a typical setting are excessive, depriving other students from getting the services they need.[159] This analytic framework requires school systems to be proactive by considering if specialized services might be transported to typical educational settings. If it is feasible to replicate services that are critical to an individual student's appropriate education, then the special setting is not the LRE.[160] The Eighth Circuit Court of Appeals also has adopted this feasibility test.[161]

In contrast, the Fifth Circuit Court of Appeals devised a different framework in its 1989 case of *Daniel R. R. v. State Board of Education*.[162] This framework considers the benefits of supplementary aids and services, and the non-academic as well as academic benefits of a general education placement. In this case, the Fifth Circuit rejected the *Roncker* portability standard, viewing the feasibility of transporting services to more integrated settings as dependent on contextual circumstances and reliant on the judgments of school officials, not of courts.

The *Daniel R.R.* framework requires a child-centered and fact-specific inquiry that asks two questions: (1) whether education in the regular classroom, with the use of supplementary aids and services, can be achieved satisfactorily for a given student, and if not, (2) whether the school has included the student to the maximum extent appropriate.[163] In making this determination, school officials must balance whether the student can benefit more from general or from special education. In doing so, school officials must consider more than token attempts at modifying instruction, but they need not offer every conceivable service nor completely alter the standard program. Undue teacher time and undue curricular modification are not required. According to the court, this inquiry focuses on the student's ability to grasp the essential elements of the general curriculum. As in the *Roncker* analysis, school officials can consider the effect this child will have on other children and the quality of their education.[164] The Second, Third, Tenth and Eleventh Circuit Courts of Appeal have adopted the *Daniel R.R.* framework.[165]

In the 1994 case of *Sacramento City Unified School District v. Rachel H.* (the "*Holland*" case),[166] the Ninth Circuit Court of Appeals outlined a framework that is clearly related to the previous two frameworks. However, the *Holland* test differs from the others by not balancing the benefits of special or general education but considering only if a student can receive education satisfactorily in regular classes.[167] This analysis addresses four issues: (1) the educational benefits of placing the student in a full-time regular education program; (2) the non-academic benefits of such a placement; (3) the effect the student would have on the teacher and other students in the regular classroom; and (4) the costs associated with this placement.[168]

In 1994, yet another federal court, the Fourth Circuit Court of Appeals, decided the case of *DeVries v. Fairfax County School Board*,[169] in which a fourth framework was established. The court noted that Congress had expressed a strong preference for students with disabilities to be educated in the mainstream, but also stated that mainstream placements would not be appropriate for every student with a disability.[170] The court cited portions of both the *Roncker* and *Daniel R.R.* tests and fashioned its own three-part test. According to the *Devries* test, mainstreaming is not required when (a) a student with a disability would not receive educational benefit from mainstreaming in a general education class; (b) any marginal benefit from mainstreaming would be significantly outweighed by benefits that could feasibly be obtained only in a separate instructional setting; or (c) the student is a disruptive force in the general education classroom.[171]

Although the circumstances surrounding each student were different in these cases, the analytical frameworks used to determine placements for them continue to guide school officials and to inform judges in making decisions that comport with both the standard of FAPE and the principle of LRE.

For example, the *Roncker* and *Daniel R. R.* frameworks were put to the test in a case addressing the disputed placement of Beth, a 13-year-old student with Rett syndrome, a rare neurological condition that severely impairs both cognitive and physical functioning. In *Beth B. v. Van Clay,* [172] the federal district court in Illinois noted that neither the Supreme Court nor the Seventh Circuit has indicated a preference among the various judicial tests. Before applying its analysis, the court discussed the merits of each framework, finding the *Daniel R. R.* test superior to the others in tracking the statutory language of the IDEA.[173] In addition, the court determined that the standard of feasibility in the *Roncker* analysis placed too much emphasis on what services could be delivered, but not enough on what the student actually learned.[174]

The district court first analyzed Beth's current regular class placement using the *Daniel R.R.* test. It first examined the central question of whether Beth could be satisfactorily educated in the general education classroom. The court noted that the school system made many attempts to accommodate her in the general education setting, including the individualized services of two teacher-aides, an inclusion facilitator, and a customized curriculum using laminated books with embossed pictures and modified text.[175] The district also provided a variety of assistive technologies and trained personnel and other students how to use these technologies in communicating with Beth. Although these were described by her parents as inadequate and by the school system as Herculean efforts, the court determined that Beth's progress in the inclusive regular class setting was best described as inconsistent.[176]

In applying the *Daniel R. R.* test, the court noted that the IDEA does not require changes so extensive that the standard curriculum becomes unrecognizable.[177] Significant alterations were made in the seventh-grade classroom to adjust to Beth's severe cognitive delays and other issues. Because of her disability, Beth frequently dozed in school, took twenty-to-thirty-minute scheduled toilet breaks, and was frequently absent. Thus, even though she remained in the general education classroom, she was not learning the same or even slightly modified material. In addition, as Beth advanced in grade levels, her interactions with other class members diminished.

The court next considered Beth's effect on both students and teachers in the learning environment, finding that only on occasion were her outbursts or needs distracting to other students.[178] However, Beth's teachers could not work with her and with other students simultaneously because of the significantly modified nature of her curriculum. For these reasons, the court determined that Beth could not be satisfactorily educated in a regular classroom.

The court next turned to the second prong of the *Daniel R. R.* analysis, finding the district's plans for reverse mainstreaming—and for inclusion in non-academic activities including art, music, lunch, and field trips—acceptable opportunities for social integration. Using the *Daniel R. R.* analytical framework, the court determined that the statutory presumption for regular class placement was overcome.

The court next analyzed Beth's placement using the *Roncker* test. The court first found that the specialized programming was superior to regular programming for Beth. The specialized setting provided her with more direct contact with teachers who were trained and experienced in educating students with cognitive disabilities. In the smaller, more specialized setting, Beth could receive close attention from the teacher without detracting from other students. Not only were the teachers specially trained to work with students like Beth, the program's administrator had previous experience with students with Rett syndrome. Although other personnel could be trained to communicate with Beth, such training was not viewed as equivalent to the specialized preparation and experience of special education teachers. According to the court, "special education is also more conducive to systematic instruction. Rather than attempting to keep pace, even in modified form, with her non-disabled classmates' lessons, Beth can repeat skills until she learns them."[179] Thus, the court found that the specialized setting was superior to placement in the general education setting. Finally, the court found that these advantages could not feasibly be duplicated in a regular education setting.

Beth's parents appealed the decision and invoked the IDEA's stay put provision[180] allowing Beth to remain in the regular class pending the resolution of the placement dispute. Upholding the judgment of the lower court, the Seventh Circuit Court expressly addressed the argument of Beth's parents that placement in the regular education classroom was mandated under LRE because she had obtained some educational benefit in the regular education classroom, thus satisfying the *Rowley* test to determine a FAPE. The Seventh Circuit characterized the FAPE-IEP determination as being the threshold for any placement inquiry.[181] It first considered the appropriateness of the IEP in terms of educational benefit and determined that the FAPE mandate was not at issue. Warning that "the FAPE provision and LRE provision are two sides of the same IEP coin,"[182] the court rejected the concept that, so long as a child obtains *some* educational benefit in the regular class, the school could not remove her from the setting. The court instructed that "the *Rowley* holding applies only to the school district's responsibility to provide a FAPE—a requirement that analyzes the appropriateness of the district's placement—not the appropriateness of its alternative, in this case, the regular setting."[183] Indeed, misapplying the *Rowley* standard to placement decisions instead of correctly applying it to decisions about an appropriate IEP would "turn the 'some educational benefit' language on its head."[184]

The court declined to adopt a formal framework for use in the Seventh Circuit, but relied on a fact-specific inquiry in finding that the school system's placement represented "an acceptable point along the continuum of services between total integration and complete segregation."[185] As long as the special program included opportunities for interaction with non-disabled peers, the placement satisfied the requirement that Beth be mainstreamed to the maximum extent appropriate. The Supreme Court denied Beth's parents' petition for a writ of certiorari.[186]

Although the Supreme Court established the standard of appropriateness in 1982, the attendant principle of instructional placement in the LRE continues to be left to members of the professional community and the courts to decide. Over the past few decades, legal analysts have developed sets of questions to guide LRE decision making[187] and established sequenced formats to ensure full consideration of the LRE placement requirements.[188] Although the IDEA prefers inclusion, it does not require inclusion; however, courts give careful scrutiny to decisions that place students in more restrictive settings. Placement decisions require thoughtful analysis because the law acknowledges a rational basis for determining, on a case-by-case basis, that a child's FAPE might be provided in specialized settings using differing treatments. All involved individuals, including particularly school administrators and parents, need to understand that when IEP teams are determining a student's placement, the primary consideration must be the unique individual needs of a student and the placement in which these needs can best be met. Moreover, "when there is uncertainty about the appropriate placement for a student, the IEP team should make a documented diligent and good-faith effort to educate the student in the least restrictive environment before considering, much less proposing, a more restrictive one."[189]

Changing Placements and Protecting Individual Rights

Fiscal resources and due process protections support the special education process, and the assurance of both funding and civil rights commands the attention of school administrators. FAPE is at risk when inadequate funding threatens the provision of costly but appropriate services. The IDEA places the fiscal burden for educating students with disabilities on school systems, and cost may not be a factor in providing a particular student with needed services. In a few cases, usually related to placements, where an appropriate education can be provided in more than one setting, school officials are permitted to select the less-expensive option.[190]

FAPE is also at risk when inadequate safeguards fail to ensure a student's right to receive an individually appropriate education. The IDEA is a child-centered law, and procedural protections surround decisions about IEPs, LRE, and placements. Parents, on behalf of their child, and students at the age of majority have the right to receive prior written notice and to participate in all meetings regarding identification, evaluation, programming, or placement. Informed consent is only required for an initial evaluation to determine if services are necessary and then only to initiate those services if the child is found eligible to receive special education. Some states have additional requirements for parents to sign annual IEPs before services for the year can begin. If parents whose children are receiving special education refuse to sign consent at any point, school officials may seek an order from a hearing officer to proceed without consent, if that action seems to be in the student's best interests. Dangers arise when school officials appease parents at the child's expense—keeping the peace, but abandoning the child's best interests.

Prior written notice is also required when school officials propose any change in educational placement, including the proposal of a student's graduation with a regular education diploma.[191] In addition, the IDEA allows parents to pursue a due process hearing when they contest a change in placement for their child. However, courts are hesitant to grant hearings in cases where parents seek to prevent school officials from making organizational or fiscal decisions that affect more than their own child, such as closing or consolidating schools.[192] In these instances, it is important for school officials and for parents to understand the differences in meaning between a "program" and a "placement" under the IDEA. Students with disabilities can be transferred from schools or classes without these transfers being regarded as changes in placement, as long as the educational program offered in each setting is comparable and equally appropriate. Only when the services prescribed in a student's current IEP cannot be implemented in the new setting has a change in placement occurred that substantially affects a student's rights to an appropriate education.

Educating students in placements that support the delivery of appropriate instruction is a critical component of the IDEA, reinforcing the supportive role of placement in providing a student with FAPE. The percentage of time indicated on a student's IEP for the receipt of special education and related services outside the regular class is presumed to result from procedures that were legally correct and considerations that were student-specific. Educational placements that result from team-based decisions are presumed to comport with the delivery of services required by the IEP. Consequently, the IDEA's "stay put" provision prevents school officials from disrupting the provision of FAPE by removing students from placements over parental objections, pending the resolution of due process review proceedings.[193] In the case of *Hale v. Poplar Bluff R-I School District*,[194] the Eighth Circuit held that the stay put provision is to be rigorously enforced to stop schools from using the unilateral authority they once employed to exclude students with disabilities from school. In *Bell v. Education in the Unorganized Territories*, a district court in Maine relied on the stay put provision in determining that graduation was grounds for a disputed change in placement. In this case, the parents of Jesse Bell, a student with autism, challenged the district's proposal that their son graduate from high school with his class. Finding that the district failed to overcome the law's strong preference for preserving the educational status quo, the court determined that the student remain in his current placement attending to the curriculum prescribed in the previous year's IEP during the pendency of further proceedings. The decision in *C.P. v. Leon County School Board*[195] clarified for states in the Eleventh Circuit that the stay put provision does not require annual updating of an IEP.

Suspension and Expulsion

The only exception to the stay put provision occurs when a hearing officer finds substantial evidence to indicate that it would be dangerous for the student to remain in the current placement.[196] The IDEA permits school officials to remove students who inflict serious bodily injury to another person while at school, and students who bring weapons or illegal drugs to school or to school functions, for forty-five days if they attend an interim alternative educational setting. The discipline setting, not the pre-dispute setting, will be the stay put placement during contested disciplinary actions.[197] With regard to suspension and expulsion, the IDEA again employs the legal strategy of a rebuttable presumption, favoring the student's placement in the present setting, but allowing the presumption to be overcome by evidence that harm or danger might ensue. Suspending special education students for more than ten consecutive days, or expelling them from school, both represent changes of placement that trigger the use of procedural safeguards. Additionally, suspensions that total over ten cumulative days in a school year can also be a change in placement if the removals constitute a pattern.[198]

In these cases, the IDEA is clear: there is to be no cessation of educational services when students are suspended or removed to alternative settings.[199] Suspending or removing a student with a disability to an alternative setting for ten cumulative days in the same school year does not require educational services. On the eleventh cumulative school day of removal, and all subsequent days, educational services must be provided.[200] FAPE cannot be denied once it has been guaranteed through eligibility and initiated through an IEP. School officials must continue to provide services that allow special education students to have access to the general curriculum and to make progress toward their goals.

Although the disciplinary procedures of the IDEA affect student placement, they are essentially issues related to the principle of zero-reject, which stipulates that a student who has a disability cannot be denied an equitable educational opportunity.[201] The IDEA's requirements that IEPs for students whose behaviors impede their learning include behavioral intervention plans are essentially issues related to the provision of an appropriate education.[202] The U.S. Department of Education has provided strong guidance to school officials, recommending that proactive measures be taken to address misconduct as soon as it appears to prevent more drastic measures from being taken at a later point.[203] Functional behavioral assessments could be conducted to determine if the present programming for a student who engages in misconduct is sufficiently specialized to provide appropriate support.[204] A detailed examination of the IDEA's disciplinary procedures is contained in Chapter 9. But, consideration of proactive measures to address the misconduct of students through the IEP process,[205] ensuring that individuals with disabilities are educated appropriately, brings this discussion of IEPs, LRE, and placement full circle.

The delivery of high-quality special education that ensures the delivery of FAPE relies greatly on educators who understand that the IDEA views a student's disability as "a distinction that usually justifies a different approach."[206] Greater alignment of the IDEA with the federal law applying to all students (i.e., ESSA) is viewed by some as the critical link enabling students with disabilities to achieve higher standards in higher-performing schools. Given the differing perspectives of these public policies, such an alignment could mean significant changes for many students with disabilities and their parents. The IDEA focuses on the performance of individuals by mandating an IEP with placements that hinge on its appropriateness and by requiring school officials to provide appropriate programming to a personalized standard. ESSA focuses on the performance of schools and subgroups of students within schools. Moreover, the ESSA mandates that states have challenging academic standards and administer annual standardized assessments based on these standards. Additionally, the law requires that states develop a common standard of academic performance, without assurance of appropriate benefit or of due process protections. Assessing the risks and benefits of a policy fusion is important because laws alone cannot create good administrators, or good teachers, or good schools, but they certainly can take away very hard-won rights.[207]

Recommendations for Practice

In making IEP and placement decisions for students with disabilities, there is no substitute for implementing the IDEA with integrity. In making decisions with confidence, educators should anchor their actions in the law's conceptual foundations. The following recommendations are grounded in the trinity of FAPE, LRE, and validated practices, so that children receive high-quality special education services in their schools.

1. Educators should make ethical and legally defensible decisions. Promote professional behavior that pays more than lip-service to providing equity, quality, and opportunity for all learners. Schools are now enrolling record numbers of students whose learning differences would have once excluded them from receiving a public education. But, for some special education students, functional exclusion is still a reality when schools fail to deliver specially designed instruction or teachers fail to follow the prescriptions of an IEP. As a result, these students "experience a different kind of segregation—the exclusion from the basic right to learn."[208]

2. All stakeholders should directly address individuality and exceptionality in learning. School leaders are in strong positions to articulate that special education is for students with disabilities who need to learn something different or who need to learn the same thing as everyone else but in a different way. Special education is not for any student who fails in the general curriculum, but for students who, because of the extent of their disability-related needs, require different ways to learn and to demonstrate what they know in order to meet with school success. Special education, with its guarantee

of an appropriate public education in the LRE, is for individuals whose disabilities threaten to handicap their future if left unnoticed and unaddressed.

3.   The delivery of special education should be both legally correct and educationally meaningful. School administrators should communicate to stakeholders the statutory purpose of the IDEA and the legal meanings of its critical components, including a FAPE and placements made in accordance with the principle of the LRE. Parents should gain an in-depth understanding of the critical concepts regarding IEP development including, particularly, the LRE principle.

4.   School administrators must provide IEPs that address the procedural and substantive requirements of the IDEA. Courts have viewed serious procedural errors as violations of FAPE if they result in harmful disruption to the delivery of appropriate instruction and educational services. Moreover, to meet the substantive requirements of the law ensure that full, individualized, and relevant assessments are conducted of every student who is eligible for special education under the IDEA, develop meaningful and measurable annual goals, determine and implement the necessary special education and related services, and monitor student progress.

5.   All IEP teams should develop IEPs that are reasonably calculated to enable a child to make progress that is appropriate in light of the child's circumstances. To confer educational benefit, students' IEPs must (a) be based on relevant and meaningful assessments; (b) include ambitious, but reasonable, measurable annual goals; (c) be comprised of special education and related services that are designed to confer benefit; and (d) involve the collection of relevant and meaningful data to monitor student progress. Parents are a critical part of their child's IEP team and should provide thoughtful feedback during the IEP development process.

6.   School administrators must develop IEPs that rely on current and relevant data about the unique educational needs of each student, not on the prerogatives of the school system or on the availability of services. Parents should review the data collected by school officials and seek clarification, if necessary, so that all members of the IEP team are using the same data to develop the child's IEP.

7.   School administrators should avoid filling IEPs with details about content standards. Focus, instead, on the necessary adjustments to be made in providing intensive and specific instruction in academics and desirable behavior, so that students can appropriately access and participate in the general curriculum and meet their disability-related goals.

8. Do not allow policies of "full inclusion" to substitute for the IDEA's requirement that school systems to make available a full continuum of alternative placements. Use student-specific IEP data, not philosophical arguments about inclusion, in making legally correct decisions about placements that constitute the LRE for each student. Remember that providing a student with a special education program that provides educational benefit, thus conferring FAPE, is the primary mandate of the IDEA. Determining the LRE in which a student will receive a FAPE is a secondary mandate that is made after the IEP is developed. The goal, for both parents and school administrators, should be that the child is placed in an educational setting that will allow the child to gain meaningful benefit from special education services, even if that placement is not a full inclusion setting.

9. If a student exhibits problem behavior, the IEP team must determine if the behavior is to be addressed in the IEP; if the team does so, IDEA requires consideration of positive behavior interventions and supports.[209] When possible, disciplinary procedures that employ in-school procedures, such as in-school suspension, should be used. Remember that services to students are not to cease because of suspension or expulsion from school. Any change of placement, for any reason, requires that parents be notified of the school's intent to remove their child from the current setting. Remember, too, that the IDEA has a strong preference for the placement that represents the status quo.

10. All stakeholders should support high expectations for positive results. School administrators must ensure that professionals use effective instructional methodologies and assessment systems that have a demonstrated record of being successful for students with disabilities. Those administrators also should ensure that special and general educators balance a student's need to be successful in the general curriculum with the need to learn from a specialized curriculum in other areas.

11. Establish productive partnerships, particularly between school personnel and parents. School personnel must notify parents in writing before taking any action regarding their child's programming or placement. Give parents a copy of procedural safeguards before IEP meetings and provide them with genuine opportunities to participate in any meetings regarding their child. Involve parents as full partners, but do not appease them by forsaking professional judgment about the best interests of their child. Parents should strive to work cooperatively with school personnel, but they should also freely propose ideas, offer opinions, and ask probing questions, all in furtherance of the shared goal of developing the most effective program for their own child.

12. Remember that schools have the best hope for meeting state standards and national goals adequately when they are vigilant in meeting the needs of their students with disabilities appropriately.

Endnotes

[1] The Individuals with Disabilities Education Improvement Act of 2004, Pub. L. No. 108-446, 118 Stat. 2647 (2004) (codified at 20 U.S.C. §§ 1400-1482 (2012)).

[2] Pub. L. No. 94-142, 89 Stat. 773 (1975).

[3] 20 U.S.C. § 1412(A)(1) (2012) (defining FAPE); 20 U.S.C. § 1414 (d) (2012) (setting forth requirements for IEPs).

[4] See 20 U.S.C. § 1412(a)(5)(A) (2012) (setting forth the statutory LRE language).

[5] See B.H. v. West Clermont Bd. of Ed., 788 F. Supp. 2d 682 (S.D. Ohio 2011) for an illustration of this principle.

[6] Pub. L. No. 108-446, 118 Stat. 2647 (2004) (codified at 20 U.S.C. §§ 1400-1482 (2012)).

[7] See 34 C.F.R., Subt. B, Chpt. III, Pt. 300 (2016).

[8] Every Student Succeeds Act, Pub. L. No. 114-95, 129 Stat 1802 (2015).

[9] Every Student Succeeds Act, Pub. L. No. 114-95, § 1111(b)(2)(B)(vii)(II), 129 Stat. 1802 (2015).

[10] Thomas Hehir, New Directions in Special Education: Eliminating Ableism In Policy and Practice 14 (2005) (asserting that able-ism, or preferring students with disabilities to do things the same way as their nondisabled peers, can result in unintentional discrimination).

[11] 20 U.S.C. § 1400(d)(1)(A) (2012). In the 2004 Amendments to IDEA, Congress added new wording to include further education as an outcome along with employment and independent living. See Pub. L. No. 108-446, § 682(d)(1)(A), 118 Stat. 2647 (2004).

[12] 20 U.S.C. § 1412(a)(1) (2012); 34 C.F.R. § 300.101(c) (2016).

[13] 20 U.S.C. § 1401(29)(A) (2012) (emphasis added).

[14] County of San Diego v. California Sp. Educ. Hrg. Office, 93 F.3d 1458 (9th Cir. 1996) (emphasis added).

[15] See 64 Fed. Reg. 12,406, 12,425 (Mar. 12, 1999).

[16] 34 C.F.R. § 300.39(b)(3) (2016).

[17] See Hehir, supra note 10, at 49 for discussion of the purpose of special education.

[18] H. Rutherford Turnbull, III, Matthew J. Stowe, Nancy E. Huerta, Free Appropriate Public Education, The Law And Children With Disabilities 36 (2007) (addressing the findings and purposes of the IDEA).

[19] See Michael K. Yudin & Melody Musgrove, Dear Colleague Letter, U.S. Dep't. of Educ. 4 (Nov. 17, 2015), https://www2.ed.gov/policy/speced/guid/idea/memosdcltrs/guidance-on-fape-11-17-2015.pdf.

[20] Karen Glasser Sharp, & Vicki M. Pitasky, The Current Legal Status of Inclusion (2002).

[21] 20 U.S.C. § 1414 et. seq. (2012). For an extended discussion of special education programming and placements see Barbara D. Bateman & Mary Anne Linden, Better IEPs: How to Develop Legally Correct and Educationally Appropriate Programs (2012).

[22] 20 U.S.C. § 1414(d)(1)(B) (2012); 34 C.F.R. § 300.321(a) (2016).

[23] 20 U.S.C. § 1401(9) (2012); 34 C.F.R. §300.17 (2016).

[24] 20 U.S.C. § 1414(d) (2012).

[25] This document is developed, reviewed, and revised in a meeting in accordance with 34 C.F.R. §§ 300.320-300.324 (2016); 20 U.S.C. § 1414(d)(1)(A)(i) (2012).

[26] 458 U.S. 176 (1982).

[27] 20 U.S.C. § 1414(d)(1)(A)(i)(I) (2012); 34 C.F.R. § 300.320(a)(1) (2016).

[28] 20 U.S.C. § 1414(d)(1)(A)(II) (2012).

[29] 20 U.S.C. § 1414(d)(1)(A)(i)(I)(cc) (2012); 34 C.F.R. § 300.320(a)(2)(B)(ii) (2016).

30 20 U.S.C. § 1414(d)(1)(A)(i)(III) (2012); Bateman & Linden, *supra* note 21, at 170 (the authors advise districts against dropping short-term objectives because they serve a progress monitoring function).

31 Mitchell L. Yell, THE LAW AND SPECIAL EDUCATION 223 (2016) (the author advises that at least one goal be written for each area of academic or non-academic need).

32 20 U.S.C. § 1414(d)(1)(A)(i)(III) (2012).

33 34 C.F.R. § 300.320(a)(3) (2016). See Yell, *supra* note 31, at 228-229 (the author advises that using appropriate means for evaluating and reporting regularly on the progress toward annual goals is essential to determining success or failure of the district's efforts to provide FAPE).

34 20 U.S.C. § 1414(d)(1)(A)(i)(IV) (2012).

35 20 U.S.C. § 1414(d)(1)(A)(i)(V) (2012); 34 C.F.R. § 300.320(a)(4) (2016). Bateman & Linden, *supra* note 21, at 15-16 (the authors advise against cluttering a student's IEP with detailed goals and services for the content standards in the general education curriculum. Instead, the IEP must indicate goals, accommodations, and adjustments focusing on how professionals will enable the student to acquire the access skills necessary to address the standards considered by the team to be most relevant to the student).

36 20 U.S.C. § 1414(d)(3)(C) (2012); 34 C.F.R. § 300.324(a)(3) (2016). Section 1414(d)(3)(C) is a statutory provision that specifically addresses the role of the regular education teacher. The regular education teacher on the IEP team is to assist in the development, review, and revision of the IEP, with particular attention to the appropriate positive behavioral interventions and strategies for the child, as well as the supplementary aids and services, program modifications, or supports for school personnel that will be provided for the child to be successful in meeting individual goals, accessing the general curriculum, and being educated and participating with other students with and without disabilities.

37 20 U.S.C. § 1414(d)(1)(A)(i)(V) (2012); 34 C.F.R. § 300.320(a)(5) (2016).

38 20 U.S.C. § 1414(d)(1)(A)(i)(V) (2012); 34 C.F.R. § 300.320(a)(5) (2016). Bateman & Linden, *supra* note 21, at 17 & 19 (the authors advise that decisions about the extent of a student's participation in the general classroom depend on the needs identified in the student's evaluation and the student's IEP).

39 20 U.S.C. § 1414(d)(1)(A)(i)(VI)(aa) (2012); 34 C.F.R. § 300.320(a)(6) (2016).

40 20 U.S.C. § 1414(d)(1)(A)(i)(VI)(bb) (2012); 34 C.F.R. § 300.320(a)(6) (2016).

41 20 U.S.C. § 1414(d)(1)(A)(i)(VII) (2012); 34 C.F.R. § 300.320(a)(7) (2016).

42 20 U.S.C. § 1414(d)(1)(A)(i)(VII) (2012); 34 C.F.R. § 300.320(a)(7) (2016). *See* Yell, *supra* note 31, at 227 (the author advises that the IEP must be implemented as soon as possible after it is written).

43 20 U.S.C. § 1414(d)(1)(A)(i)(VIII)(aa) (2012); 34 C.F.R. § 300.320(b)(1) (2016).

44 20 U.S.C. § 1414(d)(1)(A)(i)(VIII)(bb) (2012); 34 C.F.R. § 300.320(b)(2) (2016).

45 20 U.S.C. § 1414(d)(1)(A)(i)(VIII)(cc) (2012); 34 C.F.R. § 300.320(c) (2016).

46 20 U.S.C. § 1414(d)(3)(A)(i)-(iv) (2012).

47 20 U.S.C. § 1414(d)(3)(A)(i) (2012).

48 20 U.S.C. § 1414(d)(3)(A)(ii) (2012); *see also* 34 C.F.R. § 300.322 (2016) (detailing requirement of parental participation in the IEP process).

49 *See* Yell, *supra* note 31, at 227-228 (the author advises that transition services included in an IEP must address instruction, community services, employment, and other objectives of adult living. If any of these required services are not included, an explanatory note must detail the reasons for the exclusion).

50 20 U.S.C. § 1414(d)(3)(A)(iii) (2012); 34 C.F.R. § 300.324 (2007).

51 20 U.S.C. § 1414(d)(3)(A)(iv) (2012).

52 20 U.S.C. § 1414(d)((4)(B)(i)-(v) (2012); 34 C.F.R. § 300.324(a)(2)(i)-(v) (2016).

53 20 U.S.C. § 1414(d)(4)(B)(i) (2012).

54 20 U.S.C. § 1414 (d)(4)(B)(ii) (2012); 34 C.F.R. § 300.324(a)(2)(ii) (2016).

55 20 U.S.C. § 1414(d)(4)(B)(iii) 2012); 34 C.F.R. § 300.324(a)(2)(iii) (2016). Teams must also evaluate the appropriate reading and writing media for the student, including an evaluation of the student's future needs for instruction in Braille or the use of Braille.

56 20 U.S.C. § 1414(d)(4)(B)(iv) (2012).

57 20 U.S.C. § 1414(d)(4)(B)(v) (2012).

58 *Id.*; 34 C.F.R. § 300.320(a)(6)(i) (2016).

59 20 U.S.C. § 1414(d)(2)(C) (2012).

60 20 U.S.C. § 1414(d)(2)(C)(i)(II) (2012).

61 20 U.S.C. § 1414(d)(2)(C)(I) (2012); 34 C.F.R. § 300.323(e) (2016)4(a)(4).

62 20 U.S.C. § 1414 (d)(1)(c) (2012).

63 20 U.S.C. §1414 (d)(1)(D) (2012); 34 C.F.R. § 300.321(f) (2016).

64 34 C.F.R. § 300.328 (2016).

65 Scott F. Johnson, *Reexamining Rowley: A New Focus in Special Education Law*, 2003 B.Y.U. EDUC. & L.J. 561, 585 (2003). Johnson argued that the concept of FAPE is newly aligned with high expectations established in state education standards, although school systems must address more than academic needs. *Id.* at 561.

66 See the website for the National Center for Educational Outcomes, funded by the US Department of Education's Office of Special Education Programs, at https://www.osepideasthatwork.org/node/114 addressing frequently asked questions about accommodations for students with disabilities.

67 Hehir, *supra* note 10, at 131-136.

68 *See* Perry A. Zirkel, *Is it Time for Elevating the Standard for FAPE under the IDEA?* 79 EXCEPTIONAL CHILDREN, 497-508 (2013).

69 458 U.S. 176 (1982).

70 *Id.* at 200.

71 *Id.* at 202. In fact the Court expressly declined "o "attempt today to establish any one test for determining the adequacy of educational benefits," noting that the standard will vary greatly by child and disability. *Id.*

72 *Id.* at 206-07.

73 Doe v. Bd. of Educ. of Tullahoma City Sch., 9 F.3d 455, 459 (6th Cir. 1993).

74 *Id.* at 459-60.

75 *See., e.g.,* Thompson R2-J Sch. Dist. v. Luke P., 540 F.3d 1143 (10th Cir. 2008) (educational benefit must be more than de minimus).

76 In *Polk v. Central Susquehanna Intermed. Unit 16*, 853 F.2d 171, 182-184 (3d Cir. 1988), the Third Circuit held that an IEP must be calculated to offer "meaningful benefit" by providing educational services in a way that a student can best achieve success in learning. In *Hall v. Vance County Bd. of Educ.*, 774 F.2d 629, 636 (4th Cir. 1985), the Fourth Circuit allowed courts to make decisions regarding the substantive standard of an appropriate IEP on a case-by-case basis, taking into consideration the child's capacity to learn. In *J.S.K. v. Hendry Cty. Sch. Bd.*, 941 F.2d 1563, 1573 (11th Cir. 1991), the Eleventh Circuit required public schools to provide educational benefit greater than a trifle, and defined an appropriate education in terms of "making measurable and adequate gains in the classroom" based on the child's needs, potential, and efforts. Other circuit decisions in which a somewhat higher standard of meaningful benefit seems to have been used include *Deal ex. rel. Deal v. Hamilton Cty. Bd. of Educ.*, 392 F.3d 840 (6th Cir. 2004); and *Adam J. v. Keller Indep. Sch.Dist*, 328 F.3d 804 (5th Cir. 2003).

77 *See* Mitchell Yell, Jean Crockett, James Shriner, & Michael Rozalski, *Free Appropriate Public Education*, in HANDBOOK OF SPECIAL EDUCATION (J. Kauffman & D. Hallahan eds. 2017) for extended discussion of FAPE.

78 Frank G. v. Bd. of Educ. of Hyde Park, 459 F.3d 356, 364 (2d Cir. 2006) ("Grades, test scores, and regular advancement may provide evidence that a child is receiving educational benefit…").

79 In *Rowley,* the Supreme Court noted that "We do not hold today that every handicapped child who is advancing from grade to grade in a regular public school system is automatically receiving a "free appropriate public education." 458 U.S. at 203 n.25.

80 D.B. v. Bedford Cty. Sch. Bd., 708 F. Supp. 2d 564, 584 (W.D. Va. 2010) (noting that the child's promotion from grade to grade every year was, "at best, a sad case of social promotion"); Fayetteville-Perry Local Sch. Dist., 20 IDELR 1289 (SEA Ohio 1994); Tucson Unified Sch. Dist., 30 IDELR 478 (SEA Ariz. 1999).

81 774 F.2d 629 (4th Cir. 1985).

82 Florence Cty. Sch. Dist. Four v. Carter, 510 U.S. 7 (1993).

83 Cypress-Fairbanks Indep. Sch. Dist. v. Michael F., 118 F.3d 245 (5th Cir. 1997).

84 *Id.* at 253. The court noted that each of the four factors comport with the federal regulations implementing IDEA. *See* 34 C.F.R. §300.324 (academic and functional needs); 34 C.F.R. §§ 300.114-120 (least restrictive environment); 34 C.F.R. § 300.321 (team approach); and 34 C.F.R. § 300.320 (demonstrated outcomes).

85 Cypress-Fairbanks Indep. Sch. Dist., 118 F.3d at 256.

86 *Id.* at 253-54.

87 *Id.* at 251.

88 *Id.* at 254.

89 *Id.* at 258.

90 *Id.* This action was filed before the 2004 Amendments to the IDEA, which amended the IDEA to allow courts to award attorneys' fees to a prevailing school board against parents, if the court determines that the action was filed for an improper purpose, such as to harass, unnecessarily delay or needlessly increase the cost of litigation. *See* 20 U.S.C. § 1415(i)(3)(B)(i)(III) (2012); 34 C.F.R. § 300.517(a)(1)(iii) (2016).

91 200 F.3d 341 (5th Cir. 2000).

92 *Id.* at 347-48.

93 *Id.* at 349.

94 *Id.*

95 *Id.* at 350.

96 *Id.* at 349-50.

97 *Id.* at 349.

98 Endrew F. v. Douglas Cty. Sch. Dist. RE-1, 798 F.3d. 1329 (10th Cir. 2015).

99 Parents who disagree with the educational decisions regarding their child have the ability to file a "due process" complaint. *See* 20 U.S.C. § 1415(b)(6) (2012). In some states, special education due process complaints are decided by administrative law judges.

100 798 F.3d at 1333.

101 *Id.*

102 *Id.*

103 *Id.* at 1342.

104 *Id.* at 1339-40.

105 *See* Endrew F. v. Douglas Cty. Sch. Dist. RE-1, Petition for Writ of Certiorari, No. 15-827 (U.S.) (filed Dec. 22, 2015), http://www.scotusblog.com/wp-content/uploads/2016/05/15-827-Petition-for-Certiorari.pdf.

106 *Id.* at 2.

107 *See* Endrew F. v. Douglas Cty. Sch. Dist. RE-1, Brief of the United States As Amicus Curiae, No. 15-827 (U.S.) (filed Aug. 18, 2016), http://www.scotusblog.com/wp-content/uploads/2016/08/15-827-US-Amicus.pdf.

108 *See* Endrew F. v. Douglas Cty. Sch. Dist. RE-1, No. 15-827, 2016 WL 5416228 (U.S. Sept. 29, 2016). For updates on the case, visit http://www.scotusblog.com/case-files/cases/endrew-f-v-douglas-county-school-district/.

109 Endrew F. v. Douglas County School District, 137 S.Ct. 988 (2017). A pdf of the *Endrew* decision is available at https://www.supremecourt.gov/opinions/16pdf/15-827_0pm1.pdf.

110 *Id.* at 15.

111 *Id.* at 14.

[112] *Id.* at 11.

[113] *Id.* at 16.

[114] *Id.* at 16.

[115] 458 U.S. at 207-08.

[116] *See* Dixie Snow Huefner & Cynthia M. Herr, Navigating Special Education Law and Policy 132 (2012). IDEA's emphasis on adapting the content, methodology, or delivery of instruction has prompted the interest of the courts in different methodologies and the need for educators to select teaching methods responsive to a student's unique educational needs. If a student needs a particular device, service, intervention, accommodation, or modification, then that information must be placed in the IEP. If FAPE can be provided without using a specific method, then the decision to include methodology on the IEP rests with the IEP team.

[117] Nein v. Greater Clark County Sch. Corp., 95 F. Supp. 2d 961 (S.D. Ind. 2000).

[118] *Id.* at 977.

[119] *Id.* at 963.

[120] *Id.* at 977.

[121] Deal *ex rel.* Deal v. Hamilton Cty. Bd. of Educ., 392 F.3d 840 (6th Cir. 2004).

[122] *Id.* at 865.

[123] *Id.* at 861-62. Some commentators have suggested that the Sixth Circuit lacked the expertise to recognize or assess the various instructional practices, noting that the Sixth Circuit characterized the parents' teaching method—known as the "Lovaas method"—as having shown "extraordinary results, " 392 F.3d at 845, n.2, even though it was not peer-reviewed and other experts questioned the rigor of the design. *See* Tessie E. Rose & Perry Zirkel, *Orton-Gillingham Methodology for Students with Reading Disabilities: 30 Years of Case Law,* 184 J. Special Educ. 171, 184 (2007).

[124] Deal *ex. rel.* Deal v. Hamilton Cty. Dep't of Educ., 2006 WL 5667836, 46 IDELR 45 (E.D. Tenn., Apr. 3, 2006).

[125] J.P. v. West Clark Cmty. Sch., 230 F. Supp. 2d 910 (S.D. Ind. 2002).

[126] Deal *ex. rel.* Deal v. Hamilton Cty. Dep't of Educ., 2006 WL 5667836 at *24, 46 IDELR 45, 72 (E.D. Tenn., Apr. 3, 2006).

[127] J.P. v. West Clark Cmty. Sch., 230 F. Supp. 2d 910 (S.D. Ind. 2002).

[128] *Id.* at 936.

[129] *Id.* at 938.

[130] *See* Bateman & Linden, *supra* note 21, at 138 (advising school officials to carefully and critically review claims for the research base of publishers' curricular materials; pursue guidance from professional development; provide practitioner journals that publish practical articles for teachers and related service providers; consult personnel at state departments of education; and utilize professional websites that publish valid data on evidence-based practices. Additionally, the authors advise educators to shop with a critical eye because "snake oil is more readily available than research-validated remedies!"

[131] 20 U.S.C. § 1414(d)(1)(A)(i)(IV) (2012); 34 C.F.R. § 300.320(a)(4) (2016).

[132] Congress did not define peer-reviewed research, but usage of the term is consistent with *scientifically-based instruction* in NCLB, as practices tested and validated through systematic, rigorous, and objective methods. *see* 34 C.F.R. § 300.35 (2016).

[133] Schaffer v. Weast, 546 U.S. 49 (2005).

[134] For an extended discussion of this decision, *see* Charles J. Russo, & Allan G. Osborne, *The Supreme Court Clarifies the Burden of Proof in Special Education Due Process Hearings: Schaffer ex rel. Schaffer v. Weast,* 208 Educ. L. Rep. 705-717 (2006).

[135] Winkelman by Winkelman v. Parma City Sch. Dist., 550 U.S. 516 (2007).

[136] 458 U.S. at 208-09, quoting Sen. Conf. Rep. No. 94-445, at 30 (1975).

[137] For a discussion of how the tools used by educators are more than representative of intentions but are constitutive of their practice, see James P. Spillane, Richard Halverson, & John B. Diamond, *Investigating School Leadership Practice: A Distributed Perspective,* 30 Educ. Researcher 23-28 (2001).

[138] Jeffrey Champagne, "*LRE: Decisions in Sequence*," Symposium at the Annual Conference of the National Association of Private Schools for Exceptional Children, 14 (1992).

[139] 20 U.S.C. § 1412(a)(5) (2012).

[140] 34 C.F.R. § 300.115 (2016).

[141] 34 C.F.R. § 300.327 (2016); 34 C.F.R. § 300.501(c) (2016).

[142] The IDEA regulations set out fact-specific guidelines stipulating that placement decisions must be made by a group of people, including the student's parents, and others who are knowledgeable about the child, the meaning of the evaluation data, and the placement options. Placement decisions are also to be made in conformity with the LRE provisions of the federal regulations at 34 C.F.R §§ 300.114-120 (2016).

[143] 34 C.F.R. § 300.116(b)(1)-(2) (2016).

[144] 34 C.F.R. § 300.116(b)(3) (2016) (requirement that placement be as close to home as possible); 34 C.F.R. § 300.116(c) (2016) (requirement that school be the same one that the child would attend if not disabled, unless the IEP requires some other arrangement).

[145] 34 C.F.R. § 300.116(e) (2016).

[146] 20 U.S.C. § 1412(a)(10)(B) (2012).

[147] *See, e.g.,* Stacey Gordon, *Making Sense of the Inclusion Debate under IDEA*, 2006 B.Y.U. Educ. & L.J. 189, 198-99 (2006).

[148] *Id.* at 198.

[149] *Id.* at 199.

[150] 34 C.F.R. § 300.116(b) (2016) (a student's placement "must be based on the child's IEP").

[151] Roncker v. Walter, 700 F.2d 1058, 1063 (6th Cir. 1983) ("The Act does not require mainstreaming in every case but its requirement that mainstreaming be provided to the *maximum* extent appropriate indicates a very strong congressional preference").

[152] *See* Crockett & Kauffman, The Least Restrictive Environment: Its Origins and Interpretations in Special Education (1999), for a full discussion of the origins and interpretations of the LRE principle in special education.

[153] Jean B. Crockett, *The Least Restrictive Environment and the 1997 IDEA Amendments and Federal Regulations*, 28 J. L. & Educ. 543 (1999); 34 C.F.R. § 300.115 (2016).

[154] 34 C.F.R. § 300.116(d) (2016) ("In selecting the LRE, consideration must be given to any potential harmful effect on the child or on the quality of services that he or she needs").

[155] The federal circuit courts of appeal have jurisdictions over various regions of the United States. A map that depicts the jurisdictional boundaries of each circuit court of appeal can be found at http://www2.fjc.gov/sites/default/files/2012/IJR00007.pdf.

[156] The major frameworks include the *Roncker* standard, the *Daniel R. R.* two-pronged test, the four-pronged *Holland* test, and the *DeVries* three-part test. *See* Roncker v. Walter, 700 F.2d 1058 (6th Cir. 1983); Daniel R.R. v. State Bd. of Educ., 874 F 2d. 1036 (5th Cir. 1989); Sacramento City Unified Sch. Dist. v. Rachel H., 14 F.3d 1398 (9th Cir. 1994); DeVries v. Fairfax Cty. Sch. Bd., 882 F.2d 876 (4th Cir. 1989).

[157] Roncker v. Walter, 700 F.2d 1058 (6th Cir. 1983). This test also is used in the Eighth Circuit. *See* A.W. v. Northwest R-1 Sch. Dist., 813 F.2d 158 (8th Cir. 1987).

[158] 700 F.2d at 1063.

[159] *Id.*

[160] In developing the feasibility standard, the Sixth Circuit acknowledged that a student's need for an appropriate education might conflict with preferences for integration and that certain factors, including marginal benefits, disruption, and cost, could be considered in determining whether education in regular settings could be provided satisfactorily. *Id.*

[161] A.W. v. Northwest R-1 Sch. Dist., 813 F.2d 158 (8th Cir. 1987).

[162] Daniel R.R. v. State Bd. of Educ., 874 F 2d. 1036 (5th Cir. 1989). This test is used in the Second, Third, Fifth, Tenth, and Eleventh Circuits.

[163] *Id.* at 1048.

[164] The *Daniel R. R.* two-pronged analytic framework influenced the 1997 amendments to the IDEA and has had a broad impact on courts deliberating placements in the LRE. This framework requires school systems to consider more than academic achievement in place-

ment decisions and to ensure that access to general education settings will not be denied solely because the progress of the special education student will not equal that of a general education student.

[165] Greer v. Rome City Sch. Dist., 950 F.2d 688 (11th Cir. 1991), L.B. and J.B. ex rel. K.B. v. Nebo Sch. Dist., 379 F.3d 966 (10th Cir. 2004), Oberti v. Bd. of Educ. of the Borough of Clementon Sch. Dist., 995 F.2d 1204 (3rd Cir. 1993), P. v. Newington Bd. of Educ., 546 F.3d 111 (2d Cir. 2008).

[166] Sacramento City Unified Sch. Dist v. Rachel H., 14 F.3d 1398 (9th Cir. 1994). This test is used in the Ninth Circuit.

[167] 874 F.2d at 1048.

[168] 14 F.3d at 1404.

[169] DeVries v. Fairfax Cty. Sch. Bd., 882 F.2d 876 (4th Cir. 1989).

[170] *Id.* at 878-79.

[171] *Id.* at 879, quoting *Roncker*, 700 F.2d at 1063.

[172] Beth B. v. Van Clay, 211 F. Supp. 2d 1020 (N.D. Ill. 2001), *aff'd*, 282 F.3d 493 (7th Cir. 2002), *cert denied*, 537 U.S. 948 (2002).

[173] *Id.* at 1030.

[174] *Id.*

[175] *Id.* at 1031.

[176] *Id.*

[177] *Id.* at 1032.

[178] *Id.* at 1033.

[179] *Id.* at 1034.

[180] 282 F.3d 493.

[181] *Id.*

[182] *Id.* at 498.

[183] *Id.* at 497.

[184] *Id.* at 498.

[185] *Id.* at 498.

[186] *Id.*

[187] *See* Mitchell L. Yell, THE LAW AND SPECIAL EDUCATION 284 (2012). The following questions address the components embodied in the LRE frameworks and rely on student-centered data collected throughout the LRE determination process.

    (1) Has the school taken steps to maintain the child in the general education class: What supplementary aides and services were used? What interventions were attempted?

    (2) What are the benefits of placement in a general education setting with supplementary aids and services versus the benefits of placement in a special education setting: What are the academic benefits? What are the nonacademic benefits such as social communication and interactions?

    (3) What are the effects on the education of other students: If the student is disruptive, is the education of other students adversely affected? Does the student require an inordinate amount of attention from the teacher, and, as a result, adversely affect the education of others?

    (4) If a student is being educated in a setting other than the general education classroom, are there integrated experiences with nondisabled peers to the maximum extent appropriate? In what academic settings is the student integrated with nondisabled students? In what nonacademic settings is the child integrated with nondisabled students?

    (5) Is the entire continuum of alternative services available from which to choose an appropriate placement?

[188] *See* Jeffrey Champagne, *supra* note 132. Decisions about placement can be addressed by using a sequential format that begins by considering whether the appropriate educational services written in the IEP can be delivered in the regular class if modified through the use of supplementary aids and services. If the answer is yes, then the regular class is the primary placement. If not, the team would move along the continuum of alternative placements one

step at a time, from regular class to resource room to separate class to separate school residential setting hospital or home, considering whether the appropriate educational services
might be delivered with appropriate supports until the answer *yes* is obtained.

[189] Stephen E. Lake, Slippery slope! The IEP Missteps Every Team Must Know And How To
Avoid Them (2007).

[190] *See* Letter from Patricia J. Guard to Paul Veazey, U.S. Dep't. of Educ. (Nov. 26, 2001), http://
www2.ed.gov/policy/speced/guid/idea/letters/2001-4/veazey112601place.pdf.

[191] 20 USC 1415(b)(1)(C) (2012); 34 C.F.R. § 300.503 (2016).

[192] Powell v. Studstill, 441 S.E.2d 52 (Ga. 1994).

[193] 34 C.F.R. § 300.518 (2016).

[194] Hale v. Poplar Bluff R-I Sch. Dist., 280 F. 3d 831 (8th Cir. 2002).

[195] C.P. v. Leon Cty. Sch. Bd., 483 F.3d 1151 (11th Cir. 2007).

[196] 34 C.F.R. § 300.530 (2016).

[197] 20 U.S.C. § 1415(k)(1)(G) (2012); 34 C.F.R. § 300.533 (2016).

[198] To determine if suspensions in excess of 10 cumulative school days, the school principal
and a student's IEP team should, on a case-by-case basis examine such factors as (a) was the
student's behaviors that led to the suspension similar to the student's behavior in previous
incidences, (b) the length of each removal, (c) the total amount of time the student has been
removed, and (d) the proximity of the removals to one another. 34 C.F.R. § 300.536(a-d)
(2016).

[199] 34 C.F.R. § 300.530 (2016). A special education student removed from the current placement for more than ten consecutive days must continue to receive educational services and
behavioral interventions whether or not the offending behavior is a manifestation of the
disability.

[200] Steven E. Lake, What Do I Do When--: The Answer Book on Special Education Practice
and Procedures 5.7 (2d ed. 2014).

[201] Turnbull, Stowe, & Huerta, *supra* note 19, at 86.

[202] 34 C.F.R. § 300.324(a)(2)(i) (2016).

[203] Sue Swenson & Ruth Ryder, Dear Colleague Letter, U.S. Dep't. of Educ. (Aug. 1, 2016),
http://www2.ed.gov/policy/gen/guid/school-discipline/files/dcl-on-pbis-in-ieps--08-01-2016.
pdf.

[204] 34 C.F.R. § 300.530 (2016).

[205] 34 C.F.R. § 300.324(a)(IV)(2)(i) (2016).

[206] Turnbull, Stowe, & Huerta, *supra* note 18, at 98.

[207] The ESSA is discussed in Chapter 2 of this volume.

[208] Jean S. Schumm et al., *General Education Teacher Planning: What Can Students With
Learning Disabilities Expect?* 61 Exceptional Children 335 (1995).

[209] 20 U.S.C. § 1414(d)(3)(B)(i) (2012).

Chapter 7

Related Services under the IDEA

Jennifer A. Sughrue

Introduction

Since the enactment of the Individuals with Disabilities Education Act (IDEA),[1] the federal courts have attempted to bring clarification to the congressional intent of the law and to its implementation in public education—which is no small feat, in view of the number of key provisions within the law and the subsequent passage of No Child Left Behind (NCLB)[2] and, more recently, the Every Student Succeeds Act (ESSA).[3] This chapter is focused on the related services provision of IDEA and examples of the contexts in which it has been litigated. It covers the statutory definition of related services, as well as the judiciary's application of that definition. The chapter closes with a discussion of three questions that provide guidance for the IEP team in determining appropriate related services to eligible children with a disability. Those questions are: (1) Does the requested service provide the student meaningful access to special education services?; (2) Does the requested service fall under the definition of an excluded medical service?; and (3) When may a related service be modified or terminated?

Definition of Related Services

Related services are support services that students with disabilities require in order to be able to access and benefit from special education. These services include "transportation, and such developmental, corrective, and other supportive services . . . as may be required to assist a child with a disability to benefit from special education, and includes the early identification and assessment of disabling conditions in children."[4] Several examples of such services are included in the statutory definition, among them speech and audiology services, psychological services, rehabilitation therapies, recreation, therapeutic recreation, social work services, and counseling services.[5] "Medical services" are to be provided if they are for the purpose of diagnosis and evaluation of the disability in relation to qualifying for and receiving special education.[6] The examples of services as provided in the statute are not to be considered a definitive list.

To identify needed related services, a child should be "assessed in all areas related to the suspected disability, including, if appropriate, health, vision, hearing, social and emotional status, general intelligence, academic performance, communicative status, and motor abilities."[7] The IEP team then should review evaluation data to determine what related services the student will need in order to benefit from the proffered educational programming.[8] Once those services are identified, goals must be developed for each related service and included in the IEP. The IEP must also specify when the service will begin, how often it will be provided and for what amount of time for each session, and where it will be provided.[9] If the amount or type of services specified in the IEP need to be adjusted, the IEP team must convene and agree to those changes, unless the parent and the school district together agree that no meeting is necessary.[10] If any changes are made without an IEP meeting, the IEP team must be informed of the changes.[11] As long as there is no change in the overall amount of a specific service, adjustments to scheduling of the service may be made without an IEP team meeting. Scheduling is not one of the required elements to be included in the IEP, and therefore it is not a change to the IEP per se.[12] However, parents should be notified of schedule changes.

Although the statutory language seems clear on related services, the nature and extent to which these services apply are sometimes called into question as school personnel, parents, and eligible students negotiate individual educational programs. For this reason, the courts have had to further characterize related services and their function.

In 1984, the U.S. Supreme Court provided guidance by indicating that related services were those that were necessary for a child with disabilities "to remain at school during the day" in order to have "meaningful access to education."[13] The case, *Irving Independent School District v. Tatro*, centered on whether a procedure known as clean intermittent catheterization (CIC) was a related service required under IDEA, or an excluded medical service. CIC can be can be performed by non-medical personnel who have received basic instruction on the procedure.[14] The student, Amber Tatro, was an 8-year-old child with spina bifida. In order to avoid damaging her kidneys, Tatro required CIC every four hours.[15] This meant that this procedure had to be administered during school hours. In a two-part analysis, the Supreme Court held that CIC clearly fell within the statutory definition of related services. The Court considered CIC as functionally the same as transportation, inasmuch as it allowed Tatro to attend school and to benefit from special education.[16] The Court stated: "Services like CIC that permit a child to remain at school during the day are no less related to the effort to educate than are services that enable the child to reach, enter, or exit the school."[17]

In the second prong of the analysis, the Court distinguished eligible from non-eligible medical services under the IDEA. Federal implementation regulations stated that those school health services that could be performed by a school nurse or other qualified person would be considered related services.[18] Excluded medical services were those that required the services of a physician. Inasmuch as the CIC procedure did not require a physician, the Court held that it was clearly a related service.[19]

School District Fiscal Responsibility

As explicitly stated in IDEA, special education programming and related services are to be free of charge to families of students eligible under IDEA.[20] In the matter of related services, the Supreme Court has rejected any "test" that sets an artificial limit on the costs of needed related services.[21] This conclusion stemmed from a case in which the parents requested the school district bear the financial responsibility for a nurse during the school day for their quadriplegic son who was ventilator-dependent.[22] Garret F. required continuous, one-on-one nursing care in order to stay in school. He needed assistance with urinary bladder catheterization and with the suctioning of his tracheotomy tube, among other procedures. Also, it was essential that someone be available who could respond to a problem with the ventilator, or in the event Garret was to experience autonomic hyperreflexia, an "uncontrolled visceral reaction to anxiety or a full bladder . . . [during which] blood pressure increases, heart rate increases, and flushing and sweating may occur."[23]

The school district did not dispute the lower court's conclusion that the kinds of assistance that Garret required were related services under the first prong of the *Tatro* analysis.[24] It also acknowledged that other students in the district were receiving similar services; however, the district contended that the scope of services that Garret required was beyond the school district's obligation under the IDEA.[25]

The district proposed a multi-factor test that would be employed on a case-by-case basis to determine whether a school district would be responsible for an extensive collection of related services for individual students. These factors included "[1] whether the care is continuous or intermittent, [2] whether existing school health personnel can provide the service, [3] the cost of the service, and [4] the potential consequences if the service is not properly performed."[26]

The Court rejected the school district's proposed test, arguing that the test was unsubstantiated by any legal authority and that there was no reasonable explanation as to why "one service [would be] any more 'medical' than another."[27] As it regarded each of the factors, the Court noted that the test more accurately assessed the potential cost to a school district than it assessed whether needed procedures were excluded medical services.[28] It also concluded that the district was attempting to establish an "undue burden exemption."[29] In rejecting this strategy, the Court asserted that the services that Garret required were necessary to his access to free appropriate public education (FAPE), and reaffirmed its earlier conclusion in *Tatro* that the single best determinant of an excluded medical service is one that requires the services of a physician.[30]

Parents may seek reimbursement for unilateral provision of related services when they can demonstrate that services were necessary for the child to receive educational benefit and that the school district refused or failed to provide them. In an early case, *Max M. v. Illinois State Board of Education*,[31] parents successfully sued in order to recuperate the cost of providing intensive psychotherapy for their son during his junior and senior years in high school. The school district's own consultant recommended that Max receive this therapy, stating that without it, Max would not be socially, emotionally, or academically prepared to be successful in school. However, the school district failed to provide it, thereby putting the parents in the position of having to pay for it. The court determined that the school district's failure to provide Max with the recommended psychotherapy had the effect of denying him a FAPE.

In a more recent case, a public school district placed a student diagnosed with Asperger syndrome and developmental delay in a private school, with the agreement of the parent. However, the school district did not pay for the cost of tuition or related services. The designated related services were: "(1) 24 hours of specialized instruction; (2) 90 minutes of psychological counseling; (3) 2 hours and 15 minutes of speech therapy; and (4) 90 minutes of occupational therapy."[34] The father filed a due process complaint, after which the school district entered into an agreement to reimburse the father.[35] The student continued to attend the private school for another two years, but the school district did not follow up on the student's progress, did not prepare an updated IEP, and did not administer any evaluations or assessments. And, again, the school district failed to reimburse the father for the additional two years of schooling and related services.[36] The father successfully sued the school district in court for his out-of-pocket payments for tuition and related services.

Nature and Scope of Related Services

Although the Supreme Court has established a clear, two-step analysis on what services are considered related services under the IDEA, questions yet arise as to the nature and scope of such services. Decisions in recent lower court cases illustrate the breadth of the controversies.

Transportation

Transportation is a related service under IDEA, which the school district is required to provide so that a student with disabilities may access the specialized instructional program designated in the student's IEP.[37] Transportation must also be provided if the child has to travel to an off-campus location for related services that cannot be provided at the school site. The obligation is extended to cover both specialized transportation for the child, if the child's disability requires it, and to cover transportation for parents or guardians if the child has been placed in a facility that requires the parents to travel to participate in prescribed family therapy or other training.[38]

Three cases illustrate the range of transportation-related questions that surface in the courts. In the first instance, the court was asked to determine if a school district was responsible to provide transportation outside the boundaries of the school for programs unrelated to the student's IEP.[39] The IDEA plainly states that transportation is a related service. However, in this instance, there was a challenge to a school district's refusal to provide after-school transportation to a daycare center that was outside the school district's boundaries.[40] The Eighth Circuit Court of Appeals held for the school, stating that the daycare program was not a part of providing FAPE to the child.[41] The school had provided the necessary transportation for the child to and from home in order for the child to receive special education services, as required by the IDEA. The daycare center program was one of personal choice by the parents.[42]

A second transportation dispute involved a question of whether or not a school district was responsible for reimbursing the parents of a special needs student for their travel to and from their child's residential treatment center.[43] This controversy involved a boy with autism, Aaron, who resided at a private residential facility known as Boston Higashi, even though his parents lived in Illinois. This facility was chosen because of its unique, twenty-four-hour "milieu therapy."[44] The therapy is designed to teach children with autism independent living skills and to provide parents with the training necessary to help their children when they are at home and in the public.

In addition to agreeing to the placement, the school district also agreed to reimburse the parents for travel to and from the center to attend training and to pick up and return Aaron during school breaks. The per-trip reimbursement covered airfare, hotel accommodations for two days, airport parking, rental car, and two days' per diem for meals.[45] The district also covered the cost of the parental training, which was considered "vitally important if Aaron is ever to return to his home and family."[46]

For four years, the district had agreed to reimburse up to twelve trips per year. At the 1999 IEP meeting, however, the district offered to reimburse for no more than six trips per year, and asked the treatment center to arrange to have the parental training sessions just prior to or immediately following a school break.[47] The district did not ask the center to alter its training in any form.

The parents objected to this change and later filed a due process complaint. An impartial hearing officer (IHO) ruled in favor of the school district, noting that the number of tripe was appropriate to providing FAPE under the IDEA. The parents appealed the IHO's decision.[48]

The federal district court agreed with the IHO's ruling in favor of the school district. It emphasized the IHO's finding that the parents had never taken as many as twelve trips each year, yet the Boston Higashi staff reported that Aaron was making good progress and that the parents were better able to control him when he was at home. The facility's staff never indicated that they would be unable to implement Aaron's IEP with the reduced number of trips.[49] Finally, the court drew attention to the fact that the IDEA does not require the school district to provide transportation for parents if it is unrelated to a child's access to special education. The school district was only obligated to provide parental transportation for the training sessions, which were essential to Aaron's social development needs.[50]

In a 2015 case, a parent who had agreed to transport her severely disabled child to and from school until the district could arrange specialized transportation and could hire a nurse to accompany the student on the bus sued to recover additional "costs" related to her temporary transportation of her daughter to and from school. The school district had offered to cover her mileage at the district's standard reimbursement rate. The plaintiff asserted that she was entitled to hourly wages in addition to the mileage reimbursement because she had saved the district "from the necessity of incurring various expenses, including hiring a bus driver and medical support" for the period that she provided her daughter's transportation.[52] The federal court rejected her premise, stating that "the replacement costs Plaintiff has identified are merely hypothetical expenses associated with Defendant's transportation of L.L. by a means other than reimbursing Plaintiff. But Plaintiff never had to bear these hypothetical 'costs' in order to provide L.L. with transportation."[53]

In summary, school districts are obligated to provide free transportation to students with disabilities so those students may access the educational programming and services identified in their IEPs. This may include reimbursing parents for travel costs for a specified number of trips for specific purposes, (e.g., attending therapy or training sessions), if the district has placed the child in a residential facility in another city or state. The district may enter into a contractual agreement to reimburse, at business mileage rate, parents who are willing to transport their children with disabilities to school.

Medical Services

IDEA's definition of related services specifies that medical services are included only to the extent that they are for "diagnostic and evaluation purposes." However, the administrative regulations promulgated by the Department of Education also specify that the term "medical services" should mean only those services that are provided by a licensed physician.[55] As the Supreme Court specified in the *Tatro* case, the related services provisions cover medical procedures that do not require the services of a physician and are supportive services that enable a child to benefit from special education. However, disputes between parents and school districts still arise over what constitutes excluded medical services. Below are descriptions of three cases that are illustrative of the controversy.

The first case represents a particular category of disputes involving the question of whether costs of psychiatric treatment, including hospitalization, are related services under IDEA.[56] The federal district court reviewed an appeal by a school district that was ordered to reimburse parents for the cost of hospitalizing their daughter, Cari Rae, during which time she was diagnosed with "oppositional defiance disorder" and drug dependency. This diagnosis was followed by a psychological evaluation and other tests that concluded Cari Rae was emotionally impaired.[57]

The hospital stay and the subsequent evaluations preceded any action by the school district to identify Cari Rae as a student requiring special education, even though she always had struggled in high school and had been habitually absent.[58] The administrative hearing officer ruled that the school district had breached the "child find" provision of the IDEA and, therefore, was responsible to reimburse the parents for the hospitalization. The federal district court agreed with the administrative hearing officer regarding the "child find" violation, stating that the "'child find' duty requires children to be identified and evaluated 'within a reasonable time after school officials are on notice of behavior that is likely to indicate a disability.'"[59]

In the second half of the analysis, the court then explored the question of whether the school district must pay for the hospitalization under IDEA's related services provisions. The school district argued that the hospitalization was an intervention to an emotional crisis during which Cari Rae had locked herself in a bathroom and threatened her mother, and not a circumstance where supportive services were necessary to the provision of a FAPE.[60] Cari Rae's mother called the police, who then referred Cari Rae to the acute care center at the hospital. The school district believed the cost should not be recoverable because it was a medical service prompted by a "psychiatric crisis," not a diagnostic or evaluative stay mandated by an IEP.[61]

The court reasoned that while the emotional crisis led to the hospital stay, the result was the identification of Cari Rae's disability. "The stay at [the] [h]ospital was—as the hearing officer found—the beginning of, if not an integral part of, the 'evaluation and diagnosis' of the Student."[62] In fact, the court went so far as to hypothesize that Cari Rae might never have been identified had it not been for her hospitalization.

Finally, the court remarked that the IDEA and case law provided courts with considerable discretion in determining an appropriate remedy for a substantive infringement of the IDEA.[63] Specifically, the court cited a Sixth Circuit Court of Appeals ruling in which reimbursement to parents for a unilateral private placement was appropriate when the district had failed to identify a student under "child find" who was later eligible for IDEA services.[64] The court concluded that reimbursement for the hospitalization was a "preplacement"[65] expense and, therefore, should be reimbursed.

In contrast to the decision involving Cari Rae, in which the parents were reimbursed for hospitalization and psychiatric evaluation and treatment, the Third Circuit Court of Appeals denied reimbursement for expenses related to a residential hospital stay in *Mary Courtney T. v. School District.*[66] The defendant school district in this case appealed a district court's decision mandating that it reimburse the plaintiff's parents for the cost of a stay in a New York residential health care facility.

Courtney was identified as having "learning disabilities, speech and language impairments, attention deficit hyperactivity disorder, and other mental health disorders."[67] Because of the complexity and severity of Courtney's disabilities, she was placed in a private school setting at the school district's expense from the time she was in kindergarten. Her evolving needs required periodic changes in placement.

At one point, her parents unilaterally placed her in a residential education facility in New Mexico that specialized in adolescents with educational, emotional, and behavioral problems. She remained there for a year, was discharged, and returned to Philadelphia, where she was enrolled in school and did quite well for the next academic year. However, her behavior and emotional condition began to deteriorate the following school year. Her parents were notified by the school that it could no longer meet Courtney's needs, so they placed her back in the residential facility in New Mexico. Her problems worsened, including psychotic events and self-harming behaviors. This facility then notified Courtney's parents that it could no longer meet her needs.

Eventually, Courtney was placed in a long-term psychiatric residential treatment institution in New York. While this facility was licensed by the New York State Office of Mental Health and with a national accreditation organization for rehabilitation services, it offered no educational services and was not accredited to do so. After five months, Courtney's parents informed the defendant school district that she was sufficiently emotionally stable to be evaluated. Based on its evaluation, the district recommended an educational program that focused on adaptive and vocational skills. Courtney remained at the New York residential hospital for several more months.

Courtney's parents requested a due process hearing to compel the school district to reimburse them for the cost of Courtney's stays in New Mexico and New York, or to provide Courtney with compensatory education if their request for tuition reimbursement was denied The school district agreed to reimburse for the New Mexico facility, but refused to agree to pay for the New York stay, arguing that Courtney had been there solely for medical purposes. The hearing officer in the due process hearing disagreed, stating that her educational needs could not be separated from her medical needs in this instance. The school district appealed to a federal district court, which decided to divide Courtney's New York stay into two parts: the first months, when she was being treated solely for emotional and behavioral issues, and the second part of her stay, when she was transferred to the post-acute wing of the facility. The court ruled that the first part of her stay was not recoverable, but the second part was. The court found that once the school district started to provide educational services to Courtney, it was obligated to provide related services, as well. The district court ruled that Courtney's treatment was a related service and not subject to the "medical services" exception.[68]

The Third Circuit agreed with the lower court's determination regarding Courtney's stay in the acute-care ward, where Courtney received medical care and no educational services and, therefore, the costs should not be reimbursed. However, it overturned the district court's determination that the period during which Courtney was in the post-acute ward was not reimbursable It concluded that "only those residential facilities that provide special education, however, qualify for reimbursement."[69] In this particular case, the appellate court determined that the residential facility in New York addressed Courtney's medical needs, but not her educational needs, and that her medical and academic needs were severable. As a result, "Courtney's education was impeded, not by a lack of educational services or a specific kind of placement, but by a complex and acute medical condition. The School District could neither prevent the onset of such a condition nor control when it would subside."[70]

The court also rejected the district court's conclusion that the school district was responsible for the cost of the residential facility as a related service once it started to provide educational services. It concluded that it was an excluded medical service because it was care "far beyond the range of competence of any public school district or that of any school nurse."[71]

The third case represents a category of disputes involving reimbursement for services provided to students with hearing impairments. The parents of a student who was deaf requested reimbursement for insurance copayments for the services of an audiologist and for transportation costs incurred when taking their son to the audiologist.[72] Hunter was born deaf, although both parents and his siblings had normal hearing. He was initially fitted with acoustical hearing aids, but it soon became evident that he was not benefiting from them. On the advice of a physician, they chose to have Hunter fitted with a cochlear implant that would help him perceive sound that, in turn, would assist him in acquiring oral language skills.[73]

Programming the speech processor, referred to as "mapping," was essential to the proper functioning of the implant and could be performed only by a specially trained audiologist. The school staff checked daily to test if Hunter was able to perceive a range of sounds. If he did not respond as expected, they referred him to the audiologist so that the processor could be adjusted.[74]

Although Hunter's IEP included objectives that were based on the use of the cochlear implant and that he was expected to learn to hear, it neither included reimbursement for the copayments nor the cost of taking him for "mapping" visits to the audiologist, whose office was located in a neighboring city.[75] His parents sought to have these expenses reimbursed, and to have the audiologist services included in the IEP as related services.[76]

At the due process hearing, the school district asserted that the cochlear implant was not an acoustical hearing device and, therefore, not covered under the IDEA.[77] It also argued that "mapping" and other procedures related to the implant were excluded medical services, so the audiologist services should not be included in the IEP. The administrative hearing officer disagreed and ruled in favor of the parents.[78]

The federal district court upheld the administrative hearing officer's decision. It was clear from the IEP that the implant was considered necessary to Hunter's language acquisition. Without it, he would not achieve some of the IEP's stated goals, nor would he have meaningful access to special education services. "The IEP . . . confirms that the educational methodology chosen for Hunter includes the use of the conchlear [sic] implant as a necessary part of the free appropriate public education provided to him. Under these circumstances, the mapping services necessary for the use of Hunter's cochlear implant are 'related services' within the meaning of the IDEA."[79]

In 2006, following this and other similar decisions, the U.S. Department of Education amended the administrative regulations to provide clarity surrounding cochlear implants and the provision of related services.[80] Specifically, the definition of related services contained in the regulations now exclude "a medical device that is surgically implanted, the optimization of that device's functioning (e.g., mapping), maintenance of that device, [and] the replacement of that device."[81] The Department of Education also promulgated a regulation that specifically addressed school districts' responsibility for the maintenance of surgically implanted medical device. Under that regulation, school districts are responsible for ensuring that "the external components of surgically implanted medical devices are functioning properly."[82]

The regulations obligate a school district "to appropriately monitor and maintain medical devices that are needed to maintain the health and safety of the child, including breathing, nutrition, or operation of other bodily functions, while the child is transported to and from school or is at school."[83]

Furthermore, the Department emphasizes that the regulations should not be construed in such a manner that "limits the right of a child with a surgically implanted device . . . to receive related services . . . that are determined by the IEP Team to be necessary for the child to receive FAPE."[84] In 2012, the United States Court of Appeals for the D.C. Circuit held that the Department of Education had not exceeded its authority in promulgating these regulations.[85]

Examples of other excluded medical devices include G-tubes, insulin pumps, Baclofen pumps, pacemakers, and vagus nerve stimulators.[86] School districts are not required to optimize the functioning of these surgically implanted devices, but they are required to check to make sure they are functioning properly so that the child may benefit for the educational programming.

In summary, medical services that require a physician are not reimbursable expenses under IDEA. However, if physician-provided services and/or a hospital stay are demonstrated to be related to diagnosing or evaluating a disability that leads to a student's eligibility for IDEA educational programs and services, those expenses may be found to be reimbursable

Alternative Therapies

Not unlike disputes over specialized instructional approaches, parents have sought to have their choice of related services take precedence over those offered by the school. And, as in other cases, unless the parents can demonstrate that the proffered services are inadequate to ensure FAPE, the courts will uphold a school district's right to choose the programs and services it provides at public expense.

One such example concerned a child, C.M., who had profound hearing loss, whose parents opted for cochlear implants for her when it was evident she was having no success with hearing aids.[87] After the devices were activated, C.M.'s parents sought "an 'educational program that maximizes exposure to meaningful sounds ... [particularly] exposure to spoken language every day,'"[88] as recommended by the company that created the implants. While the manufacturer made no specific recommendation as to which program to follow, the parents had received professional advice to continue with auditory-verbal therapy (AVT), the very same program they had chosen for their daughter while she was using hearing aids.[89]

As a preschooler, C.M. was enrolled in a year-round program at her family's synagogue. Concurrently, she participated in the school district's Early Intervention Program (EIP), during which time her AVT was paid for by the county. After she turned three, her educational dossier from the EIP was forwarded to the school district so that it could determine whether she would be eligible for special education services.[90]

Once the school district determined that C.M. was eligible under IDEA, the parents expressed their wish to continue her schooling at the synagogue, but wanted the school district to pay for the AVT that she was still receiving. The district indicated that it had trained its personnel in the verbotonal (VT) approach, a recognized and well-established program in which hearing-impaired students learned how to communicate orally.[91] The parents objected to the change in therapies and requested a due process hearing.

In denying the family's request to be reimbursed for tuition and AVT sessions, the administrative law judge (ALJ) ruled for the school district, indicating that "VT is an accepted and proven therapy and that '[i]t is the School Board's prerogative, not the Parents', to choose which of these accepted and proven methodologies will be provided at public expense.'"[92] The Eleventh Circuit Court of Appeals agreed with the ALJ, as follows:

> C.M.'s parents may be correct that VT would confuse C.M. and that the classroom dynamics offered by the School Board would not be most suitable for C.M. However, C.M.'s parents never challenged the School Board's assertion, or the ALJ's conclusion, that VT is a well-recognized means by which to teach hearing-impaired children to speak. While C.M.'s parents may not want such a program, the IDEA does not grant them a right to select among various programs. Rather, the School Board offered C.M. what was required under the IDEA—a free *appropriate* public education. . . . The IDEA does not permit them to challenge an IEP on the grounds that it is not the best or most desirable program for their child.[93]

This ruling, however, should not be construed to imply that school districts out-of-hand can disregard therapies or other related services that were selected and paid for by parents and that have contributed to a student's significant progress in another school or district. This is especially pertinent if the receiving school district does not provide appropriate related services in their place and in a timely manner.

Such was the case for A.G., a student with emotional disturbance who had been released from a residential facility, which had been paid for by the district, after the residential staff concluded A.G. could function in a day school and live at home, provided his "wrap-around" (related) services were continued.[94] The recommended wrap-around services included, among other items, that A.G. was to be "associated with a non-parental adult to act as respite and/or prosocial facilitator outside of the home and school."[95] The accepting day school, a district-approved private school, requested an opportunity to observe A.G. prior to determining what services and instructional programming would serve his needs. In the interim, the parents scheduled and paid for the recommended therapies that A.G. needed.[96]

A year passed before the school district called an IEP meeting, at which time the district IEP team decided it would not provide the wrap-around services. The parents followed up this determination with a letter to the district requesting reimbursement for the services that they had already paid for and the provision of ongoing therapy for A.G.[97]

When they received no response from the district, the parents filed a due process complaint, which resulted in a ruling against the district. The hearing officer noted that A.G. had been denied FAPE by the school district's failure to develop an IEP that included the full range of required related services that were essential to A.G.'s continued progress[98] Upon appeal, the federal district court awarded the parents reimbursement and reasonable attorney fees and court costs.

Substituting focused therapies and training with something less structured or informal, or even nothing at all, will not satisfy the IDEA's requirement for FAPE. Parents of a young child with severe autism, S.K., filed a due process complaint after they concluded that the proffered IEP, which included a kindergarten placement in a year-around special education class, failed to meet their daughter's needs.[99] Among their complaints were deficient related services, including insufficient speech therapy, no applied behavior analysis (ABA), and no parent counseling and training.[100]

As a 2-year-old, S.K. had been evaluated and had been determined to need speech therapy by the state education department's Early Intervention Program. A year later, the department's Committee on Preschool Education (CPSE) diagnosed S.K. with severe autism, at which time she began receiving ABA services, as well as continued speech therapy. The CPSE followed this with a pre-kindergarten IEP in which it was recommended that S.K. be in a small class and that she continued to receive home ABA therapy and one-on-one speech therapy.[101] The committee also recommended one-on-one occupational therapy (language therapy), because S.K. had significant developmental delays in expressive language.

When S.K. became of age for the kindergarten program, the school district convened an IEP meeting. While the one-on-one occupational therapy and placement in a small class (in a specialized, year-round public school) continued to be recommended, the kindergarten IEP indicated that S.K. would participate in three-to-one speech therapy sessions, and that the home ABA therapy would be discontinued.[102] This latter recommendation was made even though the IEP noted S.K. had made substantial progress with the ABA therapist.

S.K.'s parents contested the changes and her school placement.[103] After searching for alternatives, the parents chose to unilaterally place S.K. in a private school that specialized in children with autism, and then pursued a claim for reimbursement of tuition and for related services.[104]

The IHO ruled that the department had failed to provide S.K. with FAPE based on the fact that, among other issues, the IEP did not provide adequate speech therapy and did not offer any parent counseling and training. The IHO also noted that the parents met their burden in demonstrating that their choice of school placement met S.K.'s educational needs. The IHO ordered the district to retroactively pay the full tuition directly to S.K.'s private school, and to provide the needed related services.[105]

The district appealed this decision to the state board of education, at which time the state review officer (SRO) overturned the IHO's rulings.[106] In addressing the parents' claim that appropriate related services were not adequately addressed in the IEP, the SRO relied on the testimony of the district's special education teacher, who said that she would be able to meet S.K.'s needs because she provided "specialized language instruction in her classroom throughout the day . . . that 'specialized language instruction takes place all throughout the day because communication is all throughout the day.'"[107] The SRO also relied on the district's psychology supervisor's assessment that the school placement "'did a great deal to support parents,' including offering a six-week parent training program provided by a non-profit agency, monthly meetings, and support groups."[108] The SRO concluded that, although the IEP did not specify provision for parental training and counseling, such offerings were available and, therefore, S.K. was not being denied FAPE.

S.K.'s parents appealed to federal district court, which ruled that S.K. was denied FAPE based on the fact that the district did not provide the necessary related services for S.K. to experience growth and success in school. The district court concluded that "the combination of terminating S.K.'s one-on-one speech and ABA therapy *and* failing to provide training to her parents deprived S.K. of a FAPE."[109] The court relied on evidence that S.K. was making significant progress, that there were consistent expert opinions that S.K. needed continued individualized speech and ABA therapy to continue to progress, and that there was no evidence to suggest that S.K. would receive meaningful educational benefit without these related services.[110]

In rejecting the SRO's ruling that S.K. was not denied FAPE, the court remarked on the absence of any expert witnesses or evidence in the SRO's reasoning that would lead one to conclude that S.K. would be successful without the related services that had served her so well prior to the kindergarten IEP.[111] The court dismissed the notion that S.K.'s speech therapy needs could be met by simple interaction with the classroom teacher, stating that "[t]his generalized approach is, simply put, not a meaningful substitute for the focused, individualized attention and instruction determined by the experts ... to be necessary for S.K.'s continued development.[112] The court also rejected the SRO's assessment that adequate parental training and counseling were available to S.K.'s parents, noting that those services referred to in the SRO's decision were designed to meet the general concerns of all parents of special needs children and were not tailored to the specialized training for parents of children with autism. Finally, the court noted the progress that S.K. was making with her ABA therapist and, again, that there was no justification for terminating the ABA therapy other than the district's policy of not offering it to children once they are 5 years old.[113]

These cases collectively indicate that, while parents may not dictate which related services they want for their child, the school district may not substitute inadequate or inappropriate services in their place. Likewise, districts may not terminate related services without sufficient evidence that the child can continue to make adequate progress and to have meaningful, or "non-trivial,"[114] educational benefit.

Service Animals

Service or assistance animals have been getting attention in the courts, but most often the controversies are litigated under Section 504 of the Rehabilitation Act or the Americans with Disabilities Act (ADA), both of which are covered in other chapters of this guide.[115] IDEA decisions involving the use of service animals have been primarily the result of due process impartial hearing officer or state review officer decisions, but none of it very clarifying.[116] There are a few cases in which appellate courts heard claims that a child was denied FAPE because the child's service dog was not allowed to come into the school, but the analyses primarily focused on whether the parents had exhausted IDEA's due process remedies prior to bringing a case to the federal court. While Chapters 10 and 11 contain more details about due process procedures, generally, courts have declined to allow plaintiffs who allege their child has been denied FAPE to circumvent the administrative remedies requirement by filing under ADA.

The U.S. Supreme Court recently ruled in *Fry, v. Napoleon Community Schools*, a case involving a school district's denial to allow a service animal to accompany a student to school.[117] The disputed point of law is whether the plaintiffs should be required to exhaust administrative remedies, as required under IDEA, prior to filing a suit in federal court. In this instance, however, the plaintiffs argued that they were not alleging that their daughter, E.F., was denied FAPE under IDEA, but rather that she was discriminated against by the school district because of her disability, a violation of both the Americans with Disabilities Act (ADA) and the Rehabilitation Act.[118] The school district refused to allow Wonder, a trained service dog, to accompany E.F. to school. Wonder performed functions like opening and closing doors to bathroom stalls that allowed E.F. to function more independently.[119] The school district argued that school personnel could perform those functions. In reality, however, E.F.'s privacy was infringed and her independence diminished under the district's proposal. As a result, her parents sought damages for the social and emotional harm she suffered.[120] The trial court and Sixth Circuit Court of

Appeals ruled in favor of the school district and dismissed the case, opining that the family must first exhaust administrative procedures under IDEA as the first step in resolving disagreements, prior to filing suit in federal court.[121]

The Supreme Court, in a 6-2 ruling, overturned the Sixth Circuit's decision and remanded the case with instructions to apply the proper analysis in determining if the substance of the complaint is indeed a denial of FAPE. If the grievance is unrelated to IDEA, but rather falls under the ADA and the Rehabilitation Act, then there is no requirement to exhaust administrative remedies. It is important to emphasize that *Fry* does not focus on the use of service dogs as a related service, something that a student may need in order to access educational services, but rather on the child's needs to be able to function more independently.

The IDEA is silent with regard to the use of service animals. Federal regulations promulgated under the ADA provide a definition of "service animal," which is a good point of reference for school leaders, teachers, parents, and others who are following legal developments in this area.[122] Only dogs are covered in this definition; however, in another section of the regulations there is a provision for miniature horses.[123] The definition is as follows:

> *Service animal* means any dog that is individually trained to do work or perform tasks for the benefit of an individual with a disability, including a physical, sensory, psychiatric, intellectual, or other mental disability. Other species of animals, whether wild or domestic, trained or untrained, are not service animals for the purposes of this definition. The work or tasks performed by a service animal must be directly related to the individual's disability. Examples of work or tasks include, but are not limited to, assisting individuals who are blind or have low vision with navigation and other tasks, alerting individuals who are deaf or hard of hearing to the presence of people or sounds, providing non-violent protection or rescue work, pulling a wheelchair, assisting an individual during a seizure, alerting individuals to the presence of allergens, retrieving items such as medicine or the telephone, providing physical support and assistance with balance and stability to individuals with mobility disabilities, and helping persons with psychiatric and neurological disabilities by preventing or interrupting impulsive or destructive behaviors. The crime deterrent effects of an animal's presence and the provision of emotional support, well-being, comfort, or companionship do not constitute work or tasks for the purposes of this definition.[124]

Access to the school or other public place may be denied for two reasons: "(1) the dog is out of control and the handler does not take effective action to control it, or (2) the dog is not housebroken."[125]

The OCR has been pressing states and school districts to alter laws, policies, and practices to allow service animals into schools, but it has not mandated consideration of service animals as a related service under IDEA. Therefore, school districts would not be responsible for providing, training, or caring for service animals. Regardless, appropriate policies should be developed to guide administrators on how to properly respond to requests by students with disabilities to allow their service animals to accompany them to school and to school events. The Civil Rights Division of the U.S. Department of Justice offers considerable information that could serve as guidance for such policies.[126]

Private Right of Action

As illustrated by the case law discussed above, students with disabilities and their parents may seek relief under IDEA when related services are not provided or paid for. However, there is no private right of action to seek monetary damages; complainants may only to seek the provision of programming and services or reimbursement of the costs they have incurred when the school district has failed to provide FAPE. There have been two other legal avenues parents and students have taken in seeking monetary damages related to special education: state law tort claims, or claims for violation of federal law, as asserted under 42 U.S.C. § 1983.

Several circuit courts have concluded that the IDEA does not provide for a private right of action for "tort-like money damages."[127] By way of example, a suit was filed by the parent of a 4-year-old, developmentally delayed boy alleging that the school district was negligently responsible for his death. The child died by asphyxiation when his tracheotomy tube became dislodged while he played. His mother claimed that the "School District . . . violated the IDEA by failing to have a person capable of reinserting Antione's tracheotomy tube ... at the time of the incident in question."[128] While noting that it was a tragic case, the court granted summary judgment for the school district, stating:

> Although the IDEA is silent about the availability of tort-like damages, "[t]ort-like damages are simply inconsistent with IDEA's statutory scheme....The purpose of the IDEA is to provide educational services, not compensation for personal injury, and a damages remedy—as contrasted with reimbursement of expenses—is fundamentally inconsistent with this goal....The IDEA's central mechanism for the remedying of perceived harms is for parents to seek changes to a student's program.[129]

In conclusion, the only private right of action under the IDEA available to parents is to force public education agencies to pay for educational services, including related services, due under the IDEA. Legal remedies for other kinds of alleged violations, such as disability discrimination or civil rights violations, are discussed in more detail in Chapters 10 and 11.

Implications

The above discussions instruct school leaders, teachers, parents, and others involved with the development of IEPs and with the delivery of special education services to follow the lead of the courts and ask three questions. The first question is: *Does the requested service provide the student meaningful access to special education services?* While the statutory definition and federal regulations enumerate several examples of related services, those examples are not to be viewed as all-inclusive. The IEP team must consider what services the student needs to be able to attend, remain at, and return home from school, and to benefit from the education being provided.

The second question is: *Does the requested service fall under the definition of an excluded medical service?* The IDEA specifies excluded medical services as those that are not for the purposes of student evaluation or diagnosis related to special education eligibility. The U.S. Supreme Court has provided a "bright line" test by defining an excluded medical service as one that requires the services of a physician. As was illustrated above, parents are likely to receive reimbursement for medical and other related costs if such expenses are the result of inaction by the school district, and if the medical services provide evaluation and diagnosis that result in a child being identified as eligible for special education services. Furthermore, school district officials are unlikely to be successful in arguing that the cost associated with a student who requires extensive related services is an undue financial burden on the school district.

The last question is: *When may a related service be modified or terminated?* The IDEA requires that an IEP specify related services that the student requires in order to experience meaningful educational benefit. IEP teams should take care in determining what those services are and how they support the student and her/his family. However, sometimes related services need to be modified or terminated. The IEP team should rely on evidence and expert reports to determine that the student will continue to make progress or that her/his educational progress will not be stymied by the recommended changes.

Essentially, the U.S. Supreme Court continues to emphasize the intent of Congress—to give students with disabilities access to a free appropriate public education and to do so in a manner that is reasonably calculated to provide them with educational benefit—through its rulings on all provisions of the IDEA, including related services. In this regard, school leaders will prevail in court challenges if they provide the supportive services students need to reach school, to stay in school, and to participate in the special education programs designed to give them meaningful educational experiences.

Endnotes

[1]   20 U.S.C. § 1401 *et. seq.* (2012).
[2]   Pub. L. No. 107-110, 115 Stat. 1425 (2002).

[3] Pub. L. No. 114-95, 129 Stat. 1802 (2015).

[4] 20 U.S.C. § 1401(26) (2012); 34 C.F.R. § 300.34 (2016).

[5] 20 U.S.C. § 1402(26)(A) (2012); 34 C.F.R. § 300.34(a) (2016). The statutory definition excludes "a medical device that is surgically implanted, or the replacement of such a device." 20 U.S.C. § 1402(26)(B) (2012).

[6] 20 U.S.C. § 1402(26)(A) (2012). Medical services is a term that is defined in the federal regulations to mean services "provided by a licensed physician."

[7] 34 C.F.R. § 300.304(c)(4) (2016).

[8] 20 U.S.C. § 1414(d)(1)(A)(i)(IV) (2012); 34 C.F.R. § 300.320(a)(4) (2016).

[9] 34 C.F.R. § 300.320(a)(7) (2016).

[10] 34 C.F.R. § 300.324(a)(4)(i) (2016).

[11] 34 C.F.R. § 300.324(a)(4)(ii)(2016).

[12] *Supra*, note 9.

[13] Irving Indep. Sch. Dist. v. Tatro, 468 U.S. 883, 891 (1984).

[14] *Id.* at 885.

[15] *Id.*

[16] *Id.* at 891.

[17] *Id.*

[18] *Id.* at 892. The current regulation can be found at . § 300.34(c)(13) (2016).

[19] *Id.*

[20] 20 U.S.C. § 1401(9) (2012) (defining "free appropriate public education" or FAPE).

[21] Cedar Rapids Cmty. Sch. Dist. v. Garret F. *ex rel.* Charlene F., 526 U.S. 66 (1999).

[22] *Id.*

[23] *Id.* at 69, n. 3.

[24] *Id.* at 72.

[25] *Id.* at 73-74.

[26] *Id.* at 75.

[27] *Id.* at 75-76.

[28] *Id.* at 76-77.

[29] *Id.* at 77.

[30] *Id.* at 79.

[31] Max M. v. Ill. St. Bd. of Educ., 629 F. Supp. 1504 (N.D. Ill. 1986).

[32] *Id.* at 1507.

[33] S.B. v. Dist. of Col., 783 F. Supp. 2d 44 (D.D.C. 2011).

[34] *Id.* at 48.

[35] *Id.*

[36] *Id.*

[37] *Supra*, note 4.

[38] Aaron M. v. Yomtoob, 2003 WL 223469 (N.D. Ill. Feb. 3, 2003).

[39] Fick *ex rel.* Fick v. Sioux Falls Sch. Dist. 49-5, 337 F.3d 968 (8th Cir. 2003).

[40] *Id.*

[41] *Id.* at 970.

[42] *Id.*

[43] Aaron M., 2003 WL 223469.

[44] *Id.* at *1.

[45] *Id.* at *3.

[46] *Id.* at *2.

[47] *Id.* at *6.

[48] *Id.* at *4.

[49] *Id.*

[50] *Id.* at *6.

[51] Ruby J. v. Jefferson Co. Bd. of Educ., 122 F. Supp. 3d 1288 (N.D. Ala. 2015).

[52] *Id.* at 1308.

[53] *Id.* at 1308-1309.

54   42 U.S.C. § 1401(26)(A) (2012).

55   34 C.F.R. § 300.34(c)(5) (2016).

56   Dep't of Educ. v. Cari Rae S., 158 F. Supp. 2d 1190 (D. Haw. 2001).

57   *Id.* at 1992.

58   *Id.* at 1997.

59   *Id.* at 1194, citing W.B. v. Matula, 67 F.3d 484, 501 (3rd Cir.1995).

60   *Id.* at 1197, citing Clovis Unified Sch. Dist. v. California Office of Admin. Hrgs., 903 F.2d 635 (9th Cir. 1990); Butler v. Evans, 225 F.3d 887 (7th Cir. 2000).

61   *Id.* at 1198, quoting Butler, 225 F.3d at 893.

62   *Id.* at 1199.

63   *Id.* at 1199. "As a remedy for a substantive violation, the Court is authorized to 'grant such relief as the court determines is appropriate,'" *Id.* at 1199, citing 20 U.S.C. § 1415(i)(2)(B) (iii) (2012). "The statute thus 'confers broad discretion' on the Court and allows for reimbursement for costs of pre-eligibility private placements (e.g., private schools), if an IDEA violation is found and a child is subsequently determined to be eligible for IDEA services." *Id.* at 1199-1200, citing Burlington Sch. Comm. v. Mass. Dep't. of Educ., 471 U.S. 359, 369 (1985).

64   *Id.* at 1200. "Similarly, authorities have approved reimbursement for costs of private placements for 'child-find' violations, if a child is subsequently determined to be eligible for IDEA services . . . 'In cases where the lack of dialogue stems from the school district's failure to conduct sufficient 'child-find,' reimbursement may be appropriate,'" *Id.*, citing Doe v. Metro. Nashville Public Schs., 133 F.3d 384, 388 (6th Cir.1998).

65   *Id.*

66   Mary Courtney T. v. Sch. Dist. of Phila., 575 F.3d 235 (3d Cir. 2009).

67   *Id.* at 239.

68   *See* Mary Courtney T. v. Sch. Dist. of Phila, 2009 WL 185426 (E.D. Pa., Jan 22, 2009).

69   575 F.3d at 244, citing Kruelle v. New Castle Cty. Sch. Dist., 642 F.2d 687, 692 (3d Cir. 1981).

70   *Id.* at 246.

71   *Id.* at 248.

72   Stratham Sch. Dist. v. Beth P., 2003 WL 260728 (D.N.H., Feb. 5, 2003).

73   *Id.* at *1.

74   *Id.* at *2.

75   *Id.*

76   *Id.*

77   *Id.* at *3.

78   *Id.*

79   *Id.* at *5.

80   *See* 71 Fed. Reg. 46,540, 46,760 (2006) (codified at 34 C.F.R. § 300.34(b)(1) (2016)).

81   34 C.F.R. § 300.34(b)(1) (2016).

82   34 C.F.R. § 300.113(b)(2) (2016).

83   34 C.F.R. § 300.34(b)(2)(ii) (2016).

84   34 C.F.R. § 300.34(b)(2)(i) (2016). For further discussion regarding school districts' obligations related to cochlear implants, *see* Petit v. U.S. Dep't of Educ., 675 F.3d 769 (D.C. Cir. 2012) (holding that U.S. Department of Education regulations regarding the mapping of cochlear implants were consistent with the statute).

85   Petit v. U.S. Dep't. of Educ., 675 F.3d 769 (D.C. Cir. 2012).

86   *See* Center for Parent Information and Resources, *Related Services: What's Excluded as a Related Service,* (http://www.parentcenterhub.org/repository/iep-relatedservices/#exclusion) (last visited June 20, 2017).

87   M.M. *ex rel.* C.M. v. Sch. Bd. of Miami-Dade County, Fla., 437 F.3d 1085 (11th Cir. 2006).

88   *Id.* at 1099.

89   *Id.* at 1090.

90   *Id.*

91   *Id.* at 1091.

[92] *Id.* at 1094.

[93] *Id.* at 1103.

[94] A.G. v. Dist. of Columbia, 794 F. Supp. 2d 133 (D.D.C. 2011).

[95] *Id.* at 136.

[96] *Id.*

[97] *Id.*

[98] *Id.* at 136-37.

[99] P.K. *ex. rel.* S.K. v. New York City Dep't. of Educ., 819 F. Supp. 2d 90 (E.D.N.Y. 2011).

[100] *Id.* at 102.

[101] *Id.* at 101.

[102] *Id.* at 102.

[103] *Id.* at 103.

[104] *Id.* at 102.

[105] *Id.* at 98. The IHO, SRO, and subsequent court rulings all applied the *Burlington-Carter* test for determining whether a school district is responsible for reimbursing parents for tuition when the parents have made a unilateral decision to place their child in a private school. Under the '*Burlington–Carter*' test, reimbursement is appropriate when (1) the school district has provided an 'inadequate or inappropriate' placement; (2) the parents' selected program is appropriate, such that the private program meets the student's special education needs; and (3) the equities favor the parents." *Id.,* citing Sch. Comm. of Burlington v. Dep't of Educ., 471 U.S. 359, 369–70 (1985); Florence Cnty. Sch. Dist. Four v. Carter. 510 U.S. 7, 12–13 (1993).

[106] *Id.* at 102.

[107] *Id.* at 110.

[108] *Id.*

[109] *Id.* at 98.

[110] *Id.* at 111.

[111] *Id.* at 11-12.

[112] *Id.* at 113.

[113] *Id.* at 112, n.10.

[114] *Id.* at 114.

[115] *See* Chapter 4, *supra.*

[116] Perry Zirkel, *Service Animals in the K-12 Schools: A Legal Update*, 327 Ed. Law Rep. 554 (2016).

[117] Fry v. Napoleon Community Schools, 137 S.Ct. 743 (2017).

[118] *Id.*

[119] *Id.*

[120] *Supra*, note 117.

[121] Fry v. Napoleon Community Schools, 2014 WL 106624 (E.D. Mich.); 788 F.3d 622 (6th Cir. 2015).

[122] 28 C.F.R. § 35.104 (2016).

[123] 28 C.F.R. § 35.136(i) (2016).

[124] *Supra*, note 122.

[125] Service animals, 28 C.F.R. § 35.136(b) (2016); see also, U.S. Dept. of Justice, Civil Rights Division, Disability Rights Section, *ADA 2010 Revised Requirements: Service Animals* (2010), https://www.ada.gov/service_animals_2010.pdf .

[126] U.S. Department of Justice, Civil Rights Division, *Frequently Asked Questions about Service Animals and the ADA*, https://www.ada.gov/regs2010/service_animal_qa.html.

[127] Ortega v. Bibbs County Sch. Dist., 397 F.3d 1321, 1324 (11th Cir. 2005); *see also* Nieves-Marquez v. Puerto Rico, 353 F.3d 108 (1st Cir. 2003); Witte v. Clark County Sch. Dist., 197 F.3d 1271(9th Cir. 1999); Charlie F. v. Bd. of Educ. of Skokie Sch. Dist., 98 F.3d 989 (7th Cir. 1996); Heidemann v. Rother, 84 F.3d 1021(8th Cir. 1996); Gean v. Hattaway, 330 F.3d 758 (6th Cir. 2003); Babicz v. Sch. Bd. of Broward County, 135 F.3d 1420 (11th Cir. 1998).

[128] *Ortega*, 397 F.3d at 1323.

[129] *Id.* at 1325.

Chapter 8

Secondary School Transition Planning

Stanley L. Swartz, Philip H. Swartz, and
Cathleen A. Geraghty-Jenkinson*

Introduction

It can be said with some confidence that the history of special education has evolved from a time when accountability was a matter of measuring *efforts*, to the current standard of accountability, where the *outcomes* for individual students are the standard to which the public schools are held. Another important change is that the responsibility of the public schools has expanded from services provided in PreK-12 to programs that ensure that students with disabilities are appropriately prepared for postsecondary opportunities and transitioned to other agencies that provide supports for independent living, employment, and even higher education. It is the goal of legislation, supported by various legal opinions, to provide a seamless transition from childhood to adulthood for students with disabilities. The public schools play a critical role in planning for and supporting the efforts to make this transition successful.

The Individuals with Disabilities Education Act (IDEA)[1] extends mandatory public education to include planning and programs to ensure a successful transition from K-12 educational experiences to community integration, including meaningful employment. The IDEA allows states to reserve a portion of federal funds received under the Act for the "[d]evelopment and implementation of transition programs, including coordination of services with agencies involved in supporting the transition of children with disabilities to postsecondary activities."[2]

The reauthorization of the IDEA in 2004 revised the definition of secondary transition services. Transition services currently are defined as:

> [A] coordinated set of activities for a child with a disability that—
>
> (a) is designed to be within a results-oriented process, that is focused on improving the academic and functional achievement of the child with a disability to facilitate the child's movement from school to post-school activities, including postsecondary education, vocational education, integrated employment (including supported employment), continuing and adult education, adult services, independent living, or community participation;
>
> (b) is based on the individual child's needs, taking into account the child's strengths, preferences and interests; and

(c) includes instruction, related services, community experiences, the development of employment and other post-school adult living objectives, and, when appropriate, acquisition of daily living skills and functional vocational education.[3]

The importance of the transition from public school educational programs to appropriate postsecondary experiences for individuals with disabilities, and the necessary support services to successfully accomplish the transition, has a history that can be traced through public policy reflected in legislation and changing professional practices. A more detailed discussion of federal legislation is set forth below. That the IEP must now include a specific statement of the needed transition services[4] is a result of research demonstrating that the absence of such planning diminishes the likelihood of a child's success.[5] Additionally, political activism directed toward establishing the need for a follow-along plan for all children with disabilities has resulted in legislation hopefully facilitating a continuum of services for individuals with disabilities throughout their lives.[6]

Transition Planning Requirements

A successful school transition program can be conceptualized as a four-step procedure: (1) foundation, (2) process, (3) culmination, and (4) follow-up.[7] The transition foundation includes all education, training, and experience that prepare an individual for adult life. An educational program is designed to develop functional skills, which are defined as skills that have a high probability of being required of someone as an adult. A foundation for children with mild educational disabilities will include academic skills that can be built upon with postsecondary vocational training or college training. For children with more severe educational disabilities, the curriculum will be more basic and functional. For all children, however, the curriculum should include training in social and vocational "survival skills."[8]

Survival skills are those that generalize across social and vocational settings. For example, social survival skills include behaviors such as responding appropriately, expressing needs such as the location of a restroom, and appropriately interacting with others in social settings.[9] Vocational survival skills include reporting to work on time, working at one's workstation for a continuous period of time, and asking for clarification if an instruction is not understood.[10] The need for these types of skills is not specific to individuals with disabilities, but is expected of all adults.

IDEA's "Findings and Purposes" section emphasizes congressional intent that transition to independent living and working is very much the goal of providing special education services to children with disabilities.[11] While the IDEA does not require formal transition planning earlier than age 16, the elementary IEP process should include some goals that build a foundation for secondary school transition planning. IEP decisions should be made in the context of how planning may affect the child's future school or post-school experiences. A July 2012 report on transition challenges that was issued by the Government Accountability Office (GAO) suggested that age 16 may be too late to begin transition services, especially when considerations need to be made as to whether the child will participate in 'diploma-track' classes or a more vocationally oriented curriculum.[12]

All children receiving special education under the IDEA must have transition services included in their individualized education program (IEP) beginning no later than age 16, and transition planning can occur earlier.[13] Secondary transition requirements may be added into an IEP before the child turns 16 if it is determined to be appropriate by the IEP team. Regardless of when the transition requirements are added into the IEP, it will be updated annually thereafter. In addition, the Rehabilitation Act Amendments of 1992[14] made clear that children eligible under Section 504 are also eligible for transition planning.

IDEA requires that the child's IEP include (1) "appropriate measurable postsecondary goals based on age appropriate transition assessments related to training, education, employment, and, where appropriate, independent living skills;" and (2) "transition services (including courses of study) needed to assist the child in reaching those goals."[15] A school district's failure to include any of these required components can result in a denial of FAPE. In addition, the failure of a school district to conduct transition assessments, including obtaining preferences and interests from the child, also can result in a denial of FAPE.[16] These statutory requirements cannot be waived or deferred until a later date.[17] The requirement to include a transition plan and provide transition services continues until the child either "ages out" of IDEA eligibility or obtains, per state law, a regular high school diploma.[18]

The transition plan should include the roles and responsibilities of teachers, agency personnel, parents, and children.[19] Some examples include:

1. Assessing child's needs, interests, or preferences for future education, employment, and adult living and devising goals in these areas;
2. Identifying, exploring, and trying out transition placements that match the child's assessment and vision and providing community experiences;
3. Instructing the child in the academic, vocational, and adult-living skills needed to achieve transition goals, including self-determination and independent living, or community participation;
4. Identifying and providing the accommodation, supports, or related services the child needs to achieve the highest level of independent living possible;
5. Coordinating with adult services and organizations, while helping families identify resources and natural supports; and
6. Providing or planning follow-up or follow-along support and activities once the child develops independence in a transition activity, or graduates.

The IDEA requires that the child be invited to the IEP team meeting if the purpose of the meeting is to discuss postsecondary goals for the child.[20] Emphasis is placed on the child's involvement in transition planning, while empowering the family to guide their child with a disability into adult living. Furthermore, the parent/guardian, child's special education teacher or related services provider, regular education teacher, and local educational agency representative are required to attend IEP meetings. If the child is 16 years old or older and unable to attend the meeting, the law requires that steps are taken to ensure the child's preferences and interests are considered.[21] With consent from parents and the child with a disability, appropriate adult-service organizations that provide or pay for transition services should be invited to attend the IEP.[22] If the adult-service organization does not attend the meeting, the local education agency (LEA) is not required to take other steps in continuing to include the participating agency in transition planning.

Other constituents such as guidance counselors, vocational educators, college counselors, related service providers, and administrators have a potential place in designing transition plans and may be invited to transition planning depending on the goals and needs of the child. If the aforementioned individuals will contribute to the transition plan, the teacher or administrator should invite those individuals.

Transition services from a secondary education environment to adult living can include no support or limited support, support that is time-limited, or specific and ongoing support. The U.S. Department of Education has published a comprehensive guide for high school educators that addresses the topic of transition to postsecondary education.[23]

Some children with mild/moderate disabilities, such as specific learning disabilities, may not require adult services, or they may benefit from context-specific accommodations such as extended time to complete college and university course examinations, services that would be determined by each particular postsecondary institution. Other children may need time-limited services, including specific training such as on-the-job support or support in finding independent living arrangements; however, the assumption is that this support will only be needed for a specific period of time. Third, some individuals will need a specific type of support on an ongoing basis, including specialized services permitting the individual to live normally within the community. Individuals with severe disabilities might be expected to need various levels of support throughout their lifetimes, including ongoing support of an extensive nature. The outcome for each of these types of support is different. For individuals needing no support, time-limited support, or specific ongoing support, the outcomes are typically competitive employment and independent living. For individuals with severe disabilities that need ongoing support of an extensive nature, the expected outcomes are unusually supported employment and supported living. In some cases, individuals with severe disabilities who need extensive and ongoing support may live independently and work in competitive employment.

Goal development must be based on an individual child and take into account the interests and preferences of that child. Minimally, goals must address instruction (including all types of education); community experiences (community services including transportation, recreation, etc.); when appropriate, employment and their post-school daily living objectives (not only does this include community based work experiences, but also functional adult activities including voting, paying taxes, and utilizing Social Security or other government benefit programs); acquisition of daily living skills (self-care, budgeting, etc.); and functional vocational evaluation (vocational skill interest or aptitude assessments). Additionally, if transition services are to be provided by a public agency other than the school district itself, and that public agency fails to meet those objectives, the IEP team must meet to find alternative strategies to try and meet the objectives.[24] These goals are part of the results-oriented process that considers all post-school activities, not exclusively employment. Often there are related services that must also be described in order for a child to access attainable outcomes (i.e., benefits from special education).

A critical component of transition goal development is personal choice. In order to facilitate lasting outcomes, child buy-in is critical. Developing choice-making skills through early child involvement in the IEP process will assist when children are later in the position of making decisions about their own lives. The law also facilitates this process by requiring LEAs to begin informing children of their rights one year prior to the age of majority under state law.[25] Children in special education programs are not required to remain in school until age 22, and cannot be coerced into doing so by agencies unwilling to take them onto their caseloads and thereby begin paying for adult services. These decisions are an important part of the transition planning process.

Transition culmination occurs with the graduation, or "aging out" of special education. The transition team is charged with the responsibility of ensuring a smooth change from school to community service agencies, including the obligation to provide a child who is exiting public school with a summary of performance (SOP).[26] The SOP is designed to provide parents and/or the child with an accurate summary of the child's performance, as well as outlining what needs to be done in order for the child to successfully meet postsecondary goals.[27] This is an opportunity for the school to provide the family and child with community resources and related wrap-around services that can help the child achieve postsecondary goals. The SOP is defined in the IDEA 2004 as follows:

> (ii) **Summary of performance** – For a child whose eligibility under this part terminates under circumstance described in clause (i), a local educational agency shall provide the child with summary of the child's academic achievement and functional performance, which shall include recommendations on how to assist the child in meeting the child's postsecondary goals.[28]

Finally, a transition follow-up is the last step. By evaluating results, school administrators can adjust the program and the process to ensure the most appropriate outcomes.

Two other significant requirements that are related to transition also deserve mention. The definition of transition was changed to emphasize that related services are to be included and that every IEP must consider whether the child requires assistive technology devices and assistance.[29] Therefore, every IEP team meeting about transition must examine related services, determine the child's needs regarding technology, and consider assistive technology and services.

Also, teams must remember that the availability of services may not be considered when developing the IEP. The Office of Special Education and Rehabilitative Services (OSERS) and the Office of Special Education Programs (OSEP) have continually reminded LEAs that if the services needed by a child are not available, it is the responsibility of the LEA to create the service or identify community resources that will meet the unique needs of the child. In the case of transition planning, many of the services that a child needs to be successful in post- secondary life may only be available outside of the traditional school setting. This cannot be used as a reason to not provide the services to the child. It is the responsibility of the school to coordinate with the necessary agencies in order to provide the child with the necessary services, or to create equitable programs.

Finally, teams must remember that the IEP is a legally binding document. If the district does not provide the listed services, including goal attainment, then they are at risk of an adverse decision regarding a lack of FAPE.

History of Federal Legislation

The need for transition services has been addressed in a variety of federal special education, vocational education, and rehabilitation legislation, including the Carl D. Perkins Career and Technical Education Act,[30] the Rehabilitation Act of 1973,[31] the IDEA,[32] and the Americans with Disabilities Act.[33] A summary of this history is instructive to the understanding of changing public attitudes and awareness and changing public policy.

The IDEA, which originally was enacted in 1975 as The Education of All Handicapped Children Act (EAHCA),[34] required that children with disabilities have available to them a free and appropriate public education, protected the rights of children with disabilities and their parents to procedural due process, and required safeguards in the evaluation and placement process. Central to this legislation was making increased federal funds available to the states for the purposes of assuring the implementation of this law. Key to the eventual recognition of the need for transition services was the provision that the effectiveness of these programs be evaluated.

In 1983, additional federal education legislation addressed the need to coordinate the education and training of youth with disabilities to assist in the transitional process from school to employment and postsecondary education.[35] Major emphases included the design of vocational programs to increase the potential for youth with disabilities to gain competitive employment and to encourage the development of cooperative training models between educational and adult service agencies. This law marked the emergence of the transition process as a major focus in programs for children with disabilities.

A number of important revisions to legislation addressing secondary education and transitional services were made in 1986.[36] Programs were expanded not only in regard to whom can be served, but also the nature of the services to be provided. Services could now be provided to children recently graduated or exited from the public schools. Reflecting Brown, Nietupski, and Hamre-Nietupski's "Criterion of Ultimate Functioning," transition was reconceptualized as an education theme throughout a child's schooling.[37]

In 1989, the National Council on Disability[38] noted the critical need to address the transition from school to adult life. Their findings included:

- Upon leaving school, children with disabilities and their families had a difficult time accessing appropriate adult services.[39]
- Effective transition planning for high school children with disabilities can facilitate their success in adult life.[40]
- Graduates with disabilities are more likely to be employed following school if comprehensive vocational training is a primary component of their high school programs and they have jobs secured at the time of graduation.[41]
- There are insufficient partnerships between the business community and schools for the purpose of enhancing employment opportunities for children with disabilities.[42]
- Parent participation during high school facilitates the successful transition of children with disabilities from school to adult life.[43]

Thus, when Congress amended and reauthorized the EAHCA, including renaming it as the Individuals with Disabilities Education Act in 1990, Congress expanded the concept of transition services to include independent living and full participation of youth with disabilities in community programs as appropriate goals.[44] This change represents a movement from education as a means to competitive employment to a broader goal of full community integration. Requirements for IEP development included a statement of needed transition services by age 16, or age 14 if appropriate, and any necessary interagency responsibilities after school exit. The 1990 amendments required the development of objectives for employment and other post-school adult living skills, thus addressing the development of job skills for transition to the workplace and social skills to enable full participation in community life.[45]

The reauthorization of the IDEA in 2004 clarified that all children eligible under the IDEA must be considered for transition services, and that transition must be considered as part of the IEP process beginning at age 16.[46] Transition became one of the required statutory elements of an IEP after age 16. Finally, the reauthorization of IDEA in both 1997 and 2004 served to strengthen the belief that transition to independent living and working is the primary goal of all special education interventions.

Vocational Education Legislation

Originally passed in 1984, the Carl D. Perkins Career and Technical Education Act[47] allocated federal funds for equipment, staff, and buildings. Ten percent of funds available under this Act were earmarked for children with disabilities, and 22 percent for the disadvantaged. This Act provided for assessment of interests and abilities related to vocational education programs; special services, including adaptation of curriculum, instruction, equipment, and facilities; guidance, counseling, and career development activities conducted by professionally trained counselors; and counseling services designed to facilitate the transition from school to post-school employment opportunities. By its very inclusion in the statute, vocational education for children with disabilities was legitimized. The focus of programming from education in the traditional academic sense to programs that emphasized employment and necessary functioning for adult life was made possible with the requirement that a portion of the funds authorized under this act be reserved for use by programs designed to benefit individuals with disabilities.

Rehabilitation Legislation

Building on a long history of the progressive expansion of services to individuals with disabilities, the Rehabilitation Amendments, passed in the 1960s, marked the entry of the Department of Rehabilitation into training for expanded employment outcomes.[48] Though earlier establishment of sheltered workshops had employment as a goal, this legislation concentrated on integrated community setting.

The Rehabilitation Act of 1973[49] provided the statutory foundations for the Rehabilitation Services Administration and established priority for rehabilitation services to those with the most severe disabilities. It also initiated and expanded programs for individuals previously being underserved, including homebound and institutionalized clients; expanded employment opportunities for individuals with disabilities; included Section 503, which eliminated architectural and transportation barriers impeding citizens with disabilities in public governmental buildings, required an individualized written rehabilitation plan (IWRP) with an annual review, which outlines, in the form of a contract developed in conjunction with the client, the conditions and responsibilities under which services will be provided; funded research and demonstration projects concerned with the rehabilitation of individuals with severe disabilities; and included Section 504, which prohibits discrimination against any individual solely by reason of the disability in any program or activity receiving federal funds.[50]

Important to the eventual emphasis on transition for school-aged children was the inclusion of education for children with disabilities as one of the major features of the Rehabilitation Act. Children served by the public schools were guaranteed similar protections as adults served by rehabilitation and other service agencies. The EAHCA, IDEA's precursor statute, was specifically referenced in the language of the law. This inclusion of school-aged children in the language of the Act set the stage for the eventual coordination of services of various agencies, because of the wide authority of this Act.

The Rehabilitation Comprehensive Services and Developmental Disabilities Amendments of 1978[51] continued and enlarged the existing trends of rehabilitation legislation. The law:

1. increased the commitment to rehabilitation research by expanding its research provisions and by stipulating the need and the means for ensuring coordination in the research enterprise;
2. continued the movement from a focus on preparation for employment to a focus on preparation, plus affirmative action for enlarging opportunities for competitive employment for individuals with disabilities;
3. continued the attempt to provide services to underserved populations, especially the individuals with developmental disabilities and other severe disabilities;[52]
4. authorized the expansion of rehabilitation to include independent living as an objective for individuals served under the Act; and
5. provided employer incentives for training and hiring individuals with disabilities.[53]

Programs that required an affirmative action-type push were encouraged by this act. Transition at its inception was this type of an effort. This Act authorized the use of funds to provide a variety of support mechanisms that allowed transition programs to be mounted.

The Vocational Rehabilitation Amendments of 1986[54] made notable changes to include the use of supported employment (defined as employment in an integrated setting with ongoing support services) as an acceptable outcome for the rehabilitation program.[55] Much of the historical emphasis of the state/federal rehabilitation agencies had been in rehabilitation that resulted in almost total independence of functioning for clients, which had the obvious effect of excluding serious efforts on behalf of individuals with moderate and severe disabilities. This Act legitimized and authorized funding for services that were supportive in nature and expected to be ongoing.

Employment-Related Legislation

The Job Training Partnership Act of 1982[56] was designed to shift training away from the public sector to the private sector. Individuals with disabilities are targeted as a special population for services under this Act. Incentives were made available to employers to accommodate individuals with disabilities in community-based employment settings.

The Supplemental Security Income Improvement Act of 1986 removed work disincentives by allowing recipients to work without loss of benefits.[57] It allowed participation in a variety of training programs, including supported employment, while still receiving income assistance.

In 2014, Congress passed the Workforce Innovation and Opportunity Act (WIOA).[58] WIOA extended out-of-school services to students with disabilities up to age 24 who are no longer attending school. New provisions in the WIOA emphasize community integrated employment opportunities, where individuals work in the actual workforce, as preferable to supported employment, where jobs sites are sheltered, individuals require long term support, and competitive employment is a low priority.[34]

Primarily, WIOA addressed four areas: (1) integrated education and training for a specific occupation or cluster; (2) financial literacy education; (3) entrepreneurial skills training; and (4) services that provide labor market information about in-demand industry sectors and occupations.

Specifically, WIOA addresses the following services:

- Tutoring, study skills training, and instruction leading to secondary school completion, including dropout prevention strategies;
- Alternative secondary school offerings or dropout recovery services;
- Paid and unpaid work experiences with an academic and occupational education component;
- Occupational skill training, with a focus on recognized postsecondary credentials and in-demand occupations;
- Leadership development activities (e.g., community service, peer-centered activities);
- Supportive services;
- Adult mentoring;
- Follow-up services for at least twelve months after program completion; and
- Comprehensive guidance and counseling, including drug and alcohol abuse counseling,

With the passage of the Assistive Technology Act of 2004,[59] each state began to receive additional money for technology programs, client protection, and advocacy services. New emphasis was placed on device demonstration and equipment loan, and there was an increased focus on training to ensure service providers have information on assistive technology. Supplemental grants are provided for equipment loan programs, and the Act authorized a comprehensive national study of the assistive technology industry.

Taken together, these pieces of legislation chart the evolution of programming for individuals with disabilities from traditional programs to a continuum of services beginning in the public schools and extending to community integration via adult service agencies. Such a movement was a public recognition of the need to coordinate efforts on behalf of individuals with disabilities as various governmental agencies assumed responsibility for service provision. It is important to remember that new initiatives built into legislation do not develop in isolation. Research demonstrating program efficacy and professional practice evolved because of field-based experience.

Continuing Concerns about Effectiveness of Transition Services

In 2002, prior to the 2004 Amendments to IDEA, poor post-school outcomes were reported by the Commission on Excellence in Special Education, a committee formed by President George W. Bush.[60] These findings helped drive changes to the IDEA 2004. Among the Commission's findings were the following:

> The Commission finds students with disabilities are significantly unemployed and have underemployment upon leaving school compared to their peers who do not have disabilities. Too many students with disabilities leave school without successfully earning any type of diploma, and they attend postsecondary programs at rates lower than their nondisabled peers. Adults with disabilities are much less likely to be employed than adults without disabilities. Unemployment rates for working-age adults with disabilities have hovered at the 70 percent level for at least the past 12 years, which the Commission finds to be wholly unacceptable. Even when employed, too many adults with disabilities who are employed earn markedly less income than their nondisabled peers. These statistics reflect failures in the present systems' structures. We find that the overriding barrier preventing a smooth transition from high school to adult living is the fundamental failure of federal policies and programs to facilitate smooth movement for students from secondary school to competitive employment and higher education.[61]

In July 2012, the United States Government Accountability Office (GAO)[62] published a document highlighting the continued need for successful transition planning for children with disabilities, due to continued poor outcomes. Specifically, as of February 2012, it is estimated that the employment rate for young adults ages 20 to 24 with disabilities was less than half the rate of their peers without disabilities.[63]

One clear concern emerging from the GAO report is lack of coordination among agencies. Children with disabilities often have difficulties navigating through the various agencies, which can result in delays in services or lack of access to services.

The four agencies that administer key transition programs are the Department of Education, the Department of Health and Human Services (HHS), the Department of Labor (Labor), and the Social Security Administration (SSA). The student's school district (the local education agency (LEA)) is specifically responsible for coordinating the child's services (e.g., IEP) so that the child can be prepared for gainful employment. However, the Department of Labor is designed to improve training and employment opportunities for individuals with disabilities. The SSA oversees Disability Insurance and Supplemental

Security Income (SSI) programs, as well as the Ticket to Work program. The aforementioned SSA programs are designed to provide supplemental cash awards, as well as to help individuals with disabilities find, enter, and retain employment. Finally, HHS manages Medicare and Medicaid services. Both home- and community-based services can be provided and can include case management, personal care attendants, or day or residential habilitation.

While there is no formal program to integrate all four agencies, in 2005 they joined together to form the Federal Partners in Transition Workgroup, which is designed to improve interagency communication and coordination in the delivery of transition services.[64] It is an informal workgroup, but involves information sharing and may serve as an invaluable resource to IEP teams. One result of the enactment of WIOA in 2014 was that the Federal Partners in Transition Workgroup would coordinate transition services for students with disabilities, to ensure a federal interagency strategy to improve the outcomes for these students.

Several key barriers make it difficult for individuals with disabilities to access transition services, including lack of adequate information or aware-ness, and lack of preparedness for postsecondary education or employment. Additionally, children in the juvenile justice system, those who are parents, and/or those who have less-visible disabilities (e.g., mild cognitive delays and learning disabilities) may also have unique challenges when it comes to accessing transition services. The lack of coordination is reported across states, with Florida's "Project 10 Transition Education Network" and Minnesota's Department of Employment and Economic Development program providing examples of ongoing collaborative efforts.[65]

Thus, it is important for IEP teams to keep in mind that children with disabilities enrolled in school are entitled to an IEP, but as an adult they must apply for federal and state services for individuals with disabilities. The IEP transition plan should be mindful of this and seek to develop goals and services that will facilitate successful application of post school services.

Case Law

In a fairly recent case, *J.L. v. Mercer Island School District*,[66] the Ninth Circuit Court of Appeals specifically addressed transition-related issues. K.L. was identified by the school district as being a child with a specific learning disability. She attended school in the district off and on from fourth through ninth grade, with her parents unilaterally placing her in private school in tenth grade. Primary points of disagreement were in regard to little to no progress being made on IEP goals from year to year, and the parents' feeling that the school was not considering their desire to have K.L. attend college instead of remaining in a vocational track. In a due process hearing, an administrative law judge originally found in favor of the district. The parents then filed suit in federal court and prevailed at both the trial and appellate court level, leading to an award of attorney fees and related costs. The federal courts found that after three years of no progress on goals, and little revision of the IEP, K.L.

had not been provided with a FAPE and had not been adequately prepared for a postsecondary transition. Additionally, the postsecondary goals of the parents and child were not reflected in the IEP goals or services. It is important to note that, in this case, the Ninth Circuit applied a "meaningful educational benefit" standard, which arguably exceeds the Supreme Court's language in *Rowley*,[67] which had stipulated that a child receive "some educational benefit." Part of this updated interpretation is most likely due to increased accountability for all children receiving special education.

This decision in *J.L.* incorporated previous cases that clarified the requirements and intent of the IEP with regard to transition services. When planning for postsecondary transition, all of the child's needs must be addressed, not just academic. In *Russell v. Jefferson School District*[68] and *Abrahamson v. Hershman*,[69] for example, the courts identified that transition plans should include services and goals that may not be academically related, but that will allow the child to access meaningful employment and facilitate transition from school to post-school activities.

In *Carrie I. v. Department of Education,* the parent of a student with disabilities filed suit alleging, among other things, that the student's IEP failed to provide a FAPE because it did not provide for appropriate transition services.[70] A federal district court determined that the IEP had failed to address the student's unique needs for the transition from school to adult life for several reasons, including the failure to include the appropriate agencies in the planning process and the failure to conduct any transition assessments of the student before drafting the IEP. Indeed, the court noted that the lack of any assessments "alone is enough to constitute a lost educational opportunity."[71] This lack of transition planning resulted in a denial of FAPE. Similarly, the federal Sixth Circuit Court of Appeals has held that the failure to consider a student's transition-related preferences, or to conduct age-appropriate transition assessments, can result in a denial of FAPE.[72]

Numerous cases have addressed the consequences of a district's failure to provide adequate transition services. In a due process matter decided by the Massachusetts Board of Special Education Appeals regarding Carver Public Schools, the board determined that a hearing officer could declare a high school diploma invalid because the district had not provided an appropriate transition plan.[73] Likewise, in a California due process hearing involving Livermore Valley Joint Unified School District, the hearing officer determined that the student's diploma should be rescinded because the school district had not yet provided transition planning and services, which are required before graduation.[74] These cases, in effect, returned the students to the district and established their continued eligibility for services. In two other due process matters involving school districts in California and Maine, the districts were required to pay for post-graduation services because of their failure to provide transition services while the student was enrolled in the district.[75]

For more information, Dean Eggert and Allison Minutelli, two lawyers who practice in New Hampshire, have compiled an excellent review of other special education cases that address issues relating to transition services.[76]

Recommendations for Practice

The focus on transition represents an important milestone in the history of efforts to serve individuals with disabilities. Past efforts were basically designed to guarantee access. Current efforts focus on the outcomes of special education. Do public school programs target eventual adult status and community participation? Have agencies with programming responsibility for individuals with disabilities developed agreements that will ensure continuous service during the transition from school to work and community living? Have the community agencies developed agreements with regard to the agency that will take primary responsibility with regard to case management? Current legislation suggests some practices that can be recommended for site-level program administration.

1. An IEP must be developed for each child. This plan must include descriptions of services and who will be responsible for providing the services. It is important to note that this plan will include a variety of activities that are other than traditional academic programming. Efforts will include cooperation with other service agencies.

2. Transition planning begins earlier rather than later, and in many cases this may be earlier than when the child turns 16. Teams should begin a dialogue with parents, child, and any other relevant parties as to whether or not the child is going to participate in a more academic or vocationally oriented track. Preparation for the skills needed for either track should be explicitly addressed in the IEP, and ongoing progress monitoring of a child's trajectory should be discussed frequently. Changes to the child's transition plan should be reflective of the child's progress.

3. The IEP should be developed carefully to ensure that all necessary information is included. Service recommendations will not be needed for each individual in all areas. The IEP should include consideration of each of the following areas: instruction, community experiences, employment and other post-school living objectives, acquisition of daily living skills, and functional vocational evaluation. Any area in which there is a recommendation must also include a statement of who will take responsibility for carrying out the action. If goals are not written in each of these areas, a statement must be provided as to why goals were not written in a particular area.

4. Transition goals should be the school district's attempt to anticipate the transition needs of the child in as many areas as possible. This process should include data collection as to how the child functions in the community, and the development of goals and services to address community participation. In the early stages of transition goal development, goals will be generic and exploratory. As chil-

dren approach graduation, goals should become more specific to the interests, needs, and desires of each child.

5. Cooperative relationships and agreements should be established with adult service agencies. Agencies should be invited to participate on an as-needed basis. Collaborative programs should be initiated to ensure that the transition from school to work or postsecondary programs will be a smooth one. An individual should be appointed with specific responsibility to serve as a liaison with community services agencies. The child's goals should be collaborative and not conflict with each other.

6. School curricula should be focused on the development of functional skills, those skills necessary for successful adult life. Programming for youth with disabilities should include some balance of attention to vocational, independent living, and recreation and leisure activities.

7. Schools must make renewed efforts to involve families in the program development process. Parents who are full participants in the program planning are less likely to initiate legal challenges that are costly both in time and resources.

8. Because transition is an outcome-based process, data collection is of increased importance. Follow-up studies of program graduates should be initiated. These data can be used to make any necessary program modifications.

9. Transitional programming for youth with disabilities should be viewed as a proactive process. Program opportunities that will enhance the likelihood of child success should be identified and supported. Schools need to take the initiative in developing community-based vocational programs. School programs that have the greatest potential for practical application in adulthood should be developed. Programs that have no demonstrable adult applications should be abandoned.

10. Efforts to educate school personnel and the public to the fact that appropriate programs for youth with disabilities are functional, rather than academic, should be initiated. The function of schooling for this group of children is to prepare for successful adulthood, and this information should be established and communicated.

11. In order for an IEP, and subsequently a transition plan, to be implemented, all individuals who work with the child should be aware of the plan, as well as trained on the instructional strategies needed to help the child achieve goals. It is the responsibility of the school to make sure the child meets IEP goals and has a transition plan that will help the child achieve postsecondary goals.

12. A final area is for transition planners to develop an awareness of community-based existing natural supports. Increasingly, these resources are receiving attention in the research literature. Exemplified by groups, including churches and economic organizations, social or athletic groups, and business clubs, there is great potential in facilitating community integration through these voluntary attachments.[59]

13. A cautionary note is that graduating a student absent adequate transition services might be subject to challenge. Even though graduation marks the end of district responsibility to provide services, this decision must have included the provision of a successful transition to appropriate support environments and programs.

Endnotes

* Contributors to earlier versions of this chapter include Jeff McNair, Joseph Turpin, and Gary Sherwin.

[1] 20 U.S.C. § 1400 *et.seq.* (2012).

[2] 34 C.F.R. § 300.704(b)(4)(vi) (2016).

[3] 20 U.S.C. § 1401(34) (2012).

[4] 20 U.S.C. § 1414(d)(1)(A)(i)(VIII) (2012).

[5] *See* President's Comm'n on Excellence in Special Educ., *A New Era: Revitalizing Special Education for Children and their Families* (2002), http://www.nectac.org/~pdfs/calls/2010/earlypartc/revitalizing_special_education.pdf (hereinafter *A New Era)*, citing *Transition and Post-School Outcomes for Youth with Disabilities: Closing the Gaps to Post-Secondary Education and Employment*, National Council on Disability (2000), available at http://www.ncd.gov/rawmedia_repository/c19e795f_e7da_4628_a673_86e2d0c6f951.pdf.

[6] Among other pieces of federal legislation that provide a continuum of services after students with disabilities exit the public school system, important protections are contained in the Americans with Disabilities Act, *See* 42 U.S.C. § 12101 *et. seq.* (2012).

[7] *See, e.g.,* Steere, *et. al., Outcome-Based School –to-Work Transition Planning for Students with Severe Disabilities,* 13 Career Development for Exceptional Individuals 57 (1990).

[8] Zigmond & Sansone, *Designing a Program for the Learning Disabled Applicant,* 7 Remedial and Special Education 13-17 (1986).

[9] *Id.*

[10] *Id.*

[11] 20 U.S.C. § 1400(c)(1) (2012) (noting Congress's finding that "[d]isability is a natural part of the human experience and in no way diminishes the right of individuals to participate in or contribute to society. Improving educational results for children with disabilities is an essential element of our national policy of ensuring equality of opportunity, full participation, independent living, and economic self-sufficiency for individuals with disabilities.").

[12] U.S. Gov't Accountability Office, *"Students with Disabilities: Better Federal Coordination Could Lessen Challenges in the Transition from High School,"* (hereinafter *"Students with Disabilities")* (July 2012) (available at http://www.gao.gov/assets/600/592329.pdf).

[13] 30 C.F.R. § 300.320(b) (2016).

[14] Rehabilitation Act Amendments of 1992, Pub. L. No. 102-569, 106 Stat.4344 (1992).

[15] 20 U.S.C. § 1414(d)(1)(A)(i)(VIII) (2012).

[16] *See infra,* discussion of Case Law.

[17] *See* Bd. of Educ. of Twp. High Sch. No. 211 v. Ross, 486 F.3d 267 (7th Cir. 2007) (noting that the IDEA's requirements cannot be deferred until a later date).

[18] Yankton Sch. Dist. v. Schramm, 92 F.3d 1369, 1276-77 (9th Cir. 1996).

[19] 34 C.F.R. § 300.321(b) (2016).

20 34 C.F.R. § 300.321(b)(1) (2016).

21 34 C.F.R. § 300.321(b)(2) (2016).

22 34 C.F.R. § 300.321(b)(3) (2016).

23 *See* Office for Civil Rights, *"Transition of Students with Disabilities to Post-Secondary Education: A Guide for High School Educators,"* (March 2011) (available at http://www2.ed.gov/about/offices/list/ocr/transitionguide.html).

24 34 C.F.R. § 300.324(c) (2016).

25 20 U.S.C. § 1414(d)(1)(A)(i)(VIII)(cc) (2012).

26 20 U.S.C. § 1414(c)(5)(B)(ii) (2012).

27 *Id.*

28 *Id.*

29 20 U.S.C. § 1401(34) (2012).

30 This legislation was originally passed as the "Carl D. Perkins Vocational Education Act," Pub. L. No. 98-524, 98 Stat. 2435 (1984).

31 Rehabilitation Act of 1973, Pub. L. No. 93-112, 87 Stat. 355 (1973).

32 20 U.S.C. § 1400 *et. seq.* (2012).

33 42 U.S.C. § 12101 *et. seq.* (2012).

34 Pub. L. No. 94-142, 89 Stat. 773, 775 (1975).

35 Education of the Handicapped Act Amendments of 1983, Pub. L. 98-199, 97 Stat. 1357 (1983).

36 Education of the Handicapped Act Amendments of 1986, Pub. L. 99-457, 100 Stat. 1145 (1986).

37 L. Brown, J. Nietupski & S. Hamre-Nietupski, *Criterion of Ultimate Functioning,* in HEY DON'T FORGET ABOUT ME!: EDUCATION'S INVESTMENT IN THE SEVERELY, PROFOUNDLY, AND MULTIPLY HANDICAPPED: A REPORT (M.A. Thomas ed., Council for Exceptional Children pub.) (1976).

38 National Council on Disability, *"The Education of Students with Disabilities: Where Do We Stand?"* (hereinafter *"Where Do We Stand?"*) (Sept. 1989) (available at http://www.ncd.gov/publications/1989/September1989).

39 *Where Do We Stand?, supra* note 39, at Finding 24.

40 *Id.* at Finding 25.

41 *Id.* at Finding 26.

42 *Id.* at Finding 27.

43 *Id.* at Finding 28.

44 Individuals with Disabilities Education Act of 1990, Pub. L. No. 101-476, 104 Stat. 1103 (1990).

45 Individuals with Disabilities Education Act of 1990, Pub. L. No. 101-476, §101(d), 104 Stat. 1103 (1990).

46 Individuals with Disabilities Education Improvement Act of 2004, Pub. L. No. 108-446, 118 Stat. 2647 (2004).

47 *See supra* note 31.

48 Vocational Rehabilitation Amendments of 1968, Pub L. No. 90-891, 82 Stat. 297 (1968).

49 Rehabilitation Act of 1973, Pub. L. No. 93-112, 87 Stat. 355 (1973).

50 *See* R.M. Garguilo, *"Litigation and Legislation for Exceptional Children: A Historical Perspective,"* Illinois Council on Exceptional Children Quarterly 29 (1) (1980); George N. Wright, TOTAL REHABILITATION (Little Brown 1980).

51 Rehabilitation, Comprehensive Services, and Developmental Disabilities Amendments of 1978, Pub. L. No. 95-602, 92 Stat. 2955 (1978).

52 Lizanne Destafano & Dale Snauwawert, *"A Value-Critical Approach to Transition Policy Analysis,"* (available at http://files.eric.ed.gov/fulltext/ED310610.pdf) (1989).

53 *See supra,* note 45.

54 Rehabilitation Act Amendments of 1986, Pub. L. No. 99-506, 100 Stat. 1807 (1986).

55 D. Braddock & G. Fujjura, *"Federal Foundations for Transitions to Adulthood,"* in TRANSITIONS TO ADULT LIFE FOR PEOPLE WITH MENTAL RETARDATION: PRINCIPLES AND PRACTICES (B. Ludlow, A. Turnbull & R. Likasson eds. 1988).

56 Job Training Partnership Act of 1982, Pub L. No. 97-300, 96 Stat. 1322 (1982).

[57] Supplemental Security Income Improvement Act of 1986, Pub. L. No. 99-643, 100 Stat. 3574 (1986).

[58] Pub. L. No. 133-148, 128 Stat. 1425 (codified at 29 U.S.C. § 3101 *et. seq.* (West. 2016)).

[59] Assistive Technology Act of 2004, Pub. L. No. 108-364, 118 Stat. 1707 (2004).

[60] *A New Era, supra* note 6.

[61] *Id.* at 43.

[62] *Students with Disabilities, supra* note 13.

[63] *Id.*

[64] This workgroup's formation and mission generally is described at http://youth.gov/feature-article/federal-partners-transition.

[65] Information about Florida's Project 10 Transition Education Network can be found at http://project10.info/ (last visited Dec. 15, 2016). Information about Minnesota's Department of Employment and Economic Development program can be found at https://mn.gov/deed/ (last visited Dec. 15, 2016).

[66] J.L. v. Mercer Island Sch. Dist., 592 F.3d 938 (9th Cir. 2010).

[67] Bd. of Ed. of Hendrick Hudson Cent. Sch. Dist. v. Rowley, 458 U.S. 176 (1982).

[68] Russell v. Jefferson Sch. Dist., 609 F. Supp. 605 (N.D. Ca. 1985).

[69] Abrahamson v. Hershman, 701 F.2d 223 (1st Cir. 1983).

[70] Carrie I. v. Department of Education, 869 F. Supp. 2d 1225 (D. Haw. 2012).

[71] *Id.* at 1247.

[72] Gibson v. Forest Hills Local Sch. Dist. Bd. of Educ., 655 Fed. Appx. 423, 440 (6th Cir. 2016).

[73] Re: Carver Public Schools, BSEA #00-2574 (Mass. Bd. of Sp. Ed. Appeals, July 9, 2001) (available at http://www.doe.mass.edu/bsea/decisions.html?yr=2000).

[74] Livermore Valley Joint Unified Sch. Dist., Case No. SN 727-00, 33 IDELR 288 (CA SEA 2000) (available at file:///C:/Users/eas68/Downloads/SEAHDSN_727-00_11_9_2016.pdf).

[75] San Diego Unified Sch. Dist., Case No. SN 2386-01, 36 IDELR 172 (SEA CA 2002) (available at file:///C:/Users/eas68/Downloads/SEAHDSN_2386-01_11_9_2016.pdf); Student v. Caribou Sch. Dep't, Case #01.135, 35 IDELR 118 (SEA ME 2001) (available at http://maine.gov/doe/specialed/support/dispute/hearings/2001/index.html).

[76] Dean B. Eggert & Alison M. Minutelli, *"That's All Folks: A Closer Look at Transition Services and Graduation under the Individuals with Disabilities Education Act,"* (available at http://www.wadleighlaw.com/wp-content/uploads/dlm_uploads/2015/02/IDEA-Transition-Services-and-Graduation.pdf).

Chapter 9

Disciplining Students with Disabilities

Mark A. Paige

Introduction

Appropriately handling behavioral and discipline issues of students with disabilities is an important part of special education. It raises significant legal questions, in addition to questions of practice. As discussed in more detail below, the IDEA (the Individuals with Disabilities Education Act) and its implementing regulations provide comprehensive rules that govern this issue. Similarly, court cases provide important guidance. Within the overall subject of special education discipline, particular areas that require careful attention include removal of students with disabilities, as well as the restraint and seclusion of these students, among others. These areas are given particular attention in the following pages.

Context matters in understanding the law and rules governing student discipline. It is important to understand that special education law on the topic of discipline attempts to balance competing interests. On the one hand, the IDEA is meant to protect the individual rights of students with disabilities. Given the history of treatment of such students in public schools, this is understandable. Unfortunately, children with disabilities were completely excluded from public education until the courts intervened to ensure that their right to a free appropriate public education was delivered. In this regard, the law rightly expresses a concern for disciplinary action that could exclude or diminish the educational opportunities afforded to students with disabilities.

The law must also consider rights of all students, with or without disabilities. In this respect, all students have a right to an orderly and safe school environment as part of their right to equal educational opportunity. Thus, the law seeks both to ensure the rights of students with disabilities and also to permit school officials the discretion to effectively manage schools. The day-to-day balancing and operationalization of these interests, in the end, is in the hands of school administrators. This chapter will outline important elements of the law and provide information to assist school officials, teachers, parents, and others to ensure the law is followed.

The chapter is organized as follows: (1) It delivers a brief overview of the general concepts of discipline in the special education context; (2) It highlights key considerations regarding discipline of students with disabilities that flow from the pertinent regulations under IDEA and case law, with particular attention to the concept of "change in placement" that can be triggered in certain circumstances; (3) It discusses the several categories of removal that may be helpful in complying with the law—short-term (less than ten-day) removals, long-term removals (including change of placements), and interim alternative educational settings (IAES). The chapter also discusses the legal issues surrounding restraint and seclusion.

Discipline and the IEP

Several principles concerning development of an individualized education program (IEP) deserve review before taking a deep dive into the rules governing the discipline of children with disabilities. To begin with, IEP teams should always carefully consider the behavioral needs of a student as they generate an IEP, regardless of whether these needs interfere with a student's learning. Creating the educational structure and services that are tailored to the child's needs simply reflects best practices, at a minimum, and helps ensure the proper development of an IEP.

With that said, there are times when good practice is required practice in the context of an IEP. An IEP team must consider the behavioral needs of a student when they develop an IEP, if that behavior impedes the child's learning.[1] In these cases, the team should consider positive behavioral interventions and supports (PBIS) that address the problematic behavior.[2] It has been the long history of special education law that behavior should be addressed proactively in a student's IEP.[3] In this way, it is important to recall that all members of the IEP team play an important role in assessing the impact of a student's behavior and developing appropriate responses. For instance, the student's regular education teacher plays an important role in developing interventions meant to address behavior that impedes a student's learning, and should be central to this process.[4] As the old saying goes "an ounce of prevention is worth a pound of cure"—in this case, when an IEP team takes a proactive step in addressing behavioral needs for children with disabilities, it reduces the risk of encountering the legal issues noted below.

General Disciplinary Authority and Short-Term Removals

The seminal Supreme Court case of *Honig v. Doe*[5] continues to provide the basis for discipline of special education students. Under *Honig,* a school district may remove a student who violates the school disciplinary code for no more than ten consecutive school days.[6] Calculating the ten days set forth under *Honig* does require careful attention, in some circumstances. Moreover, it should be noted that schools are not prohibited from enforcing their typical school procedures regarding discipline of students with disabilities when those students threaten themselves or others.[7] This principle means that, in the most straightforward case (e.g., suspension up to ten days for school disciplinary code violation), a school district does not have additional duties owed to the student. By way of federal law, the IEP team does not have to meet, services do not need to be provided, nor must a functional behavioral assessment be provided.

However, individuals in different jurisdictions should be aware of particular applicable state laws. State laws can, and many do, impose additional duties on school officials that reach beyond the procedures codified in federal law. For instance, Massachusetts law imposes several procedural and substantive requirements when a school seeks to suspend a student, regardless of classification (e.g., whether the student qualifies for special education or not).[8] Indeed, given the shift in education policy away from removal of students from an educational setting, it is quite likely that your state or district may have policies governing student removal that should supplement these materials. It is important to mention that school principals may be the focal point for enforcement and oversight of these rules, thus highlighting the significance of school leaders in this area.[9]

Long-Term Removal: More than Ten Days in Total over Time

When a suspension exceeds ten days, school officials must satisfy several obligations.[10] Sometimes this triggering event occurs somewhat unexpectedly. Indeed, a student may be suspended on numerous occasions for shorter duration, such as two- or three-day suspensions. It is conceivable that these multiple "short" suspensions could accrue to exceed the ten-day threshold under *Honig*. Speaking hypothetically, this might occur when a student is suspended on four separate occasions for unrelated infractions, with a three-day suspension for each infraction—thus, the student has been suspended for a total of twelve days. If these recurring suspensions are considered a pattern of removal, the student may have been subjected to a change in educational placement, which would trigger additional protections as discussed below.[11] If, however, the suspensions do not amount to a "pattern" of removal that might be considered a change of placement, no additional proceedings are necessary.

However, even while suspended, the student with disabilities must continue to receive educational services to be able to continue to participate in the general curriculum and make progress toward the IEP goals.[12] If appropriate, behavioral interventions (e.g., functional behavioral assessment (FBA), behavior intervention plan (BIP)) designed to address the underlying behavior must also be delivered to the student to prevent a recurrence of the violation.[13] School personnel and at least one of the child's teachers determine the services needed to enable the child to participate in the general education curriculum.[14]

Long-Term Removal: Change of Placement

The concept of "change in placement" is an important legal term that deserves careful attention. Many of the remedies the IDEA seeks to impose relate to the idea that a school district cannot unilaterally change the placement of a student, something that was the central piece of the *Honig* litigation.[15] In

Honig, students with disabilities had been summarily expelled or excluded from school, without any procedures to guard against arbitrary government action. Subsequent to this case, special education law imposes additional duties on school officials when a change in placement occurs. But, what constitutes a "change in placement"? If there are shorter-term suspensions that do not, individually, exceed the ten-day threshold, do they trigger a change of placement?

The regulations give some guidance to help understand how the concept of change in placement relates to many forms of possible removal of a student (e.g., half-day suspension). First, a change of placement occurs when a child with a disability is removed for more than ten consecutive school days.[16] This example is the more straightforward case. Removal for more than ten consecutive days triggers the numerous procedural and substantive obligations discussed below.

Second, a change of placement for disciplinary reasons occurs when a series of removals constitutes a "pattern." Of course, understanding what equates as a pattern may be difficult and, therefore, requires careful attention. In this instance, the law acknowledges that removal of a child for periods that exceed ten days for "substantially similar" behavior may create a "pattern" that is the legal equivalent of a "change of placement." Put another way, a pattern, as defined below, also triggers specific procedural and substantive protections.

The federal regulations relating to IDEA speak to what will be considered a "pattern" of removal constituting a change of placement, reading as follows:

> The child has been subjected to a series of removals that constitute a pattern—
>
> a. Because the series of removals total more than ten school days in a school year;
>
> b. Because the child's behavior is substantially similar to the child's behavior in previous incidents that resulted in the series of removals; and.
>
> c. Because of such additional factors as the length of each removal, the total amount of time the child has been removed, and the proximity of the removals to one another.[17]

What constitutes a pattern of removal (and therefore a change of placement) is not always easy or obvious. In fact, if school officials do not refer back to the prior incidents, they may completely overlook any analysis as to whether a pattern has emerged. It is quite possible that many administrators may simply refer back to the *Honig* standard of ten consecutive days. To be sure, the regulations provide some guidance, but no clear "test" as to how to understand what amounts to a pattern of removal. Importantly, the law recognizes that each case is different, and the determination of whether removals amount to a pattern and, therefore, a change of placement, is executed on a "case-by-case" basis.[18] To some extent, the nature of the infraction and timing of removal may be two variables that can assist in this determination. If, for example, the conduct is similar and the removals are close in timing, then an argument is strengthened that a pattern exists (assuming the ten-day threshold is satisfied).[19] Importantly, schools that operate under a zero-tolerance policy should also be aware that this raises a conflict with the "case-by-case" requirement. While the regulations place great deference to administrators' judgment as to whether a pattern has occurred, in the end, such a decision can be contested through special education due process proceedings and litigation.[20]

Schools should be consistent and should develop some uniform practice of assessing whether a behavioral pattern exists. They should be attentive—and have some organized system in place—to alert them as to whether a pattern is emerging, or has emerged. Moreover, they should attempt to discern the nature of the underlying behavior and its timing. Consistent and thorough record keeping and communication among the special education team may assist in this effort.

Procedural and Substantive Duties when Change of Placement Occurs

As discussed, assessing whether a change in placement has occurred is simply one in an important series of steps in the analysis. Importantly, significant procedural and substantive duties are triggered if a change of placement occurs. To begin with, within ten school days of the decision to change the placement, the IEP team must meet.[21] On the date that the decision to change placement is made, parents must be notified and receive a procedural safeguards notice.[22]

Substantive obligations are triggered if a change of placement occurs (e.g., the continuation of providing educational services).[23] Specifically, the child must continue to receive education services so as to "participate" in the general curriculum and "progress" toward IEP goals.[24] The IEP team is charged with determining the services that are needed to provide a free appropriate public education (FAPE).[25] Moreover, the regulations require, if appropriate, a functional behavioral analysis (FBA) and behavioral interventions designed to prevent a recurrence of the behavior.[26]

Services a student receives during a removal need not be precisely the services a student would receive in school;[27] services would have to be determined on a case-by-case basis.[28] Of course, with this "case-by-case" standard, it makes it impossible for districts to develop a bright-line rule. They must pay careful attention to the specific needs of the child so as to develop the services to be applied during the removal that will continue to allow the child to "participate." The nature of the student's needs should be the starting point for determining the services that must be offered out of school. Students with more sophisticated IEPs and greater needs likely will need more involved coordination of services for out-of-school suspensions. Conversely, students with more marginal needs (but still requiring special education) may need less to be able to continue to progress, notwithstanding their removal.

Importantly, a manifestation determination review (MDR) must occur in order to determine whether the misbehavior was, in fact, caused by the child's disability in cases involving a change of placement.[29] A meeting to make this determination must take place within ten school days of the decision to change placement due to a disciplinary code violation. Regulations require the LEA, parent, and "relevant members" of the IEP team to attend.[30] Significantly, this group does not include the child's entire IEP team. School officials should be careful to convene this configuration for the manifestation determination, unless state law or regulation dictates otherwise.

The attendees must determine the following:

1. If the conduct in question was caused by, or had a direct relationship to, the child's disability; or
2. If the conduct in question was the direct result of the LEA's failure to implement the IEP.[31]

If either of the above conditions is met, then the conduct is determined to be a manifestation of the child's disability.[32] Under those circumstances, the child cannot be subject to further school discipline. Further, if the manifestation was a result of the failure to implement the IEP, then the IEP team must "take immediate" steps to remedy the deficiencies. In making this determination, the manifestation determination participants should consider all relevant information in the child's file, including the IEP, teacher observations, and relevant information from parents.[33] When there is direct evidence linking the misconduct and the disability, then a conclusion that the behavior was a manifestation may follow.[34]

Additional obligations arise if the behavior was a manifestation of the disability. The IEP team (note that this is different than the manifestation determination group) must do either of the following:

1. Conduct a FBA (unless they had already done so before the behavior that resulted in the change of placement) and implement a behavior intervention plan (BIP); or
2. If a BIP has been developed, review and modify it to address the behavior.[35]

Even if the conduct was not a manifestation of the disability and the removal occurs, school districts cannot discontinue services.[36] Courts appear divided in their assessment of whether conduct was a particular manifestation of a disability.[37] However, school administrators that follow the process above and assess the situation in a fair and balanced manner stand a greater chance of having their decision upheld, should the matter ever come before the courts.[38]

Several cases provide some guidance about situations when administrative bodies have concluded that the behavior was not a manifestation of the disability. For instance, where a student exercises behavior that can be characterized as poor judgment, a manifestation may not be found.[39] Yet, in at least one case, a student's role in a drug distribution ring was, in fact, determined to be a manifestation of his disability.[40]

Unfortunately, there seems to be little guidance (from courts, at least) about what satisfactory BIPs look like. Indeed, courts and hearing officers have declined to create standards to assess the appropriateness of such plans.[41] In the absence of specific guidelines, school officials should be sure to closely follow the procedural requirements and exercise their considered and professional judgment regarding the appropriateness of a behavioral plan.

The regulations speak to placement of the child following a manifestation determination. Indeed, unless there is an agreement between the parent and the LEA, the student must return to the placement from which the removal was made.[42] A school district may challenge the return of the student to a placement, however. Here, the school district must demonstrate that there is a "substantial likelihood" of injury to the child, or others, if the student remains in the placement.[43] Presumably, the school would request an expedited hearing request or seek injunctive relief.[44] During this appeal process, the student's stay-put placement is in the interim placement.[45]

Discipline Other than Out-of-School Suspension

Schools have a variety of means for disciplining a student through suspension. In-school suspension is certainly one of these, and is used frequently. This means of discipline allows the school to maintain oversight and education of the student, yet at the same time prevents the student from being disruptive to others' education. However, the question arises as to the relationship between in-school suspensions and removal, as that term is understood in special education law. To what extent, if any, does in-school suspension count toward the ten days of suspension referenced under the IDEA's regulation? Here, the Department of Education takes the position that an in-school suspension does not count toward the ten days of suspension, under certain conditions,[46] as follows: the child must be afforded the opportunity to appropriately participate in the curriculum, receive the services under the IEP, and continue to participate with non-disabled students to the extent that their current placement directs.[47]

As one can imagine, the school bus can be the site of misconduct, and a student may be removed from bus transportation as a means to prevent the behavior. Here, the question arises: Does a bus suspension count toward the ten days under the regulations? It depends, but it is helpful to think about the extent to which the transportation relates to the child's special education. A bus suspension would count toward the removal timeline if bus transportation is required service under the child's IEP.[48] This reasoning is due to the fact that the service is required for the student to reach the location where the educational services will be delivered;[49] thus, it is a related service incorporated into the programming. If the service was not part of the IEP, then suspension from the bus is not a "suspension" within the meaning of the regulations.[50]

In this instance, the parents have the same obligation to transport the student as would the parents of a non-disabled peer similarly disciplined.[51]

Interim Alternative Educational Setting: Forty-Five-Day Removal

There are special circumstances where a school district may remove a student without regard to whether the disciplinary violation was a manifestation of the disability. School personnel may move a student to an interim alternative educational setting (IAES) for no more than forty-five school days in three situations, set forth below.[52] The student's IEP team determines the IAES.[53]

First, if the child brings to school or possesses a dangerous weapon on school premises, or at a school function under the jurisdiction of the LEA or SEA, this option may be available to a district. "Dangerous weapon" is defined as:

> [A] weapon, device, instrument, material, or substance, animate or inanimate, that is used for, or is readily capable of, causing serious death or serious bodily injury, except that term does not include a pocket knife with a blade of less than 2½ inches in length.[54]

Second, a district may remove a child for no more than forty-five school days if the child knowingly possess or uses illegal drugs, or sells or solicits the sale of a controlled substance while at school, or on school premises, or at a school function under the jurisdiction of the LEA or SEA.[55] The definition of "controlled substance" simply mirrors the Controlled Substance Act.[56] An "illegal drug" is a controlled substance that is legally possessed or used under the supervision of a licensed health care professional or legally possessed by another authority under the Controlled Substance Act.[57] Thus, school administrators must use their judgment and seek guidance, if there is doubt.

Third, a district may remove a child to an interim alternative setting for up to forty-five school days when the child inflicted serious bodily injury upon another person while at school, on school premises, or at a school function under the jurisdiction of the LEA or SEA. Here again, attention must be paid to the critical definitional term of "serious bodily injury," which means:

> [A] bodily injury that involves:
> 1. A substantial risk of death;
> 2. Extreme physical pain;
> 3. Protracted and obvious disfigurement; or protracted loss or impairment of the function of a bodily member, organ, or mental faculty.[58]

A few final notes are in order with respect to the interim alternative educational setting. Schools should still be aware of the procedural duties that arise when they make a change of placement in this or any other setting. There are important procedural notification requirements to follow. Specifically, schools must notify parents of the decision to change placement and give them the procedural safeguards notice,[59] in addition to the substantive requirements (e.g., review of the IEP, conduct FBA, etc.).

As one can imagine, a parent and school district may not agree to a change of placement based on disciplinary action, and there are routes available to resolve such a disagreement. Indeed, schools may seek injunctive relief to prevent a child from returning to a placement that it deems dangerous.[60] They may also seek review through an expedited hearing process.[61] Likewise, the same expedited appeal process is available to parents to challenge a district's decision.

Non-identified Students and Child Find

School districts must consider their disciplinary actions in relation to students who have not yet been identified as eligible for special education and related services. A key determination here is whether the district "had knowledge" that the student was a student with a disability prior to the disciplinary infraction(s)/behavior. The regulations specify when a school district will be deemed to have the requisite knowledge.

A district must be considered to have had knowledge that the student was a child with a disability under the following circumstances.

- If prior to the behavior that precipitated the disciplinary action, the parent expressed in writing that the child is in need of special education. The writing could be expressed to "supervisory or administrative personnel" or "a teacher of the child."[62]
- If prior to the behavior that precipitated the disciplinary action, the parent requested an evaluation.[63]
- If prior to the behavior that precipitated the disciplinary action, the teacher or other LEA personnel expressed specific concerns about a pattern of behavior directly to the director of special education or other supervisory personnel.[64]

However, in certain circumstances, schools will not be deemed to have knowledge that a non-identified student was a student with a disability. Indeed, when the parent of the child has not allowed an evaluation to occur,[65] or has refused services,[66] then the district cannot be said to have had knowledge of the disability. Additionally, when the child has been evaluated and determined not to have a disability, the special rules governing disciplinary actions for students with disabilities will not apply.[67] Under these situations—where there is no basis for knowledge that the child has a disability—the school district may apply the disciplinary procedures it would normally use for non-disabled students.[68] However, in the instance where a district does have knowledge, or should have had knowledge, then the student can assert the procedural protections.

What if a request is made for an evaluation during the time when the child is disciplined under the school's normal procedures—in other words, with an occurrence that may happen frequently, the child is not identified, commits an infraction, is disciplined, and then someone (e.g., a parent) requests an evaluation? In these circumstances, the evaluation must be expedited.[69] Yet, until the evaluation is complete, school authorities have the discretion to determine placement, including expulsion or suspension.[70] During this time, educational services are not required.[71] Of course, if the expedited evaluation and processes reveal that the student is a child with a disability, then the school must provide special education and related services under the IDEA.[72]

Referral to Law Enforcement and Judicial Authorities

Certain in-school behavior may be so serious as to rise to a criminal level. Indeed, the possession of a weapon or drugs is perhaps an all-too-common infraction that illustrates this point. As a result, local law enforcement officials may need to be involved. In such circumstances, the IDEA provides some guidance as to how the discipline provisions in special education interact with behavior that may involve other law enforcement agencies.

It should be clear that the IDEA and its accompanying regulations do not prevent a school district from reporting criminal or suspected criminal behavior to appropriate authorities.[73] Moreover, the discipline sections regarding special education law do not prevent state law enforcement officials from exercising their duties in applying state or federal law.[74]

With that said, school districts reporting crimes do have some obligations with respect to the student's records; namely, the school must ensure that the student's records are transmitted to the appropriate agency where the crime was reported so that they may be considered.[75] In doing so, the school must comply with the Family Educational Rights and Privacy Act (FERPA).[76] To the extent that school districts coordinate or report to the police, they should be careful to abide by constitutional requirements regarding search and seizure, as well.

Restraint and Seclusion

While this overview regarding the use of restraint and seclusion may be helpful, careful consideration must be afforded to specific state laws.[77] States may, for instance, define "restraint" differently.[78] Each state also may carve out exceptions to that definition that, again, may vary depending on the jurisdiction.[79] However, regardless of jurisdiction, the law generally disfavors physical restraint and seclusion, and that is worth repeating. These concepts are antithetical to basic freedoms and the intent of special education. Accordingly, best practices should avoid their use whenever possible.

Indeed, there have been multiple incidents in which students with disabilities have been seriously injured, or even killed, as a result of a school district's use of restraint and seclusion techniques as a means to control behavior or discipline. Use of restraints or seclusions may raise constitutional or statutory claims by parents; for example, a student who is injured as a result of a restraint may present a viable claim that her substantive due process rights have been violated.[80] The use of physical restraints and seclusion methods is disfavored by the U.S. Department of Education and, in general, the education profession. Most states have adopted specific statutes regarding restraint and seclusion, which should be carefully reviewed by all stakeholders.[81]

Of course, there are times when restraint or seclusion may be warranted, or even required, to prevent further injury of the student or others. Each case is unique, but courts have been called upon to address the use of these methods against claims that the student's constitutional or statutory rights have been violated. In one instance, a court determined that a special education teacher's use of restraints and seclusion did not violate the student's Fourth Amendment right when the IEP authorized the use of such techniques.[82] Yet, in another instance, a student presented a triable issue as to whether her Fourth Amendment right was violated where a teacher strapped the student in a "restraint chair" almost immediately upon the beginning of the school day.[83]

School districts may establish policies that govern the use of restraint and seclusion as part of their effort to comply with governing statutes and regulations. These are susceptible to court review, as well. In one case, *Hernandez v. Board of Education of Albuquerque Public Schools*, special education students argued that a district's policy violated the Americans with Disabilities Act (ADA), among other claims.[84] The district court upheld the policy. Importantly, the court noted that the policy outlines the use of restraint for all students, not simply students with disabilities; thus, it was not discriminatory against students with disabilities. Moreover, the court found that the district's policy asserted, at multiple instances, that the use of physical restraint or force was a "last resort" and that the district's adoption of the policy was, in part, intended to reduce the use of restraint, rather than promote it vis-a-vis students with disabilities.[85] The express sentiment of the policy, then, was to avoid the use of restraint or seclusion; in other words, it was intended to protect students from abuse of these techniques.

Recap and Reminders

1. School districts can remove students with disabilities for violation of the disciplinary code for a period of ten school days without triggering additional duties, such as providing services. Of course, school district should be careful here. If they typically provide services to non-disabled students when they are suspended for ten or fewer days, then those obligations apply to children with disabilities.

2. Removals that cumulate to ten days become a change of placement if they form a pattern of removal, in which case additional procedures are triggered just as they are with a ten-consecutive-day removal.

3. Careful attention should be paid to what constitutes a "suspension" and, therefore, contributes to the ten-day maximum. For instance, an in-school suspension may not be a "suspension" within the mean-

ing of the IDEA, if the student has the opportunity to appropriately participate in the general education curriculum and continues to receive services, among others.

4. There are important timelines that districts should be aware of with respect to removals that amount to change of placement. Perhaps the most important of these relates to the requirement to conduct a manifestation determination. Here, the determination must be made within ten school days of the decision to change the placement.

5. If the conduct was a manifestation of the child's disability, districts must conduct an FBA or review and modify a BIP, if warranted.

6. In terms of procedure, school districts must notify parents of a change of placement decision on the date that the decision is made. At this time, they must provide parents with information regarding procedural safeguards.

7. Schools have the authority to place students in an IAES for up to forty-five school days when the child brings a weapon, sells or possesses drugs, or inflicts serious bodily injury on another.

8. Students who have not been identified as disabled may still be entitled to additional procedural protections, but only when the school district had knowledge that the child may, in fact, have a disability.

9. Nothing in the IDEA prohibits school officials from reporting crimes or suspected crimes to the authorities.

10. The use of restraint and seclusion should be avoided, wherever possible. In addition, the rules governing these issues are determined on a state-by-state basis; you should be sure to consult your state laws and regulations on this matter.

Endnotes

[1] 34 C.F.R. § 300.324(a)(2) (2016).

[2] 20 U.S.C. §1414(d)(3)(B)(i) (2012).

[3] *See e.g.*, Neosho R-V Sch. Dist. v. Clark, 315 F.3d 1022 (8th Cir. 2003) (holding that failure to offer behavioral services amounted to denial of FAPE). *But compare with* C.J.N. v. Minneapolis Pub. Schs., 323 F.3d 630, 642 (8th Cir. 2003) (noting that failure to adopt a behavioral intervention plan did not amount to denial of FAPE where mother disagreed with components of the proposed plan and refused to sign it.); *see also* Lathrop R-II Sch. Dist. v. Gray, 611 F.3d 419 (8th Cir. 2010) (noting that IEP need not have specific goals related to behavior).

[4] 34 C.F.R. § 300.324(a)(3) (2016) (regulation requiring that the regular education teacher of a child with a disability as a member of the IEP Team must participate in developing of the IEP of the child, including behavioral interventions).

[5] 484 U.S. 305, 325 (1988) (defining that a "change of placement" occurs when a student is suspended in excess of ten days).

[6] 34 C.F.R. § 300.530(b)(1) (2016).

[7] *Honig,* 484 U.S. at 325; *see also* 71 Fed. Reg. 46540, 46715 (Aug. 14, 2006) (noting that the disciplinary measures should be applied to children with disabilities to the extent that they are applied to children without disabilities, stating "[a] primary intent of Congress in revising the [IDEA] was to provide for a uniform and fair way of disciplining all children – both for those children with disabilities and those children without disabilities,").

[8] *See, e.g.,* 603 Mass. Code Regs. 53.13 (West. 2016) (imposing numerous requirements on school officials to provide educational opportunities for all students when suspensions of any length or expulsions are issued).

[9] *Id.* The Massachusetts regulations impose the oversight and enforcement of its rules governing student removal on principals in many instances.

[10] The additional topic of "change of placement" is considered elsewhere in this chapter.

[11] *See* 34 C.F.R. § 300.536 (2016).

[12] 34 C.F.R. § 300.530(b)(2) (2016); 34 C.F.R. § 300.530(d)(i) (2016).

[13] 34 C.F.R. § 300.530(d)(ii) (2016).

[14] 34 C.F.R. § 300.530(d)(4) (2016).

[15] *See Honig, supra* note 7.

[16] 34 C.F.R. § 300.536(a)(1) (2016).

[17] 34 C.F.R. § 300.536(a)(2)(i)-(iii) (2016) (emphasis added).

[18] 34 C.F.R. § 300.536(b)(1) (2016).

[19] 34 C.F.R. § 300.536(a)(2)(ii) and (iii) (2016) (noting specifically that the behavior must be "substantially similar" and the "proximity of removals to one another").

[20] 34 C.F.R. § 300.536(b)(2) (2016).

[21] 20 U.S.C. § 1415(k)(1)(E)(i) (2012).

[22] 34 C.F.R. § 300.530(h) (2016).

[23] 34 C.F.R. § 300.530(d) (2016).

[24] 34 C.F.R. § 300.530(d)(1) (2016).

[25] 34 C.F.R. § 300.530(d)(5) (2016); *See, e.g.,* M.M. v. Special Sch. Dist. No. 1, 512 F.3d 455 (8th Cir. 2008) (holding that offer of homebound services was sufficient even though parents rejected that offer); Troy City Bd. of Educ., 27 IDELR 555 (AL 1998) (affirming district's provision of four hours of homebound tutoring per week to properly expelled middle school-aged student with a disability as consistent with the provision of FAPE).

[26] 34 C.F.R. § 300.530(d) (2016).

[27] 71 Fed. Reg. *supra* note 7, at 46716 (Aug. 14, 2006) (requiring school district to provide services so that the student can "participate" does not mean that the district must "replicate" every service a child would receive in the normal classroom).

[28] 34 C.F.R. § 300.530(d)(5) (2016) (in cases where the removal is a change of placement the IEP Team determines "appropriate" services.); *see also* Farrin v. Maine Sch. Admin. Dist. No. 59, 165 F. Supp. 2d 37 (D. Me. 2001); 71 Fed. Reg., *supra* note 7, at 46720 ("[D]ecisions regarding the manifestation determination must be made on a case-by-case basis.").

[29] It is worth repeating that manifestation determinations are only required removals that constitute a "change of placement." 71 Fed. Reg. *supra* note 7, at 46720.

[30] 34 C.F.R. § 300.530(e) (2016).

[31] *Id.*

[32] *Id.*

[33] 34 C.F.R. § 300.530(e) (2016). This list is not exhaustive, however. *See* San Diego Unified Sch. Dist., 52 IDELR 301 (SEA CA 2009).

[34] *See, e.g.,* Swansea Public Sch., 47 IDELR 278 (SEA MA 2007) (child's emotional and oppositional behavior resulted when administrator violated the terms of the BIP).

[35] 34 C.F.R. § 300.530(f) (2016).

[36] 34 C.F.R. § 300.530(d)(1)(i) (2016).

[37] *Compare* Randy M. v. Texas City Ind. Sch. Dist., 93 F. Supp. 2d 1310 (S.D. Tex. 2000) *with* Jonathan G. v. Caddo Parish Sch. Bd., 875 F. Supp. 352 (W.D. La. 1994).

[38] *See, e.g.,* Rowley v. Bd. of Educ. of Hendrick Hudson Cent. Sch. Dist., 458 U.S. 176 (1982) (noting, in dicta, that courts must be careful to avoid imposing their educational judgment on local education agencies).

[39] *See, e.g.,* Fitzgerald v. Fairfax Cty. Sch. Bd., 50 556 F. Supp. 2d 543 (E.D. Va. 2008); *see also* Lewellyn v. Sarasota Cty. Bd. of Educ., 2009 WL 5214983 (M.D. Fla. 2016) (Dec. 29, 2009) (unreported decision).

[40] Sch. Bd. of Prince William Cty. v. Malone, 762 F.2d 1210 (4th Cir. 1985) (affirming lower court decision that student's role in drug distribution was a function of his disability). *But compare with* Lancaster Elementary Sch. Dist., 49 IDELR 53 (SEA CA 2007) (bringing drugs to school was not related to specific learning disability).

[41] *See, e.g.,* Alex R. v. Forrestville Valley Comm. Sch. Dist. #221, 375 F.3d 603 (7th Cir. 2004). *See also* Susan C. Bon & Allan G. Osborne, Jr., *Does the Failure to Conduct an FBA or Develop a BIP Result in a Denial of FAPE under the IDEA?* 307 Educ. L. Rep. 581, 583 (2014) (noting that there are no substantive requirements for such plans).

[42] 34 C.F.R. § 300.530(f)(2) (2016).

[43] 34 C.F.R. § 300.532(a) (2016).

[44] 34 C.F.R. § 300.532(c) (2016).

[45] 34 C.F.R. § 300.533 (2016).

[46] 71 Fed. Reg., *supra* note 7, at 46715; *See* Delaware (OH) City Sch. Dist., 51 IDELR 257 (OCR 2008) (decision of whether in-school suspension counts as removal depends on whether educational and special services were provided during the in-school suspension).

[47] 71 Fed. Reg., *supra* note 7, at 46715.

[48] *Id.*

[49] *Id.*

[50] *Id.*

[51] The Department of Education does not take a position on this matter. *Id.*

[52] 34 C.F.R. § 300.530(g)(1)-(3) (2016).

[53] 34 C.F.R. § 330.531 (2016).

[54] 71 Fed. Reg., *supra* note 7, at 46723; *see also* 18 U.S.C. § 1356(h)(3) (2012) (defining "controlled substance"); 34 C.F.R. § 300.530(i)(4) (2016).

[55] *See* 71 Fed. Reg., *supra* note 7, at 46723 (the definition of controlled substance changes frequently and, therefore, the Department of Education refuses to attempt to offer a definition in their regulations or commentary and simply maps the definition used in the Controlled Substance Act); *see also* 34 C.F.R. § 300.530(i)(1) (2016).

[56] *See* 34 C.F.R. § 300.530(i)(1) (2016).

[57] 34 C.F.R. § 300.530(i)(2) (2016).

[58] *See* 71 Fed. Reg., *supra* note 7, at 46723.

[59] 34 C.F.R. § 300.530(h) (2016).

[60] *See Honig v. Doe,* 484 U.S. 305 (1988); 34 C.F.R. §§ 300.532 and 300.533 (2016) (school may seek injunctive relief in court to prevent dangerous student from returning to school).

[61] *See* 34 C.F.R. §§ 300.532(c) and 300.533 (2016) (outlining the appeal process for parents and school districts and requiring student to remain in the interim alternative educational setting during the pendency of the appeal, e.g., stay-put).

[62] 20 U.S.C. § 1415(k)(5)(B)(i) (2016).

[63] 20 U.S.C. § 1415(k)(5)(B)(ii) (2016).

[64] *See* 20 U.S.C. § 1415(k)(5)(B)(i) (2016); 34 C.F.R. § 300.534(b)(1)-(3) (2016).

[65] 34 C.F.R. § 300.534(c)(1)(i) (2016).

[66] 34 C.F.R. § 300.534(c)(1)(ii) (2016).

[67] 34 C.F.R. § 300.534(c)(2) (2016). However, certain circumstances may arise whereby the school district will be deemed to have had knowledge that the child qualified for special education and, therefore, the protections regarding discipline attach. *See, e.g.,* S.W. v. Holbrook Pub. Schs. 221 F. Supp. 2d 222 (D. Mass. 2002); Colvin ex. rel. Colvin v. Lowndes Cty. Sch. Dist., 114 F. Supp. 2d 504 (N.D. Miss. 2000) (ruling that the disciplinary protections afforded students with disabilities applied to student where parents had requested student be evaluated

but district ignored such requests). And, of course, there are different fact patterns where knowledge will not be imputed to the district. *See, e.g.,* Mr. and Mrs. R. v. West Haven Bd. of Educ., 36 IDELR 211 (D. Conn. 2002) (district did not have knowledge).

[68] 34 C.F.R. § 300.534(d) (2016).

[69] 34 C.F.R. § 300.534(2)(i) (2016).

[70] 34 C.F.R. § 300.534(2)(ii) (2016).

[71] *Id.* But school officials should note that if they provide services to nondisabled peers, then the same practices should follow for a student undergoing evaluation for special education.

[72] 34 C.F.R. § 300.534(2)(iii) (2016).

[73] 34 C.F.R. § 300.535(a) (2016).

[74] *Id.*

[75] 34 C.F.R. § 300.535(b) (2016).

[76] 34 C.F.R. §300.535(b)(2) (2016).

[77] For an overview of state laws, see Deanna Arivett, *The Need for Restraints in Public Schools? Keeping Students Safe in the Age of Inclusion,* 40 Dayton L. Rev. 155 (2015) available at: https://udayton.edu/law/_resources/documents/law_review/vol40_no2/40-2_the_need_for_restraints_in_public_schools.pdf.

[78] *See, e.g.,* N.H. Rev. Stat. Ann. § 126-U:I-IV (2016) (defining restraint as "bodily physical restriction, mechanical devices, or any device that unreasonably limits the freedom of movement. It includes mechanical restraint, physical restraint, and medication restraint used to control behavior in an emergency or any involuntary medication.").

[79] *Id.* (excepting from the definition of restraint actions that constitute "holding a child to calm or comfort").

[80] *See, e.g.,* Brown v. Ramsey, 121 F. Supp. 2d 911 (E.D. Va. 2000) (holding that basket hold restraint did not violate student's substantive due process rights).

[81] For an excellent resource, *see* U.S. Dep't. of Educ., *Restraint and Seclusion: Resource Document,* (May 2012), available at http://www2.ed.gov/policy/seclusion/restraints-and-seclusion-resources.pdf:

[82] C.N. v. Willmar Public Schools, 591 F.3d 624 (8th Cir. 2010).

[83] A.B. *ex rel.* B.S. v. Adams-Arapahoe Sch. Dist., 831 F. Supp. 2d 1226 (D. Colo. 2011). However, claims involving a violation Fourth Amendment rights because of a more limited use of a restraint chair by other teachers and a "basket hold" were dismissed. *Id.*

[84] Hernandez v. Board of Educ. of Albuquerque Public Sch., 124 F. Supp. 3d 1181 (D.N.M. 2015).

[85] *Id.*

Chapter 10

Parental Rights

Susan G. Clark

Introduction

Research suggests that principals have a significant impact on student success and achievement, second only to classroom teachers.[1] As instructional leaders, principals are charged with the development, implementation, and assessment of teaching and learning through data analysis and through resource allocation and supervision. Despite principals' focus on student performance outcomes, they also retain their duties as administrators charged with the responsibility to ensure that the school functions well through efficient and effective operations, policies, and procedures. Both roles require the principal to provide teachers and staff with the support, tools, and professional development they need to bring meaning to those building policies and instructional practices, and to reinforce their importance in a school-wide framework for high quality teaching and learning for all students.

However, there may be impediments to effective organizational operations and to student access and opportunity to learn. Obstacles can be the type, frequency, or quality of communication between administrators, teachers, and parents. The principal must develop and use effective interpersonal communication and relationship-building skills because the Individuals with Disabilities Education Act (IDEA)[2] includes provisions to maximize parental involvement in special education. Indeed, the U.S. Supreme Court recognized in *Board of Education of Hendrick Hudson Central School District v. Rowley* (*Rowley*)[3] that parents would "not lack ardor"[4] in their role as advocates for their children. Parents and educators may have different views of what constitutes parental involvement and child advocacy. School board policies, procedures, and building practices can help clarify for parents and educators what rights parents have under the law. By managing and nurturing relationships between and among staff and parents, a principal can improve instructional effectiveness. A hindrance to professional working relationships often is the lack of capacity that employees have in dealing with conflict and diminishing resources. Further complicating the work of the school are the unique needs of all students, and the need to address those differences in a demanding political, social, and economic climate focused on reform and improved outcomes.

The IDEA, first enacted in the 1970s, was Congress's response to strong parent political and legal advocacy.[5] Since then, the law has evolved to include not only increased educational accountability, e.g., alignment with the Family Education Rights and Privacy Act,[6] but also to ensure that students with disabilities are prepared for participation as adults in the economic world of work.[7] Today, the IDEA guarantees that all students with disabilities, no matter the nature and severity of the condition, will have a specially designed and individualized free appropriate public education (FAPE).[8]

A FAPE is defined by the Supreme Court as both a substantive right and a procedural right.[9] In *Rowley*, the Supreme Court set forth a two-pronged analysis for an alleged violation of the IDEA, which remains the standard of review used by courts today. The Court asked 1) whether the school district officials adhered to the procedural requirements of the Act, and 2) whether the individualized educational program (IEP) was reasonably calculated to confer meaningful educational benefit to the student.[10] If these two questions are answered in the affirmative, the state has met its obligation to provide a FAPE.[11] Hence, parental rights are procedural and process-oriented, leading to the substantive right to a FAPE as understood through the IEP and its implementation.

If a parent is denied an opportunity to be notified of and meaningfully participate in the special educational *process*—a procedural violation—then the final *outcome*, the IEP and/or its implementation, may be legally flawed, resulting in a denial of the child's right to a FAPE.[12] Importantly, in 2007, the Supreme Court held that the IDEA grants to parents not just procedural rights, but also independent, enforceable, substantive rights of their own, a determination that now permits them to pursue federal FAPE claims in court on their own behalf and without legal counsel.[13] The Court held that procedural rights, such as the right to pursue claims for procedural violations or to seek reimbursement and attorney fees, were "intertwined with the substantive adequacy"[14] of a child's education. Parental rights to attend meetings, to participate in decision making, to request hearings, and to transfer their IDEA rights to their child upon his or her reaching the age of majority,[15] all point to the Court's conclusion that parents have rights of their own under the statute. The Court stated:

> These provisions confirm that the IDEA, through its text and structure, creates in parents an independent stake not only in the procedures and costs implicated by this process, but also in the substantive decisions to be made…We conclude that the IDEA does not differentiate, through isolated references to various procedures and remedies, between the rights accorded to children and the rights accorded to parents.[16]

Consequently, the two elements of a FAPE—procedural and substantive— are intertwined, as are the rights of the parent and child, and the leadership and management roles of the principal. To protect a student's substantive rights, the principal must engage in strong instructional leadership skills. To ensure that parents' procedural and substantive rights are safeguarded, the principal must utilize effective management tools, strong interpersonal communication skills, and conflict resolution strategies.

Thus, the role of the principal is to identify policies, procedures, and practices that may create barriers to effective communication, use of resources, and professional development, and to remove them. The other important role of the principal is to create the conditions for student success by identifying practices that support teaching and learning, including relationship building between home and school.

Within this context, this chapter examines parental rights under the IDEA, called procedural safeguards.[17] It is the school district's adherence to the procedures that "safeguard," or protect, parental rights. Such rights include being notified of school district actions, as well as rights to give consent before school officials may take certain actions, to meaningful participation in decision making about the child, to seek independent evaluation, to access records, to file complaints, and to seek dispute resolution. In each of the sections below, parental rights are identified and discussed. The dispute resolution process—known as "due process"—also is discussed. The chapter concludes with recommendations for practice, because principals uniquely make school and family connections to ensure that student and parental rights are safeguarded.

Rights of a "Parent" Under the IDEA

While the IDEA affords parents extensive rights, a principal must first know who is a "parent" for the purpose of implementing special education protections. Of course, a biological or adoptive parent is assumed to be the parent for purposes of special education. The IDEA's definition of a parent is quite broad and also includes a foster parent (unless state law prohibits foster parents from acting as a parent); a guardian generally authorized to act as the child's parent, or authorized to make educational decisions for the child (but not the state if the child is a ward of the state); a person acting in the place of a biological or adoptive parent, such as a grandparent, stepparent, or other relative with whom the child lives; an individual who is legally responsible for the child's welfare; or a surrogate parent, if allowed under state law.[18] The IDEA requires that a surrogate parent must be appointed to protect a child's rights if a parent cannot be identified; if after reasonable efforts a parent cannot be located; if the child is a ward of the state; or if the child is defined as an unaccompanied homeless youth under the McKinney-Vento Homeless Assistance Act.[19]

Divorce, separation, and custody arrangements also may alter which parent has access to school records. For example, the Seventh Circuit Court of Appeals held that a noncustodial parent had the right to seek a due process hearing based on the school district's failure to notify him of IEP meetings because the divorce decree permitted him to communicate with district personnel about the student's progress and to participate in school activities.[20]

In contrast, a divorced mother sought to be included as a member of the IEP team, to have access to all assessment and evaluation records including test protocols, testing reports, and eligibility determinations. She also sought to amend her child's special educational records by having all references to her ex-husband's wife changed from "mother" to "stepmother" and to obtain an IEE to contest the student's identification as emotionally disturbed. The Second Circuit Court of Appeals examined whether she had standing as a noncustodial parent to assert those claims in the first place.[21] The court reasoned that the rights of a natural parent under the IDEA were those identified by state law, and in the case of divorce, by the divorce decree. Because the divorce decree did not specifically revoke her informational access, the parent was permitted to pursue her records access claim under FERPA; she was entitled under state law to reasonable information regarding the child's progress in school. The court made clear, however, an entitlement to "reasonable" records did not mean access to every single cover letter, transmittal sheet, or scrap of paper that happened to be in the files. Nor did the entitlement necessitate access to more substantive original documents or notes if the information contained in them was substantially incorporated into reports, or if the parent was otherwise informed of their content.

The court further held that the noncustodial parent had no rights to decision making or to an IEE. The Second Circuit Court of Appeals noted that the implementing regulations of federal special education law established a wide range of persons who may be considered "the parent," including stepparents and grandparents.[22] The court opined that it was illogical that all those listed in the law as "potential parents" would be expected to exercise the same parental rights under the IDEA at the same time. The court concluded that parental rights are to be informed by applicable state law. The parent in this case lacked standing to make educational decisions, as she had only the right to access information about the child's evaluation, identification, placement, and FAPE.

Although the court decided that the parent could not seek a due process hearing to challenge the appropriateness of the identification, the court did not reach the question as to whether the noncustodial parent's right to reasonable information regarding the child's progress in school encompassed the federal right to notice of IEP meetings.[23] One interpretation of this unanswered question might be that the parent who has only access rights to information be given the results of the IEP meeting–the completed IEP–but the parent afforded decision making authority be given prior notice and an opportunity to attend the meeting. Keep in mind that the focus of any decision making meeting is the wellbeing and FAPE of the child, and the principal must keep the team focused to that end in accord with state law.

In sum, court orders may remove the right of the parent to make educational decisions, and a principal should be aware that parents who are divorced are still parents and are entitled to make educational decisions for their child unless a divorce decree, separation agreement, or custody order divests a parent of the those decision-making rights. In such a case, only the parent whose educational decision-making rights have not been terminated is entitled to make decisions for the child under the IDEA, and that parent alone possesses parental rights under the IDEA.[24]

However, if a divorce decree or custody order is silent on the matter of which parent is the educational decision maker, a principal may not be sure if both parents hold parental rights under the IDEA. In this situation, the custody order assigning custody to one parent may be determinative, as the rights of a noncustodial parent turns on state law. This was the outcome in a case where the noncustodial parent did not have the right under the IDEA to challenge his child's IEP services, although he did have the right to be apprised of educational progress.[25]

Once a principal is certain of who is serving in the role of parent under the Act, the parent is entitled to a written copy of the IDEA's procedural safeguards. The procedural safeguards are the legal protections afforded to parents during the process in which school district officials engage to identify, evaluate, and educate children with disabilities. In essence, the procedural safeguards protect parental interests during the process. The procedures are so important that, under the first prong of the *Rowley* analysis, a court may find against a school district in a lawsuit if the parent is denied these rights.[26]

Parents must be given a copy of the procedural safeguards only once per school year, and whenever a parent so requests, but there are other events that trigger the obligation to provide parents with another copy, even if they have already received the annual notice. The notice of procedural rights must be given to the parents when any of these events occurs: (a) the first time the student is referred for evaluation or when a parent requests an evaluation; (b) upon the school district's receipt of the first state complaint or first request for a due process hearing filed by the parent in a school year; and (c) *on the date* a decision is made to remove a student from school for violating the student code of conduct, for which removal would constitute a change of placement.[27]

The procedural safeguards are often provided to parents in a packet or booklet. These rights must be conveyed in easily understood language, even if the parent's mode of communication is not spoken English.[28] In the event the parent uses another form of language, (e.g., sign language or a foreign language), school officials must ensure that the notice is translated appropriately. Failure to give parents a copy of their procedural rights can result in a lawsuit and a finding of a denial of FAPE.[29] The procedural safeguards may be posted on the school district's webpage; however, written evidence must be kept to show that the parent actually received the procedural safeguards notice, such as a signed receipt. Notably, guidance from the U.S. Department of Education states that posting the notice on the internet does not replace the requirement in the IDEA to provide a printed copy.[30] A parent can choose to receive procedural safeguards notices by email if that option is available.[31]

A principal should obtain a copy of these procedural safeguards and read them so as to be prepared to answer any questions a parent or teacher may have about them. Although there is nothing in the IDEA that requires a principal or any school official to sit down and review the procedural safeguards with a parent, federal regulations state that the explanation of these procedural rights must be "full."[32] So, either the writing should be self-explanatory for a parent, or a principal should be prepared to discuss the procedural safeguards with a parent.

The principal should be aware of the duality of leadership regarding procedural safeguards. School district officials are charged with the duty to inform parents of their rights under the IDEA, including the parents' right to bring a due process complaint against the school district if a dispute should arise. Some educators may be uncomfortable discussing with parents the extent of their rights because doing so could expose the district to liability, if it is determined in a due process hearing that the district failed to provide a FAPE. However, the school leader must recognize that due process is inherently about fairness. Assuring that school procedures and practices afford parents the process that is due to them is critical to creating a school culture in which partnership and communication are essential values to student success. Indeed, the process of understanding the reasons that students may not be making educational progress includes dialogue between teachers and parents.

Rights to Notice of the Law and Procedural Safeguards

Parents have the right to know what federal law guarantees to them and to their children under the IDEA. The IDEA provides for this by imposing on school districts the duty to notify parents of their "procedural safeguards" and to give parents "prior written notice" of certain actions.[33]

Prior written notice is the document that memorializes the decisions that school officials made, including descriptions of actions proposed or refused by the district, and an explanation of why the district proposes or refuses to take the action, including a description of other options considered by the IEP team, the reasons why those options were rejected, and descriptions of the factors relevant to the district's proposal or refusal.[34] The notice must also describe each evaluation procedure, assessment, record or report that the district used as a basis for the proposed or refused action.[35] This information provides both certainty to the parents about the school district's position on particular matters and clarity as to how decisions were made. It is important to understand that these requirements are detailed in IDEA itself, thus indicating Congress's emphasis on the detailed nature of the notice that parents should receive.

Prior written notice also ensures that parents are notified that they have legal protections under IDEA's procedural safeguards. If the prior written notice is not an initial referral for an evaluation, parents must be informed of the means by which a copy of a description of the procedural safeguards can be obtained, including information about sources for parents to contact to obtain assistance in understanding the law of special education and related services.

School officials should consider ways to ensure that prior written notice was actually sent, given that there is no requirement in the law for parents to acknowledge receipt of the notice. Failing to send a prior written notice or a copy of the procedural safeguards when required to do so is a procedural error of the IDEA, but it might not be a denial of FAPE.[36] If the parents have the opportunity for meaningful participation, and the student has not suffered any loss of educational opportunity, then the student may have received FAPE despite any procedural errors.

Rights Regarding Evaluation

Parents of children who are not yet receiving special education services under IDEA have a right to request that an evaluation of their child be undertaken. As set forth in more detail in Chapter 5, each local school district has a "child find" duty of school officials under the IDEA, which requires that children suspected of having disabilities and in need of special education must be located, identified, and evaluated, even if they are advancing from grade to grade. This child find obligation includes highly mobile children and migrant children.[37] The child find duty also extends to students enrolled in private and religious schools that are located within the public school district's jurisdiction, even if they or their parents are not residents within the public school district. This is an affirmative duty requiring school personnel to be aware of red flags that suggest that a student may have a disability. Consequently, administrators should inform teachers to treat a parent request for testing or evaluation as a referral for special education services and to proceed accordingly.

To determine the presence of a disability, an educational evaluation is required to identify the learning needs of the student, to determine the content of an educational program, and to determine the child's needs for involvement in, and progress in, the general education curriculum. A public agency, (e.g., the school district) or a parent of a child may request an initial evaluation to determine if the child has a disability. Parents have no legal duty to put a request to evaluate in writing.[38] However, the duty to evaluate a student in order to make a determination as to the existence of a disability requires reasonable cause to suspect a disability. There is no parental right to have a child tested merely because a parent made such a request where educators do not believe there is evidence of a disability. Notably, a request for an evaluation made by a parent based on a child's problems that are evident only at home and not manifest at school may not be sufficient reason to warrant a full evaluation, in part because testing must result in a determination of the *educational* needs of the child. It is important to recognize that the student's problems must be schooling-related before evaluation, because learning difficulties related to illegal drug use, juvenile delinquency, or family dysfunction may be construed as social maladjustments, not disabilities, and any resulting problems may be explainable by factors other than educational need.[39]

In the event that an evaluation of a student is not appropriate because school officials do not suspect that the student is a child with a disability in need of special education and related services, the principal should ensure that the parent received prior written notice of that decision and a copy of the district's procedural safeguards. A parent who disagrees with the district's decision not to test the student has the right to appeal that decision through the IDEA's due process procedures.

Once a child who is suspected of having a disability is found, and before the district may proceed with an evaluation, the parent has the right to receive a copy of the procedural safeguards and to give written consent to testing. Written consent to evaluate must be voluntary and "informed," which means that the parent has enough information to be generally informed of the nature of the activity for which he or she is providing consent.[40] Such information includes that pertinent to the evaluation process and its potential outcomes, including which tests will be administered to the student and who will have access to the results, and allows the parent to seek out additional information as to the content of the tests themselves and to the meaning of the results that will be obtained. Certainly, knowledge of the tests and the procedures in evaluation can help parents to prepare their children for the experience. Encouraging parents to explain to their child what to expect during the evaluation and to assuage any fears they may have can help make the process successful. An evaluation must be conducted within sixty days after receipt of the parent's written consent unless state law provides otherwise.[41]

While the IDEA requires that districts obtain written, informed parental consent before the initial evaluation, it also requires such consent before a reevaluation and before the initial provision of special education services.[42] Informed consent to each of these district actions also means that such consent may be revoked by the parent at any time. If the parent refuses to consent or revokes consent during the evaluation process, the principal may meet with the parents to listen to their concerns and to educate them about teachers' need to understand how the student learns. Extensive knowledge of curriculum, assessment, and teaching is fundamental to the principal acting as an instructional leader in this situation. The willingness of the principal to openly communicate the importance of evaluation depends largely upon respect for the parent's feelings, fears, and rights.

Should a parent revoke consent, that revocation is not retroactive and does not mean that the evaluation, reevaluation, or provision of special services were not initiated or provided. For example, if the parent revokes consent in writing for the provision of special education services after the child initially received special education and related services, the school district is not required to amend the child's educational records. All activity undertaken by the school district during the time the consent was in effect remains valid as an educational record.

At times, district officials may experience difficulty obtaining parental consent. Generally, where consent is required, "reasonable efforts" to obtain it must be undertaken, and evidence that the parent failed to respond will be required if a dispute arises down the road. Reasonable efforts include telephone contacts, mailings, and home and workplace visits. A prudent principal will never permit an initial evaluation to proceed without prior written informed parental consent.

Unlike revocation, if a parent refuses to consent to an evaluation, the principal may offer parents an opportunity to participate in no-cost mediation in order to convince them of the need for testing. In mediation, a trained individual with no subjective interest in the outcome works with the parents and a representative from the school to come to a mutual decision about testing. If efforts to obtain written informed parent consent for testing have been unsuccessful, the school district has the option to seek a due process hearing to ask that a hearing officer to compel the evaluation.

Informal chats between teachers and other personnel about student learning problems that may or may not implicate a disability do not constitute school officials' knowledge that the child may need special educational services. Additionally, the protections of IDEA do not apply to an unidentified student when an evaluation was conducted at some point in the student's schooling and the student was not found to have a disability, or when a formal decision was made that an evaluation was not necessary. Even in the case where the student was found eligible for services, but where the parent denied consent for the services, under the IDEA, school officials do not have knowledge that the student is a student with a disability. In all these situations, the parents were to have been included in the decision making and properly notified of their rights to appeal those decisions through due process, and were to have received a copy of the procedural safeguards.

In some circumstances, a parent may request an evaluation only after having been informed of an intended disciplinary action for a violation of the student code of conduct of an unidentified student. If it is appropriate to evaluate the child, the evaluation must be conducted in an expedited manner, and the parents are entitled to written notice of the procedures used to determine the existence of a disability and of their rights under the law.

Rights Regarding Identification

Once an evaluation is complete, the parent has the right to participate in the decision as to whether the student is eligible for special education and related services. Eligibility decisions are very important to the future of the child, yet many principals do not participate in those meetings. The principal should work closely with teachers to know the challenges they face in providing classroom instruction and the difficulties some students experience in learning. Furthermore, the principal must manage all building resources in an effective manner. The human and other resources required to evaluate and to examine a student's learning are evidence of a deep commitment to understanding the learner. The principal, therefore, should know and understand the general education curriculum, the evaluation process, and the manner in which results are interpreted so as to be a leader who can ask and answer questions appropriate to the needs of both the teacher and the student. The process by which a child is deemed eligible for special education and related services under IDEA is set forth in more detail in Chapter 5.

Parent participation in decision making is an important component of evaluation, eligibility determinations, placement, and of a FAPE. The parent, however, does not have a right to guarantee that the child will, in fact, be found to be a student with a disability.

The parent's right to participate in the decision making as to whether the student falls into one of the disability categories or is in need of special education carries the additional right to an independent educational evaluation (IEE) at public expense. The right to an IEE is invoked when the parent disagrees with the school district's evaluation or eligibility determination. When this occurs, the school administrator may ask, but not require, the parent to explain the source and nature of the disagreement. Disagreement as to eligibility permits the decision making team to determine what additional data, if any, may be necessary in order to fully consider the educational needs of the child. The principal should embrace disagreement and should lead the team to consider a variety of sources in making the determination including ability, achievement, parent input, and teacher recommendations.

In response to the parent's objection to an evaluation, school officials must either pay for the IEE or, after providing the parent with prior written notice, initiate a due process hearing to defend its evaluation. The hearing officer may deny the parent's request for an IEE if the school district's evaluation is found to be appropriate. If inappropriate, the hearing officer may order the school district to pay for the IEE. If school officials authorize an IEE, they may provide payment for it in advance of the testing or may reimburse the parent after the evaluation is completed without going to due process at all. The payment option the district chooses cannot prevent a parent from exercising the right to an IEE, and the parent has the right to have the results of any such independent evaluation considered by school officials. Once a parent obtains an IEE at public expense, or shares an evaluation obtained at private expense, the results of the evaluation must be considered by school officials.

Notably, the IDEA does not confer parents of children with disabilities, or their representatives, a general entitlement to observe their children in any current or proposed educational placement; rather, such observation will be controlled by state law or by school district policy. However, the Second Circuit Court of Appeals averred that classroom access may be necessary in the event of a due process hearing in which parents require expert testimony. "Expert testimony is often critical in IDEA cases . . . parties to IDEA proceedings have 'the right to be accompanied and advised by . . . individuals with special knowledge or training with respect to the problems of children with disabilities'. . .."[43] Parents may seek to have a trained evaluator observe their child in the school setting as part of an IEE or to prepare for decision making at an eligibility determination or IEP meeting.

Rights Regarding Decision Making

As discussed above, parents are entitled to be a member of any team assembled to make decisions about the identification, evaluation, and eligibility of the child. The decision making process does not end with the evaluation and eligibility determination, however. Once eligibility has been determined, the parent has the right to participate in the development of the student's IEP. The written IEP commits the school district's resources to the student by defining the special instructional program and services the school district will provide to the student to ensure FAPE and IEPs are to be in effect at the start of the school year. A parent is entitled to attend and to participate meaningfully in IEP decision making and to be given prior written notice of the purpose, time, location of IEP meetings, as well as the necessary attendees. In fact, the parent has the right to prior written notice of *any* change, or refusal to change, the evaluation or identification of the child subsequent to a parental request or to a school-initiated proposal.

Errors in assembling a properly constructed IEP team or failure for consideration of parent input and suggestions, transition planning, discussion of IEE results, or IEP development may result in procedural or substantive violations of the student's rights. Principals can model appropriate respect for parent opinion, no matter how unusual, and help the team to integrate what is important to the parent into the decision-making process. Principals should facilitate these decision-making meetings to ensure that voices are heard, ideas are explored, and data are used to substantiate student performance and to identify educational needs. While parents are considered to be equal participants in the IEP process, they do not have veto power over the IEP. Consensus is the goal for decision making. If the team cannot reach consensus, the parents should be given a prior written notice.[44]

Depending on state law, school district policy, or the collective bargaining agreement, the IDEA does not afford parents with a right to audio or video recording of meetings. The federal Office of Special Education and Rehabilitative Services opined that a school district can limit or prohibit recordings of IEP meetings unless recording is needed to ensure that the parent understands the process.[45] In one case, the parents of a student with a disability unsuccessfully argued that the refusal of their request to videotape the classroom denied them their right to participate in their child's education under the IDEA. The court found that the IDEA was silent on videotaping and provided no parental right to be present in the classroom during instruction.[46]

The right to participate in decision making about the child's education also does not extend to informal or unscheduled conversations involving any district personnel. Parents have no right to be privy to discussions between teachers who meet in the lunchroom or during planning periods to discuss a student. Nor does the right to participate confer upon the parent any claim to be a part of educators' professional determinations as to methodology, lesson planning, or coordination of services. Meetings scheduled for the purpose of planning meeting strategies or of working out a response to a parent proposal do not require parent participation to comply with the IDEA. In one case, parents of a ninth-grade student with obsessive compulsive disorder, Tourette syndrome, and Asperger syndrome sued the school district in part because they were not invited to a teacher in-service meeting during which the parents' consultant, hired by the district, worked to help teachers learn ways to better serve the child. The Sixth Circuit Court of Appeals held that the parents were not denied meaningful participation in their child's education when they were not included in the meeting. The court found that the parents had shared what they wanted school officials to know when they met with teachers and administrators and when the district hired the consultant to work with staff.[47]

Rights to participate in decisions about the special education programming of the child do not include rights to choose the child's teacher, to select the teaching strategies or methodologies, or to any particular learning outcome or achievement level. The Third Circuit Court of Appeals affirmed the lower court's decision that the school district's refusal to use the parents' preferred program did not result in a denial of FAPE.[48] While any special education and related services and supplementary aids and services identified in the IEP should be based on peer-reviewed research, the parent does not have to right to determine which services meet that requirement. The education and services to be provided should be researched-based to the extent practicable; however, the IDEA's reference to peer-reviewed research does not prohibit schools from using eclectic or untested teaching methodologies.[49] The *Rowley* Court stated that the choice of the educational method most suitable to the child's needs is one to be made by state and local educational agencies in cooperation with the parents.[50] Thus, decisions about what methods will be employed to meet student needs should be made by a careful consideration of the student's disability, its effect on learning, and curriculum and program expectations.

Principals should note that it is very important that educators do not predetermine the placement of a student. In one case, school district officials had invested a great deal of effort and money in training its staff in a particular autism methodology and, after they denied the parents' request for their preferred methodology, the parents successfully made a showing to the court that the educators had made its placement decision before the IEP team meeting. The denial of FAPE resulted from the school district's failure to come to the IEP meeting prepared to consider the parents' input in determining placement. Thus, the IEP team meeting is the proper venue for decision making as to appropriate placement, which must be based on an analysis of appropriate data, review of any independent evaluation reports, and meaningful consideration of parent input.

Although decisions about teaching content, methodology, and strategy are best made by professional educators and IEP teams with parental input, the courts show great deference to such decisions when they are data-based and made in good faith. There is no requirement that the team reach consensus. Certainly, consensus is desirable and the principal should work toward that end, but at some point, the school leader must ensure that a FAPE is recommended for the student by making the offer in no uncertain terms. This practice may feel threatening to parents who may insist that the district is "forcing" a decision, or is acting with complete disregard for their position. Principals should be aware of the parental view of district actions. The fact that parents and school district officials may have principled disagreement does not mean that the district failed to take parent views seriously or that the district is not offering a FAPE.[51] Of course, any dispute the parent has with the school's FAPE recommendation may be taken to due process, but during the meeting, the principal should ensure that the team articulates its rationale, that those who will implement the IEP have the necessary experience and training, and that the methodological approach taken by the district is at least adequate under the circumstances.[52]

If a student is identified as having a disability by a team that includes the parent, and the educational needs are ascertained, the informed written consent given by the parent for the initial evaluation does not imply consent for services. Informed written consent for the provision of services is separate from the informed consent required for the evaluation. Informed written consent is needed for the student's initial IEP, however, parents do not have the right to select which provisions of the IEP they consent to and which they do not.[53] Should the parent deny consent for the initial provision of special education and related services, school officials are prohibited from providing those services, from seeking mediation, or from initiating a due process hearing.

However, once the initial IEP is written and services begin, no parent signature is required to continue services without a change in placement even though subsequent IEPs may be written. This is because the school district must offer a FAPE to the child. If the parent refuses to sign an IEP for any reason, the district may continue the services under the last signed IEP, may implement that portion of the IEP with which the parent agrees, or may seek a due process hearing, all while continuing to work to resolve the disagreement.

Once a written revocation of consent is received, the student is considered a general education student and all rights under the IDEA cease. The exercise of this parental right to revoke consent may present a dilemma to school officials who believe that the student continues to need special education and related services. However, the IDEA prohibits school officials from seeking mediation[54] or filing a due process complaint in the hopes of obtaining an agreement or ruling that would prevent the parent from revoking consent. When revocation occurs, the school district must provide prior written notice within a reasonable time before it stops providing special education and related services to the child. The prior written notice should explain what changes in the educational program will result from the parents' revocation and gives parents time and information and time to consider fully the ramifications of the revocation of consent, (e.g., there is no longer a requirement to convene an IEP team meeting or to review/develop an IEP). In fact, the school district will not be considered to be in violation of the IDEA when it ceases to provide special services to the student. Notably, only one parent's revocation of consent is required to trigger the prior written notice and cessation of services, even if the other parent disagrees with the revocation.[55] Furthermore, a parent may revoke consent and then subsequently seek reinstatement of special education services.[56] This request should be treated as an initial evaluation, not a reevaluation.[57]

If the school district offers a different placement or different services than those included in the previous IEP, parents are entitled to prior written notice of the change. When parents make a suggestion for a change to the child's program or FAPE and the district considers the recommendation, but decides against it, parents must be given prior written notice of the refusal and reasons for it.

The Eighth Circuit Court of Appeals reviewed a case in which the parent brought suit against the school district for what was believed to be a denial of FAPE. The student with cerebral palsy had been on home instruction during his convalescence from surgery. After eleven months, because the parent insisted that the child continued to be unable to attend school, school district officials, believing home instruction to be inappropriate, offered the same program and the same IEP to the student but delivered in school, not at home. The parents refused to bring the child to school until the district court weighed in on the matter. The court found that the school district changed the student's placement without prior written notice and violated the stay-put provision. The school district had argued that no program or placement change had occurred, merely the location of service changed. The district court disagreed and the circuit court affirmed.[58] The appeals court averred that a transfer to a different school building for fiscal or other reasons unrelated to the child's disability is not a change in placement, whereas expulsion or other change in location made because of the student's disability or behavior is a change of placement.

Rights Regarding Reevaluation

A parent has the right to written notice of a district decision concerning reevaluation. The parent also has the right to request a reevaluation and to be given a written copy of the procedural safeguards. A reevaluation requires informed parental consent, unless the reevaluation is merely a review of existing data. If a parent refuses consent for a reevaluation, school officials may initiate a due process hearing, but they are not required to do so. Should the school district decide not to pursue a due process hearing, it will not be in violation of the IDEA for failing to provide a FAPE. However, school officials may proceed with the reevaluation without parental consent if it made reasonable efforts to obtain such consent and the parent failed to respond. If a student is homeschooled, or has been parentally placed in a private school, public school officials are prohibited from seeking mediation or initiating a due process hearing to resolve a dispute over reevaluation. They are not required to consider those children eligible for special education when parents refuse to provide consent to a reevaluation.

The purpose of a reevaluation is to determine whether the student continues to be eligible for special education and to identify educational needs. The review of continued eligibility must occur at least every three years, but may not occur more than once each school year. By mutual agreement with school officials, a parent may waive the reevaluation in writing. Even if a reevaluation is waived, conducting one will be necessary when the parent or teacher requests it, or when school officials determine that additional data are needed to address the student's needs, including those needed to meet IEP goals, or to improve academic achievement or functional performance. Importantly, no reevaluation is needed when a student graduates from high school with a regular diploma or ages out of special education (i.e., reaches the age of 22). Under those two circumstances, a parent has only the right to prior written notice of the change of placement unless the IEP team decides that reevaluation is necessary, but the parent must be given a summary of the student's academic achievement and functional performance, including recommendations as to how to assist the student to meet post-secondary goals.

Reevaluation includes a review of existing data which includes, but is not limited to, current classroom-based assessments and observations, results of district or state tests given to all students, and teacher and related services provider's records of student performance. No parent permission is required for educators to review existing data. In fact, parental consent is not required for school officials or teachers who choose to observe a student with a disability, to conduct ongoing classroom assessments, or to conduct or to review any adapted or modified assessments of the sort given to all students in any class, grade, or school.

However, the U.S. Department of Education, through its Office of Special Education Programs (OSEP),[59] opined that a functional behavior assessment (FBA) is an "evaluation," requiring informed parental consent, when it is conducted in order to determine behavioral supports and services required for an individual student and not for the whole school to assess the effectiveness of behavioral interventions in general.[60] An FBA is a process used most often in the context of student discipline after a violation of the code of conduct, but it can be utilized at any time. The FBA is a systematic method of identifying the antecedents and consequences of events that inform educators of the nature and purpose of student misconduct. If the process of FBA meets the requirement of a review of existing data or of behavior observation available to all students, as explained above, then no parental consent is required. Following

OSEP's guidance, parents may claim entitlement to an IEE if they disagree with the FBA conducted by school officials.

If a decision is made that the student continues to be eligible for special education, based on a review of existing data and without administration of any new evaluation instruments, the parent is entitled to written notice of that fact. The notice must explain to the parent that school officials believe all necessary data are available to make the decision as to continued eligibility, and why no additional data are needed. Nevertheless, the notice must also inform the parent that if the parent requests further assessments, the district will conduct those assessments irrespective of its decision that no new data are needed.

Should school officials determine that a reevaluation requiring additional testing is needed, either through its own decision making or through parent request, the parent must give informed written consent to the process. Like the initial consent for evaluation, if a parent refuses to give consent for a reevaluation involving new testing, the district may resort to mediation or to the due process mechanism in order to obtain such consent, but to do so is not required. In that case, the school district will not be in violation of the IDEA.

Rights Regarding Educational Records

The IDEA comports with the Family Education Rights and Privacy Act (FERPA), under which parents have the right to inspect and review education records maintained by the school district and to protect records from third parties, unless the parent consents to their disclosure. Educational records include any handwritten, typed, computer-generated, video- or audio-taped record kept by the school and necessary for its business. All notice requirements under FERPA apply to the IDEA.

Under FERPA, records must be disclosed to parents, upon their request, no later than forty-five days after the request, although the school's failure to do so does not provide the parent with a legal cause of action.[61] The time period allotted by law does not suggest that principals wait until the time is about to expire before making records available for parental review. Nor is the time to be spent "scrubbing" the files or redacting any information contained in them. Rather, the time period affords the principal a reasonable time in which to review the records, to gather any information necessary to clarify their meaning, and to make time to sit with the parent during the review in order to answer questions and to protect the integrity of the file.

Under the IDEA, parental access to student records is a necessary component to the provision of FAPE because such access enables a parent to meaningfully participate in the process. In one case, the Ninth Circuit Court of Appeals held that because the school district failed to disclose all the student's records to her parents in a timely fashion, including records indicating that the child may have had autism and suggesting that she be evaluated by a psychiatrist, her parents were not provided with sufficient notice of their child's condition. Because the parents did not have access to the full record of the child, the court held that they could not design an IEP that addressed the child's needs, and, as such, the parents were denied meaningful participation in the special education process.[62] Special education records that may enable meaningful parent participation in the identification, evaluation, or placement decision making, or in the provision of FAPE, may include evaluation reports, testing protocols, disciplinary records, or nurse's files. In another case, the Sixth Circuit Court of Appeals found that parents were denied meaningful participation in the development of the IEP when they were not given access to certain testing protocols so that they could be reviewed by their expert in preparation for the IEP meeting, because this violation "lessen[ed] the parents' ability to advocate for their son during the IEP process."[63]

Under FERPA or IDEA, there is no right to records kept in the principal's or teacher's sole possession, because such records are not considered to be education records and are, instead, considered to be personal notes for purposes of remembrance.[64] Nor is there a right to have the educational record amended unless the record contains information that is inaccurate or misleading, or violates the privacy or other rights of the child.

Logs must be kept by school officials to record the name, date, and purpose of those who access student records, except parents and authorized employees with legitimate educational interests. These logs constitute an educational record to which a parent may request access. Importantly, parents are entitled not only to inspect education records, but also to an explanation of them. Whenever a request for a records inspection is made, the principal should be prepared to answer any questions the parent may have.

Like FERPA, the IDEA ensures that records are confidential unless parental consent is given to authorize their disclosure. Some parents may want the IEP itself kept confidential. Under the IDEA, the child's IEP must be made available to all staff members who are responsible for its implementation. Consequently, all staff members must be informed of their duties and responsibilities related to IEP implementation, irrespective of parent demands to keep the IEP confidential.

Furthermore, the principal can facilitate appropriate communication among staff members and families if some formal system of information sharing is adopted within the school. A few ways a principal can assist in this regard are: (1) by ensuring that teachers know a student's needs before that student enters the classroom; (2) reminding teachers and staff of their recordkeeping duties; (3) expecting data-based decision making; (4) encouraging proactivity in keeping parents informed of student progress or lack of progress; (5) valuing the importance of the IEP team as a decision-making body; and (6) developing a method whereby the principal is made aware of problems, concerns, and questions that a teacher or parent may have regarding the education of the student with a disability. The importance of strong communication through data collection and reporting of developing needs and progress cannot be overstated. Indeed , even where the parent does not want information shared, the principal may need to disclose information without parental consent.

Under FERPA, records may be disclosed to third parties without parental consent pursuant to a number of regulatory exceptions, such as in the case of a health or safety emergency. Under FERPA and the IDEA, a parent does not have the right to prevent principals from sharing special educational records to appropriate authorities where the safety of the student or the school community is at stake. In one case, the principal sent explanatory letters home to parents of children who were victims of, and witnesses to, the misconduct of a student with a disability. No FERPA violation was found because the court found it reasonable that school officials would notify parents that they were taking steps at school to ensure the safety of their children.[65] Furthermore, when reporting criminal conduct to the police, the IDEA authorizes school officials to provide copies of disciplinary records to the authorities for their consideration. Additionally, records may be released without parent permission when state law permits disclosure to authorities in the juvenile justice system, to law enforcement personnel who keep records for law enforcement purposes, and with a court order or subpoena.

Although FERPA permits the school district to charge a reasonable fee for copies of records requested by parents, the IDEA requirement that special education be at no cost to parents precludes school officials from charging parents for copies of the IEP. A reasonable fee may be charged for copies of other educational records, but the fee cannot preclude parent access to those records. Generally, copies of the evaluation team report, progress reports, and other records should be provided to parents of children with disabilities at no cost to them.

The IDEA requires school officials to inform parents when personally identifiable information contained in educational records is no longer needed to provide educational services to the child. If the parents request that the information be destroyed, the school district must comply. This right extends to records maintained by third parties that are agents of the school district. However, a permanent record of the student's name, address, and phone number, grades, attendance record, classes attended, grade level completed, and year completed may be kept on file indefinitely.[66] "Destruction" under the IDEA means physical destruction or the removal of personal identifiers from the information so that it is no longer personally identifiable.[67]

Rights to Disagree Regarding Student's Program: Due Process Procedures

Parents have the right under the IDEA to complain to district or state officials about any special education services their children are, or should be, receiving. This right includes complaints about identification, evaluation, placement, and the provision of FAPE. The proper venues to resolve these student-based disputes are first with the teacher or service provider, at the IEP team, followed by administrative review or mediation options, and culminating at a due process hearing. A visit to the administrator's office should be encouraged at each step of the way, giving the principal an opportunity to defuse the situation, to clarify and articulate the various points of view, and to help the parents arrive at a decision, even if that decision is to proceed with a formal dispute. The principal should be careful to avoid interfering with the parent's right to invoke IDEA's dispute resolution mechanisms.

When a dispute arises over the identification, evaluation, placement, or provision of FAPE, the parents have the right to seek administrative review, mediation, a due process hearing, redress in civil court, and to be reimbursed the costs of their attorney fees if they are prevailing parties.[68] During any dispute, the parents have the right to ensure that their child remains in the current placement with the current services until the matter is settled. During the period of dispute resolution, the child's program or placement may not be changed until the matter is settled. Stay-put protects the child from unilateral actions taken by the school district by ensuring that the student "stays put" until the issues can be clarified and resolved.[69] The stay-put provision can be altered if the parent and school district agree otherwise.

There are several avenues to resolve disputes. Administrative review is a voluntary option for conflict resolution in which parents may present a complaint to the school district superintendent or designee regarding the identification, evaluation, or placement of a student with a disability, or the provision of a FAPE. Doing so is expedient, may result in a mutually agreed-upon solution, and is less expensive than a due process hearing.

No-cost mediation is voluntary between the parents and school officials and cannot be used to delay a due process hearing.[70] (Some states may provide for IEP facilitators as well.) During mediation, an objective third party attempts to guide each side to an understanding of each other's interests and to reach a settlement to which all can agree. Anything said during mediation may not be used in a subsequent due process hearing or in civil court; discussions are confidential and cannot be used as evidence. Because mediation is an option for parents, some state laws may require parents who refuse mediation to meet with a third party to encourage the use of mediation.[71] Mediation is a dispute resolution mechanism that can be used at any time, even after a due process complaint has been filed.

Any decisions reached through mediation are to be in writing. Often, mediation agreements contain a confidentiality provision in which both parties agree that neither party will discuss the settlement with others. However, there may be circumstances in which parents will inform other parents of the dispute and the result reached with school officials. This can happen when parents are pleased with the outcome and want to share their success with other parents, or when parents are eager to help other parents who may present similar issues. Because of the confidentiality provision, this situation may be considered a breach of contract and may cause principals to have to respond to other families that may seek similar services. In that case, the appropriate response is to convene the IEP team to discuss the appropriateness of the current program of the complaining parents' child. Should parents disagree with the decision, they, too, may seek mediation or a due process hearing. The principal should not breach the confidentiality agreement made during mediation.

If administrative review or mediation does not resolve the matter, the IDEA affords the parent the right to seek a due process hearing before an impartial hearing officer, usually assigned by the state, no later than forty-five days after the request for the hearing is made.[72] The parent has the right to request that the hearing be held in public and that the child attend. The hearing can be likened to a mini-trial in which evidence is submitted, witnesses are called, testimony is heard, cross examinations are conducted, and a decision is rendered. The hearing officer's final decision is mailed to both parties and the parent is entitled to a transcript of the proceedings.

The hearing may not proceed, however, until a mandatory resolution session either is held or waived in writing by the parent and school officials.[73] The resolution session must be conducted within fifteen days of the school district's receipt of the parent's due process complaint, for the purpose of discussing the complaint and the facts underlying it so that school officials have an opportunity to resolve it before the hearing. Information raised in the resolution session is confidential and may not be used at a due process hearing. Relevant members of the IEP team must attend the meeting; the determination of relevancy is made both by the parent and school officials. Only if the parent brings an attorney may the school district's attorney be present at the resolution session. If the matter remains unresolved, the due process hearing may proceed.

A parent must comply with all IDEA procedural requirements relative to filing a due process hearing request, or risk the possibility of losing the opportunity to appeal the hearing officer's decision to civil court. A request for a due process hearing can be made any time the school district proposes or refuses to initiate or change the identification, evaluation, or educational placement of the child or the provision of FAPE. The request must be in writing, describing the name and address of the child, the child's school of attendance, a description of the nature of the problem of the child, all related facts, and must propose a resolution. This required notice to the school district is to afford the district the opportunity to reconsider its decision, explore the parents' suggested solution, and to revise its offer, if necessary. The party that chooses to bring forward a due process complaint bears the burden to persuade the hearing officer of the validity of its argument.[74] Principals should be aware that IDEA requires every state to make available a model form of a due process complaint notice, which parents can use when they wish to file a due process complaint.[75]

If school district officials initiate a due process hearing, the parent is entitled to written notice of the request. In addition to providing all the details of the nature of the problem, the written notice also must inform the parent of the option for mediation and where to find free or low-cost legal representation; however, a resolution session is not required.

Additionally, parents must exhaust their due process privileges before filing suit in civil court. IDEA gives each state the option of creating a "one-tier" or a "two-tier" due process procedure.[76] The exhaustion requirement means that in states with one tier of administrative review, the parent must go to due process and have a decision rendered in order to appeal to civil court. In states with two tiers of review, one local and the other at the state level, parents must take their dispute to both venues before the court will hear their complaint. There are some exceptions to the exhaustion requirement, especially when to take the matter to due process would be futile. The court will decide if one of the exceptions applies.

Rights to Dispute District Practices: State Complaint Procedure

One formal complaint procedure that parents can access is the "state complaint" procedure.[77] Each state is required to adopt and implement written complaint resolution procedures, and each state may include in those procedures what are the proper subjects for complaint. The state complaint procedure provides parents a less costly and generally more efficient mechanism for resolving certain disputes than an impartial due process hearing.[78] In filing a state complaint, parents must provide a written statement explaining how the school district has violated the IDEA not more than one year prior to the complaint. The complaint must include (a) the facts on which the statement is based; (b) the signature and contact information of the parent; and (c) if alleging violations with respect to a specific student, the student's name and address of the student's residence, the name of the school the student is attending, a description of the nature of the student's problem, including facts relating to the problem, and a proposed resolution.[79]

The state complaint procedure also may be used when parents are not disputing a specific student's placement, services, or program, but are complaining about the school district's policies, practices, or procedures that affect a group of students. Problems with the operations, administrative hierarchy, and customs of the school, or the school district itself, are properly handled through the state complaint procedure, not due process. For example, parents who demanded that the public school provide special education to their son at a private school were not permitted to use due process proceedings to examine their claims; the court held that they needed to use the state complaint procedure because state law governed such entitlements, not the local school district.[80]

When a parent invokes the state complaint procedure, the state educational agency must conduct an on-site investigation and must issue a written decision with findings of fact, along with its reasons.[81] When the principal is confronted by parent concerns about general school district operations, and not the student's particular and individualized education, the parent is to be informed that the state complaint procedure is the appropriate venue for voicing such concerns. A parent may file a state complaint and concurrently file a due process complaint, as long as the issue relates to a matter regarding the identification, evaluation, or educational placement of a student with a disability, or the provision of FAPE to the student.[82]

Rights Regarding Attorney and Other Fees

A parent's right to attorney fees is not automatic; rather, attorney fees are a discretionary award if the parent is the prevailing party in an IDEA lawsuit.[83] Additionally, if a settlement offer was already made during or after mediation or hearing and was rejected, the award of attorney fees to the parent generally will not be more favorable than the offer of settlement. Parents are not eligible for attorney fees accrued during an IEP team meeting, unless that meeting was convened as a result of an administrative hearing or judicial action. The costs of a parent's expert witness are not recoupable as attorney fees.[84]

School districts may be awarded attorney fees against the parent's attorney if the court finds that the attorney filed a complaint or subsequent cause of action that is frivolous, unreasonable, or without foundation, or if the attorney continued to litigate after the litigation clearly became frivolous, unreasonable, or without foundation.[85] School districts also may be awarded such fees against the parent, if the parent's request for a due process hearing or subsequent cause of action was presented for any improper purpose, such as to harass, to cause unnecessary delay, or to needlessly increase the cost of litigation.[86]

Rights Regarding Placement in Private Schools

Parents may remove their children from public schools at any time and enroll them in private schools, religious schools, or choose homeschooling.[87] As to a student with a disability, however, parents who remove their child without giving the school district prior notice of the decision to change schools, and who later attempt to seek reimbursement for education costs, assume a financial risk.[88]

The public school has a duty to offer and to provide a FAPE. Where FAPE is in dispute and the parent unilaterally removes the child, then later sues the school district for tuition reimbursement, the court generally will not award tuition if FAPE was available in the public school. Parents may recover costs of tuition for private school if FAPE was not available at the time the child was removed, or if it was not offered in a timely manner and the private school placement was appropriate.[89] Reimbursement is available even if the private school did not meet state standards, or the student never received special education services from the public school.[90]

The decision to award tuition reimbursement, however, is contingent upon several parental actions that must precede the removal from public school.

First, parents must inform school officials at the last IEP meeting they attend before the removal of their rejection of the district's placement offer, including their concerns, and of their intent to enroll the child in a private school at public expense. Reimbursement may be denied if the parents did not give their reasons for rejecting the district's offer, their concerns, and put their notice of intent to withdraw in writing at least ten business days, including holidays that fall on business days, before they remove the child from public school.[91] Additionally, the parents may not be eligible for reimbursement if the court finds they behaved unreasonably, or if they did not make the child available for a proper request for evaluation before they removed the child from public school.

There are exceptions to the parental written notice requirement. One obvious exception is when the parents are illiterate or do not speak English.[92] Another is when the child may suffer physical or emotional harm by remaining in the public school, and the parent must act swiftly in caring for the child's health and well-being.[93] Recall that the procedural safeguards include notice to the parent that they must give notice prior to any withdrawal. Tuition reimbursement, if appropriate, generally will not be denied to the parent who did not give the required notice to the school district if school officials did not give the parent a copy of the procedural safeguards when necessary.[94] Occasionally, school officials will prevent the parent from giving the required notice if the relationship deteriorated during the decision making. Again, the court may overlook the notice requirement in that case.

When FAPE is not in dispute—that is to say, the parent chooses a private school for the child with a disability based on academic, social, philosophical, religious, or other reasons unrelated to special education—the parent has no right to expect that the public school will provide to the child some or all of the services the child would have received if enrolled in public school. In this case, the parent is not even entitled to a due process hearing, except for issues involving evaluation and child find.

Children placed in private schools by their parents, where FAPE is not in dispute, are not entitled to a FAPE. However, the school district must maintain records as to the number of students parentally placed in private schools that were evaluated, found eligible for special education, and were served. These students may be eligible to participate in the services provided to the private school that are designated by the school district. To determine what services will be provided for private school students, if any, public school officials are required to consult with private school officials on how any available money will be spent, on whom to spend it, and on where, when, how, and what services to provide. Funds to provide services to students in private schools are a proportionate amount of federal funds made available to the public school district for those students. No state or local funds are used to provide these services. The decision the public school district makes will be written as a service plan. The services, if any, can be provided on the premises of private schools, including those that are religious, to the extent that to do so is consistent with state law. If transportation is necessary, those costs can be taken from the amount allocated to the private school. If the school district fails to provide the services in the plan, parents then may file a state administrative complaint, because a due process hearing is not available to them.

Sometimes the school district will offer to place a child in a private school at the district's expense.[95] Public school officials generally will choose a private placement because, due to the child's unique needs, a FAPE is unavailable in the public school. Those students are entitled to a FAPE, and their parents are entitled to all procedural safeguards discussed above, because the rights belonging to the student and parent are no different than if the child were placed in public school.

Transfer of Rights

Each state must have rules to appoint a parent or other adult to represent the educational interests of the student with a disability who has reached the age of majority, if the student is found to be incompetent and unable to provide informed consent for his or her educational programming.[96] When a student with a disability who is found competent by a court reaches the age of majority, usually age 18 in most states, the parents' rights under the IDEA transfer to the student.[97] This can be very difficult for parents who, for years, have been advocates used to making decisions and participating in their child's special education. The situation can be especially difficult if the student chooses to exit special education or refuses to permit the parents to attend IEP meetings. However, the IDEA permits school officials to invite to IEP team meetings those persons who are knowledgeable about the student, who can be the parents.[98]

Conclusion

A violation of the IDEA can occur if the parent either is unaware of the parental rights or was prevented from exercising them. In fact, the courts will not extend an inquiry to the second prong of *Rowley* to examine the IEP if the procedural violations found through first-prong analysis alone denied the student's right to FAPE.[99] However, simple mistakes and oversights are not enough to violate the IDEA.[100] Procedural errors clearly violate the IDEA when they result in a compromise to the child's right to FAPE, when they seriously hamper the parent's opportunity to participate meaningfully in the IEP formulation process, or when they cause a deprivation of educational benefits to which the student was entitled.[101]

Recommendations for Practice

1. Parents have the right to be given a copy of their rights under the law. A written copy of the procedural safeguards must be given to parents, at a minimum, upon initial referral for evaluation, for reevaluation when new assessments are necessary, whenever a parent files the first request for due process or a state complaint during a school year, and before any disciplinary action that might result in a change of placement. Principals should have a recordkeeping mechanism in place that gives them the assurance that parents did, in fact, receive a copy of procedural safeguards. Should the school district go to due process, that information will be required for the district to prove it met its obligation under the law.

2. Before children are evaluated for a suspected disability, their parents have the right to a copy of the procedural safeguards, written notice of the assessments the school district will use to identify the existence of any disability, and to give written, informed consent to testing. Consent may be revoked at any time. In that case, should school officials desire to proceed with the evaluation, they may, but are not required to, seek mediation in order to convince the parent of the need for testing, or an order authorizing testing through the due process hearing mechanism.

3. A parent request to test a student may necessitate an evaluation. However, educators ultimately make the determination as to whether a disability is suspected through a careful analysis of student records, performance, behavior, and affect. If the team, including the parent, determines that testing is not necessary or is inappropriate, the decision and the team's rationale should be documented, and a prior written notice sent to the parents.

4. Parents are entitled to participate in the eligibility determination. Eligibility is based on a categorical definition, accompanied by the child's need for special education as determined by the entire team. A parent may contest an eligibility decision through optional mediation or due process proceedings.

5. Parents who disagree with the school district's evaluation or eligibility determination have the right to request an independent educational evaluation at public expense. The principal may ask the parent to explain the reasoning behind the request, but the parent is under no obligation to discuss it. School district policy will dictate whether the district will issue an invoice for direct payment to the approved independent evaluator, or whether the parent must pay for the evaluation and then be reimbursed. If the district believes that its evaluation is appropriate and refuses a request for an independent evaluation,

the parent is entitled to prior written notice of that decision, including the reasons for the refusal, and the district must seek a due process hearing to defend its evaluation.

6. The results of any independent evaluation conducted—paid for either by the parent or by the school district—must be considered by the team. Failure to consider the results may result in a denial of FAPE.

7. Parents have the right to meaningful participation at any meeting regarding the provision of FAPE to the child, including the IEP meeting. Educators must plan the meeting and its purpose and be ready to explain their professional judgments and to answer questions. Consequently, parents are to be given prior written notice of the purpose of the meeting, as well as the time, location, and who will be in attendance. Decision-making meetings requiring parent attendance do not include business-related, organizational, in-service, strategic, or planning meetings of teachers. To allow otherwise would undermine the educators' need to engage in professional discussion and to give thoughtful consideration to a variety of organizational and staff concerns.

8. Any proposed change to the child's identification, evaluation, placement, or provision of FAPE requires that the parent receive prior written notice of the school's proposal. Any time the school refuses to change the identification, evaluation, placement, or provision of FAPE to the child, the parent is entitled to receive prior written notice of the district's decision. The notice must include the reasons for the school district's refusal. Such advance notice provides parents with the opportunity to consider the proposal and to seek advice, if necessary.

9. Parents must provide written, informed consent before a child's placement may be changed. However, certain disciplinary removals do not require such consent, nor is consent required for conducting reevaluations or FBAs that are merely reviews of existing data, or if a part of regular classroom observation available to all students.

10. A parent may, in writing, revoke consent for the provision of special education and related services at any time. School officials must then provide the parents with prior written notice, stop the provision of services within a reasonable time, and may not use mediation or pursue a due process hearing in attempt to retain the child in special education. Revocation of consent for services is a revocation of the entire IEP, and the student then is considered a general education student.

11. Students who previously received special education and related services, and whose parents revoked consent for the continued provision

of special education and related services, should not be treated any differently in the child-find process than any other student.

12. Parents are entitled to inspect and review all educational records of their children, and to receive copies of those records, but divorce, separation, or custody may alter participation and decision-making rights, depending on state law. Principals should identify which parent(s) have access rights and which have decision-making rights, and should communicate that information to those with a legitimate need to know.

13. Parents have no right to keep a child's records confidential where school employees have a legitimate need to know and where the health and safety of student(s) or the school community are at stake, should they be necessary to provide to appropriate authorities. Concern for the safety of the entire school community is of overarching concern to the principal.

14. Parents have the right to present complaints about school district operations, policies, and procedures to the state through the state complaint procedure.

15. Parents have the right to review decisions and present complaints concerning their child's identification, evaluation, placement, and provision of FAPE, generally, first to the IEP team, then through optional mediation and/or administrative review, and finally, in a due process hearing. Parents must exhaust administrative review before they may appeal an agency decision to civil court.

16. Parents have the right to attorney fees for the costs of a due process hearing and litigation, if not limited by the court, so long as they are prevailing parties and do not fail in the requirement to properly notify school officials of their concerns before removing the child from public school. Parents do not have a right to expert witness fees.

17. Parents have the right to withdraw their children from public schools and to educate them in homeschools, private, or religious schools. They may be entitled to reimbursement for those costs if the school district's placement is inappropriate, if they properly notify school officials of their intentions. This award ensures that the appropriate education to which their children are entitled is free and at no cost to them.

Endnotes

[1] *The School Principal as Leader: Guiding Schools to Better Teaching and Learning*, THE WALLACE FOUNDATION (2013), available at http://www.wallacefoundation.org/knowledge-center/Documents/The-School-Principal-as-Leader-Guiding-Schools-to-Better-Teaching-and-Learning-2nd-Ed.pdf.

[2]   Education for All Handicapped Children Act, P.L. 91-230, Title VI §601, 84 Stat. 175 (1970), *amended* P.L. 93-380 (1974), 88 Stat. 579; *amended* P.L. 94-142, §3(a), 89 Stat. 774 (1975), *amended* P.L. 95-49, 91 Stat. 230 (1977); *amended* P.L. 98-199, 97 Stat. 1357 (1983); *amended* P.L. 101-476 (1990), *renamed* Individuals with Disabilities Act, P.L. 102-119 § 25(b), 105 Stat. 587 (1991), *amended* 20 U.S.C. §1400 *et seq.*(1997); *amended* P.L. 108-446, 118 Stat. 2647 (2004).

[3]   Board of Educ. of Hendrick Hudson Cent. Sch. Dist. v. Rowley, 458 U.S. 176, 209 (1982).

[4]   *Id.*

[5]   Pa. Ass'n for Retarded Children (PARC) v. Pennsylvania, 343 F. Supp. 279 (1972); Mills v. Bd. of Educ. of Dist. of Columbia, 348 F. Supp. 866 (D.D.C. 1972).

[6]   20 U.S.C. § 1232g (2012); 34 C.F.R. § 99.1 *et. seq.* (2016).

[7]   Chapter 8 discusses the transition from school to work in more detail.

[8]   20 U.S.C. § 1412(a) (2012).

[9]   *Rowley*, 458 U.S. at 206-07.

[10]   Chapter 6 discusses in more detail the varying interpretations of the federal appellate courts regarding *Rowley's* "educational benefit" standard.

[11]   *Rowley*, 458 U.S. at 178.

[12]   *See* Deal v. Hamilton County Bd. of Educ., 392 F.3d 894 (6th Cir. 2004), *cert. denied*, 546 U.S. 936 (2005), *on remand*, 259 F. Supp. 2d 687 (E.D. Tenn. 2006), *aff'd*, 258 Fed. Appx 863 (6th Cir. 2008).

[13]   Winkelman *ex rel.* Winkelman v. Parma City Sch. Dist., 550 U.S. 516 (2007).

[14]   *Winkelman*, 550 U.S. at 531-532.

[15]   Each of these rights is discussed in more detail, *infra*. IDEA provides that, if the student has been found to be incompetent under state law, no transfer of rights must take place. 20 U.S.C. § 1415(m) (2012); 34 C.F.R. § 300.520(b) (2016).

[16]   *Winkelman*, 550 U.S. at 531.

[17]   20 U.S.C. § 1415 *et. seq.* (2012).

[18]   20 U.S.C. § 1401(23) (2012); 34 C.F.R § 300.30(a) (2016).

[19]   34 C.F.R. § 300.519(a) (2012); *see also* 42 U.S.C. § 11434(a) (2012) (defining homeless children and youths).

[20]   Navin v. Park Ridge Sch. Dist. 64, 270 F.3d 1147 (7th Cir. 2001).

[21]   Taylor v. Vermont Dep't of Educ., 313 F.3d 768 (2d Cir. 2002).

[22]   *Id.* at 778-78.

[23]   *Id.* at 781 n.10.

[24]   Driessen v. Miami-Dade County Sch. Bd., 61 IDELR 95 (11th Cir. 2013).

[25]   Fuentes v. Bd. of Educ., City of NY, 569 F.3d 46 (2d Cir. 2009), *cert. den.* 129 S. Ct. 1357 (2009).

[26]   *Rowley*, 458 U.S. at 205.

[27]   34 C.F.R. § 300. 504 (2016).

[28]   *Id.*

[29]   Jaynes *ex rel.* Jaynes v. Newport News Sch. Bd., 13 Fed. Appx. 166 (4th Cir. 2001); Mason *ex rel.* Mason v. Schenectady City Sch. Dist., 879 F. Supp. 215 (N.D.N.Y. 1993).

[30]   71 Fed. Reg. 46540-01, 46693 (Aug. 14, 2006).

[31]   34 C.F.R. § 300.505 (2016).

[32]   34 C.F.R. § 300.504(c) (2016).

[33]   20 U.S.C. § 1415(b)(2)(B)(3) (2012) (requiring prior written notice); 20 U.S.C. § 1415(d) (2012) (requiring provision of procedural safeguards).

[34]   20 U.S.C. § 1415(c)(1) (2012).

[35]   20 U.S.C. § 1415(c)(1)(B) (2012).

[36]   M.B. *ex. rel.* Burns v. Hamilton Southeastern Sch., 668 F.3d 851, 861-62 (7th Cir. 2011).

[37]   34 C.F.R. § 300.8 (2016); 34 C.F.R. § 300.111(c) (2016).

[38]   Doe v. Nashville Pub. Schs., 133 F.3d 384, 387-88 (6th Cir. 1998).

[39]   *See, e.g.*, Indep. Sch. Dist. No. 284 v. A.C., 258 F.3d 769 (8th Cir. 2001).

[40] Letter from Alexa Posny to Deborah S. Johnson, U.S. Dep't. of Educ. (Jun. 3. 2010), available at https://www2.ed.gov/policy/speced/guid/idea/letters/2010-2/johnson060310consent2q2010.pdf.

[41] 34 C.F.R. §300.301(c) (2016).

[42] *See* 34 C.F.R. §300.300 (2016).

[43] Murphy v. Arlington Cent. Sch. Dist. Bd. of Educ., 402 F.3d 332, 338 (2d Cir. 2005), *rev'd* 126 S. Ct. 2455 (2006).

[44] 34 C.F.R. § 300.503(a) (2016); Letter from Alexa Posny to Dorothy M. Richards, U.S. Dep't. of Educ. (Jan. 7. 2010), available at http://pattan.net-website.s3.amazonaws.com/files/materials/osep/CY2010/Richards010710.pdf.

[45] *See* letter from Ruth Ryder to Diane M. Savit, , U.S. Dep't. of Educ. (Jan. 19, 2016) available at https://www2.ed.gov/policy/speced/guid/idea/memosdcltrs/savit-dcps-policies1-1-19-2016.pdf.

[46] J.P. v. County Sch. Bd. of Hanover, 447 F. Supp. 2d 553 (E.D. Va. 2006), *vacated,* 516 F.3d 254 (4th Cir. 2008).

[47] Kings Local Sch. Dist. v. Zelazny, 325 F.3d 724 (6th Cir. 2003).

[48] *See, e.g.,* Ridley Sch. Dist. v. M.R. and J.R. *ex rel.* E.R., 112 LRP 25613, 2011 WL 499966 (E.D. Pa., Feb. 14, 2011), *aff'd,* 680 F.3d 260 (3d Cir. 2012).

[49] Board of Educ. v. J.A., 56 IDELR 209, 2011 WL 1231317 (N.D. W.Va., Mar. 30, 2011).

[50] *Rowley,* 458 U.S. at 208-209.

[51] J.P. v. West Clark Cmty. Schs., 230 F. Supp. 2d 910, 916 (S.D. Ind. 2002).

[52] *Id.* at 936.

[53] G.J. v. Muscogee County Sch. Dist., 704 F. Supp. 2d 1299 (M.D. Ga. 2010), *aff'd,* 668 F.3d 1258 (11th Cir. 2012).

[54] Letter from Melody Musgrove to James Gerl, U.S. Dep't of Educ. (Jun. 6, 2012), available at https://www2.ed.gov/policy/speced/guid/idea/memosdcltrs/11-023202r-wv-gerl-revocation.pdf.

[55] Letter from Patricia Guard to H. Douglas Cox, U.S. Dep't of Educ. (Aug. 21, 2009), available at https://www2.ed.gov/policy/speced/guid/idea/letters/2009-3/cox082109revocationofconsent3q2009.pdf..

[56] 73 Fed. Reg. 73,006-01, 73014 (Dec. 1, 2008).

[57] *See* Letter from Patricia Guard, *supra* note 61.

[58] Hale *ex rel.* Hale v. Poplar Bluff R-1 Sch. Dist., 280 F.3d 831 (8th Cir. 2002).

[59] The Office of Special Education Programs has been renamed the Office of Special Education and Rehabilitative Services, also known as OSERS. *See* https://ed.gov/about/offices/list/osers/index.html.

[60] Letter from Alexa Posny to Dr. Kris Christiansen, U.S. Dep't of Educ. (Feb. 9, 2007), available at https://www2.ed.gov/policy/speced/guid/idea/letters/2007-1/christiansen020907discipline1q2007.pdf.

[61] Gonzaga Univ. v. Doe, 536 U.S. 273 (2002).

[62] Amanda J. v. Clark Cnty. Sch. Dist., 267 F.3d 877 (9th Cir. 2001).

[63] Woods v. Northport Pub. Sch., 487 Fed. Appx. 968 (6th Cir. 2012).

[64] 20 U.S.C. § 1232g(a)(4)(B)(i) (2012).

[65] Jensen *ex rel.* C.J. v. Reeves, 3 Fed. Appx. 905 (10th Cir. 2001).

[66] 34 C.F.R. §300.624 (2016).

[67] 34 C.F.R. §300.611(a) (2016).

[68] *See* 20 U.S.C. §1415(k) (2012).

[69] 20 U.S.C. § 1415(j) (2012).

[70] 20 U.S.C. § 1415(e) (2012).

[71] 20 U.S.C. § 1415(e)(2)(B) (2012).

[72] 20 U.S.C. § 1415(f) (2012).

[73] 20 U.S.C. § 1415(f)(1)(B) (2012).

[74] Schaffer v. Weast, 546 U.S. 49, 57-58 (2005).

[75] 20 U.S.C. § 1415(b)(8) (2012).

[76] 20 U.S.C. § 1415(f)(1)(A) (2012).

[77] 34 C.F.R. § 300.151-153 (2016).

[78] Memorandum from Melody Musgrove to Chief State School Officers, *"Dispute Resolution Procedures under Part B of the Individuals with Disabilities Education Act (Part B),"* U.S. DEP'T OF EDUC. (July 23, 2013), available at https://www2.ed.gov/policy/speced/guid/idea/memosdcltrs/acccombinedosersdisputeresolutionqafinalmemo-7-23-13.pdf.

[79] 34 C.F.R. § 300.153(b).

[80] E.W. v. School Bd. of Miami Dade Cty., 307 F. Supp. 2d 1363 (S.D. Fla. 2004).

[81] 34 C.F.R. § 300.152 (2016).

[82] 34 .C.F.R. § 300.152(c) (2016).

[83] 20 U.S.C. § 1415(i)(3)(B)(i) (2012).

[84] Arlington Cent. Sch. Dist. Bd. of Educ. v. Murphy, 548 U.S. 241 (2006).

[85] 20 U.S.C. § 1415(i)(3)(B)(i) (2012).

[86] *Id.*

[87] 20 U.S.C. § 1412(a)(10)(A) (2012).

[88] 20 U.S.C. § 1412(a)(10)(C) (2012).

[89] Town of Burlington v. Dep't of Educ., 471 U.S. 359 (1985); Florence Cnty. Sch. Dist. Four v. Carter, 510 U.S. 7 (1988).

[90] Forest Grove Sch. Dist. v. T.A., 557 U.S. 230 (2007).

[91] *See* W.D. v. Watchung Hills Regional High Sch. Bd. of Educ., 602 Fed. Appx. 563 (3d Cir. 2015) (failure to provide notice precluded claim for tuition reimbursement).

[92] 20 U.S.C. § 1412(a)(10)(C)(iv)(I)(bb) (2012).

[93] 20 U.S.C. § 1412(a)(10)(C)(iv)(II)(aa) (2012)

[94] 20 U.S.C. § 1412(a)(10)(C)(iv)(II)(bb) (2012).

[95] 20 U.S.C. § 1412(a)(10)(B) (2012).

[96] 20 U.S.C. § 1415(m) (2012).

[97] *Id.*

[98] 34 C.F.R. §300.321(a)(6) (2016).

[99] Amanda J. v. Clark Cnty Sch. Dist., 267 F.3d 877 (9th Cir. 2001).

[100] Burilovich v. Board of Educ., 208 F.3d 560, 566 (6th Cir. 2000).

[101] *Amanda J.*, 267 F.3d at 892.

Chapter 11

Procedural Safeguards: Resolving Family-School Disputes

Susan C. Bon

Introduction

Procedural safeguards, or dispute resolution procedures,[1] are among several key provisions in the Individuals with Disabilities Education Act (IDEA). Other provisions establish basic guarantees that protect students' rights, including a free appropriate public education (FAPE),[2] parental involvement, the least restrictive environment (LRE) principle,[3] and an individualized education program (IEP).[4] Parents of children with disabilities[5] and school officials often disagree over the interpretation and implementation of these key IDEA provisions and seek intervention by the courts to resolve their disputes.

In targeted efforts to increase cooperation among parents and school district personnel, Congress included procedural safeguards and dispute resolution that offer a unique level of parental rights protections.[6] Specifically, IDEA provides detailed procedures to resolve disputes between schools and parents, and to protect parental rights as discussed in the preceding chapter. At the center of the procedural protections for parents is the impartial due process hearing. IDEA permits parents to request a due process hearing if they disagree "with respect to any matter relating to the identification, evaluation, or educational placement of the child, or the provision of a free appropriate public education."[7]

Formal Resolution Mechanisms

The various procedures have changed over the years with each congressional reauthorization of the IDEA. In 1997, the IDEA reauthorization added a requirement for states to offer voluntary mediation when a request for a due process hearing is filed.[8] The subsequent reauthorization of IDEA in 2004 sought to enhance the use of alternative dispute resolution, specifically through mediation and resolution sessions, by expanding the 1997 provisions of IDEA. In the sections below, each of the formal resolution mechanisms will be discussed, including resolution sessions,[9] mediation,[10] administrative due process hearings,[11] judicial review,[12] and state complaints.[13]

Resolution Sessions

During the reauthorization of IDEA in 2004, resolution sessions were adopted as a way of resolving disputes between schools and parents over special education programs and services.[14] According to IDEA, school officials must schedule resolution sessions within fifteen days of receiving a parental complaint. Resolution sessions are mandatory; however, both parents and the school may waive this process if they mutually agree. The resolution sessions were anticipated to also reduce conflict and the adversarial nature of relationships between schools and parents.

School officials must schedule a resolution session before holding the impartial due process hearing[15] under the 2004 IDEA procedural safeguards provision. This resolution session must be scheduled within fifteen days of the parental notification requesting a due process hearing.[16] Several individuals must attend the meeting, including the parent and relevant members of the IEP team who are knowledgeable about the topic or issues identified in the due process complaint. Additional members should include a school or public official with decision-making authority, but should not include an attorney representing the school unless the parents elect to bring an attorney.[17] If parents do bring an attorney, fees for the attorney's services are not available under the IDEA.[18]

During the resolution session, parents are to be given an opportunity to discuss why they requested a due process hearing, and the school should have an opportunity to resolve the dispute.[19] If the school and parents are able to resolve the dispute through a resolution session, they are then required to both sign and enter a legally binding agreement, which is enforceable in court. On the other hand, if the issue is not resolved within thirty days of the due process request, the parents may proceed with the due process hearing.[20]

Although the parents may elect to waive the resolution session and opt instead for mediation, they may not unilaterally refuse to participate in the resolution session. If the parents do refuse to participate, the timelines for the resolution process and due process hearing will be delayed until a resolution meeting is held.[21] In addition, if the parents refuse to participate and the school officials have documented evidence[22] of their reasonable efforts to set up the meeting, the school may request dismissal of the due process complaint after thirty days.[23] On the other hand, the parents may request to begin the due process hearing timeline if school officials fail to schedule and meet for the resolution session as required by the fifteen-day timeline.[24]

Mediation

Unlike the mandatory resolution sessions, mediation is a voluntary process that is encouraged as an option to avoid due process.[25] Although it is voluntary, the 1997 IDEA amendments require states to provide mediation at no cost to parents and to create the procedures for purposes of settling disputes.[26] Mediation may not, however, be used to deny or delay parents' rights to administrative hearings.[27] During mediation, a neutral third party works with the school and parents to resolve their differences. This individual must be a qualified and impartial mediator, or must at a minimum be qualified and knowledgeable about special education laws and regulations.[28]

Once the resolution of a complaint is reached, the school and parents are required to form a legally binding agreement regarding the resolution; this agreement must also indicate that the discussions during the mediation process are to be confidential.[29] Both the parents and a school official with the authority to bind the school district must sign the resolution.[30] Signed mediation agreements are legally binding and may be enforced in a state or federal court.[31]

IDEA is silent with respect to attorney participation in mediation sessions; thus, attorney presence varies widely from state to state. Some states permit attorneys to be present at the mediation, although other states expressly prohibit attorney involvement.[32] Determining whether or not an attorney's presence at mediation is beneficial is a disputed matter, due to common issues such as mistrust between parents and school districts, the expense of hiring an attorney, the adversarial nature of attorneys, and the imbalance of power between schools and parents.[33]

Administrative Due Process Hearings

If parents and school districts are unable to resolve their dispute through a resolution session or mediation, then the process moves to an administrative due process hearing. Due process hearings provide an avenue for parents to exercise their rights to participate in educational decisions affecting their children. Furthermore, these hearings are a mandatory step that parents must take before they seek redress in a state or federal court; IDEA requires parents to exhaust their administrative remedies through the administrative court system first.[34] Parents may request impartial due process hearings if they disagree with the actions or recommendations of school personnel regarding the identification, evaluation, educational placement, or any aspect of FAPE.[35] Both school districts and parents must adhere to the timelines and procedural guidance established by IDEA and accompanying regulations. These details are presented in the following discussion.

Due process hearings must be requested within a two-year time period of the incident or actions that led to the complaint.[36] This time period may be extended if parents demonstrate that school officials misrepresented or withheld information about the incident or actions that were at the base of the complaint.[37] Appropriate notice of the due process complaint must be provided by whichever party requests the due process hearing, the school district or parents.[38] The due process hearing provides an opportunity for parents and school officials to share evidence supporting their respective positions with an impartial hearing officer (IHO),[39] who is responsible for making a decision regarding the issues presented. The state educational agency (e.g., state department of education) oversees the due process complaint procedures and the supervision of the administrative court system. IDEA's regulations allow the state educational agency to compensate the IHOs.[40]

The burden of persuasion in due process hearings, as affirmed by the U.S. Supreme Court in *Schaffer ex rel. Schaffer v. Weast*,[41] is placed on the parties initiating the due process complaint. *Schaffer* effectively puts the burden of proof on parents in most due process hearings, because they are the ones who typically file due process complaints. Parties appealing final administrative orders have ninety days to do so, unless state law dictates otherwise.[42]

According to IDEA, exhaustion of remedies—in other words, pursuing the administrative due process hearing—is necessary when the parents' claims are related to identification, evaluation, or educational placements for their children.[43] Even though parents are required to exhaust their administrative remedies before they initiate civil actions, the courts have granted exceptions in a number of recent cases.[44] For example, when parents file their claims under other statutes, they are typically seeking damages premised on violations of laws other than IDEA.[45] In an illustrative case from Oklahoma, the Tenth Circuit Court of Appeals determined that exhaustion is not required where parents are pursuing a common law tort claim.[46] The damages sought by the parents in this case related to a situation that allegedly occurred when school personnel used timeouts and physical abuse as disciplinary measures with their son.

Similarly, if the parents are seeking relief that would not be available under IDEA, the courts have not required the parents to first exhaust their administrative remedies. The Fifth Circuit Court of Appeals ruled in favor of Texas parents who claimed that school officials failed to prevent the sexual abuse of their child with a disability.[47] The court determined that exhaustion would not be required where IDEA does not provide adequate relief; namely, the court asserted that the injuries were non-educational and the relief sought would not be available under IDEA.

Courts may also decide to grant an exception, based on the parents' complaints, because it would be futile for the parents to exhaust their administrative remedies prior to initiating civil actions. In an illustrative Pennsylvania case, the Third Circuit Court of Appeals concluded that parents should not be required to exhaust IDEA administrative remedies.[48] According to the court, the parents' action sought enforcement of a favorable hearing officer decision; thus, the court asserted that not only would exhaustion be futile, but it also was not permitted under IDEA, which provides appeals only for aggrieved parties.

Judicial Review

Federal and state courts have authority under IDEA to review administrative proceedings, hear additional evidence, and determine whether relief is appropriate.[49] Thus, after the administrative proceedings are concluded and orders finalized, either party—parents or school district—may appeal to state or federal courts. Despite the ability of courts to review administrative decisions, the U.S. Supreme Court has cautioned judges to avoid substituting their perspectives for the decisions of school experts and authorities.[50] Therefore, a level of deference is given to both the school personnel and the administrative IHOs.

State Complaints

States are required to adopt complaint procedures that are separate from the due process procedures provided for in the IDEA.[51] The state complaint provisions[52] are primarily focused on violations of the IDEA Part B or Part B regulations by a public agency. State complaints may be brought by an individual or an organization, whereas only a parent or public agency may file a due process complaint. For state claims, the time period for alleging a violation is limited to up to one year following the alleged violation, although it is possible for the SEA to extend that time period.[53] The specific procedure for filing a state complaint varies by state but, in each case, the party will file a formal complaint with the state department of education. The complainant may be alleging a violation on behalf of one child (e.g., that the child did not receive a FAPE) or multiple children (e.g., that a district policy, procedure, or practice violates IDEA).[54]

After the state complaint is filed, the SEA usually has sixty calendar days to resolve the matter. The SEA may choose to conduct an on-site investigation, and must accept additional information about the complaint from both the complainant and the LEA. After reviewing the relevant information, the SEA issues a written decision. The decision may list corrective actions that the LEA must complete within a specified time period. For example, a LEA may be instructed to reimburse parents for an educational expense such as speech therapy. The state claims are viewed as efficient and effective means of resolving disputes between schools and parents because they offer an alternative to due process hearings, which tend to be more formal, expensive, and adversarial.[55]

Recommendations for Practice

Ideally, the special education due process provisions should function as part of an integrated system for schools and parents to work together to resolve disputes; however, this is not always the case. When parents file administrative due process complaints, school districts generally seek legal advice from attorneys. This often results in an adversarial relationship between school officials and parents, rather than allowing the opportunity to reach a more collaborative solution between both parties. Is there a better way to handle the conflict-oriented process? Given the number of states that continue to report high numbers of due process hearings, efforts to overhaul the legalistic framework in special education are still needed.[56] Instead of pointing fingers and laying blame, the involved parties should be encouraged to focus on good-faith efforts to resolve matters with constructive dialogue.

The emphasis on mediation and resolution sessions in recent years has been seen by some as a positive way to improve results for students and overcome the adversarial relationship between schools and parents in due process hearings.[57] In fact, several states reportedly have experienced significant declines in due process hearings as a result of mediation or resolution meetings.[58]

Additional strategies for de-escalating disputes may include inviting all parties to come to the table for a meeting during which they focus on student's interests. Other ideas include the facilitated IEP,[59] used in some districts as a mechanism to reduce disputes between schools and parents.[60] IDEA does not require that states or districts provide facilitated IEPs in the same manner it outlines requirements for resolution sessions and mediations. Facilitated IEPs are proposed as a non-legal approach to the IEP as an agreement-making, rather than adversarial, process. They are typically implemented before a dispute has arisen; thus, they occur prior to parents filing a due process complaint. Although overnight success is unlikely, reports thus far suggest that some states have experienced positive outcomes using the facilitated IEPs.[61]

Although it is unlikely that schools can avoid all disputes with parents regarding the educational rights of their children under the IDEA, there are many strategies that school officials can adopt to promote positive relationships with parents. For example, school officials who are responsive to parental concerns are less likely to be seen as unwilling to resolve disputes without the parents' threat of legal action. Similarly, when school officials are able to demonstrate their clear understanding of IDEA, particularly requirements that are pertinent to IEP development and implementation, they are more likely to be able to build trusting relationships with parents.

Providing special education teachers and general education teachers with the knowledge and skills needed to address the educational needs and rights of students with disabilities is another strategy that schools should adopt to promote parental trust and confidence in the school. The focus on special education legal literacy has gained increasing attention, given the growing population of students with disabilities being served in classrooms and the general education setting.[62] Similarly, parents may seek further legal training in special education in order to better understand what school districts are and are not legally required to provide to students with disabilities.

Given the nature of due process hearings as reactionary, rather than proactive, efforts to resolve disputes between parents and school officials, the alternate mechanisms—including resolution sessions, mediation, and facilitated IEPs—are just a few of the options that could have a positive impact on school and parent relationships.[63] In addition, due process hearings are accompanied by incredibly high financial (e.g., attorney fees, penalties, and remedial services) and emotional costs.[64] Many opponents of the due process system also cite concerns about how the student is not the center of attention; rather, the focus becomes the negative relationship between parents and school personnel.[65] Without an effort made to reduce this high level of conflict in the school setting, due process hearings will continue at a great cost to taxpayers and the children who need quality services.[66] Therefore, any efforts made to reduce the total number of due process hearings, and instead mediate any conflict in a positive manner, will ultimately improve the education of students with disabilities.[67]

Endnotes

[1]   20 U.S.C. § 1415 (2012).

[2]   20 U.S.C. § 1400(d) (2012).

[3]   *See* 20 U.S.C. § 1412(a)(5)(B) (2012). School districts are required to consider a range of placements, including regular classes, special classes, special schools, home instruction, and instruction in hospitals and institutions. *See also* 34 C.F.R. § 300.115(b)(1) (2017). Further, school districts must provide supplementary services in conjunction with regular class placements. 34 C.F.R. § 300.115(b)(2) (2017).

[4]   20 U.S.C. § 1414(d)(1)(A)(i) (2012); 34 C.F.R. § 300.320(a) (2017).

[5]   The term "parent" is defined through IDEA's regulations to include a biological or adoptive parent; a foster parent (legally permitting); a guardian authorized to make educational decisions for the child (but not the State if the child is a ward of the State); an individual acting in place of biological or adoptive parent (e.g., grandparent, stepparent); or an appointed surrogate parent. 34 C.F.R. §300.30(a) (2017).

[6]   *See* Susan Clark, *Parental Rights, in* A GUIDE TO SPECIAL EDUCATION LAW (Shaver & Decker, ed. 2017).

[7]   20 U.S.C. § 1415(b)(6)(A) (2012); *see also* 34 C.F.R. § 300.507(a) (2017). In addition, a school district or other educational entity may, under certain circumstances, file a request for an impartial due process hearing. *Id.* It is important to note that parents are typically the filing party in a special education due process hearing.

[8]   34 C.F.R. § 300.506(2017).

[9]   20 U.S.C. § 1415(f)(1)(B) (2012).

[10]   20 U.S.C. § 1415(e).

[11]   20 U.S.C. §§ 1415(f)-(g) (2012).

[12]   20 U.S.C. § 1415(i)(2)(A) (2012).

[13]   34 C.F.R. §§300.151-300.153 (2017).

[14]   Pub. L. No. 108-446, 118 Stat. 2467 (2004).

[15]   34 C.F.R. § 300.511 (2017).

[16]   *Id.*

[17]   20 U.S.C. § 1415(f)(1)(B)(i) (2012); 34 C.F.R. § 300.510(a) (2017) (relevant members of the IEP team are identified jointly by the parent and the school).

[18]   20 U.S.C. § 1415(i)(3)(D)(iii) (2012); 34 C.F.R. § 300.517(c)(2)(iii) (2017).

[19]   34 C.F.R. § 300.510(a)(1)-(2) (2017).

[20]   20 U.S.C. § 1415(f)(1)(B)(ii) (2012); 34 C.F.R. § 300.510(b)(1) (2017).

[21]   34 C.F.R. § 300.510(b)(3) (2017).

[22]   34 C.F.R. § 300.322(d) (2017).

[23]   34 C.F.R. § 300.510(b)(4) (2017).

[24]   34 C.F.R. §300.510(b)(5) (2017).

[25]   Candace Cortiella, *Resolving Disagreements Between Parents and Schools: Special Education Law and Resolution Meetings*, 38 EXCEPTIONAL PARENT 67 (2008).

[26]   34 C.F.R. § 300.506(a) (2017).

[27]   34 C.F.R. § 300.506(b) (2017).

[28] *Id.*

[29] 20 U.S.C. § 1415(e)(2)(F)(i) (2012).

[30] 20 U.S.C. § 1415(e)(2)(F)(ii) (2012).

[31] 20 U.S.C. § 1415(e)(2)(F)(iii) (2012).

[32] Katherine McMurtrey, *The IDEA and the Use of Mediation and Collaborative Dispute Resolution in Due Process Disputes*, 2016 J. Disp. Resol. 187, 197 (2016) (describing the role and presence of attorneys in mediation).

[33] *Id.* at 196.

[34] 20 U.S.C. § 1415(l) (2012).

[35] 20 U.S.C. § 1415(b)(6) (2012); 34 C.F.R. § 300.507(a) (2017).

[36] 20 U.S.C. § 1415(f)(3)(C) (2012).

[37] 20 U.S.C. § 1415(f)(3)(D) (2012).

[38] 34 C.F.R. § 300.508(a)(1) (2017).

[39] 34 C.F.R. § 300.511(c) (2017).

[40] 34 C.F.R. § 300.511(c)(2) (2017).

[41] 546 U.S. 49 (2005).

[42] 20 U.S.C. § 1415(i)(2)(B) (2012).

[43] 34 C.F.R. § 300.507(a) (2017).

[44] *See, e.g.*, D.M. v. N.J. Dep't of Educ., 801 F.3d 205 (3d Cir. 2015); Stewart v. Waco Indep. Sch. Dist., 711 F.3d 513 (5th Cir. 2013).

[45] F.H. *ex rel.* Hall v. Memphis City Sch., 764 F.3d 638 (6th Cir. 2014).

[46] Muskrat v. Deer Creek Pub. Sch., 715 F.3d 775 (10th Cir. 2013).

[47] Stewart v. Waco Indep. Sch. Dist., 711 F.3d 513 (5th Cir. 2013).

[48] D.E. v. Cent. Dauphin Sch. Dist., 765 F.3d 260 (3d Cir. 2014).

[49] 20 U.S.C. § 1415(i)(2)(C)(iii) (2012).

[50] Bd. of Educ. v. Rowley, 458 U.S. 176, 180–81 (1982); Endrew F. v. Douglas Cnty. Sch. Dist. RE-1, __ U.S. __, 137 S. Ct. 988 (2017).

[51] 45 C.F.R. §121a.602 (2017).

[52] 34 C.F.R. §§300.151-300.153 (2017).

[53] 34 C.F.R. §300.151 (2017).

[54] OSERS Memorandum, *Dispute Resolution Procedures under Part B of the Individuals with Disabilities Education Act (Part B)*, U.S. Dep't of Educ. (Jul. 23, 2013). https://www2. ed.gov/policy/speced/guid/idea/memosdcltrs/acccombinedosersdisputeresolutionqafinalmemo-7-23-13.pdf.

[55] *Id.*

[56] *Trends in Dispute Resolution under the Individuals with Disabilities Education Act (IDEA)*, Ctr. for Appropriate Dispute Resolution in Special Educ. (Oct. 2016), http://www.cadreworks. org/sites/default/files/resources/TrendsinDisputeResolutionundertheIDEAOCT16.pdf.

[57] *See* OSERS Memorandum, *supra* note 54.

[58] *See* McMurtrey. *supra* note 32 (proposing mediation as an alternative to due process).

[59] *See, e.g.*, Tracy G. Mueller, *IEP Facilitation: A Promising Approach to Resolving Conflicts Between Families and Schools*, 41 Teaching Exceptional Child. 60 (2009) (describing the benefits and use of facilitated IEPs).

[60] Reece Erlichman, Michael Gregory, & Alisia St. Florian, *The Settlement Conference as a Dispute Resolution Option in Special Education*, 29 Ohio St. J. on Disp. Resol. 407, 409 (2014).

[61] *Id.*

[62] *See, e.g.*, Janet R. Decker & Kevin Brady, *Increasing School Employees' Special Education Legal Literacy*, 36 J. of Sch. Public Relations 231 (2016).

[63] Ctr. for Appropriate Dispute Resolution in Special Educ. (2004), *Facilitated IEP meetings: An emerging practice*, http://www.cadreworks.org/resources/literature-article/facilitatediep-meetings-emerging-practice-0 (last visited Jun.2, 2017).

[64] *See, e.g.*, Joy Markowitz, Eileen Ahearn, & Judy Schrag, *Dispute Resolution: A Review of Systems in Selected States*, (June 2003), http://www.nasdse.org/DesktopModules/DNNspot-

Store/ProductFiles/130_6c4439ce-b83c-4dfd-8e3b-eba8f335a08a.pdf, (arguing that costs associated with due process hearings include how emotionally draining the entire process is for parents, teachers, administrators, and central office staff).

[65] *See, e.g.,* Debra Chopp, *School Districts and Families under the IDEA: Collaborative in Theory, Adversarial in Fact,* 32 J. OF NAT'L ASSN. OF ADMIN. LAW JUDICIARY 423 (2012); Cali Cope-Kasten, *Bidding (Fair)well to Due Process: The Need for a Fairer Final Stage in Special Education Dispute Resolution.* 42 J. OF LAW & EDUC. 501 (2013).

[66] Sasha Pudelski, *Rethinking Special Education Due Process: A Proposal for the Next Reauthorization of the Individuals with Disabilities Education Act,* Am. Ass'n of School Adm'rs http://www.aasa.org/uploadedFiles/Policy_and_Advocacy/Public_Policy_Resources/Special_Education/AASARethinkingSpecialEdDueProcess.pdf.

[67] *See, e.g.,* Timothy E. Gilsbach, *Special Education Due Process Hearing Requests under IDEA: A Hearing Should Not Always be Required,* B.Y.U. EDUC. & L.J. (2015) (proposing to reduce the number of due process hearings through the use of prehearing motions).

Chapter 12

Current Issues in Special Education

Allan G. Osborne, Jr. and Susan C. Bon

Introduction

In the 1970s, Congress strengthened the educational rights of students with disabilities, inspired in part by early litigation to gain equal educational opportunities on their behalf.[1] Most notably, in 1975 Congress enacted legislation requiring states, through local school boards, to guarantee all students with disabilities free appropriate public education (FAPEs) in the least restrictive environment. The Education for All Handicapped Children Act, currently known as the Individuals with Disabilities Education Act (IDEA),[2] changed the landscape in public schools. Since the enactment of the IDEA, boards have confronted the increasingly complicated task of providing necessary educational services and programs for students with a wide variety of disabilities in the face of numerous parental challenges to the services offered.

Historically, most IDEA suits centered on procedural issues and contested placements. The central issue in most 2016 cases was whether school boards offered students FAPEs. Other suits addressed a myriad of procedural issues. In addition, courts were called on to fashion equitable remedies when boards failed to live up to their statutory duties. In this respect, disputes over reimbursement of attorney fees to prevailing parents in special education cases remains a much-litigated topic.

The IDEA defines a FAPE as a program consisting of needed special education and related services.[3] The emphasis on individualization, notwithstanding, the IDEA does not establish clear-cut substantive standards by which the adequacy of those services can be measured. The IDEA directs board to provide qualified students with specially designed instruction[4] in conformance with their individualized education programs (IEPs).[5]

The Supreme Court has interpreted the IDEA as obligating school boards to furnish students with disabilities personalized instruction with support services sufficient to allow them to benefit from the education they receive.[6] At the same time, the Justices cautioned lower courts not to impose their views of preferable educational methods on school personnel.[7] Nevertheless, hearing officers and judges must decide what level of services is required to meet the IDEA's minimum standards.

As in previous years, in 2016 litigation was filed on behalf of students with disabilities under Section 504 of the Rehabilitation Act (Section 504)[8] and the Americans with Disabilities Act (ADA)[9] as well as the IDEA. The plaintiffs in these actions primarily alleged that students were subjected to discriminatory treatment based on their disabilities.

Entitlement to Services

As a condition of receiving federal funds under the IDEA, states must make ensure that a FAPE is available to all resident children with disabilities between the ages of three and twenty-one, inclusive.[10] The IDEA does contain two significant limitations to this requirement, though. First, states do not have to provide services to students aged three through five and eighteen through twenty-one if doing so is inconsistent with their laws, practices, or court orders with respect to the provision of public education to children in those age ranges.[11] Second, states are not obligated to provide special education to youth between the ages of eighteen through twenty-one who are incarcerated in adult facilities if they had not been previously identified as having disabilities and did not have IEPs at the time of being incarcerated.[12] Further, students who graduated from high school with regular diplomas are no longer eligible under the IDEA.[13]

The IDEA defines students with disabilities as those who have at least one statutorily identified impairment and need special education and related services due to those impairments.[14] The IDEA's regulations[15] further define the identified disabilities.

As a group, while students attending nonpublic schools are entitled to some benefits under the IDEA, individual children do not have such a right. Under the IDEA, school boards are required to spend only a proportionate share of their federal special education dollars to provide services to children whose parents unilaterally placed them in nonpublic schools.[16]

Eligibility

The First Circuit held that a child with a reading fluency deficit was still eligible for special education services even though her overall performance level was excellent.[17] Reversing an order of the federal trial court in Maine, the panel pointed out that while the student's overall academic performance may have been a relevant factor to the extent it was an indicator of her reading fluency skills, her eligibility determination should have considered the nexus between academic measures and the area of her deficiency. The record revealed that the child's academic record was excellent but she scored low on tests that specifically measured her reading fluency.

In a case from Kentucky, the Sixth Circuit affirmed that educational performance may encompass more than academic achievement but did not include a child's behavior at home or in the community.[18] The court agreed that a child whose condition did not adversely affect his educational performance was ineligible for special education.

The Ninth Circuit found that a child from California who exhibited serious behavioral problems but performed satisfactorily in academics was eligible for special education under the IDEA.[19] The court observed that the child had been receiving services that were not normally offered to general education students which eased his impairments. The court also commented that the student's disabilities adversely affected his attendance.

When a mother in Virginia disagreed with an IEP team's assessment that her child's primary disability was intellectual and requested a due process hearing, a hearing officer rejected her challenge because she had not consented to the eligibility determination pursuant to commonwealth law. Reversing a trial court's order that the child was not disabled, an appellate panel reasoned that the child's entitlement to special education and related services could not be contingent on parental consent to her eligibility review.[20]

Classification

The federal trial court in the District of Columbia decreed that a child involved in many disciplinary incidents and attempted suicide met the criteria for classification as seriously emotionally disturbed under the IDEA.[21] The court acknowledged that the student exhibited inappropriate behavior under normal circumstances by attempting to kill himself, was unable to build or keep satisfactory interpersonal relationships, and generally had a pervasive mood of unhappiness.

Procedural Safeguards

The IDEA includes a system of due process safeguards to ensure that students with disabilities are properly identified, evaluated, and placed according to the law's requirements.[22] The IDEA directs school boards to give parents or guardians of children with disabilities opportunities to participate in the development of the IEPs for and placement of their children.[23] Moreover, the IDEA requires school board officials to provide written notice and obtain parental consent prior to evaluating children[24] or making initial placements.[25] Once students are placed in special education, boards need to provide parents with proper notice before initiating changes in their placements.[26] While administrative or judicial actions are pending, boards may not change student placements without parental consent,[27] orders of hearing officers,[28] or judicial decrees.[29]

The IDEA imposes an affirmative obligation on school board officials to identify, locate, and evaluate all children with disabilities who reside within their districts.[30] This includes children whose parents have placed their children in nonpublic schools.[31] As to students in nonpublic students, the IDEA's regulations place the child find obligation on the boards in the districts where their schools are located.[32]

School personnel must conduct initial evaluations before placing students in special education programs.[33] Evaluators need to complete all assessments within 60 days of when parents consented to the evaluations.[34] All evaluations must be multidisciplinary, meaning they should consist of a variety of assessment tools and strategies to obtain relevant information in the suspected areas of disability.[35]

Students with disabilities may be entitled to independent evaluations at public expense if their parents disagree with their school boards' evaluations.[36] Boards can challenge requests for independent evaluations via administrative hearings and parents are not entitled to obtain independent evaluations at public expense if the board evaluations are shown to be appropriate.[37]

The IDEA requires IEPs to contain statements of students' current educational performance, annual goals and short term objectives, specific educational services to be provided, the extent to which they can participate in general education, the dates of initiation and duration of services, and evaluation criteria to measure whether they are meeting their objectives.[38] Also, IEPs must include statements about how students' impairments affect their abilities to be involved in and progress in general education curricula along with addressing modifications needed to allow them to participate in those curricula. IEP teams must review the status of all students with IEPs at least annually[39] and reevaluate them at least every three years unless their parent(s) and school officials agree that doing so is unnecessary.[40]

Child Find

In another installment of a long-running class-action dispute, the federal trial court in the District of Columbia was of the opinion that the school board failed to adhere to the IDEA's child find requirements as to students with disabilities between the ages of three and five.[41] The court declared that the board separately and specifically failed to identify substantial numbers of children in need of special education, timely evaluate them or make eligibility determinations, and provide smooth and effective transitions for them from Part C to Part B of the IDEA. The court recognized that although the board made good faith efforts and reforms, it still did not have effective policies in place to meet its legal obligations to all students of the identified subclasses.

The federal trial court in the District of Columbia ascertained that a child's suicide attempt put charter school officials on notice that he potentially had a disability qualifying him for services under the IDEA. The court concluded that the failure of board officials to evaluate the student at that time violated the IDEA's child find requirements.[42]

A school board in New York developed a Section 504 service plan for a student who was diagnosed as having Tourette syndrome. After the child was diagnosed as also having obsessive compulsive disorder and attention deficit hyperactivity disorder, board officials provided him with special education services pursuant to his IEP. A federal trial court, remarking that the child had done exceptionally well on his Section 504 plans, posited that school personnel had no evidence to suspect he needed special education earlier.[43]

In another case, the same court in New York maintained that although school board officials had reason to suspect that a child had a disability, they had no basis on which to think he required special education.[44] Conceding that the child's failure to perform in school was due to his absences, the court added that the IDEA's child find provision do not require boards to evaluate every child who has academic difficulties.

A federal trial court in Texas was convinced that a mother's request for a FAPE gave school board officials reason to suspect that her child had a disability and so needed special education.[45] Yet, the court treated the delay of three months in evaluating the child as reasonable and as not violating the board's child find obligations.

Evaluation

The Fifth Circuit vacated and remanded an order of a federal trial court in Louisiana denying a parental request for reimbursement for an independent evaluation.[46] Noting that such a need not adhere perfectly with state standards, the panel contended that the trial court had not squarely addressed whether the independent evaluation was substantially compliant.

In the first of three cases from California, the Ninth Circuit was of the view that school officials failed to conduct a proper evaluation of a child who exhibited signs of developmental disabilities and autism in all areas of suspected disability.[47] Because the board did not assess the child for autism using sound and reliable methods, the court asserted that it denied him a FAPE insofar as his IEP goals were likely inappropriate. The Ninth Circuit next court affirmed that a child with autism was not entitled to an independent evaluation because his guardian entered into a settlement agreement with the school board in which she stipulated that specified assessments were all that were needed to create an IEP.[48]

The Ninth Circuit then stated that school board officials were remiss in not conducting a health assessment as part of the eligibility evaluation of a child with multiple disabilities.[49] The court was persuaded that by not assessing how the child's health and medications impacted his performance, the board denied him a FAPE because had they done so, they would have more seriously considered alternative services.

According to the Eleventh Circuit, school officials in Florida did not deny a mother's request for an independent evaluation because she chose an evaluator whose fee exceeded the amount the board approved.[50] The court emphasized that the mother's actions, not the board's denial, sabotaged the process.

In Illinois, a federal trial court ruled that school board officials did not fail to evaluate a young child in all areas of disability by not conducting a behavioral assessment despite concerns expressed by his parents and preschool staff.[51] The court did not treat those concerns as substantial enough to warrant a formal evaluation for a behavioral impairment. Likewise, the federal trial court in Hawaii indicated that a child's in-home behavioral issues did not establish that he needed a behavioral reevaluation.[52]

A federal trial court in New York was satisfied that although school board officials failed to reevaluate a child within three years, it did not deny her a FAPE.[53] The court held that the IEP team had sufficient evaluative materials with which to develop the child's IEP.

In the first of three cases from the District of Columbia, the federal trial court decided that school board officials had the raw information necessary to develop a child's IEP because his evaluations sufficiently identified his specific deficits.[54] The court next observed that a reevaluation the board conducted fell short of the IDEA's standards because it did not include a new round of tests and analysis.[55] Further, the court directed officials at a charter school to either fund a requested independent evaluation or seek a hearing to demonstrate the appropriateness of its evaluation.[56] Because school officials had done neither, the court awarded reimbursement for an evaluation the mother obtained privately.

The federal trial court in Connecticut found that a mother's seeking a more in-depth analysis of the assessments conducted by her school board was sufficient to reveal her disagreement with its evaluation.[57] The court thus granted the mother's request for reimbursement for an independent evaluation because board officials had not sought a due process hearing to adjudicate the questions of the independent evaluation.

Rights of Parents or Guardians

A federal trial court in New York decreed that a school board violated parents' rights to be involved in the IEP process by failing to provide them with copies of their daughter's evaluation reports ahead of an IEP meeting.[58] The court also faulted the board for failing to conform to the IDEA's notice requirements about a proposed change in the child's IEP and for not giving them information about the class to which she was assigned until shortly before the start of the school year. The court pointed out that collectively these violations displayed an indifference to the IDEA's procedural requirements that frustrated the parents' rights to be informed about and involved in the decision-making process and to challenge the IEP on substantive grounds.

Developing Individualized Education Programs

The Ninth Circuit wrote that a school board in California violated a mother's right to informed consent by failing to provide her with copies of all of her child's assessments, treatment plans, and progress notes.[59] Specifying that the IDEA gives parents the right to examine all pertinent educational records, the court commented that this interfered with her right to participate fully in the process. The same court, in another case from California, reasoned that educational officials violated parents' rights to fully participate in the IEP process when they failed to evaluate their child completely, thereby depriving them of information necessary to allow them to participate meaningfully.[60]

The Eleventh Circuit affirmed that a school board in Florida did not fail to include a parent in an IEP meeting.[61] Acknowledging that the IDEA allows boards to conduct IEP meetings if parents refuse to attend, the court maintained that under the circumstances, the team was justified in conducting the meeting without the mother. The mother either missed or refused to attend four scheduled meeting and declined an invitation to attend via telephone. Similarly, Second Circuit explained that a board in Connecticut did not violate parents' rights by convening an IEP meeting in their absence because they had ample opportunities to participate.[62]

In the first of five cases from New York City, the Second Circuit affirmed that the New York City Board of Education (NYCBOE) violated the parental rights to participate in the development of the IEP of a child who was bullied.[63] The court remarked that the IEP team's refusal to discuss the bullying significantly impeded the parents' right to participate and consequently impaired the substance of the IEP, thereby prevented them from assessing the adequacy of the final document. In the second case from New York City, a federal trial court ascertained that officials of the NYCBOE denied parents' meaningful participation in the IEP process by failing to provide them with an IEP and placement notification in a timely fashion.[64]

The third IEP dispute from New York City resulted in a federal trial court's granting the NYCBOE's motion for summary judgment in response to a parental claim officials denied them the opportunity to participate fully in the development of their child's IEP.[65] The court determined that the parental failure to persuade the IEP team to adopt their placement recommendation did not translate to a deprivation of their rights. The court was also swayed that the IEP team used appropriate evaluative materials to formulate the child's IEP.

A federal trial court in New York, in the fourth case, was convinced that an IEP team, although improperly constituted, had enough accurate information on which to develop a child's IEP.[66] In the final case from New York, a federal trial court recognized that insofar as procedural errors in the development of a child's IEP, such as the absence of a general education teacher at the meeting, were harmless, they did not deny him a FAPE.[67]

In Illinois, a federal trial court declared that an IEP team did not predetermine a child's placement in an emotional support program.[68] The court was of the opinion that parental disagreement with the placement did not mean it was predetermined, especially because school personnel incorporated recommendations from an independent evaluation into his IEP.

The federal trial court in Connecticut uncovered little evidence supporting a mother's claim that she was prevented from participating fully in the development of her daughter's IEP.[69] Rather, the court thought board officials provided evidence showing that the mother, child, and their expert consultant were all allowed to speak at the meeting.

Change in Placement

In a case with atypical circumstances, a school board developed a two-stage IEP calling for a student to receive the services of a full-time teacher and paraprofessional for the last few weeks of one school year but to be placed in a self-contained special education class at the beginning of the next school year. After the family moved over the summer, the parents objected when their new school board proposed an IEP comparable to the second part of the child's former school's IEP. A federal trial court in Washington stated that the self-contained classroom was the child's placement for stay-put purposes. The Ninth Circuit affirmed that insofar as the parents had not challenged the IEP prepared in their son's former school, it constituted the status quo.[70]

In another case involving a move over the summer, a child with intellectual disabilities went to live with relatives after his mother passed away. When the new school board developed an IEP substantially reducing the services the child would receive, his father sought a temporary restraining order for a stay-put placement. In the meantime, the father re-enrolled his son in his former school temporarily so his services would continue. Although a federal trial court in California viewed it as likely that the father would prevail on the merits, the balance of equities did not favor him to the extent it would justify the granting of a restraining order.[71] The court emphasized while the IDEA requires new boards to implement IEPs similar to the students' former ones when they transfer during school years, it is silent about transfers between school years. Even so, the court did not interpret the IDEA's silence regarding between-year transfers as indicating that such students are exempted from stay-put protections.

The mother of a child with autism enrolled him in a neighboring school district pursuant to Colorado's school-choice law, seeking a stay-put order when officials in that district refused to re-enroll the child the following year. The Tenth Circuit affirmed the stay-put order, agreeing that the neighboring district was the child's school of attendance.[72]

In a case from the District of Columbia, the trial court treated a child's private school placement as her then-current placement because she was there as a result of a due process hearing.[73] The court noted that a reimbursement order was sufficient to establish placement for stay-put purposes because the hearing officer decided that the placement was appropriate. Similarly, the federal trial court in Hawaii issued a stay-put ordering allowing a child to continue in a private school placement throughout proceedings challenging the education department's proposal to return him to his home school.[74]

According to a federal trial court in Illinois, school personnel did not violate the IDEA's stay-put provision by separating a child who exhibited behavioral problems from his peers during lunch and recess.[75] The court concluded that the lunch and recess arrangements were consistent with the child's IEP behavior intervention plan.

Dispute Resolution

Even though Congress envisioned cooperative efforts to develop IEPs, it recognized that insofar as disputes between school officials and parents were possible, it included detailed mechanisms in the IDEA to resolve disagreements between the parties including resolution meetings,[76] mediation,[77] administrative due process hearings,[78] and, as a final resort, appeals to the courts.[79] The IDEA obligates school officials to schedule resolution sessions with parents within 15 days of the receipt of complaints. While resolution sessions are mandatory unless waived by mutual consent, mediation is voluntary and may not be used to deny or delay parental rights to administrative hearings.

Parents may request impartial due process hearings if they disagree with the actions or recommendations school personnel about proposed IEPs or other aspects of FAPEs for their children. Parties must request hearings within two years of the dates they knew or should have known about the actions on which the complaints are based.[80] Even so, parents can be excused from meeting this timeline if they can show that school officials misrepresented that the problems complained of had been resolved or withheld required information from the parents.[81] A party not satisfied with the outcome of administrative proceedings has the right to appeal to state or federal courts. However, all administrative remedies must be exhausted prior to resort to the courts unless it is futile to do so. Appeals must be filed within 90 days of final administrative decisions.[82]

The Supreme Court, in *Schaffer ex rel. Schaffer v. Weast*,[83] placed the burden of proof in administrative proceedings on the parties challenging the IEPs, thereby effectively placing the burden of proof on parents in most disputes because they, rather than boards, typically challenge IEPs. The IDEA empowers the judiciary to review the records of the administrative proceedings, hear additional evidence, and "grant such relief as the courts determine appropriate"[84] based on the preponderance of evidence standard. Still, the Justices cautioned lower courts not to substitute their views of proper educational methodology for that of competent school authorities.[85] Parties appealing final administrative orders have 90 days to do so unless state laws dictates otherwise.

Resolution Sessions and Mediation

After the mother of a child with disabilities filed a due process complaint but began negotiations with her daughter's charter school via a resolution session, the parties reached an agreement, but only after the resolution period expired. When the mother later filed suit seeking to enforce the agreement, a federal trial court in Pennsylvania rejected the claim on the basis it lacked jurisdiction because the agreement was finalized outside of the resolution period.[86]

Administrative Hearings

As in the past, in 2016 school boards moved to dismiss multiple cases, often claiming parents had not complied with the IDEA by exhausting administrative remedies. Four courts refused to allow parents to circumvent the IDEA's procedures by filing suit under Section 504 or the ADA.

The Second Circuit agreed that a mother in New York had to first exhaust the IDEA's administrative remedies because it provides relief for her grievance.[87] The Third Circuit upheld the dismissal of a suit from New Jersey on the basis that the nature of the parental allegations implicated a potential need for special education and related services.[88] In like fashion, the Sixth Circuit affirmed the dismissal of a case from Ohio because the parental request for damages was available in an administrative hearing.[89] The court added that the parents could not avoid exhaustion by seeking damages under other statutes that were not permitted under the IDEA.[90] Using an analogous rationale, a federal trial court in Texas dismissed a case brought under Title IX by the parents of a student who was sexually assaulted.[91]

In contrast, a federal trial court in Virginia denied a school board's motion to dismiss a suit for damages brought under Section 504. The parents convinced the court that exhaustion would have been futile because monetary damages were unavailable under the IDEA.[92] Further, a federal trial court in Pennsylvania was satisfied that once parents utilized the IDEA's administrative process and obtained a final order for compensatory education, they could proceed with damages claims under Section 504 and the ADA.[93]

Given the amount of time it takes for disputes to reach final resolution, it is not unusual for challenged IEPs to expire while appeals are pending, necessitating the development of subsequent plans. In one such instance, a federal trial court in Washington held that parents did not need to exhaust administrative remedies on the second IEP because it was substantially like the first.[94] The court reflected that requiring exhaustion of the subsequent IEP would have been unduly burdensome, a waste of resources, inadequate, and potentially futile.

Three courts addressed whether parents had, in fact, exhausted administrative remedies. In the first, the federal trial court in Massachusetts decided parents who procured an order from a hearing but chose to file an ADA claim rather than appeal had exhausted administrative remedies.[95]

Next, the federal trial court in New Mexico deemed that parents whose son was disciplined exhausted administrative remedies even though they had not requested an expedited hearing, but rather, filed a due process complaint under the IDEA's usual procedures.[96] The court ruled that the expedited process was an available, but not mandatory, procedure. In the court's view, the parents were not required to seek judicial review of their IDEA claim before bringing the ADA suit. In the third case, the federal trial court in Hawaii dismissed a mother's claim that the IEP team committed a procedural error because she failed to raise it at the administrative hearing.[97]

The Ninth Circuit affirmed that an administrative law judge (ALJ) had the authority to order the California Children's Services (CCS) to provide additional occupational therapy to a child with severe disabilities.[98] The child received special education from his local school board along with related services from CCS. The court maintained that occupational therapy services in a child's IEP, whether medically or educationally necessary, were related services subject to administrative hearing review.

In an appeal of an adverse hearing order, a parent from Connecticut alleged that the hearing officer was biased. The federal trial court found that throughout the proceedings the hearing officer made comments regarding the parent's comportment and her daughter while their attorney made repeated attempts to get them to respect the process.[99] Although the court conceded that the hearing officer may have been unnecessarily curt and harsh at times, this was insufficient to render the process biased.

Administrative hearings in Puerto Rico are conducted in Spanish while federal cases are conducted in English. As such, the federal trial court reasoned that the commonwealth's education department was responsible for the costs of translating administrative hearing records from Spanish to English when hearing decisions are appealed to the court.[100]

In a second case from Puerto Rico, an ALJ dismissed a mother's complaint that the Department of Education had not provided her child with an appropriate IEP or placement as moot because the school year ended. On further review, the federal trial court observed that the ALJ erred because a school year is too short a time to litigate an IEP dispute fully and such a controversy is likely to evade review because the ponderous administrative and judicial processes are usually not completed until after a school year has ended.[101] The court indicated it was likely the parental concerns would have been re-occurred in subsequent IEPs.

The District of Columbia Circuit affirmed that parents cannot seek judicial enforcement of a hearing officer's order.[102] The trial court had ascertained that while the IDEA creates a right to challenge an adverse administrative action, it does not provide a cause of action to challenge the implementation of a favorable order. Rather, in the court's opinion, such a complaint must be resolved by a jurisdiction's education agency.

The first of two cases from Pennsylvania involved a defunct charter school and the commonwealth's education agency. A federal trial court explained that the complaint against the department was not moot, even though officials agreed to provide compensatory services if ordered to do so, because it was required to remedy the charter school's FAPE violations and could be required to respond to the complaint.[103] In a separate case, also involving a closed charter school, the court acknowledged that a hearing officer erred by not rendering a substantive order on whether the children had been denied a FAPE.[104] The parents had reached a settlement agreement with officials before the school closed but claimed that they breached the agreement.

Judicial Actions

The Tenth Circuit, vacating an order of the federal trial court in Utah, posited that the IDEA does not allow judges to remand placement issues to IEP teams for resolution.[105] The court pointed out that an IEP team cannot assume the authority of a hearing officer, specifying that affording the agency that failed to provide a FAPE to devise a remedy for its violation was at odds with the IDEA's review scheme.

A federal trial court in Washington granted parents' motion to supplement the record with evidence of events that occurred after an administrative hearing.[106] In admitting the extra evidence, the court decreed that some of it was created by and was in the control of the school board while other material simply mirrored, in an updated form, evidence submitted at the hearing.

In the District of Columbia, the federal trial court would not allow a parent to submit evidence that was available at the hearing but was not presented at that time. The court did allow evidence that became available only one day before the hearing to be admitted.[107] Similarly, a federal trial court in Florida would not allow a parent to submit additional evidence because she failed to show that it could not have been introduced at the hearing.[108]

Commenting that courts have allowed both parents and children to proceed anonymously in IDEA cases, the federal trial court in the District of Columbia thought that the parents' names did not need to be revealed in an appeal of an adverse administrative hearing order.[109] The court agreed with the parents that disclosure of their names could have impacted their son's right to privacy.

A federal trial court in California wrote that a father's request for a stay-put order was not moot even though his son was receiving services from his former school district.[110] The child's domicile changed but he re-enrolled in his former school during the pendency of administrative proceedings over the adequacy of the IEP his new school board proposed. Insofar as the father's intent was for his son to live with relatives and attend the new school, the court agreed that there was a live controversy.

Standing to Sue

A federal trial court in Illinois declared that a noncustodial parent lacked standing to bring a substantive complaint regarding her child's education.[111] Granting the father custody and educational decision-making authority, the court concluded that although the mother retained the right to access records and receive notices, she had no standing to challenge the way the school board provided services.

Statute of Limitations

As discussed above, the IDEA establishes two separate limitations periods: two-years for requesting administrative hearings[112] and 90-days for appealing final administrative orders.[113] Even so, if state law provides an alternative limitations periods, the state law prevails.

Limitations Period for Requesting a Hearing

The federal trial court in the District of Columbia agreed with a hearing officer that claims arising more than two years before a mother filed an administrative complaint were time-barred.[114] The court determined that the claim accrued when the mother was apprised of evaluations demonstrating the extent to which her son had fallen behind his peers.

Limitations Period for Appealing a Final Administrative Decision

A federal trial court in Pennsylvania applied the IDEA's two-year statute of limitations to a suit under Section 504 and the ADA because it was based on the deprivation of a FAPE under the IDEA.[115] However, because the parents failed to allege that the school board intentionally misled them or knowingly deceived them regarding the child's progress, and they knew, or should have known, of alleged violations, the court would not allow them to present claims arising more than two years prior to the date they filed suit.

Placement

The IDEA regulations require school boards to ensure that a "continuum of alternative placements" exists to meet the needs of students with disabilities for special education and related services.[116] The continuum must range from placements in general education to private residential facilities and includes homebound services. Still, the placements chosen for all students must be in the least restrictive environment (LRE) for each child and removal from general education can occur only to the extent necessary for boards to provide special education and related services.[117]

All placements must both be at public expense and meet state educational standards.[118] IEP teams must review all placements at least annually and revise them when necessary.[119] The Supreme Court, in *Rowley*, defined an appropriate education as one developed in compliance with the IDEA's procedures and is reasonably calculated to enable a child to receive educational benefits.[120] Although states, at a minimum, must adopt policies and procedures consistent with the IDEA, they may provide greater benefits than those required by the federal law. If states do establish higher standards, courts consider those standards along with the IDEA when evaluating the appropriateness of IEPs.[121]

Appropriate Educational Placement

In the first of a series of involving the NYCBOE, the Second Circuit reasoned that while the substantive aspects of the IEPs for a child with autism were appropriate, procedural errors denied him a FAPE.[122] The court decided that the IEPs were consistent with evaluative data, properly identified goals and strategies, and contained objectives related to the child's needs. However, the court insisted that procedural errors, such as identifying which evaluation materials were reviewed at each IEP meeting and the failure to conduct a functional behavioral assessment, when taken together, denied him a FAPE.[123]

The Second Circuit next affirmed that an IEP calling for placement in an integrated co-teaching class was appropriate for a child with Tourette syndrome where he had progressed in the past in a similar setting.[124] In yet another case, the Second Circuit affirmed that the NYCBOE's failure to discuss and address bullying experienced by a child with learning disabilities deprived her of a FAPE.[125]

In five cases federal trial courts in New York upheld IEPs proposed by the NYCBOE. In the first, the parents of a student with multiple disabilities requested a placement in a private specialized school but NYCBOE officials disagreed because it lacked state approval. Instead, officials recommended a placement in a public-school class in a specialized facility with a one-to-one paraprofessional and related services. The court agreed with a state review officer that the recommended placement was likely to produce progress.[126] In the second case, the court also sustained a state review officer's order that, overall, a proposed placement in a public-school program was appropriate for a child with autism despite some deficiencies in her IEP.[127] The court was convinced that the deficiencies did not deny the child educational benefit.

Courts in the third and fourth cases agreed with state review officers that the NYCBOE's recommendations to place children with autism in specialized programs in the public schools offered FAPEs because their IEPs provided sufficient support services.[128] In the final case in which the court sustained the NYCBOE's recommendations, a federal trial court held that a public-school class placement offered a FAPE to a student with a speech and language impairment who exhibited some autistic features in light of his academic, language, social/ emotional, fine motor, attentional, and sensory regulation needs.[129] The court noted that the child's IEP also utilized strategies to address his management needs along with related services.

In other disputes arising in New York City, federal trial courts struck down the NYCBOE's proposals. In the first case, the court found that the NYCBOE failed to meet its burden of providing evidence that its proposed placement had the ability to implement the child's IEP.[130] In the second, the court ruled that the IEP team failed to take the child's progress into account and so developed goals not meeting his present levels of performance.[131] The court remarked that using goals due to expire by the time the IEP was implemented was unlikely to produce progress.

Another federal trial court in New York, in reviewing the administrative record, could uncover no evidence in the record supporting the NYCBOE's claim that a special education class with a ratio of 6:1:1 was reasonably calculated to provide more than trivial advancement.[132] Rejecting school officials' argument that other students with autism made progress in such a classroom, the court contended that the recommended placement did not reasonably relate to this child's identified needs. By the same token, the court discerned that another proposed IEP calling for a 6:1:1 class placement, would not produce progress because it failed to address the child's needs.[133] In the final case, the court agreed with a hearing officer that in recommending the movement of a child with learning disabilities to a class with a larger staff to student ratio, the NYCBOE did not engage in meaningful discussions about why he was ready for such an environment.[134]

Federal trial courts in New York upheld proposed IEPs from three other school boards. First, a court concurred that an IEP was appropriate to a student's cognitive and academic skills as well as his social/emotional functioning.[135] In a second case involving the same board, a court observed that the preponderance of evidence supported its IEP as appropriate for a child with developmental disabilities.[136] The evidence indicated that the child made progress in the past and achieved many of his IEP's goals. In the final dispute, the court was of the view that a child's condition worsened due to changes to his medication regimen and not a failure by school officials.[137] Moreover, the court reasoned that evidence showed that the child made progress in the past and a similar program was likely to produce progress, not regression, in the future.

In the first of eight cases before it, the federal trial court in the District of Columbia was persuaded that the school board denied FAPEs to children with disabilities. In three of those orders the courts judged that the board denied FAPEs by materially failing to implement IEPs. In one case, the court calculated that the board failed to provide 83% of the services required by a child's IEP[138] and in another that charter school officials completely failed to implement the student's IEP.[139] In the third case, the court decreed that the board had not altered a child's schedule after her IEP team increased her specialized instruction time.[140] Even though the child still made progress, the court refused to allow this to excuse the board's failure to provide the services her IEP team considered necessary.

The same court explained that the school board denied a FAPE to a student who was shot eight times by failing to convene an IEP team meeting to consider the disability-related effects of his shooting.[141] The court acknowledged that as a result of the shooting, the student's needs may have changed. Next, the court chastised the board for not revising a child's IEP to address his lack of expected progress toward his annual goals, instead persisting in following an ineffectual path.[142] Even worse, the court exclaimed, the IEP team decreased some /of the child's services.

Conversely, in three cases the court put its stamp of approval on the IEPs proposed by the school board. First, the court agreed that placement in a general education class with special education support was appropriate for a child who with multiple disabilities due to brain damage he suffered at birth because he made academic and social progress while the disputed IEPs were in effect.[143] The court maintained that the child received educational benefit in the general education setting during that time.

In a second case, the court specified that although the proposed IEP may not have been perfect, it was adequate.[144] The court saw no evidence that keeping the child in a public-school program was not a viable option. In the final dispute, the court conceded that an IEP calling for more hours of services would have provided a FAPE because the child made progress under her previous IEP with less specialized instruction.[145]

A parent from Maine challenged a recommended placement in an alternative school alleging that its abbreviated day would deprive her son of a FAPE. The First Circuit, emphasizing that school officials provided the same amount of instructional time as a traditional high school, affirmed in favor of the placement.[146]

In Illinois, a federal trial court believed placement in an emotional-support program would provide a FAPE to a child diagnosed as having disruptive mood dysregulation disorder and attention deficit hyperactivity disorder, given his academic and behavioral challenges.[147] A federal trial court in Texas asserted that a school board failed to offer a FAPE in a timely manner to a student with specific learning disabilities whose family moved to the state in her senior year.[148] At the time of the move, the student was enrolled in a private school pursuant to an IEP developed by her former school board. However, the board in Texas did not formalize a new IEP until seven days before the student was scheduled to graduate.

Pointing out that an IEP team was faced with conflicting reports, the federal trial court in Connecticut refused to invalidate the resultant IEP because the team gave more weight to one report over another.[149] Although the parent preferred a reading intervention program over the one chosen by school personnel, the court was satisfied that the program selected by the IEP team was sufficient to address the child's needs and would provide a FAPE.

According to the federal trial court in Maryland, a school board offered an appropriate IEP and placement to a student who was diagnosed with attention deficit hyperactivity disorder and anxiety disorder.[150] As an initial matter, the court ascertained that the board could not be responsible for delays in the IEP process because they resulted from a lack of parental cooperation which frustrated its attempts to identify an appropriate placement. Further, the court wrote that the parents failed to provide evidence demonstrating that the board's IEPs were inadequate or denied their son a FAPE.

Similarly, the federal trial court in Massachusetts was of the opinion that the school committee offered a FAPE to a child with a hearing impairment, but his mother resisted educators' recommendations.[151] The court attributed the child's slow progress to the mother's resistance rather than inappropriate IEPs.

The federal trial court in Hawaii approved the IEP recommended by the state department of education calling for a child who had been attending a private school to be returned to his neighborhood school.[152] The child's mother removed her son from the neighborhood school because he had been bullied there. Still, the court thought that the crisis plan incorporated into the student's IEP was sufficient to address any bullying he experienced.

Least Restrictive Environment

In a case from California, the Ninth Circuit affirmed that board officials met their duty under the IDEA by placing a child with autism in a small group setting after he returned to the public schools from a private placement.[153] The court determined that the child's academic needs weighed heavily against placement in a mainstream environment and saw no evidence he would have benefitted from a typical classroom setting.

The parents of a child with disabilities disagreed with a school board's proposal to place her in special education classes for a portion of the day but an ALJ and a federal trial court in Georgia agreed that it was the LRE.[154] The Eleventh Circuit concurred, commenting that the child need instruction significantly different from what she was offered in a general education classroom such that her schooling could not have been satisfactorily achieved in such as environment even with supplemental aids and services. In a separate order, the same court affirmed that a board in Florida was not required to create a mainstream summer school program to serve the needs of one student.[155]

A federal trial court in Illinois agreed with a school board that an emotional-support program was the LRE for a child who experienced behavior problems in a general education setting.[156] The court relied on evidence that the child regressed academically and was not meeting his behavioral goals in the general education class and that no further adjustments could be made in that setting. Moreover, the court declared that school personnel created multiple opportunities for mainstreaming the child in the social-emotional class.

Private Facilities

The federal trial court in the District of Columbia found that a child with attention deficit hyperactivity disorder and various learning disabilities required a private school placement.[157] The court posited that the child needed full-time specialized instruction throughout the school day because her significant disabilities affected all facets of her education.

Extended School Year

In a case from Hawaii, the federal trial court decided that a child's IEP team considered all necessary factors in determining that he did not require extended school year services.[158] Additionally, the court commented that the team's statement that the services were not required to provide the child with educational benefit was reasonable.

Related Services

Under the IDEA, in addition to special education, students with disabilities are entitled to related services, defined as the supplementary aids and services necessary for them to make progress toward annual goals in general education curricula and to participate with their peers who are not disabled.[159] These services, addressed in students' IEPs, include transportation, developmental, corrective, and supportive services necessary for students to benefit from special education.[160]

The Second Circuit, consistent with its own precedent, held that the NYCBOE did not deny a child with autism a FAPE by failing to include parent counseling and training in his IEP because it was required by state law.[161] The court noted that the parent had not shown how this omission deprived the child of educational benefit.

Transition Services

The IDEA requires transition services for students with disabilities to improve their academic, functional, and transition opportunities as they move from school to post-school settings.[162] The IDEA mandates the identification of transition services to enable children with disabilities to move into post-secondary educational or workplace environments, including, for example, community colleges, post-secondary education, employment, or independent living.[163] In order to provide the necessary transition services, boards must conduct age-appropriate assessments to meet the students' needs with respect to training, education, employment, or possibly independent living skills.[164] These transitions must be introduced by IEP teams when children turn sixteen and must identify post-secondary goals and services.[165]

The federal trial court in the District of Columbia granted the school board's motion for summary judgment in response to a mother's claim that her daughter's transition plan was deficient.[166] The court rejected the mother's claim absent evidence of harm due to the alleged deficiency resulting in the denial of FAPE.

On the other hand, the Sixth Circuit, in a case from Ohio, reasoned that a school board's three procedural violations of the transition services provision amounted to a denial of FAPE.[167] First, the school board failed to invite the student to the IEP team meeting when transition services were discussed.[168] Second, the board did not consider the student's transition-related interests,[169] instead relying on informal assessments and limited workplace opportunities that were insufficient to reveal any meaningful insight into the student's preferences beyond school. Finally, because the board failed to conduct age-appropriate postsecondary transition assessments,[170] the court concluded that it had insufficient information to identify measurable postsecondary goals related to the student's current or future abilities.

Discipline

Significant questions have arisen regarding disciplinary responses when students with disabilities violate codes of conduct. In 1997 and 2004, the IDEA amendments provided specific guidance for school officials responding to student misconduct.[171] Previously, the Supreme Court's guidelines established clear limits for school boards to follow in the disciplinary process when students with disabilities violated conduct codes.[172]

The 1997 and 2004 IDEA disciplinary provisions permit school officials to enforce codes of conduct when students with disabilities possess drugs or weapons or inflict serious bodily injury or the threat thereof.[173] The IDEA established specific guidelines for handling placement and stay put issues for students with disabilities. For example, although a disciplinary exclusion can last up to 45 days, students must receive educational services throughout the period of exclusion.[174] Additional requirements include conducting functional behavioral assessments (FBAs) and developing behavior intervention plans (BIPs) for students with disabilities in identified situations.[175] Despite the added flexibility, in all disciplinary situations the IDEA requires schools to protect students' educational rights throughout the periods of exclusion.

In New York, responses by school boards to behavioral challenges are complicated by state regulations requiring specific actions to address behavioral deficiencies.[176] The Second Circuit ruled that a board's failure to conduct an FBA was a serious procedural violation of the IDEA because the student's behaviors interfered significantly with his learning.[177] In order to ensure the student's IEP provided him with a FAPE, the court ordered the board to adopt a BIP based on the results of an FBA. Further, the court explained that the FBA needed to identify the root causes of the student's behavioral deficiencies in order for officials to adopt intervention strategies and positive behavioral supports to address the behavior.

The federal trial court in the District of Columbia was convinced that the school board's failure to follow its own physical restraint policies denied a child a FAPE.[178] The court thought that by not reconvening the IEP within five days of a physical restraint, as required by the policy, the board impeded the child's parent's opportunity to participate in the decision-making process.

Remedies

Students with disabilities who were denied FAPEs are entitled to an array of remedies pursuant to the IDEA's enforcement provisions. Remedies may include tuition reimbursement, compensatory services, and attorney fees.[179] The courts select the appropriate remedies and award equitable relief for students once plaintiffs have exhausted administrative remedies under the IDEA unless they meet the limited exceptions to exhaustion addressed elsewhere in this chapter.[180]

Tuition Reimbursement

Parents seeking tuition reimbursement are subjected to the three-pronged *Burlington/ Carter* test,[181] which boards meet when school officials demonstrate that IEPs provide students with FAPEs.[182] If boards meet this test, parents must prove that their unilateral placements were appropriate and the equities favor tuition reimbursement.[183]

A complex case arose in Texas over tuition reimbursement where a federal trial court observed that a board was obligated to provide a FAPE when a student with a disability became a state resident, even though her mother failed to enroll her in a public school.[184] On the other hand, in another case from Texas, the Fifth Circuit affirmed that where parents' single-minded all-or-nothing refusal to work with school officials to identify an appropriate placement for their daughter and to develop an IEP was the primary cause of their inability to offer a FAPE, the parents were not entitled to tuition reimbursement.[185]

In four different claims by parents against school boards in New York, federal trial courts granted requests for tuition reimbursement for children with autism who were placed in private schools after being denied Applied Behavioral Analysis (ABA) therapy which resulted in the denial of FAPEs.[186] In three of these cases, the courts maintained that state review officers (SROs) rendered flawed adjudications about the type of support needed, resulting in their forgoing the customary judicial deference afforded to the actions of SROs. As such, the court relied on the original well-reasoned orders of the hearing officers as to the violations of FAPEs.

As to the fourth claim, a federal trial court in New York court reached a similar outcome. However, rather than being diagnosed with autism, the child suffered from severe migraines and psychological problems that led his parents to place him in a private school.[187] The court overturned an order by the SRO denying tuition reimbursement to the parents in light of the original hearing officer's well-reasoned order.

In another case against the NYCBOE, the federal trial court entered an order in favor of parents who sought tuition reimbursement following a series of procedural and substantive violations of the IDEA.[188] The court determined that the various procedural violations did not rise to the level of a denial of FAPE. Even so, the court was of the view that the procedural violations in combination with the failure to provide prior written notice, a substantive violation, led to a denial of FAPE. As a result of the NYCBOE's denial of FAPE and the parental action in enrolling the child in a private school offering an appropriate education, the court granted the request for tuition reimbursement.

At issue in another case from New York over tuition reimbursement was a prospective claim by parents that the NYCBOE's suggested placement was in a school lacking the capacity to implement their child's IEP.[189] Even though the parents never enrolled their child in the district, the federal trial court asserted that the board failed to meet the burden of presenting evidence of the appropriateness of its proposed placement.

As reflected by a case from the District of Columbia, although the merits of a parental claim regarding a child's eligibility for services under the IDEA may be unresolved, a stay-put order may still result in the payment of private school tuition fees. The federal trial court found that a stay-put order was necessary to ensure that a child received a FAPE regardless of the pendency of administrative or judicial proceedings in her IDEA case.[190] Recognizing the private school as the current placement, the court explained that the board had to pay the full tuition pursuant to the IDEA's stay-put mandate.

Compensatory Services

Pursuant to the IDEA, courts are responsible for awarding appropriate relief such as compensatory education and may consider the equitable aspects of granting such relief for violations of the IDEA.[191] In selecting relief, courts must engage in a fact-specific inquiries to evaluate the educational benefits that would have accrued to children if they had received the necessary special education services they required.[192]

In the first of four cases on point before it, the federal trial court in the District of Columbia granted an award of compensatory education where a student's behavior significantly impacted his academic progress.[193] According to the court, the board's failure to provide the student with behavioral support services directly impacted his academic success.

The court next overturned a hearing officer's order dismissing a parental complaint alleging school board officials failed to provide their son with a FAPE for seven months.[194] The court directed the board to offer compensatory education that would put the student in the educational position he would be in prior to the denial of a FAPE.

In the third case, the federal trial court in the District of Columbia granted a request for compensatory education due to the school board's failure to provide a student with a FAPE.[195] In treating the board's procedural defect of failing to discuss both the LRE and an alternate placement in the student's IEP as having amounted to the denial of FAPE, the court granted the parental request for tuition and transportation funding. In the final case, the court awarded compensatory services because the board failed to evaluate a child in a timely fashion.[196]

Attorney Fees

The party requesting an attorney fees award is responsible for presenting evidence of the reasonableness of an attorney's hourly rate pursuant to the IDEA.[197] Such submissions must establish the reasonableness of the requested fees along with information about the billing practices, skills, experiences, reputations, and prevailing market rates of attorneys in the relevant community. Prevailing parties may be awarded fees-on-fees representing a reasonable amount of the attorney fees incurred in recovering attorney fees awarded to the prevailing party.[198] Overall, attorney fees cases continue to arise predominantly in the District of Columbia, focusing primarily on how courts set the applicable rate for awards of attorney fees.

A variety of the cases in the District of Columbia focused on how to calculate awards of attorney fees for parents who were prevailing parties against their school board. The federal trial court typically refers to the *Laffey* matrix[199] in setting awards of attorney fees in IDEA cases.[200] The frequency of these cases is well-documented, but has not resulted in the federal trial court's sympathizing with the local school board.

As illustrated in one case from the federal trial court, the best way to avoid litigation over attorney fees under the IDEA is to comply with its provisions.[201] Yet, in light of the steady flow of litigation, board officials seemingly appear to fail to heed this advice.

The federal trial court in the District of Columbia frequently awards fees based on a reduction of the hourly rates set by the *Laffey* fee matrix.[202] In one case, the court reduced the award due to the parent's limited success on the merits.[203] In another case the court rejected an award at the full *Laffey* rate as unwarranted due to the lack of complexity of the IDEA claims.[204]

In multiple orders the federal trial court in the District of Columbia decided that as to fee-collection or fees-on-fees litigation in IDEA cases, it is well settled that the straightforward nature of such routine proceedings warrants awards at one-half of attorneys' applicable *Laffey* rates.[205] In related cases the court awarded one-half of the attorney fees in fees-on-fees cases in light of the general rule that the full *Laffey* rate is for complex cases. [206] On the other hand, the court awarded reimbursement at the full *Laffey* rate to prevailing parents.[207]

The previous judgments in the District of Columbia relied solely on the *Laffey* Matrix in setting awards of attorney fees. In one case, though, the court pointed out that the United States Attorney's Office (USAO) replaced the *Laffey* Matrix with a new methodology, the USAO Matrix. [208] Of importance to the present case is that the *Laffey* Matrix set a lower rate for attorney fees and that the litigation commenced before the USAO Matrix was officially adopted. In light of the complexity of the case, the court awarded the fess between 75%-100% of the *Laffey* and USAO Matrix rates. A second issue related to the attorney fees award addressed the interrelatedness of the issues. The court acknowledged the interrelationship but held that when the plaintiffs withdrew their prior complaints, they prolonged the overall litigation and so were not entitled to full reimbursement.

In another case, the federal trial court in the District of Columbia noted that the plaintiffs were substantially justified in rejecting a settlement offer from the school board.[209] In so doing, the court referenced the IDEA mandate requiring boards to include provisions for attorney fees in settlement offers.[210] The court accepted the three-quarters USAO *Laffey* rates but refused to reduce the attorney fees award by another 25% due to the failure of the plaintiff's counsel to bill consistently in six-minute increments rather than the prohibited quarter-hour time-frames. Finally, the court granted a 35% fee reduction of the attorney fees because of the mixed success insofar as the mother succeeded on only one of her three claims.

The final case from the District of Columbia involved a joint request for attorney fees from parents who filed seven due process hearings against the school board. The court remarked that although the parents were the prevailing

parties but achieved only partial success, their fee awards could be reduced.
[211] In addition, the court rejected the parents' claims that the complexity of their cases justified an enhanced *Laffey* Matrix rate, instead adhering to the norm of a reduced *Laffey* rate percentage. The court affirmed that attorney fees were not recoverable for an educational advocate even though he was an attorney because he was not acting as such.

The Third Circuit rejected a school board in Pennsylvania's effort to reduce the attorney fees awarded to prevailing parents in a dispute over the provision of FAPE to their child.[212] The court was of the opinion that the hours charged were not excessive, the parents' success on four of the six claims did not warrant a fee lodestar reduction based on the degree of success, and the board's financial condition was not a factor to consider in awarding attorney fees.

Parents of a child with disabilities sought attorney fees from their school board in Louisiana on obtaining a stay-put order in a due process hearing.[213] The Fifth Circuit explained that insofar as a stay-put order is interim relief, it does not qualify parents as prevailing parties for purposes of recovering attorney fees. Conversely, a federal trial court in Tennessee awarded fees for parents who obtained a stay-put order because it was important relief.[214]

The Ninth Circuit significantly reduced the attorney fees awarded to the mother of a child with disabilities in California because she unreasonably rejected the school board's timely settlement offer.[215] Although the board violated the IDEA's child find provisions by failing to identify the child as a student with a disability, the court affirmed that the mother's rejection of its settlement offer was unjustified. The court added that the board's subsequent provision of appropriate special education services further demonstrated its efforts to address the child's special education needs.

In a case from New Mexico, the Tenth Circuit awarded full attorney fees even though a mother was not successful on all claims.[216] Insofar as the mother prevailed in a due process hearing, the court affirmed her award of the full amount of attorney fees.

A dispute over attorney fees emerged following a mother's claim that her son with a disability who was enrolled in a charter school was denied a FAPE. The mother sought relief from the Pennsylvania Department of Education (PDE) because the direct service provider, the charter school, was no longer in existence. A federal trial court in the commonwealth rejected the PDE's claim it were not responsible for attorney fees, on the basis that such a reimbursement is expressly authorized for prevailing parties and there is no distinction in the IDEA between state and local education agencies.[217]

Section 1983

Pursuant to the federal civil rights statute, Section 1983,[218] aggrieved parties can seek monetary, declaratory, or injunctive relief from state actors, including public school boards or employees, who violate their civil rights.

Section 1983 provides relief for violations of federal statutory or constitutional rights. However, courts tend to limit awards when relief is available via federal statutes providing procedural and substantive remedies for violations.

According to the Supreme Court, Section 1983 prohibits individual enforcement when comprehensive statutory protections have been established.[219] Consequently, insofar as the IDEA includes administrative remedies and extensive exhaustion requirements, parties may not bypass these provisions in efforts to pursue money damages.[220]

Section 1983 claims by parents of children with disabilities face significant barriers in court and must prove the deprivations of federal rights pursuant to state policies or customs. Courts are generally hesitant to award remedies pursuant to Section 1983 claims. For example, in a case from Michigan, the Sixth Circuit affirmed the denial of a mother's claim of disparate treatment based on disability in violation of the Equal Protection Clause.[221] In its analysis, the court rejected the mother's claim that she failed to present evidence of her son's having been treated differently from peers who were not disabled and were similarly situated.

In a second case before it, the Sixth Circuit, in a dispute from Ohio, affirmed that a special education teacher's inappropriate conduct did not rise to the level of a Fourteenth Amendment due process violation. [222] The court specified that the school board had no supervisory liability for the teacher's behavior under Section 1983.

A federal trial court in Washington rejected a mother's broad claims that the use of aversive interventions violated Section 1983 by transgressing her son's protected rights to due process and the unreasonable seizures clauses under the Fourth and Fourteenth Amendments, respectively. [223] The court observed that the mother's vague claims failed to provide sufficient evidence about whether her son had clearly established rights.

On the other hand, a federal trial court in California largely rejected motions to dismiss parental Section 1983 claims against a teacher, aide, and various defendants given evidence the educators' use of excessive force against their daughter.[224] The court was convinced that allegedly kicking student in response to various symptoms of her disability and putting inedible objects in her mouth were sufficient to allege that the defendants were deliberately indifferent to her rights under Section 504 and the ADA.

Discrimination under Section 504 of the Rehabilitation Act and the Americans with Disabilities Act

Section 504[225] and the ADA[226] provide additional protections to individuals and students with disabilities. Pursuant to these laws, persons with disabilities may not be discriminated against or excluded from participation in federally funded programs and activities.

It is not uncommon for courts to consider Section 504 and ADA claims jointly in light of congressional intent to interpret these civil rights statutes consistently.[227] Plaintiffs may pursue Section 504 and ADA claims through the Office for Civil Rights in light of the its congressional authority to investigate disability discrimination claims and complaints. As defined by Section 504 and the ADA, individuals with disabilities or impairments may qualify under both laws if they have physical or mental impairments substantially limiting one or more major life activities, have records of such impairments, and/ or are regarded as having such impairments.[228]

Section 504 protects the rights of individuals with disabilities who meet the statutory definition to not be discriminated against or excluded from programs or activities receiving federal financial aid. The ADA extends protection to private as well as public institutions, thereby offering additional coverage to individuals who may experience discrimination due to their disabilities.

As demonstrated in the cases discussed below, parents continue to initiate litigation on behalf of their children with disabilities concurrently under the IDEA, Section 504, and the ADA. Although some courts have recognized that students may have multiple claims, it is important to note they have also ruled that students who qualify as individuals with disabilities under Section 504 are not automatically eligible under the IDEA.

Students at the Elementary and Secondary Levels

In the first of a pair of cases before it, the Second Circuit refused to excuse parental failure to exhaust IDEA and Section 1983 remedies because they did not demonstrate how exhaustion would have been futile.[229] The parents unsuccessfully alleged that the board failed to implement IEP services and immediately claimed the school board violated Section 504 and the ADA, without first seeking relief pursuant to the IDEA's administrative remedies.

Parents of a student in New York who committed suicide filed claims against their school board and various officials under Section 1983, constitutional provisions, Section 504, and the ADA, alleging they failed to stop or prevent harassment and bullying to which their son was subjected. The parents challenged the dismissal of all counts against the board and officials while seeking to amend their Section 504 and ADA claims. In light of the relaxation of the standard for substantial limits on major life activities, pursuant to the ADA Amendments Act of 2008, the Second Circuit found that insofar as the federal trial court should have granted the leave to amend Section 504 and ADA, the case had to be remanded with orders to permit them to do so.[230]

The Ninth Circuit permitted parents of a child with a disability from Arizona to proceed with their Section 504 and ADA claims against their board for the alleged failure by school officials to provide reasonable accommodations.[231] Reversing an earlier order for summary judgment in favor of the board and remanding for further proceedings, the court reasoned that the parents may present evidence the board had notice of the need for an accommodation yet failed to make reasonable modifications to have enabled the child to have had meaningful educational access.

In a second case from the Ninth Circuit premised on Section 504 and the ADA, a parent claimed her son was discriminated against when he was denied admission to a charter school in California. The mother's discrimination claim failed because the court decided that that officials denied the child admission due to a valid, nondiscriminatory admissions policy granting admissions preference to current students.[232] By the same token, the Fifth Circuit affirmed that parents from Texas did not sufficiently allege that school officials transferred their child to an alternative program for any reason other than his disciplinary infractions.[233]

Addressing multiple claims under Section 504, the ADA, and the IDEA, a federal trial court in Pennsylvania determined that because parents exhausted their administrative remedies under the IDEA, they could proceed under Section 504 and the ADA.[234] Further, although the student was receiving services at a private school, the court was satisfied that the parents presented sufficient evidence this did not qualify as a private school placement such that the private school was required to provide FAPE under subject to Section 504 the ADA.

In a second case from Pennsylvania, after a student's suicide, his parents sought compensatory damages under Section 504 and the ADA, alleging that he took his own life following the school board's failure to implement and follow an appropriate educational plan for their son. A federal trial court dismissed on the basis that the suicide was not foreseeable.[235] The court added that the failure of officials to alert the student's parents about his academic failures as set forth in his 504 Plan did not constitute affirmative action or deliberate indifference under Section 504.

Aversive intervention efforts such as time-outs and seclusion, which may be used to address aggressive or dangerous behaviors of students with disabilities, have led to conflicts and litigation between parents and school boards. The mother of a child with a disability claimed that her son was discriminated against in violation of Section 504 and ADA when the board allowed the continued use of aversive interventions without ensuring they were used properly. A federal trial court in Washington rejected the board's motion to dismiss because it was not clear officials acted to confirm whether the aversive interventions were use appropriately.[236]

In the first of two similar cases from California, the parents of six minor students with disabilities, ranging from three to six years old, sought compensatory damages under Section 504 and the ADA from their school board alleging that their children were exposed to a hostile educational environment. After examining the parents' claims that the board denied meaningful educational access and discriminated against the students because of their disabilities, the court granted its motion for summary judgment because the parents failed to present a triable issue.[237]

Another federal trial court in California rejected a school board's motion for summary judgment in the face of parental claims filed under Section 504 and the ADA alleging that officials knew of the harm a teacher subjected their daughter to but failed to act.[238] At the same time, the court rejected the parents' Section 1983 claims alleging that the teacher violated the student's rights to substantive due process.

The Sixth Circuit affirmed the denial of the claims a mother in Michigan filed against a teacher and school board under Section 504 and the ADA as a result of the alleged emotional and physical abuse he inflicted on her son.[239] Despite the bad and possibly abusive acts of the teacher, the court agreed that in light of the child's participation in and benefit from his educational program, neither the board nor the teacher violated his educational rights.

In long running case from Kentucky, the Sixth Circuit affirmed that a school board and superintendent did not discriminate against a student with Type 1 diabetes by placing him in a school other than the one in his neighborhood because there was a full-time nurse on staff.[240] The court rejected the parental claim that the placement violated Section 504 and the ADA absent evidence of deliberate indifference toward the student due to his disability.

A female high school para-athlete in Missouri, in a Section 504 and ADA case, alleged she should have been able to earn points when she competed in track team events. A federal trial court denied the student's request for a preliminary injunction against the state high school activities association board of directors because they were individuals and not a public entity subject to the ADA.[241] The court rejected the student's claim under Section 504 because the association did not receive federal financial assistance.

A federal trial court in Virginia thought that parents plausibly demonstrated that their child was discriminated against due to his disability.[242] The court commented that parental allegations that school personnel engaged in conduct departing substantially from accepted professional judgment, practice, or standards supported both claims for discrimination and that board officials acted in bad faith or with gross misjudgment.

Other Section 504 and ADA Issues

While student placements may implicate the ADA, the courts must consider whether its protections are separate from the IDEA mandates. In light of a hearing officer's order that a school committee in Massachusetts complied with the IDEA and provided a student with a FAPE in the LRE, the parents of a child with emotional disabilities claimed that officials violated their son's ADA rights on removing him from a neighborhood school and placing him in a segregated day school.[243] The federal trial court concluded that the parents presented sufficient facts to support a claim under the ADA, explaining that it and IDEA not coextensive. The court thus denied the school committee's motion to dismiss the parental ADA claims.

Conclusion

In an effort to define and protect the educational rights of students with disabilities, plaintiffs, overwhelmingly parents, turn to the courts to interpret state and federal legislation as well as special education regulations and guidelines. The cases consistently focus on the IDEA's provisions about FAPEs, parental rights, stay-put provisions, and attorney fees. Other remedies parents sought include compensatory services and tuition reimbursement as when violations of the IDEA, whether procedural and/or substantive, amount to the denial of FAPEs.

Additional areas of dispute between parents and school boards involve the rights of students with disabilities under Section 504 and the ADA. While these cases are generally less successful than the IDEA claims, the courts have acknowledged that the three statutes are not coextensive with one another. Consequently, Section 504 and ADA claims may be permitted along with both successful and unsuccessful IDEA claims.

Endnotes

[1] *See, e.g.,* Pa. Ass'n for Retarded Children v. Pa., 343 F. Supp. 279 (E.D. Pa. 1972); Mills v. Bd. of Educ. of Dist. of Columbia, 348 F. Supp. 866 (D.D.C. 1972).

[2] 20 U.S.C. §§ 1400-1485 (2012).

[3] 20 U.S.C. §§ 1401(9), 1412(a)(1)(A).

[4] 20 U.S.C. § 1401(29).

[5] 20 U.S.C. §§ 1401(14), 1414(d).

[6] Bd. of Educ. of Hendrick Hudson Cent. Sch. Dist. v. Rowley, 458 U.S. 176 [5 Educ. L. Rep. 34] (1982).

[7] *Id.*

[8] 29 U.S.C. § 794.

[9] 42 U.S.C. §§ 12101 - 12213.

[10] 20 U.S.C. § 1412(a)(1)(A).

[11] 20 U.S.C. § 1412(a)(1)(B)(i).

[12] 20 U.S.C. § 1412(a)(1)(B)(ii).

[13] 34 C.F.R. § 300.102(a)(2)(B).

[14] 20 U.S.C. § 1401(3).

[15] 34 C.F.R. § 300.8.

[16] 20 U.S.C. § 1412(a)(10)(A).

[17] Mr. and Mrs. Doe v. Cape Elizabeth Sch. Dist., 832 F.3d 695 [335 Educ. L. Rep. 21] (1st Cir. 2016).

[18] Q.W. *ex rel.* M.W. v. Bd. of Educ. of Fayette Cnty., 630 F. App'x 580 [327 Educ. L. Rep. 639] (6th Cir. 2015).

[19] L.J. *ex rel.* Hudson v. Pittsburg Unified Sch. Dist., 835 F.3d 1168 [336 Educ. L. Rep. 47] (9th Cir. 2016).

[20] J.V. *ex rel.* Veldhuyzen v. Stafford Cty. Sch. Bd., 782 S.E.2d 286 [337 Educ. L. Rep. 536] (Va. Ct. App. 2016).

[21] Horne v. Potomac Preparatory P.C.S., 209 F. Supp.3d 146 [341 Educ. L. Rep.] (D.D.C. 2016).

[22] 20 U.S.C. § 1415.

[23] 20 U.S.C. §§ 1414(d)(1)(B)(i), 1414(f).

[24] 20 U.S.C. § 1414(a)(1)(D).

[25] 20 U.S.C. § 1415(b)(3).

26 20 U.S.C. § 1415(b)(3)(A).
27 20 U.S.C. § 1415(j).
28 20 U.S.C. § 1415(k)(3)(B)(ii).
29 Honig v. Doe, 484 U.S. 305 [43 Educ. L. Rep. 857] (1988).
30 20 U.S.C. § 1412(a)(3).
31 20 U.S.C. § 1412(a)(10)(A)(ii)(I).
32 34 C.F.R. § 300.131.
33 20 U.S.C. § 1414(a)(1)(A).
34 20 U.S.C. § 1414(a)(1)(C)(i)(I).
35 20 U.S.C. § 1414(b)(2), (3).
36 20 U.S.C. § 1415(b)(1).
37 34 C.F.R. § 300.502(b).
38 20 U.S.C. § 1414(d)(1)(A).
39 20 U.S.C. § 1414(d)(4)(A).
40 20 U.S.C. § 1414(a)(2).
41 DL v. Dist. of Columbia, 194 F. Supp.3d 30 (D.D.C. 2016).
42 Horne v. Potomac Preparatory P.C.S., 209 F. Supp.3d 146 [341 Educ. L. Rep.] (D.D.C. 2016).
43 R.E. ex rel. M.E. v. Brewster Cent. Sch. Dist., 180 F. Supp.3d 262 [337 Educ. L. Rep. 62] (S.D.N.Y. 2016).
44 W.A. and M.S. ex rel. W.E. v. Hendrick Hudson Cent. Sch. Dist., 2016 WL 6915271 (S.D.N.Y. 2016).
45 Dallas Indep. Sch. Dist. v. Woody, 178 F. Supp.3d 443 [336 Educ. L. Rep. 786] (N.D. Tex. 2016).
46 Seth B. v. Orleans Parish Sch. Bd., 810 F.3d 961 [326 Educ. L. Rep. 620] (5th Cir. 2016).
47 Timothy O. v. Paso Robles Unified Sch. Dist., 822 F.3d 1105 [331 Educ. L. Rep. 673] (9th Cir. 2016).
48 Baquerizo v. Garden Grove Unified Sch. Dist., 826 F.3d 1179 [333 Educ. L. Rep. 556] (9th Cir. 2016).
49 L.J. ex rel. Hudson v. Pittsburg Unified Sch. Dist., 835 F.3d 1168 [336 Educ. L. Rep. 47] (9th Cir. 2016).
50 A.L. v. Jackson Cnty. Sch. Bd., 635 F. App'x 774 [330 Educ. L. Rep. 60] (11th Cir. 2015).
51 Jason O. v. Manhattan Sch. Dist. No. 114, 173 F. Supp.3d 744 [335 Educ. L. Rep. 868] (N.D. Ill. 2016).
52 Dep't of Educ., State of Haw. v. Leo W., 2016 WL 7478960 (D. Haw. 2016).
53 S.Y. and R.Y. ex rel. R.Y. v. N.Y. City Dep't of Educ., 210 F. Supp.3d 556 [341 Educ. L. Rep. 739] (S.D.N.Y. 2016).
54 Damarcus S. v. Dist. of Columbia, 190 F. Supp.3d 35 [338 Educ. L. Rep. 823] (D.D.C. 2016).
55 James v. Dist. of Columbia, 194 F. Supp.3d 131 [339 Educ. L. Rep. 189] (D.D.C. 2016).
56 Horne v. Potomac Preparatory P.C.S., 209 F. Supp.3d 146 [341 Educ. L. Rep. 273] (D.D.C. 2016).
57 Genn v. New Haven Bd. of Educ., 2016 WL 7015610 (D. Conn. 2016).
58 S.Y. and R.Y. ex rel. R.Y. v. N.Y. City Dep't of Educ., 210 F. Supp.3d 556 [341 Educ. L. Rep. 739] (S.D.N.Y. 2016).
59 L.J. ex rel. Hudson v. Pittsburg Unified Sch. Dist., 835 F. Supp.3d 1168 [336 Educ. L. Rep. 47] (9th Cir. 2016).
60 Timothy O. v. Paso Robles Unified Sch. Dist., 822 F.3d 1105 [331 Educ. L. Rep. 673] (9th Cir. 2016).
61 A.L. v. Jackson Cnty. Sch. Bd., 635 F. App'x 774 [330 Educ. L. Rep. 60] (11th Cir. 2015).
62 Dervishi ex rel. T.D. v. Stamford Bd. of Educ., 653 F. App'x 55 [336 Educ. L. Rep. 194] (2d Cir. 2016).
63 T.K. and S.K. ex rel. L.K. v. N.Y. City Dep't of Educ., 810 F.3d 869 [326 Educ. L. Rep. 609] (2d Cir. 2016).
64 E.H. ex rel. M.K. v. N.Y. City Dep't of Educ., 164 F. Supp.3d 539 [334 Educ. L. Rep. 230] (S.D.N.Y. 2016).

[65] M.T. & R.T. *ex rel.* E.T. v. N.Y. City Dep't of Educ., 165 F. Supp.3d 106 [334 Educ. L. Rep. 286] (S.D.N.Y. 2016).

[66] C.R. and A.R. *ex rel.* L.R. v. N.Y. City Dep't of Educ., 211 F. Supp.3d 583 [341 Educ. L. Rep. 815] (S.D.N.Y. 2016).

[67] C.W. and W.W. *ex rel.* W.W. v. City Sch. Dist. of the City of N.Y., 171 F. Supp.3d 126 [335 Educ. L. Rep. 262] (S.D.N.Y. 2016).

[68] Jason O. v. Manhattan Sch. Dist. No. 114, 173 F. Supp.3d 744 [335 Educ. L. Rep. 868] (N.D. Ill. 2016).

[69] Genn v. New Haven Bd. of Educ., 2016 WL 7015610 (D. Conn. 2016). *See also* Forest Grove Sch. Dist. v. Student, 665 F. App'x 612 [340 Educ. L. Rep. 74] (9th Cir. 2016) (affirming that evidence reflected active parental participation in the formation of their child's IEP).

[70] N.E. *ex rel.* C.E. and P.E. v. Seattle Sch. Dist., 842 F.3d 1093 [337 Educ. L. Rep. 620] (9th Cir. 2016).

[71] R.F. *ex rel.* Frankel v. Delano Union Sch. Dist., 2016 WL 7338597 (E.D. Cal. 2016).

[72] Smith v. Cheyenne Mountain Sch. Dist. 12, 652 F. App'x 697 [335 Educ. L. Rep. 182] (10th Cir. 2016).

[73] Wimbish v. Dist. of Columbia, 153 F. Supp.3d 4 [332 Educ. L. Rep. 118] (D.D.C. 2015).

[74] J.M. *ex rel.* Mandeville v. Dep't of Educ., State of Haw., 2016 WL 7029825 (D. Haw. 2016).

[75] Jason O. v. Manhattan Sch. Dist. No. 114, 173 F. Supp.3d 744 [335 Educ. L. Rep. 868] (N.D. Ill. 2016).

[76] 20 U.S.C. § 1415(f)(1)(B).

[77] 20 U.S.C. § 1415(e).

[78] 20 U.S.C. §§ 1415(f), (g).

[79] 20 U.S.C. § 1415(i)(2)(A).

[80] 20 U.S.C. § 1415(f)(3)(C).

[81] 20 U.S.C. § 1415(f)(3)(D).

[82] 20 U.S.C. § 1415(i)(2)(B).

[83] 546 U.S. 49 [203 Educ. L. Rep. 29] (2005).

[84] 20 U.S.C. § 1415(i)(2)(C)(iii).

[85] Bd. of Educ. of Hendrick Hudson Cent. Sch. Dist. v. Rowley, 458 U.S. 176 [5 Educ. L. Rep. 34] (1982).

[86] T.L. *ex rel.* Latisha G. v. Penn. Leadership Charter Sch., 2016 WL 7188226 (E.D. Pa. 2016).

[87] L.K. *ex rel.* N.S. and S.S. v. Sewanhaka Cent. High Sch. Dist., 641 F. App'x 56 [332 Educ. L. Rep. 29] (2d Cir. 2016). *See also* C.K., T.K. *ex rel.* A.K. v. Bd. of Educ. of Westhampton Beach Sch. Dist., 185 F. Supp.3d 317 [338 Educ. L. Rep. 128] (E.D.N.Y. 2016) (holding that the issue of placement fell within the ambit of the IDEA's administrative process.)

[88] S.D. *ex rel.* AD. v. Haddon Heights Bd. of Educ., 833 F.3d 389 [335 Educ. L. Rep. 123] (3d Cir. 2016).

[89] W.R. *ex rel.* N.R. v. Ohio Health Dep't, 651 F. App'x 514 [335 Educ. L. Rep. 147 (6th Cir. 2016).

[90] *See also* B.C. *ex rel.* J.C. v. Mt. Vernon Sch. Dist., 660 F. App'x 93 [338 Educ. L. Rep. 699] (2d Cir. 2016) (affirming that a suit for money damages was subject to the IDEA's exhaustion requirement).

[91] Doe *ex rel.* T.W. v. Dallas Indep. Sch. Dist., 194 F. Supp.3d 551 [339 Educ. L. Rep. 220] (N.D. Tex. 2016).

[92] D.N. *ex rel.* Nolen v. Louisa Cnty. Pub. Schs., 156 F. Supp.3d 767 [332 Educ. L. Rep. 738 (W.D. Va. 2016).

[93] A.C. *ex rel.* Jerry C. v. Scranton Sch. Dist. and Salisbury Behavioral Health, 191 F. Supp.3d 375 [338 Educ. L. Rep. 882] (M.D. Pa. 2016).

[94] D.M. and J.M. v. Seattle Sch. Dist., 170 F. Supp.3d 1328 [335 Educ. L. Rep. 249] (W.D. Wash. 2016).

[95] S.S. *ex rel.* S.Y. v. Springfield, 146 F. Supp. 3d 414 [331 Educ. L. Rep. 214] (D. Mass. 2015)

[96] Molina *ex rel.* D.M. v. Bd. of Educ. of Los Lunas Schs., 157 F. Supp.3d 1064 [332 Educ. L. Rep. 795] (D.N.M. 2015).

[97] J.M. *ex rel.* Mandeville v. Dep't of Educ., State of Haw., 2016 WL 7029825 (D. Haw. 2016).

[98] Douglas v. Cal. Office of Admin. Hearings, 650 F. App'x 312 [334 Educ. L. Rep. 856] (9th Cir. 2016).

[99] Genn v. New Haven Bd. of Educ., 2016 WL 7015610 (D. Conn. 2016).

[100] Torres-Serrant v. Dep't of Educ. of P.R., 100 F. Supp.3d 138 [323 Educ. L. Rep. 806] (D.P.R. 2015).

[101] Arroyo-Delgado v. Dep't of Educ. of P.R., 199 F. Supp.3d 548 [339 Educ. L. Rep. 892] (D.P.R. 2016).

[102] B.D. *ex rel.* Davis v. Dist. of Columbia, 817 F.3d 792 [329 Educ. L. Rep. 612] (D.C. Cir. 2016).

[103] R.V. *ex rel.* S.V-W. v. Rivera, 2016 WL 7048953 (E.D. Pa. 2016).

[104] H.E. *ex rel.* H.F. v. Palmer Leadership Learning Partners, 2016 WL 6276418 (E.D. Pa. 2016).

[105] M.S. *ex rel.* J.S. v. Utah Schs. for the Deaf and Blind, 822 F.3d 1128 [331 Educ. L. Rep. 696] (10th Cir. 2016).

[106] D.M. and J.M. v. Seattle Sch. Dist., 170 F. Supp.3d 1328 [335 Educ. L. Rep. 249] (W.D. Wash. 2016).

[107] Carson v. Dist. of Columbia, 187 F. Supp.3d 197 [338 Educ. L. Rep. 371] (D.D.C. 2016).

[108] J.C. *ex rel.* M.C. v. Sch. Bd. of St. Johns Cnty., 210 F. Supp.3d 1318 [341 Educ. L. Rep. 772] (M.D. Fla. 2016).

[109] J.W. v. Dist. of Columbia, 318 F.R.D. 196 [340 Educ. L. Rep. 907] (D.D.C. 2016).

[110] R.F. *ex rel.* Frankel v. Delano Union Sch. Dist., 2016 WL 7338597 (E.D. Cal. 2016).

[111] Smith v. Meeks, 2016 WL 7049057 (N.D. Ill. 2016).

[112] 20 U.S.C. § 1415(f)(3)(C). This limitations period may be tolled if parents can show that school officials misrepresented that the problem had been resolved or withheld required information. 20 U.S.C. § 1415(f)(3)(D).

[113] 20 U.S.C. § 1415(i)(2)(B).

[114] Damarcus S. v. Dist. of Columbia, 190 F. Supp.3d 35 [338 Educ. L. Rep. 823] (D.D.C. 2016).

[115] A.C. *ex rel.* Jerry C. v. Scranton Sch. Dist. and Salisbury Behavioral Health, 191 F. Supp.3d 375 [338 Educ. L. Rep. 882] (M.D. Pa. 2016).

[116] 34 C.F.R. § 300.115.

[117] 20 U.S.C. § 1412(a)(5).

[118] 20 U.S.C. § 1401(9).

[119] 20 U.S.C. § 1414(d)(4).

[120] Bd. of Educ. of Hendrick Hudson Cent. Sch. Dist. v. Rowley, 458 U.S. 176 [5 Educ. L. Rep. 34] (1982).

[121] *See, e.g.,* David D. v. Dartmouth Sch. Comm., 775 F.2d 411 [28 Educ. L. Rep. 70] (1st Cir. 1985); Geis v. Bd. of Educ. of Parsippany-Troy Hills, Morris Cnty., 774 F.2d 575 [27 Educ. L. Rep. 1093] (3d Cir. 1985).

[122] L.O. *ex rel.* K.T. v. N.Y. City Dep't of Educ., 822 F.3d 95 [331 Educ. L. Rep. 609] (2d Cir. 2016).

[123] *See also* S.Y. and R.Y. *ex rel.* R.Y. v. N.Y. City Dep't of Educ., 210 F. Supp.3d 556 [341 Educ. L. Rep. 739] (S.D.N.Y. 2016) (treating the cumulative effect of nine procedural errors as displaying a pattern of indifference to the IDEA's procedures that and, when taken together, denied a FAPE).

[124] J.S. & L.S. v. N.Y. City Dep't of Educ., 648 F. App'x 96 [333 Educ. L. Rep. 645] (2d Cir. 2016).

[125] T.K. and S.K. *ex rel.* L.K. v. N.Y. City Dep't of Educ., 810 F.3d 869 [326 Educ. L. Rep. 609] (2d Cir. 2016).

[126] M.T. & R.T. *ex rel.* E.T. v. N.Y. City Dep't of Educ., 165 F. Supp.3d 106 [334 Educ. L. Rep. 286] (S.D.N.Y. 2016).

[127] J.M. and N.M. *ex rel.* L.M. v. N.Y. City Dep't of Educ., 171 F. Supp.3d 236 [335 Educ. L. Rep. 273] (S.D.N.Y. 2016).

[128] M.T. *ex rel.* N.M. v. N.Y. City Dep't of Educ., 200 F. Supp.3d 447 [339 Educ. L. Rep. 938] (S.D.N.Y. 2016); Z.C. *ex rel.* E.C. v. N.Y. Dep't of Educ., 2016 WL 7410783 (S.D.N.Y. 2016).

[129] C.R. and A.R. *ex rel.* L.R. v. N.Y. City Dep't of Educ., 211 F Supp.3d 583 [341 Educ. L. Rep. 815] (S.D.N.Y. 2016).

[130] W.W. and D.C. *ex rel.* M.C. v. N.Y. City Dep't of Educ., 160 F. Supp.3d 618 [333 Educ. L. Rep. 235] (S.D.N.Y. 2016).

[131] E.H. *ex rel.* M.K. v. N.Y. City Dep't of Educ., 164 F. Supp.3d 539 [334 Educ. L. Rep. 230] (S.D.N.Y. 2016).

[132] W.S. *ex rel.* A.S. v. City Sch. Dist. of N.Y. City, 188 F. Supp.3d 293 [338 Educ. L. Rep. 736] (S.D.N.Y. 2016).

[133] T.Y. and K.Y. *ex rel.* T.Y. v. N.Y. City Dep't of Educ., 2016 WL 6988811 (S.D.N.Y. 2016).

[134] L.R. *ex rel.* L.R. v. N.Y. City Dep't of Educ., 193 F. Supp.3d 209 [339 Educ. L. Rep. 173] (E.D.N.Y. 2016).

[135] C.W.L. and E.L. *ex rel.* v. Pelham Union Free Sch. Dist., 149 F. Supp. 3d 451 [331 Educ. L. Rep. 769] (S.D.N.Y. 2015).

[136] M.H. and S.H. *ex rel.* S.H. v. Pelham Union Free Sch. Dist., 168 F. Supp.3d 667 [334 Educ. L. Rep. 915] (S.D.N.Y. 2016).

[137] R.E. *ex rel.* M.E. v. Brewster Cent. Sch. Dist., 180 F. Supp.3d 262 [337 Educ. L. Rep. 62] (S.D.N.Y. 2016).

[138] Holman v. Dist. of Columbia, 153 F. Supp.3d 386 [332 Educ. L. Rep. 145] (D.D.C. 2016).

[139] James v. Dist. of Columbia, 194 F. Supp.3d 131 [339 Educ. L. Rep. 189] (D.D.C. 2016).

[140] Beckwith v. Dist. of Columbia, 208 F. Supp.3d 34 [341 Educ. L. Rep. 186] (D.D.C. 2016).

[141] Brown v. Dist. of Columbia, 179 F. Supp.3d 15 [336 Educ. L. Rep. 873] (D.D.C. 2016).

[142] Damarcus S. v. Dist. of Columbia, 190 F. Supp.3d 35 [338 Educ. L. Rep. 823] (D.D.C. 2016).

[143] Moradnejad v. Dist. of Columbia, 177 F. Supp.3d 260 [336 Educ. L. Rep. 262 (D.D.C. 2016).

[144] Z.B. v. Dist. of Columbia, 202 F. Supp.3d 64 [340 Educ. L. Rep. 247] (D.D.C. 2016).

[145] Garris v. Dist. of Columbia, 210 F. Supp.3d 187 [341 Educ. L. Rep. 695] (D.D.C. 2016).

[146] M.S. *ex rel.* B.S. v. Reg'l Sch. Unit 72, 829 F.3d 95 [334 Educ. L. Rep. 63] (1st Cir. 2016).

[147] Jason O. v. Manhattan Sch. Dist. No. 114, 173 F. Supp.3d 744 [335 Educ. L. Rep. 868] (N.D. Ill. 2016).

[148] Dallas Indep. Sch. Dist. v. Woody, 178 F. Supp.3d 443 [336 Educ. L. Rep. 786] (N.D. Tex. 2016).

[149] Genn v. New Haven Bd. of Educ., 2016 WL 7015610 (D. Conn. 2016). *See also* Forest Grove Sch. Dist. v. Student, 665 F. App'x 612 [340 Educ. L. Rep. 74] (9th Cir. 2016) (affirming that a board was not obligated to conform all of a child's classes to her parents' preferred teaching method).

[150] M.K. v. Starr, 185 F. Supp.3d 679 [338 Educ. L. Rep. 166] (D. Md. 2016).

[151] Johnson v. Boston Pub. Schs., 201 F. Supp.3d 187 [340 Educ. L. Rep. 133] (D. Mass. 2016).

[152] J.M. *ex rel.* Mandeville v. Dep't of Educ., State of Haw., 2016 WL 7029825 (D. Haw. 2016).

[153] Baquerizo v. Garden Grove Unified Sch. Dist., 826 F.3d 1179 [333 Educ. L. Rep. 556] (9th Cir. 2016).

[154] S.M. *ex rel.* T.M. and B.M. v. Gwinnet Cnty. Sch. Dist., 646 F. App'x 763 [333 Educ. L. Rep. 131] (11th Cir. 2016).

[155] A.L. v. Jackson Cnty. Sch. Bd., 635 F. App'x 774 [330 Educ. L. Rep. 60] (11th Cir. 2016).

[156] Jason O. v. Manhattan Sch. Dist. No. 114, 173 F. Supp.3d 744 [335 Educ. L. Rep. 868] (N.D. Ill. 2016).

[157] Q.C-C. v. Dist. of Columbia, 164 F. Supp.3d 35 [334 Educ. L. Rep. 194] (D.D.C. 2016).

[158] Dep't of Educ, State of Haw. v. Leo W., 2016 WL 7478960 (D. Haw. 2016).

[159] 20 U.S. C. § 1414(d)(1)(A)(i)(IV).

[160] 20 U.S. C. § 1401(26); (IDEA further defines supportive services as including speech-language pathology and audiology services, interpreting services, psychological services, physical and occupational therapy, recreation, including therapeutic recreation, social work services, school nurse services, counseling services, including rehabilitation counseling, orientation and mobility services, and medical services for diagnostic and evaluation purposes only).

[161] L.O. *ex rel.* K.T. v. New York City Dep't of Educ., 822 F.3d 95 [331 Educ. L. Rep. 609] (2d Cir. 2016).

[162] 34 C.F.R. § 300.43(a)(1).

[163] 20 U.S.C. § 1401(34).

[164] 20 U.S.C. § 1414(d)(1)(A)(i)(VIII)(aa).

[165] 20 U.S.C. § 1414(d)(1)(A)(i)(VIII).

[166] Garris v. Dist. of Columbia, 210 F. Supp.3d 187 (D.D.C. 2016).

[167] Gibson v. Forest Hills Local Sch. Dist. Bd. of Educ., 655 F. App'x 423 [337 Educ. L. Rep. 21] (6th Cir. 2016).

[168] 34 C.F.R. § 300.321.

[169] 34 C.F.R. § 300.321(b)(2).

[170] 34 C.F.R. § 300.320(b)(1).

[171] 20 U.S.C. § 1415(k).

[172] Honig v. Doe, 484 U.S. 305 [43 Educ. L. Rep. 857] (1988).

[173] 20 U.S.C. § 1415(k)(1)(E), (G).

[174] 20 U.S.C. § 1415(k)(1)(D).

[175] 20 U.S.C. § 1415(k)(1)(D), (E).

[176] N.Y. Comp. Codes R. & Regs. tit. 8, § 200.4(b)(1)(v).

[177] L.O. *ex rel.* K.T. v. New York City Dep't of Educ., 822 F.3d 95 [331 Educ. L. Rep. 609] (2d Cir. 2016), *rev'g* 94 F. Supp. 3d 530 [322 Educ. L. Rep. 792] (S.D.N.Y. 2015). *See also* E.H. *ex rel.* M.K. v. New York City Dep't of Educ., 164 F. Supp.3d 539 [334 Educ. L. Rep. 230] (S.D.N.Y. 2016) (rejecting a BIP not adequately addressing a child's behavioral needs as inadequate).

[178] Beckwith v. Dist. of Columbia, 208 F. Supp.3d 34 [341 Educ. L. Rep. 186] (D.D.C. 2016).

[179] 20 U.S.C. § 1415(i)(2)(C)(iii).

[180] 20 U.S.C. § 1415(l).

[181] Burlington Sch. Comm. v. Dep't of Educ., Commw. of Mass., 471 U.S. 359 [23 Educ. L. Rep. 1189] (1985); Florence Cnty. Sch. Dist. Four v. Carter, 510 U.S. 7 [86 Educ. L. Rep. 41] (1993).

[182] 20 U.S.C.A. § 1415(g).

[183] L.R. *ex rel.* L.R. v. New York City Dep't of Educ., 193 F. Supp.3d 209 [339 Educ. L. Rep. 172] (E.D.N.Y. 2016).

[184] Dallas Indep. Sch. Dist. v. Woody, 178 F. Supp.3d 443 [336 Educ. L. Rep. 786] (N.D. Tex. 2016).

[185] Rockwall Indep. Sch. v. M.C., 816 F.3d 329 [329 Educ. L. Rep. 30] (5th Cir. 2016).

[186] S.B. *ex rel.* S.B. and D.B. v. New York City Dep't of Educ., 174 F. Supp.3d 798 [335 Educ. L. Rep. 998] (S.D.N.Y. 2016); S.C. and J.C. *ex rel.* T.C. v. Katonah-Lewisboro Cent. Sch. Dist., 175 F. Supp.3d 237, 335 Educ. L. Rep. 1025 (S.D.N.Y. 2016); T.Y. and K.Y. *ex rel.* T.Y. v. New York City Dep't of Educ., 2016 WL 6988811 (E.D.N.Y. 2016); W.A. and M.S. *ex rel.* W.E. v. Hendrick Hudson Cent. Sch. Dist., 2016 WL 6915271 (S.D.N.Y. 2016).

[187] W.A. and M.S. *ex rel.* W.E. v. Hendrick Hudson Cent. Sch. Dist., 2016 WL 6915271 (S.D.N.Y. 2016); *See* also T.K. and S.K. *ex rel.* L.K. v. New York City Dep't of Educ., 810 F.3d 869 [326 Educ. L. Rep. 609] (2d Cir. 2016); E.H. *ex rel.* M.K. v. New York City Dep't of Educ., 164 F. Supp.3d 539 [334 Educ. L. Rep. 230] (S.D.N.Y. 2016); W.S. *ex rel.* A.S. v. City Sch. Dist. of City of N.Y., 188 F. Supp.3d 293 [338 Educ. L. Rep. 736] (S.D.N.Y. 2016).

[188] S.Y. and R.Y. *ex rel.* R.Y. v. New York City Dep't of Educ., 210 F. Supp.3d 556 [341 Educ. L. Rep. 739] (S.D.N.Y. 2016).

[189] W.W. and D.C. *ex rel.* M.C. v. New York City Dep't of Educ., 160 F. Supp. 3d 618 [333 Educ. L. Rep. 235] (S.D.N.Y. 2016).

[190] Wimbish v. Dist. of Columbia, 153 F. Supp. 3d 4 [332 Educ. L. Rep. 118] (D.D.C. 2015).

[191] 20 U.S.C. § 1415(i)(2)(C)(iii). See also Florence Cnty. Sch. Dist. Four v. Carter, 510 U.S. 7, 16 [86 Educ. L. Rep. 41] (1993); Sch. Comm. of the Town of Burlington, Mass. v. Dep't of Educ. of Mass., 471 U.S. 359, 374 [23 Educ. L. Rep. 1189] (1985).

[192] Florence Cnty. Sch. Dist. Four v. Carter, 510 U.S. 7, 16, 114 S. Ct. 361, 126 L.Ed.2d 284 (1993); Burlington Sch. Comm. v. Dep't of Educ., Commw. of Mass., 471 U.S. 359, 374, 105 S. Ct. 1996, 85 L.Ed.2d 385 (1985).

[193] Damarcus S. v. Dist. of Columbia, 190 F. Supp.3d 35 [338 Educ. L. Rep. 823] (D.D.C. 2016).

[194] B.D. *ex rel.* Davis v. Dist. of Columbia, 75 F. Supp. 3d 225 [319 Educ. L. Rep. 321] (D.D.C. 2014) *aff'd in part, rev'd in part and remanded* 817 F.3d 792 [329 Educ. L. Rep. 612] (D.C. Cir. 2016).

[195] Brown v. Dist. of Columbia, 179 F. Supp.3d 15 [336 Educ. L. Rep. 873] (D.D.C. 2016).

[196] Lopez-Young v. Dist. of Columbia, 211 F. Supp.3d 42 [341 Educ. L. Rep. 784] (D.D.C. 2016).

[197] 20 U.S.C.A. § 1415(i)(3)(B)(i).

[198] 20 U.S.C. § 1415(i)(3)(B)(i).

[199] The *Laffey* matrix is "a schedule of charges based on years of experience developed in Laffey v. Northwest Airlines., 572 F. Supp. 354 (D.D.C.1983), rev'd on other grounds, 746 F.2d 4 (D.C.Cir.1984), cert. denied, 472 U.S. 1021, 105 S. Ct. 3488, 87 L.Ed.2d 622 (1985)." Covington v. Dist. of Columbia, 57 F.3d 1101, 1105 (D.C.Cir.1995).

[200] 20 U.S.C.A. § 1415(i)(3)(B)(i).

[201] Joaquin v. Friendship Pub. Charter Sch., 188 F. Supp.3d 1 [338 Educ. L. Rep. 714] (D.D.C. 2016).

[202] Hammond v. Dist. of Columbia, 183 F. Supp.3d [337 Educ. L. Rep. 805]; Jackson-Johnson v. Dist. of Columbia, 174 F. Supp.3d 109 [335 Educ. L. Rep. 935] (D.D.C. 2016); Joaquin v. Friendship Pub. Charter Sch., 188 F. Supp.3d 1 [338 Educ. L. Rep. 714] (D.D.C. 2016);

[203] Taylor v. Dist. of Columbia, 187 F. Supp.3d 46 [338 Educ. L. Rep. 353] 205 F. Supp. 3d 75 [340 Educ. L. Rep. 649] (D.D.C. 2016). *See also* Collins v. Dist., of Columbia, 146 F. Supp. 3d 32 [331 Educ. L. Rep. 199] (D.D.C. 2015) (reducing an award by 35% to reflect limited parental success).

[204] Platt v. Dist. of Columbia, 168 F. Supp.3d 253 [334 Educ. L. Rep. 882] (D.D.C. 2016). *See also* Wilhite v. Dist. of Columbia, 196 F. Supp.3d 1 [339 Educ. L. Rep. 709] (D.D.C. 2016).

[205] Briggs v. Dist. of Columbia, 174 F. Supp.3d 15 [335 Educ. L. Rep. 929] (D.D.C. 2016); Jones v. Dist. of Columbia, 153 F. Supp. 3d 114 [332 Educ. L. Rep. 128] (D.D.C. 2015); Kelsey v. Dist. of Columbia, 2016 WL 7017252 (D.D.C. 2016). *See also* Kaseman v. Dist. of Columbia, 444 F.3d 637 (D.C. Cir. 2006).

[206] McAllister v. Dist. of Columbia, 160 F. Supp. 3d 273 [333 Educ. L. Rep. 198] (D.D.C. 2016); Reed v. Dist. of Columbia, 134 F. Supp. 3d 122 [329 Educ. L. Rep. 77] (D.D.C. 2015), *aff'd in part, rev'd in part, rem'd* 843 F.3d 517 [338 Educ. L. Rep. 592] (D.C. Cir. 2016).

[207] Copeland v. Dist. of Columbia, 208 F. Supp.3d [341 Educ. L. Rep. 211] (D.D.C. 2016); Flood v. Dist. of Columbia, 172 F. Supp.3d 197 [335 Educ. L. Rep. 639] (D.D.C. 2016); Shaw v. Dist. of Columbia, 210 F. Supp.3d 46 [341 Educ. L. Rep. 674] (D.D.C. 2016).

[208] Damarcus S. v. Dist. of Columbia, 206 F. Supp.3d 459 [340 Educ. L. Rep. 738] (D.D.C. 2016). *See* USAO Attorney Fees Matrix—2015–2016, https://www.justice.gov/usao-dc/file/796471/download.

[209] Daniel v. Dist. of Columbia, 174 F. Supp.3d 532 [335 Educ. L. Rep. 976] (D.D.C. 2016).

[210] 20 U.S.C.A. 1415(i)(3)(D)(i)

[211] Salmeron v. Dist. of Columbia, 195 F. Supp.3d 153 [339 Educ. L. Rep. 990] (D.D.C. 2016).

[212] E.C., C.O. *ex rel.* C.C.O. v. Philadelphia Sch. Dist., 91 F. Supp. 3d 598 [321 Educ. L. Rep. 971] (E.D. Pa. 2015), aff'd 644 F. App'x 154 [333 Educ. L. Rep. 64] (3d Cir. 2016). *See also* Rena C. *ex rel.* A.D. v. Colonial Sch. Dist., 2016 WL 737 WL 7374547 (E.D. Pa. 2016) (holding that a parent was not entitled to attorney fees beyond the point at which the board made a settlement offer).

[213] Tina M. *ex rel.* S.M. v. St. Tammany Parish Sch. Bd., 816 F.3d 57 [328 Educ. L. Rep. 512] (5th Cir. 2016).

[214] A.P. *ex rel.* Pursley v. Bd. of Educ. for Tullahoma, 160 F. Supp.3d 1024 [333 Educ. L. Rep. 264] (E.D. Tenn. 2015).

[215] Beauchamp v. Anaheim Union High Sch. Dist., 816 F.3d 1216 [329 Educ. L. Rep. 43] (9th Cir. 2016).

[216] R.M-G. *ex rel.* A.R. v. Bd. of Educ. for Las Vegas, 645 F. App'x 672 [333 Educ. L. Rep. 113] (10th Cir. 2016).

[217] R.V. *ex rel.* S.V-W. v. Rivera, 2016 WL 7048953 (E.D. Pa. 2016).

[218] 42 U.S.C. § 1983.

[219] Rancho Palos Verdes v. Abrams, 544 U.S. 113, 120 S. Ct. 1453, 161 L. Educ. 2d 316 (2005).

[220] 20 U.S.C. § 1415(i)(3)(B)(i)(I); 20 U.S.C. 1401(3)(A).

[221] Gohl *ex rel.* J.G. v. Livonia Pub. Schs., 836 F.3d 672 [336 Educ. L. Rep. 114] (6th Cir. 2016).

[222] Domingo v. Kowalski, 810 F.3d 403 [326 Educ. L. Rep. 16] (2016) (6th Cir. 2016).

[223] Miller v. Monroe Sch. Dist., 159 F. Supp. 3d 1238 [332 Educ. L. Rep. 945] (W.D. Wash. 2016).

[224] K.T. v. Pittsburg Unified Sch. Dist., 2016 WL 6599466 (N.D. Cal. 2016).

[225] 29 U.S.C. § 794.

[226] 42 U.S.C. § 12101 *et seq.*

[227] *See* 42 U.S.C.§§ 12134(b), 12201(a).

[228] 42 U.S.C. §12102(1); 34 C.F. R. §104.3(j)(1).

[229] B.C. *ex rel.* J.C. v. Mount Vernon Sch. Dist., 837 F.3d 152 [336 Educ. L. Rep. 141] (2d Cir. 2016) (2d Cir. 2016).

[230] Spring v. Allegany-Limestone Cent. Sch. Dist., 655 F. App'x 25 [337 Educ. L. Rep. 16] (2d Cir. 2016).

[231] A.G. *ex rel.* Grundemann v. Paradise Valley Unified Sch. Dist. No. 69, 815 F.3d 1195 [328 Educ. L. Rep. 495] (9th Cir. 2016).

[232] J.C. *ex rel.* W.P. v. Cambrian Sch. Dist., 648 F. App'x 652 [333 Educ. L. Rep. 661] (9th Cir. 2016).

[233] C.C. *ex rel.* Cripps v. Hurst-Euless-Bedford Indep. Sch. Dist., 641 F. App'x 423 [332 Educ. L. Rep. 40] (5th Cir. 2016). *See also* Thurmon v. Mt. Carmel High Sch., 191 F. Supp.3d 894 [338 Educ. L. Rep. 910] (N.D. Ill. 2016).

[234] A.C. *ex rel.* v. Scranton Sch. Dist. and Salisbury Behavioral Health, 191 F. Supp.3d 375 [338 Educ. L. Rep. 882] (M.D. Pa. 2016).

[235] Beam v. Western Wayne Sch. Dist., 165 F. Supp.3d 200 [334 Educ. L. Rep. 303] (M.D. Penn. 2016).

[236] Miller v. Monroe Sch. Dist., 159 F. Supp.3d 1238 [332 Educ. L. Rep. 945] (W.D. Wash. 2016).

[237] Garedakis v. Brentwood Union Sch. Dist., 183 F. Supp.3d 1032 [337 Educ. L. Rep. 869] (N.D. Cal. 2016).

[238] K.T. v. Pittsburg Unified Sch. Dist., 2016 WL 6599466 (N.D. Cal. 2016).

[239] Gohl *ex rel.* J.G. v. Livonia Pub. Schs., 836 F.3d 672 [336 Educ. L. Rep. 114] (6th Cir. 2016).

[240] R.K. *ex rel.* J.K. v. Bd. of Educ. of Scott Cnty., 494 F. App'x 589 [289 Educ. L. Rep. 563] (6th Cir. 2012), *vacating* 755 F. Supp. 2d 800 [266 Educ. L. Rep. 193] (E.D. Ky. 2010), *aff'd* 637 F. App'x 922 [330 Educ. L. Rep. 521] (6th Cir. 2016).

[241] K.L. *ex rel.* Ladlie v. Mo. State High Sch. Activities Ass'n, 178 F. Supp.3d 792 [336 Educ. L. Rep. 820] (E.D. Mo. 2016).

[242] D.N. *ex rel.* Nolen v. Louisa Cnty. Pub. Schs., 156 F. Supp.3d 767 [332 Educ. L. Rep. 738] (W.D. Va. 2016).

[243] S.S. *ex rel.* S.Y. v. Springfield, 146 F. Supp. 3d 414 [331 Educ. L. Rep. 214] (D. Mass. 2015).

Appendix

U.S. Supreme Court Cases: Special Education

Edited by Julie F. Mead and Sean Bielmeier

This appendix includes edited majority opinions from cases decided by the United States Supreme Court that considered disputes arising under Section 504 of the Rehabilitation Act and the Individuals with Disabilities Education Act. When cases were resolved by a divided Court, a notation is included to indicate the concurring and/or dissenting opinions that accompany the case, though only majority opinions are presented here. Ellipses are used to denote when portions of sentences or paragraphs have been omitted and three stars [***] mark instances when entire paragraphs were omitted during editing. The reader should also be aware that internal citations and footnotes were omitted during the editing of the cases. The cases are presented in chronological order as noted in the following list, with the corresponding page number.

SOUTHEASTERN COMMUNITY COLLEGE v. DAVIS,
442 U.S. 397 (1979).

Mr. Justice Powell delivered the opinion of the Court.

This case presents a matter of first impression for this Court: Whether § 504 of the Rehabilitation Act of 1973, which prohibits discrimination against an "otherwise qualified handicapped individual" in federally funded programs "solely by reason of his handicap," forbids professional schools from imposing physical qualifications for admission to their clinical training programs.

I

Respondent, who suffers from a serious hearing disability, seeks to be trained as a registered nurse. During the 1973–1974 academic year she was enrolled in the College Parallel program of Southeastern Community College, a state institution that receives federal funds. Respondent hoped to progress to Southeastern's Associate Degree Nursing program, completion of which would make her eligible for state certification as a registered nurse. In the course of her application to the nursing program, she was interviewed by a member of the nursing faculty. It became apparent that respondent had difficulty understanding questions asked, and on inquiry she acknowledged a history of hearing problems and dependence on a hearing aid. She was advised to consult an audiologist.

On the basis of an examination at Duke University Medical Center, respondent was diagnosed as having a "bilateral, sensori-neural hearing loss." A change in her hearing aid was recommended, as a result of which it was expected that she would be able to detect sounds "almost as well as a person would who has normal hearing." But this improvement would not mean that she could discriminate among sounds sufficiently to understand normal spoken speech. Her lipreading skills would remain necessary for effective communication: "While wearing the hearing aid, she is well aware of gross sounds occurring in the listening environment. However, she can only be responsible for speech spoken to her, when the talker gets her attention and allows her to look directly at the talker."

Southeastern next consulted Mary McRee, Executive Director of the North Carolina Board of Nursing. On the basis of the audiologist's report, McRee recommended that respondent not be admitted to the nursing program. In McRee's view, respondent's hearing disability made it unsafe for her to practice as a nurse. In addition, it would be impossible for respondent to participate safely in the normal clinical training program, and those modifications that would be necessary to enable safe participation would prevent her from realizing the benefits of the program: "To adjust patient learning experiences in keeping with [respondent's] hearing limitations could, in fact, be the same as denying her full learning to meet the objectives of your nursing programs." After respondent was notified that she was not qualified for nursing study because of her hearing disability, she requested reconsideration of the decision. The entire nursing staff of Southeastern was assembled, and McRee again was consulted. McRee repeated her conclusion that on the basis of the available evidence, respondent "has hearing limitations which could interfere with her safely caring for patients." Upon further deliberation, the staff voted to deny respondent admission.

Respondent then filed suit in the United States District Court for the Eastern District of North Carolina, alleging both a violation of § 504 of the Rehabilitation Act of 1973 and a denial of equal protection and due process. After a bench trial, the District Court entered judgment in favor of Southeastern. It confirmed the findings of the audiologist that even with a hearing aid respondent cannot understand speech directed to her except through lipreading, and further found:

> "[I]n many situations such as an operation room intensive care unit, or post-natal care unit, all doctors and nurses wear surgical masks which would make lip reading impossible. Additionally, in many situations a Registered Nurse would be required to instantly follow the physician's instructions concerning procurement of various types of instruments and drugs where the physician would be unable to get the nurse's attention by other than vocal means."

Accordingly, the court concluded:

> "[Respondent's] handicap actually prevents her from safely performing in both her training program and her proposed profession. The trial testimony indicated numerous situations where [respondent's] particular disability would render her unable to function properly. Of particular concern to the court in this case is the potential of danger to future patients in such situations."

Based on these findings, the District Court concluded that respondent was not an "otherwise qualified handicapped individual" protected against discrimination by § 504. In its view, "[o]therwise qualified, can only be read to mean otherwise able to function sufficiently in the position sought in spite of the handicap, if proper training and facilities are suitable and available." Because respondent's disability would prevent her from functioning "sufficiently" in Southeastern's nursing program, the court held that the decision to exclude her was not discriminatory within the meaning of § 504.

On appeal, the Court of Appeals for the Fourth Circuit reversed. It did not dispute the District Court's findings of fact, but held that the court had misconstrued § 504. In light of administrative regulations that had been promulgated while the appeal was pending, the appellate court believed that § 504 required Southeastern to "reconsider plaintiff's application for admission to the nursing program without regard to her hearing ability." It concluded that the District Court had erred in taking respondent's handicap into account in determining whether she was "otherwise qualified" for the program, rather than confining its inquiry to her "academic and technical qualifications." The Court of Appeals also suggested that § 504 required "affirmative conduct" on the part of Southeastern to modify its program to accommodate the disabilities of applicants, "even when such modifications become expensive."

Because of the importance of this issue to the many institutions covered by § 504, we granted certiorari. We now reverse.

II

As previously noted, this is the first case in which this Court has been called upon to interpret § 504. ... Section 504 by its terms does not compel educational institutions to disregard the disabilities of handicapped individuals or to make substantial modifications in their programs to allow disabled persons to participate. Instead, it requires only that an "otherwise qualified handicapped individual" not be excluded from participation in a federally funded program "solely by reason of his handicap," indicating only that mere possession of a handicap is not a permissible ground for assuming an inability to function in a particular context.

The court below, however, believed that the "otherwise qualified" persons protected by § 504 include those who would be able to meet the requirements of a particular program in every respect except as to limitations imposed by their handicap. Taken literally, this holding would prevent an institution from taking into account any limitation resulting from the handicap, however disabling. It assumes, in effect, that a person need not meet legitimate physical requirements in order to be "otherwise qualified." We think the understanding of the District Court is closer to the plain meaning of the statutory language. An otherwise qualified person is one who is able to meet all of a program's requirements in spite of his handicap.

The regulations promulgated by the Department of HEW to interpret § 504 reinforce, rather than contradict, this conclusion. According to these regulations, a "[q]ualified handicapped person" is, "[w]ith respect to postsecondary and vocational education services, a handicapped person who meets the academic and technical standards requisite to admission or participation in the [school's] education program or activity . . . ." 45 CFR § 84.3(k)(3) (1978). An explanatory note states:

> "The term 'technical standards' refers to *all* nonacademic admissions criteria that are essential to participation in the program in question."
> 45 CFR pt. 84, App. A, p. 405 (1978) (emphasis supplied).

A further note emphasizes that legitimate physical qualifications may be essential to participation in particular programs.[7] We think it clear, therefore, that HEW interprets the "other" qualifications which a handicapped person may be required to meet as including necessary physical qualifications.

III

The remaining question is whether the physical qualifications Southeastern demanded of respondent might not be necessary for participation in its nursing program. It is not open to dispute that, as Southeastern's Associate Degree Nursing program currently is constituted, the ability to understand speech without reliance on lipreading is necessary for patient safety during the clinical phase of the program. As the District Court found, this ability also is indispensable for many of the functions that a registered nurse performs.

Respondent contends nevertheless that § 504, properly interpreted, compels Southeastern to undertake affirmative action that would dispense with the need for effective oral communication. First, it is suggested that respondent can be given individual supervision by faculty members whenever she attends patients directly. Moreover, certain required courses might be dispensed with altogether for respondent. It is not necessary, she argues, that Southeastern train her to undertake all the tasks a registered nurse is licensed to perform. Rather, it is sufficient to make § 504 applicable if respondent might be able to perform satisfactorily some of the duties of a registered nurse or to hold some of the positions available to a registered nurse.

Respondent finds support for this argument in portions of the HEW regulations discussed above. In particular, a provision applicable to postsecondary educational programs requires covered institutions to make "modifications" in their programs to accommodate handicapped persons, and to provide "auxiliary aids" such as sign-language interpreters. Respondent argues that this regulation imposes an obligation to ensure full participation in covered programs by handicapped individuals and, in particular, requires Southeastern to make the kind of adjustments that would be necessary to permit her safe participation in the nursing program.

We note first that on the present record it appears unlikely respondent could benefit from any affirmative action that the regulation reasonably could be interpreted as requiring. Section 84.44(d)(2), for example, explicitly excludes "devices or services of a personal nature" from the kinds of auxiliary aids a school must provide a handicapped individual. Yet the only evidence in the record indicates that nothing less than close, individual attention by a nursing instructor would be sufficient to ensure patient safety if respondent took part in the clinical phase of the nursing program. Furthermore, it also is reasonably clear that § 84.44(a) does not encompass the kind of curricular changes that would be necessary to accommodate respondent in the nursing program. In light of respondent's inability to function in clinical courses without close supervision, Southeastern, with prudence, could allow her to take only academic classes. Whatever benefits respondent might realize from such a course of study, she would not receive even a rough equivalent of the training a nursing program normally gives. Such a fundamental alteration in the nature of a program is far more than the "modification" the regulation requires.

Moreover, an interpretation of the regulations that required the extensive modifications necessary to include respondent in the nursing program would raise grave doubts about their validity. If these regulations were to require substantial adjustments in existing programs beyond those necessary to eliminate discrimination against otherwise qualified individuals, they would do more than clarify the meaning of § 504. Instead, they would constitute an unauthorized extension of the obligations imposed by that statute.

The language and structure of the Rehabilitation Act of 1973 reflect a recognition by Congress of the distinction between the evenhanded treatment of qualified handicapped persons and affirmative efforts to overcome the disabilities caused by handicaps. ... Section 504 does not refer at all to affirmative action, and except as it applies to federal employers it does not provide for implementation by administrative action. ... Here, neither the language, purpose, nor history of § 504 reveals an intent to impose an affirmative-action obligation on all recipients of federal funds. ...

IV

We do not suggest that the line between a lawful refusal to extend affirmative action and illegal discrimination against handicapped persons always will be clear. It is possible to envision situations where an insistence on continuing past requirements and practices might arbitrarily deprive genuinely qualified handicapped persons of the opportunity to participate in a covered program. Technological advances can be expected to enhance opportunities to rehabilitate the handicapped or otherwise to qualify them for some useful employment. Such advances also may enable attainment of these goals without imposing undue financial and administrative burdens upon a

State. Thus, situations may arise where a refusal to modify an existing program might become unreasonable and discriminatory. Identification of those instances where a refusal to accommodate the needs of a disabled person amounts to discrimination against the handicapped continues to be an important responsibility of HEW.

In this case, however, it is clear that Southeastern's unwillingness to make major adjustments in its nursing program does not constitute such discrimination. The uncontroverted testimony of several members of Southeastern's staff and faculty established that the purpose of its program was to train persons who could serve the nursing profession in all customary ways. This type of purpose, far from reflecting any animus against handicapped individuals is shared by many if not most of the institutions that train persons to render professional service. It is undisputed that respondent could not participate in Southeastern's nursing program unless the standards were substantially lowered. Section 504 imposes no requirement upon an educational institution to lower or to effect substantial modifications of standards to accommodate a handicapped person.

One may admire respondent's desire and determination to overcome her handicap, and there well may be various other types of service for which she can qualify. In this case, however, we hold that there was no violation of § 504 when Southeastern concluded that respondent did not qualify for admission to its program. Nothing in the language or history of § 504 reflects an intention to limit the freedom of an educational institution to require reasonable physical qualifications for admission to a clinical training program. Nor has there been any showing in this case that any action short of a substantial change in Southeastern's program would render unreasonable the qualifications it imposed.

V

Accordingly, we reverse the judgment of the court below, and remand for proceedings consistent with this opinion.

So ordered.

**BOARD OF EDUCATION OF THE HENDRICK HUDSON
CENTRAL SCHOOL DISTRICT v. ROWLEY,
458 U.S. 176 (1982).**

Opinion
Justice Rehnquist delivered the opinion of the Court.

This case presents a question of statutory interpretation. Petitioners contend that the Court of Appeals and the District Court misconstrued the requirements imposed by Congress upon States which receive federal funds under the Education of the Handicapped Act. We agree and reverse the judgment of the Court of Appeals.

I

The Education of the Handicapped Act (Act), 20 U.S.C. § 1401 *et seq.*, provides federal money to assist state and local agencies in educating handicapped children, and conditions such funding upon a State's compliance with extensive goals and procedures. The Act represents an ambitious federal effort to promote the education of handicapped children, and was passed in response to Congress' perception that a majority of handicapped children in the United States "were either totally excluded from schools or [were] sitting idly in regular classrooms awaiting the time when they were old enough to 'drop out.'" The Act's evolution and major provisions shed light on the question of statutory interpretation which is at the heart of this case.

Congress first addressed the problem of educating the handicapped in 1966 when it amended the Elementary and Secondary Education Act of 1965 to establish a grant program "for the purpose of assisting the States in the initiation, expansion, and improvement of programs and projects ... for the education of handicapped children." That program was repealed in 1970 by the Education of the Handicapped Act, Part B of which established a grant program similar in purpose to the repealed legislation. Neither the 1966 nor the 1970 legislation contained specific guidelines for state use of the grant money; both were aimed primarily at stimulating the States to develop educational resources and to train personnel for educating the handicapped.

Dissatisfied with the progress being made under these earlier enactments, and spurred by two District Court decisions holding that handicapped children should be given access to a public education, Congress in 1974 greatly increased federal funding for education of the handicapped and for the first time required recipient States to adopt "a goal of providing full educational opportunities to all handicapped children." The 1974 statute was recognized as an interim measure only, adopted "in order to give the Congress an additional year in which to study what if any additional Federal assistance [was] required to enable the States to meet the needs of handicapped children." The ensuing year of study produced the Education for All Handicapped Children Act of 1975.

In order to qualify for federal financial assistance under the Act, a State must demonstrate that it "has in effect a policy that assures all handicapped children the right to a free appropriate public education." 20 U.S.C. § 1412(1). ...

The "free appropriate public education" required by the Act is tailored to the unique needs of the handicapped child by means of an "individualized educational program" (IEP). The IEP, which is prepared at a meeting between a qualified representative of the local educational agency, the child's teacher, the child's parents or guardian, and, where appropriate, the child, consists of a written document containing

> "(A) a statement of the present levels of educational performance of such child, (B) a statement of annual goals, including short-term instructional objectives, (C) a statement of the specific educational services to be provided to such child, and the extent to which such child will be able to participate in regular educational programs, (D) the projected date for initiation and anticipated duration of such services, and (E) appropriate objective criteria and evaluation procedures and schedules for determining, on at least an annual basis, whether instructional objectives are being achieved." § 1401(19).

Local or regional educational agencies must review, and where appropriate revise, each child's IEP at least annually.

In addition to the state plan and the IEP already described, the Act imposes extensive procedural requirements upon States receiving federal funds under its provisions. Parents or guardians of handicapped children must be notified of any proposed change in "the identification, evaluation, or educational placement of the child or the provision of a free appropriate public education to such child," and must be permitted to bring a complaint about "any matter relating to" such evaluation and education. Complaints brought by parents or guardians must be resolved at "an impartial due process hearing," and appeal to the state educational agency must be provided if the initial hearing is held at the local or regional level. Thereafter, "[a]ny party aggrieved by the findings and decision" of the state administrative hearing has "the right to bring a civil action with respect to the complaint ... in any State court of competent jurisdiction or in a district court of the United States without regard to the amount in controversy."

Thus, although the Act leaves to the States the primary responsibility for developing and executing educational programs for handicapped children, it imposes significant requirements to be followed in the discharge of that responsibility. Compliance is assured by provisions permitting the withholding of federal funds upon determination that a participating state or local agency has failed to satisfy the requirements of the Act, and by the provision for judicial review. ...

II

This case arose in connection with the education of Amy Rowley, a deaf student at the Furnace Woods School in the Hendrick Hudson Central School District, Peekskill, N.Y. Amy has minimal residual hearing and is an excellent lipreader. During the year before she began attending Furnace Woods, a meeting between her parents and school administrators resulted in a decision to place her in a regular kindergarten class in order to determine what supplemental services would be necessary to her education. Several members of the school administration prepared for Amy's arrival by attending a course in sign-language interpretation, and a teletype machine was installed in the principal's office to facilitate communication with her parents who are also deaf. At the end of the trial period it was determined that Amy should remain in the kindergarten class, but that she should be provided with an FM hearing aid which would amplify words spoken into a wireless receiver by the teacher or fellow students during certain classroom activities. Amy successfully completed her kindergarten year.

As required by the Act, an IEP was prepared for Amy during the fall of her first-grade year. The IEP provided that Amy should be educated in a regular classroom at Furnace Woods, should continue to use the FM hearing aid, and should receive instruction from a tutor for the deaf for one hour each day and from a speech therapist for three hours each week. The Rowleys agreed with parts of the IEP, but insisted that Amy also be provided a qualified sign-language interpreter in all her academic classes in lieu of the assistance proposed in other parts of the IEP. Such an interpreter had been placed in Amy's kindergarten class for a 2-week experimental period, but the interpreter had reported that Amy did not need his services at that time. The school administrators likewise concluded that Amy did not need such an interpreter in her first-grade classroom. They reached this conclusion after consulting the school district's Committee on the Handicapped, which had received expert evidence from Amy's parents on the importance of a sign-language interpreter, received testimony from Amy's teacher and other persons familiar with her academic and social progress, and visited a class for the deaf.

When their request for an interpreter was denied, the Rowleys demanded and received a hearing before an independent examiner. After receiving evidence from both sides, the examiner agreed with the administrators' determination that an interpreter was not necessary because "Amy was achieving educationally, academically, and socially" without such assistance. The examiner's decision was affirmed on appeal by the New York Commissioner of Education on the basis of substantial evidence in the record. Pursuant to the Act's provision for judicial review, the Rowleys then brought an action in the United States District Court for the Southern District of New York, claiming that the administrators' denial of the sign-language interpreter constituted a denial of the "free appropriate public education" guaranteed by the Act.

The District Court found that Amy "is a remarkably well-adjusted child" who interacts and communicates well with her classmates and has "developed an extraordinary rapport" with her teachers. It also found that "she performs better than the average child in her class and is advancing easily from grade to grade," but "that she understands considerably less of what goes on in class than she could if she were not deaf" and thus "is not learning as much, or performing as well academically, as she would without her handicap." This disparity between Amy's achievement and her potential led the court to decide that she was not receiving a "free appropriate public education," which the court defined as "an opportunity to achieve [her] full potential commensurate with the opportunity provided to other children." According to the District Court, such a standard "requires that the potential of the handicapped child be measured and compared to his or her performance, and that the resulting differential or 'shortfall' be compared to the shortfall experienced by nonhandicapped children." The District Court's definition arose from its assumption that the responsibility for "giv [ing] content to the requirement of an 'appropriate education' " had "been left entirely to the [federal] courts and the hearing officers."

A divided panel of the United States Court of Appeals for the Second Circuit affirmed. ...

> We granted certiorari to review the lower courts' interpretation of the Act. Such review requires us to consider two questions: What is meant by the Act's requirement of a "free appropriate public education"? And what is the role of state and federal courts in exercising the review granted by 20 U.S.C. § 1415? We consider these questions separately.

III

A

This is the first case in which this Court has been called upon to interpret any provision of the Act. As noted previously, the District Court and the Court of Appeals concluded that "[t]he Act itself does not define 'appropriate education,'" but leaves "to the courts and the hearing officers" the responsibility of "giv[ing] content to the requirement of an 'appropriate education.'" Petitioners contend that the definition of the phrase "free appropriate public education" used by the courts below overlooks the definition of that phrase actually found in the Act. Respondents agree that the Act defines "free appropriate public education," but contend that the statutory definition is not "functional" and thus "offers judges no guidance in their consideration of controversies involving 'the identification, evaluation, or educational placement of the child or the provision of a free appropriate public education.'" ...

We are loath to conclude that Congress failed to offer any assistance in defining the meaning of the principal substantive phrase used in the Act. It is beyond dispute that, contrary to the conclusions of the courts below, the Act does expressly define "free appropriate public education":

> "The term 'free appropriate public education' means *special education* and *related services* which (A) have been provided at public expense, under public supervision and direction, and without charge, (B) meet the standards of the State educational agency, (C) include an appropriate preschool, elementary, or secondary school education in the State involved, and (D) are provided in conformity with the individualized education program required under section 1414(a)(5) of this title." § 1401(18) (emphasis added).

"Special education," as referred to in this definition, means "specially designed instruction, at no cost to parents or guardians, to meet the unique needs of a handicapped child, including classroom instruction, instruction in physical education, home instruction, and instruction in hospitals and institutions." "Related services" are defined as "transportation, and such developmental, corrective, and other supportive services ... as may be required to assist a handicapped child to benefit from special education."

Like many statutory definitions, this one tends toward the cryptic rather than the comprehensive, but that is scarcely a reason for abandoning the quest for legislative intent. Whether or not the definition is a "functional" one, as respondents contend it is not, it is the principal tool which Congress has given us for parsing the critical phrase of the Act. We think more must be made of it than either respondents or the United States seems willing to admit.

According to the definitions contained in the Act, a "free appropriate public education" consists of educational instruction specially designed to meet the unique needs of the handicapped child, supported by such services as are necessary to permit the child "to benefit" from the instruction. Almost as a checklist for adequacy under the Act, the definition also requires that such instruction and services be provided at public expense and under public supervision, meet the State's educational standards, approximate the grade levels used in the State's regular education, and comport with the child's IEP. Thus, if personalized instruction is being provided with sufficient supportive services to permit the child to benefit from the instruction, and the other items on the definitional checklist are satisfied, the child is receiving a "free appropriate public education" as defined by the Act.

Other portions of the statute also shed light upon congressional intent. Congress found that of the roughly eight million handicapped children in the United States at the time of enactment, one million were "excluded entirely from the public school system" and more than half were receiving an inappropriate education. ... When these express statutory findings and priorities are read together with the Act's extensive procedural requirements and its definition of "free appropriate public education," the face of the statute evinces a congressional intent to bring previously excluded handicapped children into the public education systems of the States and to require the States to adopt *procedures* which would result in individualized consideration of and instruction for each child.

Noticeably absent from the language of the statute is any substantive standard pre-scribing the level of education to be accorded handicapped children. Certainly the language of the statute contains no requirement like the one imposed by the lower courts—that States maximize the potential of handicapped children "commensurate with the opportunity provided to other children." That standard was expounded by the District Court without reference to the statutory definitions or even to the legislative history of the Act. Although we find the statutory definition of "free appropriate public education" to be helpful in our interpretation of the Act, there remains the question of whether the legislative history indicates a congressional intent that such education meet some additional substantive standard. For an answer, we turn to that history.

B
(i)

As suggested in Part I, federal support for education of the handicapped is a fairly recent development. Before passage of the Act some States had passed laws to im-prove the educational services afforded handicapped children, but many of these children were excluded completely from any form of public education or were left to fend for themselves in classrooms designed for education of their nonhandicapped peers. As previously noted, the House Report begins by emphasizing this exclusion and misplacement, noting that millions of handicapped children "were either totally excluded from schools or [were] sitting idly in regular classrooms awaiting the time when they were old enough to 'drop out.'" One of the Act's two principal sponsors in the Senate urged its passage in similar terms:

> "While much progress has been made in the last few years, we can take no solace in that progress until all handicapped children are, in fact, receiving an education. The most recent statistics provided by the Bureau of Education for the Handicapped estimate that ... 1.75 million handicapped children do not receive any educational services, and 2.5 million handicapped children are not receiving an appropriate educa-tion." (remarks of Sen. Williams).

This concern, stressed repeatedly throughout the legislative history, confirms the im-pression conveyed by the language of the statute: By passing the Act, Congress sought primarily to make public education available to handicapped children. But in seeking to provide such access to public education, Congress did not impose upon the States any greater substantive educational standard than would be necessary to make such access meaningful. Indeed, Congress expressly "recognize[d] that in many instances the process of providing special education and related services to handicapped children is not guaranteed to produce any particular outcome." Thus, the intent of the Act was more to open the door of public education to handicapped children on appropriate terms than to guarantee any particular level of education once inside.

Both the House and the Senate Reports attribute the impetus for the Act and its predecessors to two federal-court judgments rendered in 1971 and 1972. As the Senate Report states, passage of the Act "followed a series of landmark court cases establishing in law the right to education for all handicapped children." The first case, *Pennsylvania Assn. for Retarded Children v. Commonwealth*, 334 F.Supp. 1257 (Ed Pa.1971) and 343 F.Supp. 279 (1972) (*PARC*), was a suit on behalf of retarded children challenging the constitutionality of a Pennsylvania statute which acted to exclude them from public education and training. The case ended in a consent decree which enjoined the State from "deny[ing] to any mentally retarded child *access* to a free public program of education and training."

PARC was followed by *Mills v. Board of Education of District of Columbia*, 348 F.Supp. 866 (D.C.1972), a case in which the plaintiff handicapped children had been excluded from the District of Columbia public schools. The court's judgment ... provided that

> "no [handicapped] child eligible for a publicly supported education in the District of Columbia public schools shall be *excluded* from a regular school assignment by a Rule, policy, or practice of the Board of Education of the District of Columbia or its agents unless such child is provided (a) *adequate* alternative educational services suited to the child's needs, which may include special education or tuition grants, and (b) a constitutionally adequate prior hearing and periodic review of the child's status, progress, and the *adequacy* of any educational alternative."

Mills and *PARC* both held that handicapped children must be given *access* to an adequate, publicly supported education. Neither case purports to require any particular substantive level of education. Rather, like the language of the Act, the cases set forth extensive procedures to be followed in formulating personalized educational programs for handicapped children. The fact that both *PARC* and *Mills* are discussed at length in the legislative Reports suggests that the principles which they established are the principles which, to a significant extent, guided the drafters of the Act. Indeed, immediately after discussing these cases the Senate Report describes the 1974 statute as having "incorporated the major principles of the right to education cases." Those principles in turn became the basis of the Act, which itself was designed to effectuate the purposes of the 1974 statute.

That the Act imposes no clear obligation upon recipient States beyond the requirement that handicapped children receive some form of specialized education is perhaps best demonstrated by the fact that Congress, in explaining the need for the Act, equated an "appropriate education" to the receipt of some specialized educational services. The Senate Report states: "[T]he most recent statistics provided by the Bureau of Education for the Handicapped estimate that of the more than 8 million children ... with handicapping conditions requiring special education and related services, only 3.9 million such children are receiving an appropriate education." This statement, which reveals Congress' view that 3.9 million handicapped children were "receiving an appropriate education" in 1975, is followed immediately in the Senate Report by a table showing that 3.9 million handicapped children were "served" in 1975 and a slightly larger number were "unserved." A similar statement and table appear in the House Report.

It is evident from the legislative history that the characterization of handicapped children as "served" referred to children who were receiving some form of specialized educational services from the States, and that the characterization of children as "unserved" referred to those who were receiving no specialized educational services. For example, a letter sent to the United States Commissioner of Education by the House Committee on Education and Labor, signed by two key sponsors of the Act in the House, asked the Commissioner to identify the number of handicapped "children served" in each State. The letter asked for statistics on the number of children "being served" in various types of "special education program[s]" and the number of children who were not "receiving educational services.". Similarly, Senator Randolph, one of the Act's principal sponsors in the Senate, noted that roughly one-half of the handicapped children in the United States "are receiving special educational services." By characterizing the 3.9 million handicapped children who were "served" as children who were "receiving an appropriate education," the Senate and House Reports unmistakably disclose Congress' perception of the type of education required by the Act: an "appropriate education" is provided when personalized educational services are provided.

(ii)

Respondents contend that "the goal of the Act is to provide each handicapped child with an equal educational opportunity." We think, however, that the requirement that a State provide specialized educational services to handicapped children generates no additional requirement that the services so provided be sufficient to maximize each child's potential "commensurate with the opportunity provided other children." Respondents and the United States correctly note that Congress sought "to provide assistance to the States in carrying out their responsibilities under ... the Constitution of the United States to provide equal protection of the laws." But we do not think that such statements imply a congressional intent to achieve strict equality of opportunity or services.

The educational opportunities provided by our public school systems undoubtedly differ from student to student, depending upon a myriad of factors that might affect a particular student's ability to assimilate information presented in the classroom. The requirement that States provide "equal" educational opportunities would thus seem to present an entirely unworkable standard requiring impossible measurements and comparisons. Similarly, furnishing handicapped children with only such services as are available to nonhandicapped children would in all probability fall short of the statutory requirement of "free appropriate public education"; to require, on the other hand, the furnishing of every special service necessary to maximize each handicapped child's potential is, we think, further than Congress intended to go. Thus to speak in terms of "equal" services in one instance gives less than what is required by the Act and in another instance more. The theme of the Act is "free appropriate public education," a phrase which is too complex to be captured by the word "equal" whether one is speaking of opportunities or services.

The legislative conception of the requirements of equal protection was undoubtedly informed by the two District Court decisions referred to above. But cases such as *Mills* and *PARC* held simply that handicapped children may not be excluded entirely from public education. In *Mills*, the District Court said:

> "If sufficient funds are not available to finance all of the services and programs that are needed and desirable in the system then the available funds must be expended equitably in such a manner that no child is entirely excluded from a publicly supported education consistent with his needs and ability to benefit therefrom."

The *PARC* court used similar language, saying "[i]t is the commonwealth's obligation to place each mentally retarded child in a free, public program of education and training appropriate to the child's capacity...." The right of access to free public education enunciated by these cases is significantly different from any notion of absolute equality of opportunity regardless of capacity. To the extent that Congress might have looked further than these cases which are mentioned in the legislative history, at the time of enactment of the Act this Court had held at least twice that the Equal Protection Clause of the Fourteenth Amendment does not require States to expend equal financial resources on the education of each child.

In explaining the need for federal legislation, the House Report noted that "no congressional legislation has required a precise guarantee for handicapped children, i.e. a basic floor of opportunity that would bring into compliance all school districts with the constitutional right of equal protection with respect to handicapped children." Assuming that the Act was designed to fill the need identified in the House Report—that is, to provide a "basic floor of opportunity" consistent with equal protection—neither the Act nor its history persuasively demonstrates that Congress thought that equal protection required anything more than equal access. Therefore, Congress' desire to provide specialized educational services, even in furtherance of "equality," cannot be read as imposing any particular substantive educational standard upon the States.

The District Court and the Court of Appeals thus erred when they held that the Act requires New York to maximize the potential of each handicapped child commensurate with the opportunity provided nonhandicapped children. Desirable though that goal might be, it is not the standard that Congress imposed upon States which receive funding under the Act. Rather, Congress sought primarily to identify and evaluate handicapped children, and to provide them with access to a free public education.

(iii)

Implicit in the congressional purpose of providing access to a "free appropriate public education" is the requirement that the education to which access is provided be sufficient to confer some educational benefit upon the handicapped child. It would do little good for Congress to spend millions of dollars in providing access to a public education only to have the handicapped child receive no benefit from that education. The statutory definition of "free appropriate public education," in addition to requiring that States provide each child with "specially designed instruction," expressly requires the provision of "such ... supportive services ... as may be required to assist a handicapped child *to benefit* from special education." § 1401(17) (emphasis added). We therefore conclude that the "basic floor of opportunity" provided by the Act consists of access to specialized instruction and related services which are individually designed to provide educational benefit to the handicapped child.

The determination of when handicapped children are receiving sufficient educational benefits to satisfy the requirements of the Act presents a more difficult problem. The Act requires participating States to educate a wide spectrum of handicapped children, from the marginally hearing-impaired to the profoundly retarded and palsied. It is clear that the benefits obtainable by children at one end of the spectrum will differ dramatically from those obtainable by children at the other end, with infinite variations in between. One child may have little difficulty competing successfully in an academic setting with nonhandicapped children while another child may encounter great difficulty in acquiring even the most basic of self-maintenance skills. We do not attempt today to establish any one test for determining the adequacy of educational benefits conferred upon all children covered by the Act. Because in this case we are presented with a handicapped child who is receiving substantial specialized instruction and related services, and who is performing above average in the regular classrooms of a public school system, we confine our analysis to that situation.

The Act requires participating States to educate handicapped children with nonhandicapped children whenever possible. When that "mainstreaming" preference of the Act has been met and a child is being educated in the regular classrooms of a public school system, the system itself monitors the educational progress of the child. Regular examinations are administered, grades are awarded, and yearly advancement to higher grade levels is permitted for those children who attain an adequate knowledge of the course material. The grading and advancement system thus constitutes an important factor in determining educational benefit. Children who graduate from our public school systems are considered by our society to have been "educated" at least to the grade level they have completed, and access to an "education" for handicapped children is precisely what Congress sought to provide in the Act.

C

When the language of the Act and its legislative history are considered together, the requirements imposed by Congress become tolerably clear. Insofar as a State is required to provide a handicapped child with a "free appropriate public education," we hold that it satisfies this requirement by providing personalized instruction with sufficient support services to permit the child to benefit educationally from that instruction. Such instruction and services must be provided at public expense, must meet the State's educational standards, must approximate the grade levels used in the State's regular education, and must comport with the child's IEP. In addition, the IEP, and therefore the personalized instruction, should be formulated in accordance with the requirements of the Act and, if the child is being educated in the regular classrooms of the public education system, should be reasonably calculated to enable the child to achieve passing marks and advance from grade to grade.

IV

A

As mentioned in Part I, the Act permits "[a]ny party aggrieved by the findings and decision" of the state administrative hearings "to bring a civil action" in "any State court of competent jurisdiction or in a district court of the United States without regard to the amount in controversy." § 1415(e)(2). The complaint, and therefore the civil action, may concern "any matter relating to the identification, evaluation, or educational placement of the child, or the provision of a free appropriate public education to such child." In reviewing the complaint, the Act provides that a court "shall receive the record of the [state] administrative proceedings, shall hear additional evidence at the request of a party, and, basing its decision on the preponderance of the evidence, shall grant such relief as the court determines is appropriate."

The parties disagree sharply over the meaning of these provisions, petitioners contending that courts are given only limited authority to review for state compliance with the Act's procedural requirements and no power to review the substance of the state program, and respondents contending that the Act requires courts to exercise *de novo* review over state educational decisions and policies. We find petitioners' contention unpersuasive, for Congress expressly rejected provisions that would have so severely restricted the role of reviewing courts. In substituting the current language of the statute for language that would have made state administrative findings conclusive if supported by substantial evidence, the Conference Committee explained that courts were to make "independent decision[s] based on a preponderance of the evidence."

But although we find that this grant of authority is broader than claimed by petitioners, we think the fact that it is found in § 1415, which is entitled "Procedural safeguards," is not without significance. When the elaborate and highly specific procedural safeguards embodied in § 1415 are contrasted with the general and somewhat imprecise substantive admonitions contained in the Act, we think that the importance Congress attached to these procedural safeguards cannot be gainsaid. It seems to us no exaggeration to say that Congress placed every bit as much emphasis upon compliance with procedures giving parents and guardians a large measure of participation at every stage of the administrative process as it did upon the measurement of the resulting IEP against a substantive standard. We think that the congressional emphasis upon full participation of concerned parties throughout the development of the IEP, as well as the requirements that state and local plans be submitted to the Secretary for approval, demonstrates the legislative conviction that adequate compliance with the procedures prescribed would in most cases assure much if not all of what Congress wished in the way of substantive content in an IEP.

Thus the provision that a reviewing court base its decision on the "preponderance of the evidence" is by no means an invitation to the courts to substitute their own notions of sound educational policy for those of the school authorities which they review. The very importance which Congress has attached to compliance with certain procedures in the preparation of an IEP would be frustrated if a court were permitted simply to set state decisions at nought. The fact that § 1415(e) requires that the reviewing court "receive the records of the [state] administrative proceedings" carries with it the implied requirement that due weight shall be given to these proceedings. And we find nothing in the Act to suggest that merely because Congress was rather sketchy in establishing substantive requirements, as opposed to procedural requirements for the preparation of an IEP, it intended that reviewing courts should have a free hand to impose substantive standards of review which cannot be derived from the Act itself. In short, the statutory authorization to grant "such relief as the court determines is appropriate" cannot be read without reference to the obligations, largely procedural in nature, which are imposed upon recipient States by Congress.

Therefore, a court's inquiry in suits brought under § 1415(e)(2) is twofold. First, has the State complied with the procedures set forth in the Act? And second, is the individualized educational program developed through the Act's procedures reasonably calculated to enable the child to receive educational benefits? If these requirements are met, the State has complied with the obligations imposed by Congress and the courts can require no more.

B

In assuring that the requirements of the Act have been met, courts must be careful to avoid imposing their view of preferable educational methods upon the States. The primary responsibility for formulating the education to be accorded a handicapped child, and for choosing the educational method most suitable to the child's needs, was left by the Act to state and local educational agencies in cooperation with the parents or guardian of the child. The Act expressly charges States with the responsibility of "acquiring and disseminating to teachers and administrators of programs for handicapped children significant information derived from educational research, demonstration, and similar projects, and [of] adopting, where appropriate, promising educational practices and materials." § 1413(a)(3). In the face of such a clear statutory directive, it seems highly unlikely that Congress intended courts to overturn a State's choice of appropriate educational theories in a proceeding conducted pursuant to § 1415(e)(2).

We previously have cautioned that courts lack the "specialized knowledge and experience" necessary to resolve "persistent and difficult questions of educational policy." *San Antonio Independent School Dist. v. Rodriguez*, 411 U.S. [1], at 42. We think that Congress shared that view when it passed the Act. As already demonstrated, Congress' intention was not that the Act displace the primacy of States in the field of education, but that States receive funds to assist them in extending their educational systems to the handicapped. Therefore, once a court determines that the requirements of the Act have been met, questions of methodology are for resolution by the States.

V

Entrusting a child's education to state and local agencies does not leave the child without protection. Congress sought to protect individual children by providing for parental involvement in the development of state plans and policies, and in the formulation of the child's individual educational program. As the Senate Report states:

> "The Committee recognizes that in many instances the process of providing special education and related services to handicapped children is not guaranteed to produce any particular outcome. By changing the language [of the provision relating to individualized educational programs] to emphasize the process of parent and child involvement and to provide a written record of reasonable expectations, the Committee intends to clarify that such individualized planning conferences are a way to provide parent involvement and protection to assure that appropriate services are provided to a handicapped child."

As this very case demonstrates, parents and guardians will not lack ardor in seeking to ensure that handicapped children receive all of the benefits to which they are entitled by the Act.

VI

Applying these principles to the facts of this case, we conclude that the Court of Appeals erred in affirming the decision of the District Court. Neither the District Court nor the Court of Appeals found that petitioners had failed to comply with the procedures of the Act, and the findings of neither court would support a conclusion that Amy's educational program failed to comply with the substantive requirements of the Act. On the contrary, the District Court found that the "evidence firmly establishes that Amy is receiving an 'adequate' education, since she performs better than the average child in her class and is advancing easily from grade to grade." In light of this finding, and of the fact that Amy was receiving personalized instruction and related services calculated by the Furnace Woods school administrators to meet her educational needs, the lower courts should not have concluded that the Act requires the provision of a sign-language interpreter. Accordingly, the decision of the Court of Appeals is reversed, and the case is remanded for further proceedings consistent with this opinion.

So ordered.

Justice Blackmun filed separate opinion concurring in the judgment.

Justice White filed dissenting opinion in which Justice Brennan and Justice Marshall joined.

IRVING INDEPENDENT SCHOOL DISTRICT v. TATRO, 468 U.S. 883 (1984).

Chief Justice Burger delivered the opinion of the Court.

We granted certiorari to determine whether the Education of the Handicapped Act or the Rehabilitation Act of 1973 requires a school district to provide a handicapped child with clean intermittent catheterization during school hours.

I

Amber Tatro is an 8–year–old girl born with a defect known as spina bifida. As a result, she suffers from orthopedic and speech impairments and a neurogenic bladder, which prevents her from emptying her bladder voluntarily. Consequently, she must be catheterized every three or four hours to avoid injury to her kidneys. In accordance with accepted medical practice, clean intermittent catheterization (CIC), a procedure involving the insertion of a catheter into the urethra to drain the bladder, has been prescribed. The procedure is a simple one that may be performed in a few minutes by a layperson with less than an hour's training. Amber's parents, babysitter, and teenage brother are all qualified to administer CIC, and Amber soon will be able to perform this procedure herself.

In 1979 petitioner Irving Independent School District agreed to provide special education for Amber, who was then three and one-half years old. In consultation with her parents, who are respondents here, petitioner developed an individualized education program for Amber under the requirements of the Education of the Handicapped Act, as amended significantly by the Education for All Handicapped Children Act of 1975. The individualized education program provided that Amber would attend early childhood development classes and receive special services such as physical and occupational therapy. That program, however, made no provision for school personnel to administer CIC.

Respondents unsuccessfully pursued administrative remedies to secure CIC services for Amber during school hours. In October 1979 respondents brought the present action in District Court against petitioner, the State Board of Education, and others. They sought an injunction ordering petitioner to provide Amber with CIC and sought damages and attorney's fees. First, respondents invoked the Education of the Handicapped Act. Because Texas received funding under that statute, petitioner was required to provide Amber with a "free appropriate public education," which is defined to include "related services." Respondents argued that CIC is one such "related service." Second, respondents invoked § 504 of the Rehabilitation Act of 1973, 29 U.S.C. § 794, which forbids an individual, by reason of a handicap, to be "excluded from participation in, be denied the benefits of, or be subjected to discrimination under" any program receiving federal aid.

The District Court denied respondents' request for a preliminary injunction. That court concluded that CIC was not a "related service" under the Education of the Handicapped Act because it did not serve a need arising from the effort to educate. It also held that § 504 of the Rehabilitation Act did not require "the setting up of governmental health care for people seeking to participate" in federally funded programs.

The Court of Appeals reversed. (Tatro I) First, it held that CIC was a "related service" under the Education of the Handicapped Act, because without the procedure Amber could not attend classes and benefit from special education. Second, it held that petitioner's refusal to provide CIC effectively excluded her from a federally funded educational program in violation of § 504 of the Rehabilitation Act. The Court of Appeals remanded for the District Court to develop a factual record and apply these legal principles.

On remand petitioner stressed the Education of the Handicapped Act's explicit provision that "medical services" could qualify as "related services" only when they served the purpose of diagnosis or evaluation. The District Court held that under Texas law a nurse or other qualified person may administer CIC without engaging in the unauthorized practice of medicine, provided that a doctor prescribes and supervises the procedure. The District Court then held that, because a doctor was not needed to administer CIC, provision of the procedure was not a "medical service" for purposes of the Education of the Handicapped Act. Finding CIC to be a "related service" under that Act, the District Court ordered petitioner and the State Board of Education to modify Amber's individualized education program to include provision of CIC during school hours. It also awarded compensatory damages against petitioner.

...[T]he District Court then held that respondents had proved a violation of § 504 of the Rehabilitation Act. Although the District Court did not rely on this holding to authorize any greater injunctive or compensatory relief, it did invoke the holding to award attorney's fees against petitioner and the State Board of Education. The Rehabilitation Act, unlike the Education of the Handicapped Act, authorizes prevailing parties to recover attorney's fees.

The Court of Appeals affirmed. (Tatro II) That court accepted the District Court's conclusion that state law permitted qualified persons to administer CIC without the physical presence of a doctor, and it affirmed the award of relief under the Education of the Handicapped Act. In affirming the award of attorney's fees based on a finding of liability under the Rehabilitation Act, the Court of Appeals held that no change of circumstances since Tatro I justified a different result.

We granted certiorari and we affirm in part and reverse in part.

II

This case poses two separate issues. The first is whether the Education of the Handicapped Act requires petitioner to provide CIC services to Amber. The second is whether § 504 of the Rehabilitation Act creates such an obligation. We first turn to the claim presented under the Education of the Handicapped Act.

States receiving funds under the Act are obliged to satisfy certain conditions. A primary condition is that the state implement a policy "that assures all handicapped children the right to a free appropriate public education." 20 U.S.C. § 1412(1). Each educational agency applying to a state for funding must provide assurances in turn that its program aims to provide "a free appropriate public education to all handicapped children." § 1414(a)(1)(C)(ii).

A "free appropriate public education" is explicitly defined as "special education and related services." § 1401(18). The term "special education" means

> "specially designed instruction, at no cost to parents or guardians, to meet the unique needs of a handicapped child, including classroom instruction, instruction in physical education, home instruction, and instruction in hospitals and institutions."

"Related services" are defined as "transportation, and such developmental, corrective, and other supportive services (including speech pathology and audiology, psychological services, physical and occupational therapy, recreation, and medical and counseling services, except that such medical services shall be for diagnostic and evaluation purposes only) as may be required to assist a handicapped child to benefit from special education, and includes the early identification and assessment of handicapping conditions in children."

The issue in this case is whether CIC is a "related service" that petitioner is obliged to provide to Amber. We must answer two questions: first, whether CIC is a "supportive servic[e] ... required to assist a handicapped child to benefit from special education"; and second, whether CIC is excluded from this definition as a "medical servic[e]" serving purposes other than diagnosis or evaluation.

A

The Court of Appeals was clearly correct in holding that CIC is a "supportive servic[e] ... required to assist a handicapped child to benefit from special education." It is clear on this record that, without having CIC services available during the school day, Amber cannot attend school and thereby "benefit from special education." CIC services therefore fall squarely within the definition of a "supportive service."

As we have stated before, "Congress sought primarily to make public education available to handicapped children" and "to make such access meaningful." Board of Education of Hendrick Hudson Central School District v. Rowley, 458 U.S. 176, 192 (1982). A service that enables a handicapped child to remain at school during the day is an important means of providing the child with the meaningful access to education that Congress envisioned. The Act makes specific provision for services, like transportation, for example, that do no more than enable a child to be physically present in class, and the Act specifically authorizes grants for schools to alter buildings and equipment to make them accessible to the handicapped. Services like CIC that permit a child to remain at school during the day are no less related to the effort to educate than are services that enable the child to reach, enter, or exit the school.

We hold that CIC services in this case qualify as a "supportive servic[e] ... required to assist a handicapped child to benefit from special education."

B

We also agree with the Court of Appeals that provision of CIC is not a "medical servic[e]," which a school is required to provide only for purposes of diagnosis or evaluation. We begin with the regulations of the Department of Education, which are entitled to deference. The regulations define "related services" for handicapped children to include "school health services," which are defined in turn as "services provided by a qualified school nurse or other qualified person." "Medical services" are defined as "services provided by a licensed physician." Thus, the Secretary has determined that the services of a school nurse otherwise qualifying as a "related service" are not subject to exclusion as a "medical service," but that the services of a physician are excludable as such.

This definition of "medical services" is a reasonable interpretation of congressional intent. Although Congress devoted little discussion to the "medical services" exclusion, the Secretary could reasonably have concluded that it was designed to spare schools from an obligation to provide a service that might well prove unduly expensive and beyond the range of their competence. From this understanding of congressional purpose, the Secretary could reasonably have concluded that Congress intended to impose the obligation to provide school nursing services.

Congress plainly required schools to hire various specially trained personnel to help handicapped children, such as "trained occupational therapists, speech therapists, psychologists, social workers and other appropriately trained personnel." S.Rep. No. 94–168. School nurses have long been a part of the educational system, and the Secretary could therefore reasonably conclude that school nursing services are not the sort of burden that Congress intended to exclude as a "medical service." By limiting the "medical services" exclusion to the services of a physician or hospital, both far more expensive, the Secretary has given a permissible construction to the provision.

Petitioner's contrary interpretation of the "medical services" exclusion is unconvincing. In petitioner's view, CIC is a "medical service," even though it may be provided by a nurse or trained layperson; that conclusion rests on its reading of Texas law that confines CIC to uses in accordance with a physician's prescription and under a physician's ultimate supervision. Aside from conflicting with the Secretary's reasonable interpretation of congressional intent, however, such a rule would be anomalous. Nurses in petitioner School District are authorized to dispense oral medications and administer emergency injections in accordance with a physician's prescription. This kind of service for nonhandicapped children is difficult to distinguish from the provision of CIC to the handicapped. It would be strange indeed if Congress, in attempting to extend special services to handicapped children, were unwilling to guarantee them services of a kind that are routinely provided to the nonhandicapped.

To keep in perspective the obligation to provide services that relate to both the health and educational needs of handicapped students, we note several limitations that should minimize the burden petitioner fears. First, to be entitled to related services, a child must be handicapped so as to require special education. In the absence of a handicap that requires special education, the need for what otherwise might qualify as a related service does not create an obligation under the Act.

Second, only those services necessary to aid a handicapped child to benefit from special education must be provided, regardless how easily a school nurse or layperson could furnish them. For example, if a particular medication or treatment may appropriately be administered to a handicapped child other than during the school day, a school is not required to provide nursing services to administer it.

Third, the regulations state that school nursing services must be provided only if they can be performed by a nurse or other qualified person, not if they must be performed by a physician. It bears mentioning that here not even the services of a nurse are required; as is conceded, a layperson with minimal training is qualified to provide CIC.

Finally, we note that respondents are not asking petitioner to provide equipment that Amber needs for CIC. They seek only the services of a qualified person at the school.

We conclude that provision of CIC to Amber is not subject to exclusion as a "medical service," and we affirm the Court of Appeals' holding that CIC is a "related service" under the Education of the Handicapped Act.

III

Respondents sought relief not only under the Education of the Handicapped Act but under § 504 of the Rehabilitation Act as well. After finding petitioner liable to provide CIC under the former, the District Court proceeded to hold that petitioner was similarly liable under § 504 and that respondents were therefore entitled to attorney's fees under § 505 of the Rehabilitation Act. We hold today, in Smith v. Robinson, 468 U.S. 992, that § 504 is inapplicable when relief is available under the Education of the Handicapped Act to remedy a denial of educational services. Respondents are therefore not entitled to relief under § 504, and we reverse the Court of Appeals' holding that respondents are entitled to recover attorney's fees. In all other respects, the judgment of the Court of Appeals is affirmed.

It is so ordered.

Justice Brennan filed a statement concurring in part and dissenting in part in which Justice Marshall joined.

Justice Stevens filed a statement concurring in part and dissenting in part.

[Editor's note: In 1986, Congress passed the Handicapped Children's Protection Act that amended what is now the Individuals with Disabilities Education Act (IDEA) by adding a provision that explicitly made available attorney's fees as a remedy for a prevailing party under the IDEA. The Court's ruling in *Smith v. Robinson* that plaintiffs must first exhaust administrative remedies under the IDEA before seeking judicial intervention remains good law.]

SMITH v. ROBINSON,
468 U.S. 992 (1984).

Justice Blackmun delivered the opinion of the Court.

This case presents questions regarding the award of attorney's fees in a proceeding to secure a "free appropriate public education" for a handicapped child. At various stages in the proceeding, petitioners asserted claims for relief based on state law, on the Education of the Handicapped Act (EHA), on § 504 of the Rehabilitation Act of 1973, and on the Due Process and Equal Protection Clauses of the Fourteenth Amendment to the United States Constitution. The United States Court of Appeals for the First

Circuit concluded that because the proceeding, in essence, was one to enforce the provisions of the EHA, a statute that does not provide for the payment of attorney's fees, petitioners were not entitled to such fees. Petitioners insist that this Court's decision in Maher v. Gagne, 448 U.S. 122, (1980), compels a different conclusion.

I

The procedural history of the case is complicated, but it is significant to the resolution of the issues. Petitioner Thomas F. Smith III (Tommy), suffers from cerebral palsy and a variety of physical and emotional handicaps. When this proceeding began in November 1976, Tommy was eight years old. In the preceding December, the Cumberland School Committee had agreed to place Tommy in a day program at Emma Pendleton Bradley Hospital in East Providence, R.I., and Tommy began attending that program. In November 1976, however, the Superintendent of Schools informed Tommy's parents... that the School Committee no longer would fund Tommy's placement because, as it construed Rhode Island law, the responsibility for educating an emotionally disturbed child lay with the State's Division of Mental Health, Retardation and Hospitals (MHRH).

Petitioners took an appeal from the decision of the Superintendent to the School Committee. In addition, petitioners filed a complaint under 42 U.S.C. § 1983 in the United States District Court for the District of Rhode Island against the members of the School Committee, asserting that due process required that the Committee comply with "Article IX—Procedural Safeguards" of the Regulations adopted by the State Board of Regents regarding Education of Handicapped Children (Regulations) and that Tommy's placement in his program be continued pending appeal of the Superintendent's decision. ...

***

They sought a declaratory judgment that the procedural safeguards contained in Article IX of the Regulations did not comply with the Due Process Clause of the Fourteenth Amendment or with the requirements of the EHA, 20 U.S.C. § 1415, and its accompanying regulations. They also sought an injunction prohibiting the Commissioner and Associate Commissioner from conducting any more hearings in review of decisions of the Rhode Island local education agencies (LEA's) unless and until the Board of Regents adopted regulations that conformed to the requirements of § 1415 and its regulations. Finally, they sought reasonable attorney's fees and costs.

***

On January 12, 1981, the District Court issued an order declaring petitioners' rights, entering a permanent injunction against the School Committee defendants, and approving an award of attorney's fees against those defendants. The court ordered the School Committee to pay the full cost of Tommy's attendance at Harmony Hill School, Tommy's then-current placement. ...

***

On April 30, 1982, the District Court ruled orally that petitioners were entitled to fees and costs in the amount of $32,109 for the hours spent in the state administrative process both before and after the state defendants were named as parties to the federal litigation. ...[T]he court reasoned that because petitioners were required to exhaust their EHA remedies before bringing their § 1983 and § 504 claims, they were entitled to fees for those procedures. ...

The Court of Appeals reversed. The court first noted that, under what is labeled the "American Rule," attorney's fees are available as a general matter only when statutory authority so provides. Here the action and relief granted in this case fell within the reach of the EHA, a federal statute that establishes a comprehensive federal-state scheme for the provision of special education to handicapped children, but that does not provide for attorney's fees. ...

***

[W]e granted certiorari.

II

Petitioners insist that the Court of Appeals simply ignored the guidance of this Court in Maher v. Gagne, that a prevailing party who asserts substantial but unaddressed constitutional claims is entitled to attorney's fees under 42 U.S.C. § 1988. ...

Resolution of this dispute requires us to explore congressional intent, both in authorizing fees for substantial unaddressed constitutional claims and in setting out the elaborate substantive and procedural requirements of the EHA, with no indication that attorney's fees are available in an action to enforce those requirements. We turn first to petitioners' claim that they were entitled to fees under 42 U.S.C. § 1988 because they asserted substantial constitutional claims.

III

As the legislative history illustrates and as this Court has recognized, § 1988 is a broad grant of authority to courts to award attorney's fees to plaintiffs seeking to vindicate federal constitutional and statutory rights. Congress did not intend to have that authority extinguished by the fact that the case was settled or resolved on a nonconstitutional ground. As the Court also has recognized, however, the authority to award fees in a case where the plaintiff prevails on substantial constitutional claims is not without qualification. Due regard must be paid, not only to the fact that a plaintiff "prevailed," but also to the relationship between the claims on which effort was expended and the ultimate relief obtained. Thus, for example, fees are not properly awarded for work done on a claim on which a plaintiff did not prevail and which involved distinctly different facts and legal theories from the claims on the basis of which relief was awarded. Although, in most cases, there is no clear line between hours of work that contributed to a plaintiff's success and those that did not, district courts remain charged with the responsibility, imposed by Congress, of evaluating the award requested in light of the relationship between particular claims for which work is done and the plaintiff's success.

A similar analysis is appropriate in a case like this, where the prevailing plaintiffs rely on substantial, unaddressed constitutional claims as the basis for an award of attorney's fees. The fact that constitutional claims are made does not render automatic an award of fees for the entire proceeding. Congress' purpose in authorizing a fee award for an unaddressed constitutional claim was to avoid penalizing a litigant for the fact that courts are properly reluctant to resolve constitutional questions if a nonconstitutional claim is dispositive. That purpose does not alter the requirement that a claim for which fees are awarded be reasonably related to the plaintiff's ultimate success. It simply authorizes a district court to assume that the plaintiff has prevailed on his fee-generating claim and to award fees appropriate to that success.

In light of the requirement that a claim for which fees are awarded be reasonably related to the plaintiff's ultimate success, it is clear that plaintiffs may not rely simply on the fact that substantial fee-generating claims were made during the course of the litigation. Closer examination of the nature of the claims and the relationship between those claims and petitioners' ultimate success is required.

Besides making a claim under the EHA, petitioners asserted at two different points in the proceedings that procedures employed by state officials denied them due process. They also claimed that Tommy was being discriminated against on the basis of his handicapping condition, in violation of the Equal Protection Clause of the Fourteenth Amendment.

A

The first due process claim may be disposed of briefly. Petitioners challenged the refusal of the School Board to grant them a full hearing before terminating Tommy's funding. Petitioners were awarded fees against the School Committee for their efforts in obtaining an injunction to prevent that due process deprivation. The award was not challenged on appeal and we therefore assume that it was proper.

The fact that petitioners prevailed on their initial due process claim, however, by itself does not entitle them to fees for the subsequent administrative and judicial proceedings. The due process claim that entitled petitioners to an order maintaining Tommy's placement throughout the course of the subsequent proceedings is entirely separate from the claims petitioners made in those proceedings. Nor were those proceedings necessitated by the School Committee's failings. Even if the School Committee had complied with state regulations and had guaranteed Tommy's continued placement pending administrative review of its decision, petitioners still would have had to avail themselves of the administrative process in order to obtain the permanent relief they wanted—an interpretation of state law that placed on the School Committee the obligation to pay for Tommy's education. Petitioners' initial due process claim is not sufficiently related to their ultimate success to support an award of fees for the entire proceeding. We turn, therefore, to petitioners' other § 1983 claims.

As petitioners emphasize, their § 1983 claims were not based on alleged violations of the EHA, but on independent claims of constitutional deprivations. As the Court of Appeals recognized, however, petitioners' constitutional claims, a denial of due process and a denial of a free appropriate public education as guaranteed by the Equal Protection Clause, are virtually identical to their EHA claims. The question to be asked, therefore, is whether Congress intended that the EHA be the exclusive avenue through which a plaintiff may assert those claims.

B

We have little difficulty concluding that Congress intended the EHA to be the exclusive avenue through which a plaintiff may assert an equal protection claim to a publicly financed special education. The EHA is a comprehensive scheme set up by Congress to aid the States in complying with their constitutional obligations to provide public education for handicapped children. Both the provisions of the statute and its legislative history indicate that Congress intended handicapped children with constitutional claims to a free appropriate public education to pursue those claims through the carefully tailored administrative and judicial mechanism set out in the statute.

In the statement of findings with which the EHA begins, Congress noted that there were more than 8 million handicapped children in the country, the special education needs of most of whom were not being fully met. Congress also recognized that in a series of "landmark court cases," the right to an equal education opportunity for handicapped children had been established. The EHA was an attempt to relieve the fiscal burden placed on States and localities by their responsibility to provide education for all handicapped children. At the same time, however, Congress made clear that the EHA is not simply a funding statute. The responsibility for providing the required education remains on the States. And the Act establishes an enforceable substantive right to a free appropriate public education. Finally, the Act establishes an elaborate procedural mechanism to protect the rights of handicapped children. The procedures not only ensure that hearings conducted by the State are fair and adequate. They also effect Congress' intent that each child's individual educational needs be worked out through a process that begins on the local level and includes ongoing parental involvement, detailed procedural safeguards, and a right to judicial review.

In light of the comprehensive nature of the procedures and guarantees set out in the EHA and Congress' express efforts to place on local and state educational agencies the primary responsibility for developing a plan to accommodate the needs of each individual handicapped child, we find it difficult to believe that Congress also meant to leave undisturbed the ability of a handicapped child to go directly to court with an equal protection claim to a free appropriate public education. Not only would such a result render superfluous most of the detailed procedural protections outlined in the statute, but, more important, it would also run counter to Congress' view that the needs of handicapped children are best accommodated by having the parents and the local education agency work together to formulate an individualized plan for each handicapped child's education. No federal district court presented with a constitutional claim to a public education can duplicate that process.

We do not lightly conclude that Congress intended to preclude reliance on § 1983 as a remedy for a substantial equal protection claim. Since 1871, when it was passed by Congress, § 1983 has stood as an independent safeguard against deprivations of federal constitutional and statutory rights. Nevertheless, § 1983 is a statutory remedy and Congress retains the authority to repeal it or replace it with an alternative remedy. The crucial consideration is what Congress intended.

In this case, we think Congress' intent is clear. Allowing a plaintiff to circumvent the EHA administrative remedies would be inconsistent with Congress' carefully tailored scheme. The legislative history gives no indication that Congress intended such a result. Rather, it indicates that Congress perceived the EHA as the most effective vehicle for protecting the constitutional right of a handicapped child to a public education. We conclude, therefore, that where the EHA is available to a handicapped child asserting a right to a free appropriate public education, based either on the EHA or on the Equal Protection Clause of the Fourteenth Amendment, the EHA is the exclusive avenue through which the child and his parents or guardian can pursue their claim.

C

Petitioners also made a due process challenge to the partiality of the state hearing officer. The question whether this claim will support an award of attorney's fees has two aspects—whether the procedural safeguards set out in the EHA manifest Congress' intent to preclude resort to § 1983 on a due process challenge and, if not, whether petitioners are entitled to attorney's fees for their due process claim. We find it unnecessary to resolve the first question, because we are satisfied that even if an independent due process challenge may be maintained, petitioners are not entitled to attorney's fees for their particular claim.

***

We conclude that where, as here, petitioners have presented distinctly different claims for different relief, based on different facts and legal theories, and have prevailed only on a nonfee claim, they are not entitled to a fee award simply because the other claim was a constitutional claim that could be asserted through § 1983. ...

IV

We turn, finally, to petitioners' claim that they were entitled to fees under § 505 of the Rehabilitation Act, because they asserted a substantial claim for relief under § 504 of that Act.

***

There is no suggestion that § 504 adds anything to petitioners' substantive right to a free appropriate public education. The only elements added by § 504 are the possibility of circumventing EHA administrative procedures and going straight to court with a § 504 claim, the possibility of a damages award in cases where no such award is available under the EHA, and attorney's fees. As discussed above, Congress' intent to place on local and state educational agencies the responsibility for determining the most appropriate educational plan for a handicapped child is clear. To the extent § 504 otherwise would allow a plaintiff to circumvent that state procedure, we are satisfied that the remedy conflicts with Congress' intent in the EHA.

Congress did not explain the absence of a provision for a damages remedy and attorney's fees in the EHA. Several references in the statute itself and in its legislative history, however, indicate that the omissions were in response to Congress' awareness of the financial burden already imposed on States by the responsibility of providing education for handicapped children. As noted above, one of the stated purposes of the statute was to relieve this financial burden. Discussions of the EHA by its proponents reflect Congress' intent to "make every resource, or as much as possible, available to the direct activities and the direct programs that are going to benefit the handicapped." The Act appears to represent Congress' judgment that the best way to ensure a free appropriate public education for handicapped children is to clarify and make enforceable the rights of those children while at the same time endeavoring to relieve the financial burden imposed on the agencies responsible to guarantee those rights. Where § 504 adds nothing to the substantive rights of a handicapped child, we cannot believe that Congress intended to have the careful balance struck in the EHA upset by reliance on § 504 for otherwise unavailable damages or for an award of attorney's fees.

We emphasize the narrowness of our holding. We do not address a situation where the EHA is not available or where § 504 guarantees substantive rights greater than those available under the EHA. We hold only that where, as here, whatever remedy might be provided under § 504 is provided with more clarity and precision under the EHA, a plaintiff may not circumvent or enlarge on the remedies available under the EHA by resort to § 504.

***

V

The judgment of the Court of Appeals is affirmed.
It is so ordered.

Justice Brennan filed dissenting opinion in which Justice Marshall and Justice Stevens joined.

[Editor's note: In 1986, Congress passed the Handicapped Children's Protection Act that amended what is now the Individuals with Disabilities Education Act (IDEA) by adding a provision that explicitly made available attorney fees as a remedy for a prevailing party under the IDEA. The Court's ruling in *Smith v. Robinson* that plaintiffs must first exhaust administrative remedies under the IDEA before seeking judicial intervention remains good law.]

SCHOOL COMMITTEE of the TOWN OF BURLINGTON, MASSACHUSETTS v. DEPARTMENT OF EDUCATION of the COMMONWEALTH of MASSACHUSETTS, 471 U.S. 359 (1985).

Justice Rehnquist delivered the opinion of the Court.

The Education of the Handicapped Act (Act), 20 U.S.C. § 1401 *et seq.,* requires participating state and local educational agencies "to assure that handicapped children and their parents or guardians are guaranteed procedural safeguards with respect to the provision of free appropriate public education" to such handicapped children. § 1415(a). These procedures include the right of the parents to participate in the development of an "individualized education program" (IEP) for the child and to challenge in administrative and court proceedings a proposed IEP with which they disagree. Where as in the present case review of a contested IEP takes years to run its course—years critical to the child's development—important practical questions arise concerning interim placement of the child and financial responsibility for that placement. This case requires us to address some of those questions.

Michael Panico, the son of respondent Robert Panico, was a first grader in the public school system of petitioner Town of Burlington, Mass., when he began experiencing serious difficulties in school. It later became evident that he had "specific learning disabilities" and thus was "handicapped" within the meaning of the Act. This entitled him to receive at public expense specially designed instruction to meet his unique needs, as well as related transportation. The negotiations and other proceedings between the Town and the Panicos, thus far spanning more than eight years, are too involved to relate in full detail; the following are the parts relevant to the issues on which we granted certiorari.

In the spring of 1979, Michael attended the third grade of the Memorial School, a public school in Burlington, Mass., under an IEP calling for individual tutoring by a reading specialist for one hour a day and individual and group counselling. Michael's continued poor performance and the fact that Memorial School was not equipped to handle his needs led to much discussion between his parents and Town school officials about his difficulties and his future schooling. Apparently the course of these discussions did not run smoothly; the upshot was that the Panicos and the Town agreed that Michael was generally of above average to superior intelligence, but had special educational needs calling for a placement in a school other than Memorial. They disagreed over the source and exact nature of Michael's learning difficulties, the Town believing the source to be emotional and the parents believing it to be neurological.

In late June, the Town presented the Panicos with a proposed IEP for Michael for the 1979–1980 academic year. It called for placing Michael in a highly structured class of six children with special academic and social needs, located at another Town public school, the Pine Glen School. On July 3, Michael's father rejected the proposed IEP and sought review under § 1415(b)(2) by respondent Massachusetts Department of Education's Bureau of Special Education Appeals (BSEA). A hearing was initially scheduled for August 8, but was apparently postponed in favor of a mediation session on August 17. The mediation efforts proved unsuccessful.

Meanwhile the Panicos received the results of the latest expert evaluation of Michael by specialists at Massachusetts General Hospital, who opined that Michael's "emotional difficulties are secondary to a rather severe learning disorder characterized by perceptual difficulties" and recommended "a highly specialized setting for children with learning handicaps ... such as the Carroll School," a state-approved private school for special education located in Lincoln, Mass. Believing that the Town's proposed placement of Michael at the Pine Glen School was inappropriate in light of Michael's needs, Mr. Panico enrolled Michael in the Carroll School in mid-August at his own expense, and Michael started there in September.

The BSEA held several hearings during the fall of 1979, and in January 1980 the hearing officer decided that the Town's proposed placement at the Pine Glen School was inappropriate and that the Carroll School was "the least restrictive adequate program within the record" for Michael's educational needs. The hearing officer ordered the Town to pay for Michael's tuition and transportation to the Carroll School for the 1979–1980 school year, including reimbursing the Panicos for their expenditures on these items for the school year to date.

The Town sought judicial review of the State's administrative decision in the United States District Court for the District of Massachusetts pursuant to 20 U.S.C. § 1415(e)(2) and a parallel state statute, naming Mr. Panico and the State Department of Education as defendants. In November 1980, the District Court granted summary judgment against the Town ...The court also set the federal claim for future trial. The Court of Appeals vacated the judgment on the state-law claim, holding that review under the state statute was pre-empted by § 1415(e)(2), which establishes a "preponderance of the evidence" standard of review and which permits the reviewing court to hear additional evidence.

In the meantime, the Town had refused to comply with the BSEA order, the District Court had denied a stay of that order, and the Panicos and the State had moved for preliminary injunctive relief. The State also had threatened outside of the judicial proceedings to freeze all of the Town's special education assistance unless it complied with the BSEA order. Apparently in response to this threat, the Town agreed in February 1981 to pay for Michael's Carroll School placement and related transportation for the 1980–1981 term, none of which had yet been paid, and to continue paying for these expenses until the case was decided. But the Town persisted in refusing to reimburse Mr. Panico for the expenses of the 1979–1980 school year. ...

On remand, the District Court entered an extensive pretrial order on the Town's federal claim. In denying the Town summary judgment, it ruled that 20 U.S.C. § 1415(e)(3) did not bar reimbursement despite the Town's insistence that the Panicos violated that provision by changing Michael's placement to the Carroll School during the pendency of the administrative proceedings. The court reasoned that § 1415(e)(3) concerned the physical placement of the child and not the right to tuition reimbursement or to procedural review of a contested IEP. The court also dealt with the problem that no IEP had been developed for the 1980–1981 or 1981–1982 school years. It held that its power under § 1415(e)(2) to grant "appropriate" relief upon reviewing the contested IEP for the 1979–1980 school year included the power to grant relief for subsequent school years despite the lack of IEPs for those years. In this connection, however, the court interpreted the statute to place the burden of proof on the Town to upset the BSEA decision that the IEP was inappropriate for 1979–1980 and on the Panicos and the State to show that the relief for subsequent terms was appropriate.

After a 4-day trial, the District Court in August 1982 overturned the BSEA decision, holding that the appropriate 1979–1980 placement for Michael was the one proposed by the Town in the IEP and that the parents had failed to show that this placement would not also have been appropriate for subsequent years. Accordingly, the court concluded that the Town was "not responsible for the cost of Michael's education at the Carroll School for the academic years 1979–80 through 1981–82."

In contesting the Town's proposed form of judgment embodying the court's conclusion, Mr. Panico argued that, despite finally losing on the merits of the IEP in August 1982, he should be reimbursed for his expenditures in 1979–1980, that the Town should finish paying for the recently completed 1981–1982 term, and that he should not be required to reimburse the Town for its payments to date, apparently because the school terms in question fell within the pendency of the administrative and judicial review contemplated by § 1415(e)(2). The case was transferred to another District Judge and consolidated with two other cases to resolve similar issues concerning the reimbursement for expenditures during the pendency of review proceedings.

In a decision on the consolidated cases, the court rejected Mr. Panico's argument that the Carroll School was the "current educational placement" during the pendency of the review proceedings and thus that under § 1415(e)(3) the Town was obligated to maintain that placement. The court reasoned that the Panicos' unilateral action in placing Michael at the Carroll School without the Town's consent could not "confer thereon the imprimatur of continued placement," even though strictly speaking there was no actual placement in effect during the summer of 1979 because all parties agreed Michael was finished with the Memorial School and the Town itself proposed in the IEP to transfer him to a new school in the fall.

The District Court next rejected an argument, apparently grounded at least in part on a state regulation, that the Panicos were entitled to rely on the BSEA decision upholding their placement contrary to the IEP, regardless of whether that decision were ultimately reversed by a court. With respect to the payments made by the Town after the BSEA decision, under the State's threat to cut off funding, the court criticized the State for resorting to extrajudicial pressure to enforce a decision subject to further review. Because this "was not a case where the town was legally obliged under section 1415(e)(3) to continue payments preserving the status quo," the State's coercion could not be viewed as "the basis for a final decision on liability," and could only be "regarded as other than wrongful ... on the assumption that the payments were to be returned if the order was ultimately reversed." The court entered a judgment ordering the Panicos to reimburse the Town for its payments for Michael's Carroll placement and related transportation in 1980–1981 and 1981–1982. The Panicos appealed.

In a broad opinion, most of which we do not review, the Court of Appeals for the First Circuit remanded the case a second time. The court ruled, among other things, that the District Court erred in conducting a full trial *de novo,* that it gave insufficient weight to the BSEA findings, and that in other respects it did not properly evaluate the IEP. The court also considered several questions about the availability of reimbursement for interim placement. The Town argued that § 1415(e)(3) bars the Panicos from any reimbursement relief, even if on remand they were to prevail on the merits of the IEP, because of their unilateral change of Michael's placement during the pendency of the § 1415(e)(2) proceedings. The court held that such unilateral parental change of placement would not be "a bar to reimbursement of the parents if their actions are held to be appropriate at final judgment." In dictum the court suggested, however, that a lack of parental consultation with the Town or "attempt to achieve a negotiated compromise and agreement on a private placement," as contemplated by the Act, "may be taken into account in a district court's computation of an award of equitable reimbursement." To guide the District Court on remand, the court stated that "whether to order reimbursement, and at what amount, is a question determined by balancing the equities." The court also held that the Panicos' reliance on the BSEA decision would estop the Town from obtaining reimbursement "for the period of reliance and requires that where parents have paid the bill for the period, they must be reimbursed."

The Town filed a petition for a writ of certiorari in this Court challenging the decision of the Court of Appeals on numerous issues, including the scope of judicial review of the administrative decision and the relevance to the merits of an IEP of violations by local school authorities of the Act's procedural requirements. We granted certiorari only to consider the following two issues: whether the potential relief available under § 1415(e)(2) includes reimbursement to parents for private school tuition and related expenses, and whether § 1415(e)(3) bars such reimbursement to parents who reject a proposed IEP and place a child in a private school without the consent of local school authorities. We express no opinion on any of the many other views stated by the Court of Appeals.

Congress stated the purpose of the Act in these words:

> "to assure that all handicapped children have available to them ... a free appropriate public education which emphasizes special education and related services designed to meet their unique needs [and] to assure that the rights of handicapped children and their parents or guardians are protected." 20 U.S.C. § 1400(c).

The Act defines a "free appropriate public education" to mean

> "special education and related services which (A) have been provided
> at public expense, under public supervision and direction, and without
> charge, (B) meet the standards of the State educational agency, (C)
> include an appropriate preschool, elementary, or secondary school
> education in the State involved, and (D) are provided in conformity
> with [an] individualized education program." 20 U.S.C. § 1401(18).

To accomplish this ambitious objective, the Act provides federal money to state and
local educational agencies that undertake to implement the substantive and procedural
requirements of the Act.

The *modus operandi* of the Act is the already mentioned "individualized educational
program." The IEP is in brief a comprehensive statement of the educational needs of
a handicapped child and the specially designed instruction and related services to be
employed to meet those needs. The IEP is to be developed jointly by a school official
qualified in special education, the child's teacher, the parents or guardian, and, where
appropriate, the child. In several places, the Act emphasizes the participation of the
parents in developing the child's educational program and assessing its effectiveness.

Apparently recognizing that this cooperative approach would not always produce a
consensus between the school officials and the parents, and that in any disputes the
school officials would have a natural advantage, Congress incorporated an elaborate
set of what it labeled "procedural safeguards" to insure the full participation of the
parents and proper resolution of substantive disagreements. Section 1415(b) entitles
the parents "to examine all relevant records with respect to the identification, evaluation, and educational placement of the child," to obtain an independent educational
evaluation of the child, to notice of any decision to initiate or change the identification,
evaluation, or educational placement of the child, and to present complaints with respect to any of the above. The parents are further entitled to "an impartial due process
hearing," which in the instant case was the BSEA hearing, to resolve their complaints.

The Act also provides for judicial review in state or federal court to "[a]ny party aggrieved by the findings and decision" made after the due process hearing. The Act
confers on the reviewing court the following authority:

> "[T]he court shall receive the records of the administrative proceedings,
> shall hear additional evidence at the request of a party, and, basing its
> decision on the preponderance of the evidence, shall grant such relief
> as the court determines is appropriate." § 1415(e)(2).

The first question on which we granted certiorari requires us to decide whether this
grant of authority includes the power to order school authorities to reimburse parents
for their expenditures on private special education for a child if the court ultimately
determines that such placement, rather than a proposed IEP, is proper under the Act.

We conclude that the Act authorizes such reimbursement. The statute directs the
court to "grant such relief as [it] determines is appropriate." The ordinary meaning
of these words confers broad discretion on the court. The type of relief is not further
specified, except that it must be "appropriate." Absent other reference, the only possible interpretation is that the relief is to be "appropriate" in light of the purpose of the
Act. As already noted, this is principally to provide handicapped children with "a free

appropriate public education which emphasizes special education and related services designed to meet their unique needs." The Act contemplates that such education will be provided where possible in regular public schools, with the child participating as much as possible in the same activities as nonhandicapped children, but the Act also provides for placement in private schools at public expense where this is not possible. In a case where a court determines that a private placement desired by the parents was proper under the Act and that an IEP calling for placement in a public school was inappropriate, it seems clear beyond cavil that "appropriate" relief would include a prospective injunction directing the school officials to develop and implement at public expense an IEP placing the child in a private school.

If the administrative and judicial review under the Act could be completed in a matter of weeks, rather than years, it would be difficult to imagine a case in which such prospective injunctive relief would not be sufficient. As this case so vividly demonstrates, however, the review process is ponderous. A final judicial decision on the merits of an IEP will in most instances come a year or more after the school term covered by that IEP has passed. In the meantime, the parents who disagree with the proposed IEP are faced with a choice: go along with the IEP to the detriment of their child if it turns out to be inappropriate or pay for what they consider to be the appropriate placement. If they choose the latter course, which conscientious parents who have adequate means and who are reasonably confident of their assessment normally would, it would be an empty victory to have a court tell them several years later that they were right but that these expenditures could not in a proper case be reimbursed by the school officials. If that were the case, the child's right to a *free* appropriate public education, the parents' right to participate fully in developing a proper IEP, and all of the procedural safeguards would be less than complete. Because Congress undoubtedly did not intend this result, we are confident that by empowering the court to grant "appropriate" relief Congress meant to include retroactive reimbursement to parents as an available remedy in a proper case.

In this Court, the Town repeatedly characterizes reimbursement as "damages," but that simply is not the case. Reimbursement merely requires the Town to belatedly pay expenses that it should have paid all along and would have borne in the first instance had it developed a proper IEP. ...

Regardless of the availability of reimbursement as a form of relief in a proper case, the Town maintains that the Panicos have waived any right they otherwise might have to reimbursement because they violated § 1415(e)(3), which provides:

> "During the pendency of any proceedings conducted pursuant to [§ 1415], unless the State or local educational agency and the parents or guardian otherwise agree, the child shall remain in the then current educational placement of such child ...."

***

As an initial matter, we note that the section calls for agreement by *either* the *State or* the *local educational agency.* The BSEA's decision in favor of the Panicos and the Carroll School placement would seem to constitute agreement by the State to the change of placement. The decision was issued in January 1980, so from then on the Panicos were no longer in violation of § 1415(e)(3). This conclusion, however, does not entirely resolve the instant dispute because the Panicos are also seeking reimbursement for Michael's expenses during the fall of 1979, prior to the State's concurrence in the Carroll School placement.

We do not agree with the Town that a parental violation of § 1415(e)(3) constitutes a waiver of reimbursement. The provision says nothing about financial responsibility, waiver, or parental right to reimbursement at the conclusion of judicial proceedings. Moreover, if the provision is interpreted to cut off parental rights to reimbursement, the principal purpose of the Act will in many cases be defeated in the same way as if reimbursement were never available. As in this case, parents will often notice a child's learning difficulties while the child is in a regular public school program. If the school officials disagree with the need for special education or the adequacy of the public school's program to meet the child's needs, it is unlikely they will agree to an interim private school placement while the review process runs its course. Thus, under the Town's reading of § 1415(e)(3), the parents are forced to leave the child in what may turn out to be an inappropriate educational placement or to obtain the appropriate placement only by sacrificing any claim for reimbursement. The Act was intended to give handicapped children both an appropriate education and a free one; it should not be interpreted to defeat one or the other of those objectives.

The legislative history supports this interpretation, favoring a proper interim placement pending the resolution of disagreements over the IEP:

> "The conferees are cognizant that an impartial due process hearing may be required to assure that the rights of the child have been completely protected. We did feel, however, that the placement, or change of placement should not be unnecessarily delayed while long and tedious administrative appeals were being exhausted. Thus the conference adopted a flexible approach to try to meet the needs of both the child and the State." 121 Cong.Rec. 37412 (1975) (Sen. Stafford).

We think at least one purpose of § 1415(e)(3) was to prevent school officials from removing a child from the regular public school classroom over the parents' objection pending completion of the review proceedings. As we observed in *Rowley*, 458 U.S., at 192, the impetus for the Act came from two federal-court decisions, *Pennsylvania Assn. for Retarded Children v. Commonwealth*, 334 F.Supp. 1257 (ED Pa.1971), and 343 F.Supp. 279 (1972), and *Mills v. Board of Education of District of Columbia*, 348 F.Supp. 866 (DC 1972), which arose from the efforts of parents of handicapped children to prevent the exclusion or expulsion of their children from the public schools. Congress was concerned about the apparently widespread practice of relegating handicapped children to private institutions or warehousing them in special classes. We also note that § 1415(e)(3) is located in a section detailing procedural safeguards which are largely for the benefit of the parents and the child.

This is not to say that § 1415(e)(3) has no effect on parents. While we doubt that this provision would authorize a court to order parents to leave their child in a particular placement, we think it operates in such a way that parents who unilaterally change their child's placement during the pendency of review proceedings, without the consent of state or local school officials, do so at their own financial risk. If the courts ultimately determine that the IEP proposed by the school officials was appropriate, the parents would be barred from obtaining reimbursement for any interim period in which their child's placement violated § 1415(e)(3). ...

We thus resolve the questions on which we granted certiorari; ...

The judgment of the Court of Appeals is

Affirmed.

SCHOOL BOARD OF NASSAU COUNTY, FLORIDA v. ARLINE, 480 U.S. 273 (1987).

Justice Brennan delivered the opinion of the Court.

Section 504 of the Rehabilitation Act of 1973, 29 U.S.C. § 794 (Act), prohibits a federally funded state program from discriminating against a handicapped individual solely by reason of his or her handicap. This case presents the questions whether a person afflicted with tuberculosis, a contagious disease, may be considered a "handicapped individual" within the meaning of § 504 of the Act, and, if so, whether such an individual is "otherwise qualified" to teach elementary school.

I

From 1966 until 1979, respondent Gene Arline taught elementary school in Nassau County, Florida. She was discharged in 1979 after suffering a third relapse of tuberculosis within two years. After she was denied relief in state administrative proceedings, she brought suit in federal court, alleging that the school board's decision to dismiss her because of her tuberculosis violated § 504 of the Act.[1]

A trial was held in the District Court, at which the principal medical evidence was provided by Marianne McEuen, M.D., an assistant director of the Community Tuberculosis Control Service of the Florida Department of Health and Rehabilitative Services. According to the medical records reviewed by Dr. McEuen, Arline was hospitalized for tuberculosis in 1957. For the next 20 years, Arline's disease was in remission. Then, in 1977, a culture revealed that tuberculosis was again active in her system; cultures taken in March 1978 and in November 1978 were also positive.

The superintendent of schools for Nassau County, Craig Marsh, then testified as to the school board's response to Arline's medical reports. After both her second relapse, in the spring of 1978, and her third relapse in November 1978, the school board suspended Arline with pay for the remainder of the school year. At the end of the 1978-1979 school year, the school board held a hearing, after which it discharged Arline, "not because she had done anything wrong," but because of the "continued reoccurence [*sic*] of tuberculosis."

In her trial memorandum, Arline argued that it was "not disputed that the [school board dismissed her] solely on the basis of her illness. Since the illness in this case qualifies the Plaintiff as a 'handicapped person' it is clear that she was dismissed solely as a result of her handicap in violation of Section 504." The District Court held, however, that although there was "[n]o question that she suffers a handicap," Arline was nevertheless not "a handicapped person under the terms of that statute." The court found it "difficult ... to conceive that Congress intended contagious diseases to be included within the definition of a handicapped person." The court then went on to state that, "even assuming" that a person with a contagious disease could be deemed a handicapped person, Arline was not "qualified" to teach elementary school.

The Court of Appeals reversed, holding that "persons with contagious diseases are within the coverage of section 504," and that Arline's condition "falls ... neatly within the statutory and regulatory framework" of the Act. The court remanded the case "for further findings as to whether the risks of infection precluded Mrs. Arline from being 'otherwise qualified' for her job and, if so, whether it was possible to make some reasonable accommodation for her in that teaching position" or in some other position. We granted certiorari and now affirm.

II

In enacting and amending the Act, Congress enlisted all programs receiving federal funds in an effort "to share with handicapped Americans the opportunities for an education, transportation, housing, health care, and jobs that other Americans take for granted." To that end, Congress not only increased federal support for vocational rehabilitation, but also addressed the broader problem of discrimination against the handicapped by including § 504, an antidiscrimination provision patterned after Title VI of the Civil Rights Act of 1964. Section 504 of the Rehabilitation Act reads in pertinent part:

> "No otherwise qualified handicapped individual in the United States, ... shall, solely by reason of his handicap, be excluded from participation in, be denied the benefits of, or be subjected to discrimination under any program or activity receiving Federal financial assistance...." 29 U.S.C. § 794.

In 1974 Congress expanded the definition of "handicapped individual" for use in § 504 to read as follows:

> "[A]ny person who (i) has a physical or mental impairment which substantially limits one or more of such person's major life activities, (ii) has a record of such an impairment, or (iii) is regarded as having such an impairment." 29 U.S.C. § 706(7)(B).

The amended definition reflected Congress' concern with protecting the handicapped against discrimination stemming not only from simple prejudice, but also from "archaic attitudes and laws" and from "the fact that the American people are simply unfamiliar with and insensitive to the difficulties confront [ing] individuals with handicaps." To combat the effects of erroneous but nevertheless prevalent perceptions about the handicapped, Congress expanded the definition of "handicapped individual" so as to preclude discrimination against "[a] person who has a record of, or is regarded as having, an impairment [but who] may at present have no actual incapacity at all."

In determining whether a particular individual is handicapped as defined by the Act, the regulations promulgated by the Department of Health and Human Services are of significant assistance. The regulations are particularly significant here because they define two critical terms used in the statutory definition of handicapped individual. "Physical impairment" is defined as follows:

> "[A]ny physiological disorder or condition, cosmetic disfigurement, or anatomical loss affecting one or more of the following body systems:

> neurological; musculoskeletal; special sense organs; respiratory, in-
> cluding speech organs; cardiovascular; reproductive, digestive, genito-
> urinary; hemic and lymphatic; skin; and endocrine."

In addition, the regulations define "major life activities" as

> "functions such as caring for one's self, performing manual tasks,
> walking, seeing, hearing, speaking, breathing, learning, and working."

III

Within this statutory and regulatory framework, then, we must consider whether Arline can be considered a handicapped individual. According to the testimony of Dr. McEuen, Arline suffered tuberculosis "in an acute form in such a degree that it affected her respiratory system," and was hospitalized for this condition. Arline thus had a physical impairment as that term is defined by the regulations, since she had a "physiological disorder or condition ... affecting [her] ... respiratory [system]." This impairment was serious enough to require hospitalization, a fact more than sufficient to establish that one or more of her major life activities were substantially limited by her impairment. Thus, Arline's hospitalization for tuberculosis in 1957 suffices to establish that she has a "record of ... impairment" ... and is therefore a handicapped individual.

Petitioners concede that a contagious disease may constitute a handicapping condition to the extent that it leaves a person with "diminished physical or mental capabilities," and concede that Arline's hospitalization for tuberculosis in 1957 demonstrates that she has a record of a physical impairment. Petitioners maintain, however, that Arline's record of impairment is irrelevant in this case, since the school board dismissed Arline not because of her diminished physical capabilities, but because of the threat that her relapses of tuberculosis posed to the health of others.

We do not agree with petitioners that, in defining a handicapped individual under § 504, the contagious effects of a disease can be meaningfully distinguished from the disease's physical effects on a claimant in a case such as this. Arline's contagious-ness and her physical impairment each resulted from the same underlying condition, tuberculosis. It would be unfair to allow an employer to seize upon the distinction between the effects of a disease on others and the effects of a disease on a patient and use that distinction to justify discriminatory treatment.

Nothing in the legislative history of § 504 suggests that Congress intended such a result. That history demonstrates that Congress was as concerned about the effect of an impairment on others as it was about its effect on the individual. Congress extended coverage to those individuals who are simply "regarded as having" a physical or mental impairment. The Senate Report provides as an example of a person who would be covered under this subsection "a person with some kind of visible physi-cal impairment which in fact does not substantially limit that person's functioning." Such an impairment might not diminish a person's physical or mental capabilities, but could nevertheless substantially limit that person's ability to work as a result of the negative reactions of others to the impairment.

Allowing discrimination based on the contagious effects of a physical impairment would be inconsistent with the basic purpose of § 504, which is to ensure that handicapped individuals are not denied jobs or other benefits because of the prejudiced attitudes or the ignorance of others. By amending the definition of "handicapped individual" to include not only those who are actually physically impaired, but also those who are regarded as impaired and who, as a result, are substantially limited in a major life activity, Congress acknowledged that society's accumulated myths and fears about disability and disease are as handicapping as are the physical limitations that flow from actual impairment. Few aspects of a handicap give rise to the same level of public fear and misapprehension as contagiousness. Even those who suffer or have recovered from such noninfectious diseases as epilepsy or cancer have faced discrimination based on the irrational fear that they might be contagious. The Act is carefully structured to replace such reflexive reactions to actual or perceived handicaps with actions based on reasoned and medically sound judgments: the definition of "handicapped individual" is broad, but only those individuals who are both handicapped *and* otherwise qualified are eligible for relief. The fact that *some* persons who have contagious diseases may pose a serious health threat to others under certain circumstances does not justify excluding from the coverage of the Act *all* persons with actual or perceived contagious diseases. Such exclusion would mean that those accused of being contagious would never have the opportunity to have their condition evaluated in light of medical evidence and a determination made as to whether they were "otherwise qualified." Rather, they would be vulnerable to discrimination on the basis of mythology-precisely the type of injury Congress sought to prevent. We conclude that the fact that a person with a record of a physical impairment is also contagious does not suffice to remove that person from coverage under § 504.

IV

The remaining question is whether Arline is otherwise qualified for the job of elementary schoolteacher. To answer this question in most cases, the district court will need to conduct an individualized inquiry and make appropriate findings of fact. Such an inquiry is essential if § 504 is to achieve its goal of protecting handicapped individuals from deprivations based on prejudice, stereotypes, or unfounded fear, while giving appropriate weight to such legitimate concerns of grantees as avoiding exposing others to significant health and safety risks. The basic factors to be considered in conducting this inquiry are well established. In the context of the employment of a person handicapped with a contagious disease, we agree with *amicus* American Medical Association that this inquiry should include

> "[findings of] facts, based on reasonable medical judgments given the state of medical knowledge, about (a) the nature of the risk (how the disease is transmitted), (b) the duration of the risk (how long is the carrier infectious), (c) the severity of the risk (what is the potential harm to third parties) and (d) the probabilities the disease will be transmitted and will cause varying degrees of harm."

In making these findings, courts normally should defer to the reasonable medical judgments of public health officials. The next step in the "otherwise-qualified" inquiry is for the court to evaluate, in light of these medical findings, whether the employer could reasonably accommodate the employee under the established standards for that inquiry.

Because of the paucity of factual findings by the District Court, we, like the Court of Appeals, are unable at this stage of the proceedings to resolve whether Arline is "otherwise qualified" for her job. The District Court made no findings as to the duration and severity of Arline's condition, nor as to the probability that she would transmit the disease. Nor did the court determine whether Arline was contagious at the time she was discharged, or whether the School Board could have reasonably accommodated her. Accordingly, the resolution of whether Arline was otherwise qualified requires further findings of fact.

V

We hold that a person suffering from the contagious disease of tuberculosis can be a handicapped person within the meaning of § 504 of the Rehabilitation Act of 1973, and that respondent Arline is such a person. We remand the case to the District Court to determine whether Arline is otherwise qualified for her position. The judgment of the Court of Appeals is

Affirmed.

Chief Justice Rehnquist filed a dissenting opinion in which Justice Scalia joined.

HONIG v. DOE, 484 U.S. 305 (1988).

Justice Brennan delivered the opinion of the Court.

As a condition of federal financial assistance, the Education of the Handicapped Act requires States to ensure a "free appropriate public education" for all disabled children within their jurisdictions. In aid of this goal, the Act establishes a comprehensive system of procedural safeguards designed to ensure parental participation in decisions concerning the education of their disabled children and to provide administrative and judicial review of any decisions with which those parents disagree. Among these safeguards is the so-called "stay-put" provision, which directs that a disabled child "shall remain in [his or her] then current educational placement" pending completion of any review proceedings, unless the parents and state or local educational agencies otherwise agree. 20 U.S.C. § 1415(e)(3). Today we must decide whether, in the face of this statutory proscription, state or local school authorities may nevertheless unilaterally exclude disabled children from the classroom for dangerous or disruptive conduct growing out of their disabilities. In addition, we are called upon to decide whether a district court may, in the exercise of its equitable powers, order a State to provide educational services directly to a disabled child when the local agency fails to do so.

I

In the Education of the Handicapped Act (EHA or the Act), Congress sought "to assure that all handicapped children have available to them ... a free appropriate public education which emphasizes special education and related services designed to meet their unique needs, [and] to assure that the rights of handicapped children and their parents or guardians are protected." [20 U.S.C.] § 1400(c). When the law was passed in 1975, Congress had before it ample evidence that such legislative assurances were sorely needed: 21 years after this Court declared education to be "perhaps the most important function of state and local governments," *Brown v. Board of Education,* 347 U.S. 483, 493 (1954), congressional studies revealed that better than half of the

Nation's 8 million disabled children were not receiving appropriate educational services. Indeed, one out of every eight of these children was excluded from the public school system altogether; many others were simply "warehoused" in special classes or were neglectfully shepherded through the system until they were old enough to drop out. Among the most poorly served of disabled students were emotionally disturbed children: Congressional statistics revealed that for the school year immediately preceding passage of the Act, the educational needs of 82 percent of all children with emotional disabilities went unmet.

Although these educational failings resulted in part from funding constraints, Congress recognized that the problem reflected more than a lack of financial resources at the state and local levels. Two federal-court decisions, which the Senate Report characterized as "landmark," demonstrated that many disabled children were excluded pursuant to state statutes or local rules and policies, typically without any consultation with, or even notice to, their parents. See *Mills v. Board of Education of District of Columbia,* 348 F.Supp. 866 (DC 1972); *Pennsylvania Assn. for Retarded Children v. Pennsylvania,* 334 F.Supp. 1257 (ED Pa.1971), and 343 F.Supp. 279 (1972) (*PARC*). Indeed, by the time of the EHA's enactment, parents had brought legal challenges to similar exclusionary practices in 27 other States.

In responding to these problems, Congress did not content itself with passage of a simple funding statute. Rather, the EHA confers upon disabled students an enforceable substantive right to public education in participating States and conditions federal financial assistance upon a State's compliance with the substantive and procedural goals of the Act. Accordingly, States seeking to qualify for federal funds must develop policies assuring all disabled children the "right to a free appropriate public education," and must file with the Secretary of Education formal plans mapping out in detail the programs, procedures, and timetables under which they will effectuate these policies. Such plans must assure that, "to the maximum extent appropriate," States will "mainstream" disabled children, *i.e.,* that they will educate them with children who are not disabled, and that they will segregate or otherwise remove such children from the regular classroom setting "only when the nature or severity of the handicap is such that education in regular classes ... cannot be achieved satisfactorily."

The primary vehicle for implementing these congressional goals is the "individualized educational program" (IEP), which the EHA mandates for each disabled child. Prepared at meetings between a representative of the local school district, the child's teacher, the parents or guardians, and, whenever appropriate, the disabled child, the IEP sets out the child's present educational performance, establishes annual and short-term objectives for improvements in that performance, and describes the specially designed instruction and services that will enable the child to meet those objectives. The IEP must be reviewed and, where necessary, revised at least once a year in order to ensure that local agencies tailor the statutorily required "free appropriate public education" to each child's unique needs.

Envisioning the IEP as the centerpiece of the statute's education delivery system for disabled children, and aware that schools had all too often denied such children appropriate educations without in any way consulting their parents, Congress repeatedly emphasized throughout the Act the importance and indeed the necessity of parental participation in both the development of the IEP and any subsequent assessments of its effectiveness. Accordingly, the Act establishes various procedural safeguards that guarantee parents both an opportunity for meaningful input into all decisions affecting their child's education and the right to seek review of any decisions they think inappropriate. These safeguards include the right to examine all relevant records pertaining to the identification, evaluation, and educational placement of their child; prior written notice whenever the responsible educational agency proposes (or refuses) to change the child's placement or program; an opportunity to present complaints concerning any aspect of the local agency's provision of a free appropriate public education; and an opportunity for "an impartial due process hearing" with respect to any such complaints.

At the conclusion of any such hearing, both the parents and the local educational agency may seek further administrative review and, where that proves unsatisfactory, may file a civil action in any state or federal court. In addition to reviewing the administrative record, courts are empowered to take additional evidence at the request of either party and to "grant such relief as [they] determine[ ] is appropriate." The "stay-put" provision at issue in this case governs the placement of a child while these often lengthy review procedures run their course. It directs that:

> "During the pendency of any proceedings conducted pursuant to [§ 1415], unless the State or local educational agency and the parents or guardian otherwise agree, the child shall remain in the then current educational placement of such child...." § 1415(e)(3).

The present dispute grows out of the efforts of certain officials of the San Francisco Unified School District (SFUSD) to expel two emotionally disturbed children from school indefinitely for violent and disruptive conduct related to their disabilities. In November 1980, respondent John Doe assaulted another student at the Louise Lombard School, a developmental center for disabled children. Doe's April 1980 IEP identified him as a socially and physically awkward 17-year-old who experienced considerable difficulty controlling his impulses and anger. Among the goals set out in his IEP was "[i]mprovement in [his] ability to relate to [his] peers [and to] cope with frustrating situations without resorting to aggressive acts." Frustrating situations, however, were an unfortunately prominent feature of Doe's school career: physical abnormalities, speech difficulties, and poor grooming habits had made him the target of teasing and ridicule as early as the first grade; his 1980 IEP reflected his continuing difficulties with peers, noting that his social skills had deteriorated and that he could tolerate only minor frustration before exploding.

On November 6, 1980, Doe responded to the taunts of a fellow student in precisely the explosive manner anticipated by his IEP: he choked the student with sufficient force to leave abrasions on the child's neck, and kicked out a school window while being escorted to the principal's office afterwards. Doe admitted his misconduct and the school subsequently suspended him for five days. Thereafter, his principal referred the matter to the SFUSD Student Placement Committee (SPC or Committee) with the recommendation that Doe be expelled. On the day the suspension was to end, the SPC notified Doe's mother that it was proposing to exclude her child permanently from SFUSD and was therefore extending his suspension until such time as the expulsion proceedings were completed. The Committee further advised her that she was entitled to attend the November 25 hearing at which it planned to discuss the proposed expulsion.

After unsuccessfully protesting these actions by letter, Doe brought this suit against a host of local school officials and the State Superintendent of Public Instructions.

Alleging that the suspension and proposed expulsion violated the EHA, he sought a temporary restraining order canceling the SPC hearing and requiring school officials to convene an IEP meeting. The District Judge granted the requested injunctive relief and further ordered defendants to provide home tutoring for Doe on an interim basis; shortly thereafter, she issued a preliminary injunction directing defendants to return Doe to his then current educational placement at Louise Lombard School pending completion of the IEP review process. Doe reentered school on December 15, 5 ½ weeks, and 24 school-days, after his initial suspension.

Respondent Jack Smith was identified as an emotionally disturbed child by the time he entered the second grade in 1976. School records prepared that year indicated that he was unable "to control verbal or physical outburst[s]" and exhibited a "[s]evere disturbance in relationships with peers and adults." Further evaluations subsequently revealed that he had been physically and emotionally abused as an infant and young child and that, despite above average intelligence, he experienced academic and social difficulties as a result of extreme hyperactivity and low self-esteem. Of particular concern was Smith's propensity for verbal hostility; one evaluator noted that the child reacted to stress by "attempt [ing] to cover his feelings of low self worth through aggressive behavior [,] ... primarily verbal provocations."

Based on these evaluations, SFUSD placed Smith in a learning center for emotionally disturbed children. His grandparents, however, believed that his needs would be better served in the public school setting and, in September 1979, the school district acceded to their requests and enrolled him at A.P. Giannini Middle School. His February 1980 IEP recommended placement in a Learning Disability Group, stressing the need for close supervision and a highly structured environment. Like earlier evaluations, the February 1980 IEP noted that Smith was easily distracted, impulsive, and anxious; it therefore proposed a half-day schedule and suggested that the placement be undertaken on a trial basis.

At the beginning of the next school year, Smith was assigned to a full-day program; almost immediately thereafter he began misbehaving. School officials met twice with his grandparents in October 1980 to discuss returning him to a half-day program; although the grandparents agreed to the reduction, they apparently were never apprised of their right to challenge the decision through EHA procedures. The school officials also warned them that if the child continued his disruptive behavior—which included stealing, extorting money from fellow students, and making sexual comments to female classmates—they would seek to expel him. On November 14, they made good on this threat, suspending Smith for five days after he made further lewd comments. His principal referred the matter to the SPC, which recommended exclusion from SFUSD. As it did in John Doe's case, the Committee scheduled a hearing and extended the suspension indefinitely pending a final disposition in the matter. On November 28, Smith's counsel protested these actions on grounds essentially identical to those raised by Doe, and the SPC agreed to cancel the hearing and to return Smith to a half-day program at A.P. Giannini or to provide home tutoring. Smith's grandparents chose the latter option and the school began home instruction on December 10; on January 6, 1981, an IEP team convened to discuss alternative placements.

After learning of Doe's action, Smith sought and obtained leave to intervene in the suit. The District Court subsequently entered summary judgment in favor of respondents on their EHA claims and issued a permanent injunction. In a series of decisions, the District Judge found that the proposed expulsions and indefinite suspensions of respondents for conduct attributable to their disabilities deprived them of their congressionally mandated right to a free appropriate public education, as well as their right to have that education provided in accordance with the procedures set out in the EHA. The District Judge therefore permanently enjoined the school district from taking any disciplinary action other than a 2- or 5-day suspension against any disabled child for disability-related misconduct, or from effecting any other change in the educational placement of any such child without parental consent pending completion of any EHA proceedings. In addition, the judge barred the State from authorizing unilateral placement changes and directed it to establish an EHA compliance-monitoring system or, alternatively, to enact guidelines governing local school responses to disability-related misconduct. Finally, the judge ordered the State to provide services directly to disabled children when, in any individual case, the State determined that the local educational agency was unable or unwilling to do so.

On appeal, the Court of Appeals for the Ninth Circuit affirmed the orders with slight modifications. Agreeing with the District Court that an indefinite suspension in aid of expulsion constitutes a prohibited "change in placement" under § 1415(e)(3), the Court of Appeals held that the stay-put provision admitted of no "dangerousness" exception and that the statute therefore rendered invalid those provisions of the California Education Code permitting the indefinite suspension or expulsion of disabled children for misconduct arising out of their disabilities. The court concluded, however, that fixed suspensions of up to 30 schooldays did not fall within the reach of § 1415(e) (3), and therefore upheld recent amendments to the state Education Code authorizing such suspensions. Lastly, the court affirmed that portion of the injunction requiring the State to provide services directly to a disabled child when the local educational agency fails to do so.

Petitioner Bill Honig, California Superintendent of Public Instruction, sought review in this Court, claiming that the Court of Appeals' construction of the stay-put provision conflicted with that of several other Courts of Appeals which had recognized a dangerousness exception and that the direct services ruling placed an intolerable burden on the State. We granted certiorari to resolve these questions and now affirm.

II

At the outset, we address the suggestion, raised for the first time during oral argument, that this case is moot. ...

***

... Because we believe that respondent Smith has demonstrated both "a sufficient likelihood that he will again be wronged in a similar way," *Los Angeles v. Lyons,* 461 U.S. [95], at 111, 103 S.Ct. [1660], at 1670 [(1983)], and that any resulting claim he may have for relief will surely evade our review, we turn to the merits of his case.

III

The language of § 1415(e)(3) is unequivocal. It states plainly that during the pendency of any proceedings initiated under the Act, unless the state or local educational agency and the parents or guardian of a disabled child otherwise agree, "the child *shall* remain in the then current educational placement." § 1415(e)(3) (emphasis added). Faced with this clear directive, petitioner asks us to read a "dangerousness" exception into the stay-put provision on the basis of either of two essentially inconsistent assumptions: first, that Congress thought the residual authority of school officials to exclude dangerous students from the classroom too obvious for comment; or second, that Congress inadvertently failed to provide such authority and this Court must therefore remedy the oversight. Because we cannot accept either premise, we decline petitioner's invitation to rewrite the statute.

Petitioner's arguments proceed, he suggests, from a simple, commonsense proposition: Congress could not have intended the stay-put provision to be read literally, for such a construction leads to the clearly unintended, and untenable, result that school districts must return violent or dangerous students to school while the often lengthy EHA proceedings run their course. We think it clear, however, that Congress very much meant to strip schools of the *unilateral* authority they had traditionally employed to exclude disabled students, particularly emotionally disturbed students, from school. In so doing, Congress did not leave school administrators powerless to deal with dangerous students; it did, however, deny school officials their former right to "self-help," and directed that in the future the removal of disabled students could be accomplished only with the permission of the parents or, as a last resort, the courts.

As noted above, Congress passed the EHA after finding that school systems across the country had excluded one out of every eight disabled children from classes. In drafting the law, Congress was largely guided by the recent decisions in *Mills v. Board of Education of District of Columbia,* 348 F.Supp. 866 (1972), and *PARC,* 343 F.Supp. 279 (1972), both of which involved the exclusion of hard-to-handle disabled students. *Mills* in particular demonstrated the extent to which schools used disciplinary measures to bar children from the classroom. There, school officials had labeled four of the seven minor plaintiffs "behavioral problems," and had excluded them from classes without providing any alternative education to them or any notice to their parents. After finding that this practice was not limited to the named plaintiffs but affected in one way or another an estimated class of 12,000 to 18,000 disabled students, the District Court enjoined future exclusions, suspensions, or expulsions "on grounds of discipline."

Congress attacked such exclusionary practices in a variety of ways. It required participating States to educate *all* disabled children, regardless of the severity of their disabilities and included within the definition of "handicapped" those children with serious emotional disturbances. It further provided for meaningful parental participation in all aspects of a child's educational placement, and barred schools, through the stay-put provision, from changing that placement over the parent's objection until all review proceedings were completed. Recognizing that those proceedings might prove long and tedious, the Act's drafters did not intend § 1415(e)(3) to operate inflexibly and they therefore allowed for interim placements where parents and school officials are able to agree on one. Conspicuously absent from § 1415(e)(3), however, is any emergency exception for dangerous students. This absence is all the more telling in light of the injunctive decree issued in *PARC,* which permitted school officials unilaterally to remove students in " 'extraordinary circumstances.' " Given the lack of any similar exception in *Mills,* and the close attention Congress devoted to these "landmark" decisions, we can only conclude that the omission was intentional; we are therefore not at liberty to engraft onto the statute an exception Congress chose not to create.

Our conclusion that § 1415(e)(3) means what it says does not leave educators hamstrung. The Department of Education has observed that, "[w]hile the [child's] placement may not be changed [during any complaint proceeding], this does not preclude the agency from using its normal procedures for dealing with children who are endangering themselves or others." Comment following 34 CFR § 300.513 (1987). Such procedures may include the use of study carrels, timeouts, detention, or the restriction of privileges. More drastically, where a student poses an immediate threat to the safety of others, officials may temporarily suspend him or her for up to 10 schooldays. This authority, which respondent in no way disputes, not only ensures that school administrators can protect the safety of others by promptly removing the most dangerous of students, it also provides a "cooling down" period during which officials can initiate IEP review and seek to persuade the child's parents to agree to an interim placement. And in those cases in which the parents of a truly dangerous child adamantly refuse to permit any change in placement, the 10–day respite gives school officials an opportunity to invoke the aid of the courts under § 1415(e)(2), which empowers courts to grant any appropriate relief.

Petitioner contends, however, that the availability of judicial relief is more illusory than real, because a party seeking review under § 1415(e)(2) must exhaust time-consuming administrative remedies, and because under the Court of Appeals' construction of § 1415(e)(3), courts are as bound by the stay-put provision's "automatic injunction," as are schools. It is true that judicial review is normally not available under § 1415(e)(2) until all administrative proceedings are completed, but as we have previously noted, parents may bypass the administrative process where exhaustion would be futile or inadequate. While many of the EHA's procedural safeguards protect the rights of parents and children, schools can and do seek redress through the administrative review process, and we have no reason to believe that Congress meant to require schools alone to exhaust in all cases, no matter how exigent the circumstances. The burden in such cases, of course, rests with the school to demonstrate the futility or inadequacy of administrative review, but nothing in § 1415(e)(2) suggests that schools are completely barred from attempting to make such a showing. Nor do we think that § 1415(e)(3) operates to limit the equitable powers of district courts such that they cannot, in appropriate cases, temporarily enjoin a dangerous disabled child from attending school. As the EHA's legislative history makes clear, one of the evils Congress sought to remedy was the unilateral exclusion of disabled children by *schools,* not courts, and one of the purposes of § 1415(e)(3), therefore, was "to prevent *school* officials from removing a child from the regular public school classroom over the parents' objection pending completion of the review proceedings." *Burlington School Committee v. Massachusetts Dept. of Education,* 471 U.S., at 373, 105 S.Ct., at 2004 (emphasis added). The stay-put provision in no way purports to limit or pre-empt the authority conferred on courts by § 1415(e)(2); indeed, it says nothing whatever about judicial power.

In short, then, we believe that school officials are entitled to seek injunctive relief under § 1415(e)(2) in appropriate cases. In any such action, § 1415(e)(3) effectively creates a presumption in favor of the child's current educational placement which school officials can overcome only by showing that maintaining the child in his or her current placement is substantially likely to result in injury either to himself or herself, or to others. In the present case, we are satisfied that the District Court, in enjoining the state and local defendants from indefinitely suspending respondent or otherwise unilaterally altering his then current placement, properly balanced respondent's interest in receiving a free appropriate public education in accordance with the procedures and requirements of the EHA against the interests of the state and local school officials in maintaining a safe learning environment for all their students.[10]

IV

We believe the courts below properly construed and applied § 1415(e)(3), except insofar as the Court of Appeals held that a suspension in excess of 10 schooldays does not constitute a "change in placement." We therefore affirm the Court of Appeals' judgment on this issue as modified herein. Because we are equally divided on the question whether a court may order a State to provide services directly to a disabled child where the local agency has failed to do so, we affirm the Court of Appeals' judgment on this issue as well.

Affirmed.

Chief Justice Rehnquist, concurred and filed opinion.

Justice Scalia, dissented and filed opinion in which Justice O'Connor joined.

FLORENCE COUNTY SCHOOL DISTRICT FOUR v. CARTER, 510 U.S. 7 (1993).

Justice O'Connor delivered the opinion of the Court.

The Individuals with Disabilities Education Act (IDEA or Act), 20 U.S.C. § 1400 *et seq.* (1988 ed. and Supp. IV), requires States to provide disabled children with a "free appropriate public education." This case presents the question whether a court may order reimbursement for parents who unilaterally withdraw their child from a public school that provides an inappropriate education under IDEA and put the child in a private school that provides an education that is otherwise proper under IDEA, but does not meet all the requirements of § 1401(a)(18). We hold that the court may order such reimbursement, and therefore affirm the judgment of the Court of Appeals.

I

Respondent Shannon Carter was classified as learning disabled in 1985, while a ninth grade student in a school operated by petitioner Florence County School District Four. School officials met with Shannon's parents to formulate an individualized education program (IEP) for Shannon, as required under IDEA. The IEP provided that Shannon would stay in regular classes except for three periods of individualized instruction per week, and established specific goals in reading and mathematics of four months' progress for the entire school year. Shannon's parents were dissatisfied, and requested a hearing to challenge the appropriateness of the IEP. Both the local educational officer and the state educational agency hearing officer rejected Shannon's parents' claim and concluded that the IEP was adequate. In the meantime, Shannon's parents had placed her in Trident Academy, a private school specializing in educating children with disabilities. Shannon began at Trident in September 1985 and graduated in the spring of 1988.

Shannon's parents filed this suit in July 1986, claiming that the school district had breached its duty under IDEA to provide Shannon with a "free appropriate public education," and seeking reimbursement for tuition and other costs incurred at Trident. After a bench trial, the District Court ruled in the parents' favor. The court held that the school district's proposed educational program and the achievement goals of the IEP "were wholly inadequate" and failed to satisfy the requirements of the Act. The court further held that "[a]lthough [Trident Academy] did not comply with all of the procedures outlined in [IDEA]," the school "provided Shannon an excellent education in substantial compliance with all the substantive requirements" of the statute. The court found that Trident "evaluated Shannon quarterly, not yearly as mandated in [IDEA], it provided Shannon with low teacher-student ratios, and it developed a plan which allowed Shannon to receive passing marks and progress from grade to grade." The court also credited the findings of its own expert, who determined that Shannon had made "significant progress" at Trident and that her reading comprehension had risen three grade levels in her three years at the school. The District Court concluded that Shannon's education was "appropriate" under IDEA, and that Shannon's parents were entitled to reimbursement of tuition and other costs.

The Court of Appeals for the Fourth Circuit affirmed. The court agreed that the IEP proposed by the school district was inappropriate under IDEA. It also rejected the school district's argument that reimbursement is never proper when the parents choose a private school that is not approved by the State or that does not comply with all the terms of IDEA. According to the Court of Appeals, neither the text of the Act nor its legislative history imposes a "requirement that the private school be approved by the state in parent-placement reimbursement cases." To the contrary, the Court of Appeals concluded, IDEA's state-approval requirement applies only when a child is placed in a private school by public school officials. Accordingly, "when a public school system has defaulted on its obligations under the Act, a private school placement is 'proper under the Act' if the education provided by the private school is 'reasonably calculated to enable the child to receive educational benefits.' " quoting *Board of Ed. of Hendrick Hudson Central School Dist. Westchester Cty. v. Rowley,* 458 U.S. 176, 207 (1982).

The court below recognized that its holding conflicted with *Tucker v. Bay Shore Union Free School Dist.,* 873 F.2d 563, 568 (1989), in which the Court of Appeals for the Second Circuit held that parental placement in a private school cannot be proper under the Act unless the private school in question meets the standards of the state education agency. We granted certiorari to resolve this conflict among the Courts of Appeals.

II

In *School Comm. of Burlington v. Department of Ed. of Mass.,* 471 U.S. 359, 369 (1985), we held that IDEA's grant of equitable authority empowers a court "to order school authorities to reimburse parents for their expenditures on private special education for a child if the court ultimately determines that such placement, rather than a proposed IEP, is proper under the Act." Congress intended that IDEA's promise of a "free appropriate public education" for disabled children would normally be met by an IEP's provision for education in the regular public schools or in private schools chosen jointly by school officials and parents. In cases where cooperation fails, however, "parents who disagree with the proposed IEP are faced with a choice: go along with the IEP to the detriment of their child if it turns out to be inappropriate or pay for what they consider to be the appropriate placement." For parents willing and able to make the latter choice, "it would be an empty victory to have a court tell them several years later that they were right but that these expenditures could not in a proper case be reimbursed by the school officials." Because such a result would be contrary to IDEA's guarantee of a "free appropriate public education," we held that "Congress meant to include retroactive reimbursement to parents as an available remedy in a proper case."

As this case comes to us, two issues are settled: (1) the school district's proposed IEP was inappropriate under IDEA, and (2) although Trident did not meet the § 1401(a)(18) requirements, it provided an education otherwise proper under IDEA. This case presents the narrow question whether Shannon's parents are barred from reimbursement because the private school in which Shannon enrolled did not meet the § 1401(a)(18) definition of a "free appropriate public education." We hold that they are not, because § 1401(a)(18)'s requirements cannot be read as applying to parental placements.

Section 1401(a)(18)(A) requires that the education be "provided at public expense, under public supervision and direction." Similarly, § 1401(a)(18)(D) requires schools to provide an IEP, which must be designed by "a representative of the local educational agency," and must be "establish[ed]," "revise[d]," and "review[ed]" by the agency. These requirements do not make sense in the context of a parental placement. In this case, as in all *Burlington* reimbursement cases, the parents' rejection of the school district's proposed IEP is the very reason for the parents' decision to put their child in a private school. In such cases, where the private placement has necessarily been made over the school district's objection, the private school education will not be under "public supervision and direction." Accordingly, to read the § 1401(a)(18) requirements as applying to parental placements would effectively eliminate the right of unilateral withdrawal recognized in *Burlington.* Moreover, IDEA was intended to ensure that children with disabilities receive an education that is both appropriate and free. To read the provisions of § 1401(a)(18) to bar reimbursement in the circumstances of this case would defeat this statutory purpose.

Nor do we believe that reimbursement is necessarily barred by a private school's failure to meet state education standards. Trident's deficiencies, according to the school district, were that it employed at least two faculty members who were not state-certified and that it did not develop IEP's. As we have noted, however, the § 1401(a)(18) requirements—including the requirement that the school meet the standards of the state educational agency,—do not apply to private parental placements. Indeed, the school district's emphasis on state standards is somewhat ironic. As the Court of Appeals noted, "it hardly seems consistent with the Act's goals to forbid parents from educating their child at a school that provides an appropriate education simply because that school lacks the stamp of approval of the same public school system that failed to meet the child's needs in the first place." Accordingly, we disagree with the Second Circuit's theory that "a parent may not obtain reimbursement for a unilateral placement if that placement was in a school that was not on [the State's] approved list of private" schools. *Tucker,* 873 F.2d, at 568 (internal quotation marks omitted). Parents' failure to select a program known to be approved by the State in favor of an unapproved option is not itself a bar to reimbursement.

Furthermore, although the absence of an approved list of private schools is not essential to our holding, we note that parents in the position of Shannon's have no way of knowing at the time they select a private school whether the school meets state standards. South Carolina keeps no publicly available list of approved private schools, but instead approves private school placements on a case-by-case basis. In fact, although public school officials had previously placed three children with disabilities at Trident, Trident had not received blanket approval from State. South Carolina's case-by-case approval system meant that Shannon's parents needed the cooperation of state officials before they could know whether Trident was state-approved. As we recognized in *Burlington,* such cooperation is unlikely in cases where the school officials disagree with the need for the private placement.

III

The school district also claims that allowing reimbursement for parents such as Shannon's puts an unreasonable burden on financially strapped local educational authorities. The school district argues that requiring parents to choose a state approved private school if they want reimbursement is the only meaningful way to allow States to control costs; otherwise States will have to reimburse dissatisfied parents for any private school that provides an education that is proper under the Act, no matter how expensive it may be.

There is no doubt that Congress has imposed a significant financial burden on States and school districts that participate in IDEA. Yet public educational authorities who want to avoid reimbursing parents for the private education of a disabled child can do one of two things: give the child a free appropriate public education in a public setting, or place the child in an appropriate private setting of the State's choice. This is IDEA's mandate, and school officials who conform to it need not worry about reimbursement claims.

Moreover, parents who, like Shannon's, "unilaterally change their child's placement during the pendency of review proceedings, without the consent of state or local school officials, do so at their own financial risk." *Burlington, supra,* at 373–374. They are entitled to reimbursement *only* if a federal court concludes both that the public placement violated IDEA and that the private school placement was proper under the Act.

Finally, we note that once a court holds that the public placement violated IDEA, it is authorized to "grant such relief as the court determines is appropriate." 20 U.S.C. § 1415(e)(2). Under this provision, "equitable considerations are relevant in fashioning relief," and the court enjoys "broad discretion" in so doing. Courts fashioning discretionary equitable relief under IDEA must consider all relevant factors, including the appropriate and reasonable level of reimbursement that should be required. Total reimbursement will not be appropriate if the court determines that the cost of the private education was unreasonable.

Accordingly, we affirm the judgment of the Court of Appeals.

So ordered.

CEDAR RAPIDS COMMUNITY SCHOOL DISTRICT v. GARRET F.,
526 U.S. 66 (1999).

Justice Stevens delivered the opinion of the Court.

The Individuals with Disabilities Education Act (IDEA) was enacted, in part, "to assure that all children with disabilities have available to them ... a free appropriate public education which emphasizes special education and related services designed to meet their unique needs." 20 U.S.C. § 1400(c). Consistent with this purpose, the IDEA authorizes federal financial assistance to States that agree to provide disabled children with special education and "related services." The question presented in this case is whether the definition of "related services" in § 1401(a)(17)[1] requires a public school district in a participating State to provide a ventilator-dependent student with certain nursing services during school hours.

I

Respondent Garret F. is a friendly, creative, and intelligent young man. When Garret was four years old, his spinal column was severed in a motorcycle accident. Though paralyzed from the neck down, his mental capacities were unaffected. He is able to speak, to control his motorized wheelchair through use of a puff and suck straw, and to operate a computer with a device that responds to head movements. Garret is currently a student in the Cedar Rapids Community School District (District), he attends regular classes in a typical school program, and his academic performance has been a success. Garret is, however, ventilator dependent, and therefore requires a responsible individual nearby to attend to certain physical needs while he is in school.[2,3]

During Garret's early years at school his family provided for his physical care during the schoolday. When he was in kindergarten, his 18–year–old aunt attended him; in the next four years, his family used settlement proceeds they received after the ac-

---

[1]   "The term 'related services' means transportation, and such developmental, corrective, and other supportive services (including speech pathology and audiology, psychological services, physical and occupational therapy, recreation, including therapeutic recreation, social work services, counseling services, including rehabilitation counseling, and medical services, except that such medical services shall be for diagnostic and evaluation purposes only) as may be required to assist a child with a disability to benefit from special education, and includes the early identification and assessment of disabling conditions in children." 20 U.S.C. § 1401(a)(17). ...

[2,3]   "He needs assistance with urinary bladder catheterization once a day, the suctioning of his tracheotomy tube as needed, but at least once every six hours, with food and drink at lunchtime, in getting into a reclining position for five minutes of each hour, and ambu bagging occasionally as needed when the ventilator is checked for proper functioning. He also needs assistance from someone familiar with his ventilator in the event there is a malfunction or electrical problem, and someone who can perform emergency procedures in the event he experiences autonomic hyperreflexia. Autonomic hyperreflexia is an uncontrolled visceral reaction to anxiety or a full bladder. Blood pressure increases, heart rate increases, and flushing and sweating may occur. Garret has not experienced autonomic hyperreflexia frequently in recent years, and it has usually been alleviated by catheterization. He has not ever experienced autonomic hyperreflexia at school. Garret is capable of communicating his needs orally or in another fashion so long as he has not been rendered unable to do so by an extended lack of oxygen." [App. to Pet. for Cert.], at 20a.

cident, their insurance, and other resources to employ a licensed practical nurse. In 1993, Garret's mother requested the District to accept financial responsibility for the health care services that Garret requires during the schoolday. The District denied the request, believing that it was not legally obligated to provide continuous one-on-one nursing services.

Relying on both the IDEA and Iowa law, Garret's mother requested a hearing before the Iowa Department of Education. An Administrative Law Judge (ALJ) received extensive evidence concerning Garret's special needs, the District's treatment of other disabled students, and the assistance provided to other ventilator-dependent children in other parts of the country. In his 47–page report, the ALJ found that the District has about 17,500 students, of whom approximately 2,200 need some form of special education or special services. Although Garret is the only ventilator-dependent student in the District, most of the health care services that he needs are already provided for some other students. "The primary difference between Garret's situation and that of other students is his dependency on his ventilator for life support." The ALJ noted that the parties disagreed over the training or licensure required for the care and supervision of such students, and that those providing such care in other parts of the country ranged from nonlicensed personnel to registered nurses. However, the District did not contend that only a licensed physician could provide the services in question.

The ALJ explained that federal law requires that children with a variety of health impairments be provided with "special education and related services" when their disabilities adversely affect their academic performance, and that such children should be educated to the maximum extent appropriate with children who are not disabled. In addition, the ALJ explained that applicable federal regulations distinguish between "school health services," which are provided by a "qualified school nurse or other qualified person," and "medical services," which are provided by a licensed physician. See 34 C.F.R. §§ 300.16(a), (b)(4), (b)(11) (1998). The District must provide the former, but need not provide the latter (except, of course, those "medical services" that are for diagnostic or evaluation purposes. According to the ALJ, the distinction in the regulations does not just depend on "the title of the person providing the service"; instead, the "medical services" exclusion is limited to services that are "in the special training, knowledge, and judgment of a physician to carry out." The ALJ thus concluded that the IDEA required the District to bear financial responsibility for all of the services in dispute, including continuous nursing services.

The District challenged the ALJ's decision in Federal District Court, but that court approved the ALJ's IDEA ruling and granted summary judgment against the District. The Court of Appeals affirmed. It noted that, as a recipient of federal funds under the IDEA, Iowa has a statutory duty to provide all disabled children a "free appropriate public education," which includes "related services." The Court of Appeals read our opinion in *Irving Independent School Dist. v. Tatro*, 468 U.S. 883 (1984), to provide a two-step analysis of the "related services" definition in § 1401(a)(17)—asking first, whether the requested services are included within the phrase "supportive services"; and second, whether the services are excluded as "medical services." The Court of Appeals succinctly answered both questions in Garret's favor. The Court found the first step plainly satisfied, since Garret cannot attend school unless the requested services are available during the schoolday. As to the second step, the court reasoned that *Tatro* "established a bright-line test: the services of a physician (other than for diagnostic and evaluation purposes) are subject to the medical services exclusion, but services that can be provided in the school setting by a nurse or qualified layperson are not."

In its petition for certiorari, the District challenged only the second step of the Court of Appeals' analysis. The District pointed out that some federal courts have not asked whether the requested health services must be delivered by a physician, but instead have applied a multifactor test that considers, generally speaking, the nature and extent of the services at issue. We granted the District's petition to resolve this conflict.

II

The District contends that § 1401(a)(17) does not require it to provide Garret with "continuous one-on-one nursing services" during the schoolday, even though Garret cannot remain in school without such care. However, the IDEA's definition of "related services," our decision in *Irving Independent School Dist. v. Tatro,* 468 U.S. 883 (1984), and the overall statutory scheme all support the decision of the Court of Appeals.

The text of the "related services" definition broadly encompasses those supportive services that "may be required to assist a child with a disability to benefit from special education." As we have already noted, the District does not challenge the Court of Appeals' conclusion that the in-school services at issue are within the covered category of "supportive services." As a general matter, services that enable a disabled child to remain in school during the day provide the student with "the meaningful access to education that Congress envisioned." *Tatro,* 468 U.S., at 891. ...

This general definition of "related services" is illuminated by a parenthetical phrase listing examples of particular services that are included within the statute's coverage. "[M]edical services" are enumerated in this list, but such services are limited to those that are "for diagnostic and evaluation purposes." The statute does not contain a more specific definition of the "medical services" that are excepted from the coverage of § 1401(a)(17).

The scope of the "medical services" exclusion is not a matter of first impression in this Court. In *Tatro* we concluded that the Secretary of Education had reasonably determined that the term "medical services" referred only to services that must be performed by a physician, and not to school health services. Accordingly, we held that a specific form of health care (clean intermittent catheterization) that is often, though not always, performed by a nurse is not an excluded medical service. We referenced the likely cost of the services and the competence of school staff as justifications for drawing a line between physician and other services, but our endorsement of that line was unmistakable. It is thus settled that the phrase "medical services" in § 1401(a)(17) does not embrace all forms of care that might loosely be described as "medical" in other contexts, such as a claim for an income tax deduction.

The District does not ask us to define the term so broadly. Indeed, the District does not argue that any of the items of care that Garret needs, considered individually, could be excluded from the scope of 20 U.S.C. § 1401(a)(17). It could not make such an argument, considering that one of the services Garret needs (catheterization) was at issue in *Tatro,* and the others may be provided competently by a school nurse or other trained personnel. As the ALJ concluded, most of the requested services are already provided by the District to other students, and the in-school care necessitated by Garret's ventilator dependency does not demand the training, knowledge, and judgment of a licensed physician. While more extensive, the in-school services Garret needs are no more "medical" than was the care sought in *Tatro*.

Instead, the District points to the combined and continuous character of the required care, and proposes a test under which the outcome in any particular case would "depend upon a series of factors, such as [1] whether the care is continuous or intermittent, [2] whether existing school health personnel can provide the service, [3] the cost of the service, and [4] the potential consequences if the service is not properly performed."

The District's multifactor test is not supported by any recognized source of legal authority. The proposed factors can be found in neither the text of the statute nor the regulations that we upheld in *Tatro*. Moreover, the District offers no explanation why these characteristics make one service any more "medical" than another. The continuous character of certain services associated with Garret's ventilator dependency has no apparent relationship to "medical" services, much less a relationship of equivalence. Continuous services may be more costly and may require additional school personnel, but they are not thereby more "medical." Whatever its imperfections, a rule that limits the medical services exemption to physician services is unquestionably a reasonable and generally workable interpretation of the statute. Absent an elaboration of the statutory terms plainly more convincing than that which we reviewed in *Tatro*, there is no good reason to depart from settled law.

Finally, the District raises broader concerns about the financial burden that it must bear to provide the services that Garret needs to stay in school. The problem for the District in providing these services is not that its staff cannot be trained to deliver them; the problem, the District contends, is that the existing school health staff cannot meet all of their responsibilities and provide for Garret at the same time. Through its multifactor test, the District seeks to establish a kind of undue-burden exemption primarily based on the cost of the requested services. The first two factors can be seen as examples of cost-based distinctions: Intermittent care is often less expensive than continuous care, and the use of existing personnel is cheaper than hiring additional employees. The third factor-the cost of the service-would then encompass the first two. The relevance of the fourth factor is likewise related to cost because extra care may be necessary if potential consequences are especially serious.

The District may have legitimate financial concerns, but our role in this dispute is to interpret existing law. Defining "related services" in a manner that *accommodates* the cost concerns Congress may have had is altogether different from using cost *itself* as the definition. Given that § 1401(a)(17) does not employ cost in its definition of "related services" or excluded "medical services," accepting the District's cost-based standard as the sole test for determining the scope of the provision would require us to engage in judicial lawmaking without any guidance from Congress. It would also create some tension with the purposes of the IDEA. The statute may not require public schools to maximize the potential of disabled students commensurate with the opportunities provided to other children, and the potential financial burdens imposed on participating States may be relevant to arriving at a sensible construction of the IDEA, see *Tatro*, 468 U.S., at 892. But Congress intended "to open the door of public education" to all qualified children and "require[d] participating States to educate handicapped children with nonhandicapped children whenever possible."

Rowley, 458 U.S., at 192, see also *Honig v. Doe,* 484 U.S. 305, 310–311, 324, (1988); §§ 1412(1), (2)(C), (5)(B).

This case is about whether meaningful access to the public schools will be assured, not the level of education that a school must finance once access is attained. It is undisputed that the services at issue must be provided if Garret is to remain in school. Under the statute, our precedent, and the purposes of the IDEA, the District must fund such "related services" in order to help guarantee that students like Garret are integrated into the public schools.

The judgment of the Court of Appeals is accordingly

Affirmed.

Justice Thomas filed dissenting opinion in which Justice Kennedy joined.

SCHAFFER v. WEAST,
546 U.S. 49 (2005).

Justice O'Connor delivered the opinion of the Court.

The Individuals with Disabilities Education Act (IDEA or Act) is a Spending Clause statute that seeks to ensure that "all children with disabilities have available to them a free appropriate public education," § 1400(d)(1)(A). Under IDEA, school districts must create an "individualized education program" (IEP) for each disabled child. If parents believe their child's IEP is inappropriate, they may request an "impartial due process hearing." The Act is silent, however, as to which party bears the burden of persuasion at such a hearing. We hold that the burden lies, as it typically does, on the party seeking relief.

I

A

Congress first passed IDEA as part of the Education of the Handicapped Act in 1970, and amended it substantially in the Education for All Handicapped Children Act of 1975. At the time the majority of disabled children in America were "either totally excluded from schools or sitting idly in regular classrooms awaiting the time when they were old enough to 'drop out,' " H. R. Rep. No. 94–332, p. 2 (1975). IDEA was intended to reverse this history of neglect. As of 2003, the Act governed the provision of special education services to nearly 7 million children across the country.

IDEA is "frequently described as a model of 'cooperative federalism.' " *Little Rock School Dist. v. Mauney,* 183 F.3d 816, 830 (C.A.8 1999). It "leaves to the States the primary responsibility for developing and executing educational programs for handicapped children, [but] imposes significant requirements to be followed in the discharge of that responsibility." *Board of Ed. of Hendrick Hudson Central School Dist., Westchester Cty. v. Rowley,* 458 U.S. (1982). For example, the Act mandates cooperation and reporting between state and federal educational authorities. Participating States must certify to the Secretary of Education that they have "policies and procedures" that will effectively meet the Act's conditions. State educational agencies, in turn, must ensure that local schools and teachers are meeting the State's educational standards. Local educational agencies (school boards or other administrative bodies) can receive IDEA funds only if they certify to a state educational agency that they are acting in accordance with the State's policies and procedures.

The core of the statute, however, is the cooperative process that it establishes between parents and schools. The central vehicle for this collaboration is the IEP process. State educational authorities must identify and evaluate disabled children, develop an IEP for each one, and review every IEP at least once a year. Each IEP must include an assessment of the child's current educational performance, must articulate measurable educational goals, and must specify the nature of the special services that the school will provide.

Parents and guardians play a significant role in the IEP process. They must be informed about and consent to evaluations of their child under the Act. Parents are included as members of "IEP teams." They have the right to examine any records relating to their child, and to obtain an "independent educational evaluation of the[ir] child." They must be given written prior notice of any changes in an IEP and be notified in writing of the procedural safeguards available to them under the Act. If parents believe that an IEP is not appropriate, they may seek an administrative "impartial due process hearing." School districts may also seek such hearings, as Congress clarified in the 2004 amendments. They may do so, for example, if they wish to change an existing IEP but the parents do not consent, or if parents refuse to allow their child to be evaluated. As a practical matter, it appears that most hearing requests come from parents rather than schools.

Although state authorities have limited discretion to determine who conducts the hearings and responsibility generally for establishing fair hearing procedures, Congress has chosen to legislate the central components of due process hearings. It has imposed minimal pleading standards, requiring parties to file complaints setting forth "a description of the nature of the problem," and "a proposed resolution of the problem to the extent known and available ... at the time." At the hearing, all parties may be accompanied by counsel, and may "present evidence and confront, cross-examine, and compel the attendance of witnesses." After the hearing, any aggrieved party may bring a civil action in state or federal court. Prevailing parents may also recover attorney's fees. Congress has never explicitly stated, however, which party should bear the burden of proof at IDEA hearings.

B

This case concerns the educational services that were due, under IDEA, to petitioner Brian Schaffer. Brian suffers from learning disabilities and speech-language impairments. From prekindergarten through seventh grade he attended a private school and struggled academically. In 1997, school officials informed Brian's mother that he needed a school that could better accommodate his needs. Brian's parents contacted respondent Montgomery County Public Schools System (MCPS) seeking a placement for him for the following school year.

MCPS evaluated Brian and convened an IEP team. The committee generated an initial IEP offering Brian a place in either of two MCPS middle schools. Brian's parents were not satisfied with the arrangement, believing that Brian needed smaller classes and more intensive services. The Schaffers thus enrolled Brian in another private school, and initiated a due process hearing challenging the IEP and seeking compensation for the cost of Brian's subsequent private education.

In Maryland, IEP hearings are conducted by administrative law judges (ALJs). After a 3–day hearing, the ALJ deemed the evidence close, held that the parents bore the burden of persuasion, and ruled in favor of the school district. The parents brought a civil action challenging the result. The United States District Court for the District of Maryland reversed and remanded, after concluding that the burden of persuasion is on the school district. Around the same time, MCPS offered Brian a placement in a high school with a special learning center. Brian's parents accepted, and Brian was educated in that program until he graduated from high school. The suit remained alive, however, because the parents sought compensation for the private school tuition and related expenses.

Respondents appealed to the United States Court of Appeals for the Fourth Circuit. While the appeal was pending, the ALJ reconsidered the case, deemed the evidence truly in "equipoise," and ruled in favor of the parents. The Fourth Circuit vacated and remanded the appeal so that it could consider the burden of proof issue along with the merits on a later appeal. The District Court reaffirmed its ruling that the school district has the burden of proof. On appeal, a divided panel of the Fourth Circuit reversed. Judge Michael, writing for the majority, concluded that petitioners offered no persuasive reason to "depart from the normal rule of allocating the burden to the party seeking relief." We granted certiorari to resolve the following question: At an administrative hearing assessing the appropriateness of an IEP, which party bears the burden of persuasion?

II

A

The term "burden of proof" is one of the "slipperiest member[s] of the family of legal terms." 2 J. Strong, McCormick on Evidence § 342, p. 433 (5th ed.1999) (hereinafter McCormick). Part of the confusion surrounding the term arises from the fact that historically, the concept encompassed two distinct burdens: the "burden of persuasion," *i.e.,* which party loses if the evidence is closely balanced, and the "burden of production," *i.e.,* which party bears the obligation to come forward with the evidence at different points in the proceeding. We note at the outset that this case concerns only the burden of persuasion, as the parties agree and when we speak of burden of proof in this opinion, it is this to which we refer.

When we are determining the burden of proof under a statutory cause of action, the touchstone of our inquiry is, of course, the statute. The plain text of IDEA is silent on the allocation of the burden of persuasion. We therefore begin with the ordinary default rule that plaintiffs bear the risk of failing to prove their claims.

Thus, we have usually assumed without comment that plaintiffs bear the burden of persuasion regarding the essential aspects of their claims. For example, Title VII of the Civil Rights Act of 1964, does not directly state that plaintiffs bear the "ultimate" burden of persuasion, but we have so concluded. In numerous other areas, we have presumed or held that the default rule applies. Congress also expressed its approval of the general rule when it chose to apply it to administrative proceedings under the Administrative Procedure Act.

The ordinary default rule, of course, admits of exceptions. For example, the burden of persuasion as to certain elements of a plaintiff's claim may be shifted to defendants, when such elements can fairly be characterized as affirmative defenses or exemptions. Under some circumstances this Court has even placed the burden of persuasion over an entire claim on the defendant. But while the normal default rule does not solve all cases, it certainly solves most of them. Decisions that place the *entire* burden of persuasion on the opposing party at the *outset* of a proceeding—as petitioners urge us to do here—are extremely rare. Absent some reason to believe that Congress intended otherwise, therefore, we will conclude that the burden of persuasion lies where it usually falls, upon the party seeking relief.

B

Petitioners contend first that a close reading of IDEA's text compels a conclusion in their favor. They urge that we should interpret the statutory words "due process" in light of their constitutional meaning, and apply the balancing test established by *Mathews v. Eldridge,* 424 U.S. 319 (1976). Even assuming that the Act incorporates constitutional due process doctrine, *Eldridge* is no help to petitioners because "[o]utside the criminal law area, where special concerns attend, the locus of the burden of persuasion is normally not an issue of federal constitutional moment." *Lavine v. Milne,* 424 U.S. 577 (1976).

Petitioners next contend that we should take instruction from the lower court opinions of *Mills v. Board of Education,* 348 F.Supp. 866 (D.D.C.1972), and *Pennsylvania Association for Retarded Children v. Pennsylvania,* 334 F.Supp. 1257 (E.D.Pa.1971) (hereinafter *PARC*). IDEA's drafters were admittedly guided "to a significant extent" by these two landmark cases. As the court below noted, however, the fact that Congress "took a number of the procedural safeguards from *PARC* and *Mills* and wrote them directly into the Act" does not allow us to "conclude ... that Congress intended to adopt the ideas that it failed to write into the text of the statute."

Petitioners also urge that putting the burden of persuasion on school districts will further IDEA's purposes because it will help ensure that children receive a free appropriate public education. In truth, however, very few cases will be in evidentiary equipoise. Assigning the burden of persuasion to school districts might encourage schools to put more resources into preparing IEPs and presenting their evidence. But IDEA is silent about whether marginal dollars should be allocated to litigation and administrative expenditures or to educational services. Moreover, there is reason to believe that a great deal is already spent on the administration of the Act. Litigating a due process complaint is an expensive affair, costing schools approximately $8,000-to-$12,000 per hearing. Congress has also repeatedly amended the Act in order to reduce its administrative and litigation-related costs. For example, in 1997 Congress mandated that States offer mediation for IDEA disputes. In 2004, Congress added a mandatory "resolution session" prior to any due process hearing. It also made new findings that "[p]arents and schools should be given expanded opportunities to resolve their disagreements in positive and constructive ways," and that "[t]eachers, schools, local educational agencies, and States should be relieved of irrelevant and unnecessary paperwork burdens that do not lead to improved educational outcomes."

Petitioners in effect ask this Court to assume that every IEP is invalid until the school district demonstrates that it is not. The Act does not support this conclusion. IDEA relies heavily upon the expertise of school districts to meet its goals. It also includes a so-called "stay-put" provision, which requires a child to remain in his or her "then-current educational placement" during the pendency of an IDEA hearing. Congress could have required that a child be given the educational placement that a parent requested during a dispute, but it did no such thing. Congress appears to have presumed instead that, if the Act's procedural requirements are respected, parents will prevail when they have legitimate grievances.

Petitioners' most plausible argument is that "[t]he ordinary rule, based on considerations of fairness, does not place the burden upon a litigant of establishing facts peculiarly within the knowledge of his adversary." *United States v. New York, N.H. & H.R. Co.,* 355 U.S. 253, 256, n. 5, (1957). But this "rule is far from being universal, and has many qualifications upon its application." *Greenleaf's Lessee v. Birth,* 6 Pet. 302, 312 (1832). School districts have a "natural advantage" in information and expertise, but Congress addressed this when it obliged schools to safeguard the procedural rights of parents and to share information with them. As noted above, parents have the right to review all records that the school possesses in relation to their child. They also have the right to an "independent educational evaluation of the[ir] child." The regulations clarify this entitlement by providing that a "parent has the right to an independent educational evaluation at public expense if the parent disagrees with an evaluation obtained by the public agency." IDEA thus ensures parents access to an expert who can evaluate all the materials that the school must make available, and who can give an independent opinion. They are not left to challenge the government without a realistic opportunity to access the necessary evidence, or without an expert with the firepower to match the opposition.

Additionally, in 2004, Congress added provisions requiring school districts to answer the subject matter of a complaint in writing, and to provide parents with the reasoning behind the disputed action, details about the other options considered and rejected by the IEP team, and a description of all evaluations, reports, and other factors that the school used in coming to its decision. Prior to a hearing, the parties must disclose evaluations and recommendations that they intend to rely upon. IDEA hearings are deliberately informal and intended to give ALJs the flexibility that they need to ensure that each side can fairly present its evidence. IDEA, in fact, requires state authorities to organize hearings in a way that guarantees parents and children the procedural protections of the Act. Finally, and perhaps most importantly, parents may recover attorney's fees if they prevail. These protections ensure that the school bears no unique informational advantage.

III

Finally, respondents and several States urge us to decide that States may, if they wish, override the default rule and put the burden always on the school district. Several States have laws or regulations purporting to do so, at least under some circumstances. Because no such law or regulation exists in Maryland, we need not decide this issue today. ...

We hold no more than we must to resolve the case at hand: The burden of proof in an administrative hearing challenging an IEP is properly placed upon the party seeking relief. In this case, that party is Brian, as represented by his parents. But the rule applies with equal effect to school districts: If they seek to challenge an IEP, they will in turn bear the burden of persuasion before an ALJ. The judgment of the United States Court of Appeals for the Fourth Circuit is, therefore, affirmed.

It is so ordered.

Justice Stevens concurred and filed opinion.

Justice Ginsburg dissented and filed opinion.

Justice Breyer dissented and filed opinion.

Chief Justice Roberts took no part in the consideration or decision of the case.

The Chief Jsutice took no part in the consideration or decision of this case.

ARLINGTON CENTRAL SCHOOL DISTRICT BOARD OF EDUCATION v. MURPHY, 548 U.S. 291 (2006).

Justice Alito delivered the opinion of the Court.

The Individuals with Disabilities Education Act (IDEA or Act) provides that a court "may award reasonable attorneys' fees as part of the costs" to parents who prevail in an action brought under the Act. 20 U.S.C. § 1415(i)(3)(B). We granted certiorari to decide whether this fee-shifting provision authorizes prevailing parents to recover fees for services rendered by experts in IDEA actions. We hold that it does not.

I

Respondents Pearl and Theodore Murphy filed an action under the IDEA on behalf of their son, Joseph Murphy, seeking to require petitioner Arlington Central School District Board of Education to pay for their son's private school tuition for specified school years. Respondents prevailed in the District Court and the Court of Appeals for the Second Circuit affirmed.

As prevailing parents, respondents then sought $29,350 in fees for the services of an educational consultant, Marilyn Arons, who assisted respondents throughout the IDEA proceedings. The District Court granted respondents' request in part. It held that only the value of Arons' time spent between the hearing request and the ruling in respondents' favor could properly be considered charges incurred in an "action or proceeding brought" under the Act. This reduced the maximum recovery to $8,650. The District Court also held that Arons, a nonlawyer, could be compensated only for time spent on expert consulting services, not for time spent on legal representation, but it concluded that all the relevant time could be characterized as falling within the compensable category, and thus allowed compensation for the full $8,650.

The Court of Appeals for the Second Circuit affirmed. Acknowledging that other Circuits had taken the opposite view, the Court of Appeals for the Second Circuit held that "Congress intended to and did authorize the reimbursement of expert fees in IDEA actions." The court ... noted, a cost- or fee-shifting provision will not be read to permit a prevailing party to recover expert fees without " 'explicit statutory authority' indicating that Congress intended for that sort of fee-shifting."

Ultimately, though, the court was persuaded by a statement in the Conference Committee Report relating to 20 U.S.C. § 1415(i)(3)(B)... Based on these authorities, the court concluded that it was required to interpret the IDEA to authorize the award of the costs that prevailing parents incur in hiring experts.

We granted certiorari to resolve the conflict among the Circuits with respect to whether Congress authorized the compensation of expert fees to prevailing parents in IDEA actions. We now reverse.

II

Our resolution of the question presented in this case is guided by the fact that Congress enacted the IDEA pursuant to the Spending Clause. Like its statutory predecessor, the IDEA provides federal funds to assist state and local agencies in educating children with disabilities "and conditions such funding upon a State's compliance with extensive goals and procedures." *Board of Ed. of Hendrick Hudson Central School Dist., Westchester Cty. v. Rowley,* 458 U.S. 176, 179, (1982).

Congress has broad power to set the terms on which it disburses federal money to the States, but when Congress attaches conditions to a State's acceptance of federal funds, the conditions must be set out "unambiguously," see *Pennhurst State School and Hospital v. Halderman,* 451 U.S. 1, 17, (1981). "[L]egislation enacted pursuant to the spending power is much in the nature of a contract," and therefore, to be bound by "federally imposed conditions," recipients of federal funds must accept them "voluntarily and knowingly." *Pennhurst,* 451 U.S., at 17. States cannot knowingly accept conditions of which they are "unaware" or which they are "unable to ascertain." Thus, in the present case, we must view the IDEA from the perspective of a state official who is engaged in the process of deciding whether the State should accept IDEA funds and the obligations that go with those funds. We must ask whether such a state official would clearly understand that one of the obligations of the Act is the obligation to compensate prevailing parents for expert fees. In other words, we must ask whether the IDEA furnishes clear notice regarding the liability at issue in this case.

III

A

In considering whether the IDEA provides clear notice, we begin with the text. We have "stated time and again that courts must presume that a legislature says in a statute what it means and means in a statute what it says there." *Connecticut Nat. Bank v. Germain,* 503 U.S. 249, 253–254 (1992). When the statutory "language is plain, the sole function of the courts—at least where the disposition required by the text is not absurd—is to enforce it according to its terms." *Hartford Underwriters Ins. Co. v. Union Planters Bank, N. A.,* 530 U.S. 1, 6, (2000).

The governing provision of the IDEA provides that "[i]n any action or proceeding brought under this section, the court, in its discretion, may award reasonable attorneys' fees as part of the costs" to the parents of "a child with a disability" who is the "prevailing party." While this provision provides for an award of "reasonable attorneys' fees," this provision does not even hint that acceptance of IDEA funds makes a State responsible for reimbursing prevailing parents for services rendered by experts.

Respondents contend that we should interpret the term "costs" in accordance with its meaning in ordinary usage and that § 1415(i)(3)(B) should therefore be read to "authorize reimbursement of all costs parents incur in IDEA proceedings, including expert costs."

This argument has multiple flaws. For one thing, as the Court of Appeals in this case acknowledged, " 'costs' is a term of art that generally does not include expert fees." The use of this term of art, rather than a term such as "expenses," strongly suggests that § 1415(i)(3)(B) was not meant to be an open-ended provision that makes participating States liable for all expenses incurred by prevailing parents in connection with an IDEA case—for example, travel and lodging expenses or lost wages due to time taken off from work. Moreover, contrary to respondents' suggestion, § 1415(i)(3)(B) does not say that a court may award "costs" to prevailing parents; rather, it says that a court may award reasonable attorney's fees "as part of the costs" to prevailing parents. This language simply adds reasonable attorney's fees incurred by prevailing parents to the list of costs that prevailing parents are otherwise entitled to recover. This list of otherwise recoverable costs is obviously the list set out in 28 U.S.C. § 1920, the general statute governing the taxation of costs in federal court, and the recovery of witness fees under § 1920 is strictly limited by § 1821, which authorizes travel reimbursement and a $40 per diem. Thus, the text of 20 U.S.C. § 1415(i)(3)(B) does not authorize an award of any additional expert fees, and it certainly fails to provide the clear notice that is required under the Spending Clause.

Other provisions of the IDEA point strongly in the same direction. While authorizing the award of reasonable attorney's fees, the Act contains detailed provisions that are designed to ensure that such awards are indeed reasonable. The absence of any comparable provisions relating to expert fees strongly suggests that recovery of expert fees is not authorized. Moreover, the lack of any reference to expert fees in § 1415(d)(2) gives rise to a similar inference. This provision, which generally requires that parents receive "a full explanation of the procedural safeguards" available under § 1415 and refers expressly to "attorneys' fees," makes no mention of expert fees.

B

Respondents contend that their interpretation of § 1415(i)(3)(B) is supported by a provision of the Handicapped Children's Protection Act of 1986 that required the General Accounting Office (GAO) to collect certain data, (hereinafter GAO study provision), but this provision is of little significance for present purposes. The GAO study provision directed the Comptroller General, acting through the GAO, to compile data on, among other things: "(A) the specific amount of attorneys' fees, costs, and expenses awarded to the prevailing party" in IDEA cases for a particular period of time, and (B) "the number of hours spent by personnel, including attorneys and consultants, involved in the action or proceeding, and expenses incurred by the parents and the State educational agency and local educational agency."

Subparagraph (A) would provide some support for respondents' position if it directed the GAO to compile data on awards to prevailing parties of the expense of hiring consultants, but that is not what subparagraph (A) says. Subparagraph (A) makes no mention of consultants or experts or their fees.

Subparagraph (B) similarly does not help respondents. Subparagraph (B), which directs the GAO to study "the number of hours spent [in IDEA cases] by personnel, including ... consultants," says nothing about the award of fees to such consultants. Just because Congress directed the GAO to compile statistics on the hours spent by consultants in IDEA cases, it does not follow that Congress meant for States to compensate prevailing parties for the fees billed by these consultants.

Respondents maintain that "Congress' direction to the GAO would be inexplicable if Congress did not anticipate that the expenses for 'consultants' would be recoverable," but this is incorrect. There are many reasons why Congress might have wanted the GAO to gather data on expenses that were not to be taxed as costs. Knowing the costs incurred by IDEA litigants might be useful in considering future procedural amendments (which might affect these costs) or a future amendment regarding fee shifting. And, in fact, it is apparent that the GAO study provision covered expenses that could not be taxed as costs. For example, the GAO was instructed to compile statistics on the hours spent by all attorneys involved in an IDEA action or proceeding, even though the Act did not provide for the recovery of attorney's fees by a prevailing state or local educational agency. Similarly, the GAO was directed to compile data on "expenses incurred by the parents," not just those parents who prevail and are thus eligible to recover taxed costs.

In sum, the terms of the IDEA overwhelmingly support the conclusion that prevailing parents may not recover the costs of experts or consultants. Certainly the terms of the IDEA fail to provide the clear notice that would be needed to attach such a condition to a State's receipt of IDEA funds.

IV

Thus far, we have considered only the text of the IDEA, but perhaps the strongest support for our interpretation of the IDEA is supplied by our decisions and reasoning in *Crawford Fitting,* 482 U.S. 437, and *Casey,* 499 U.S. 83. In light of those decisions, we do not see how it can be said that the IDEA gives a State unambiguous notice regarding liability for expert fees.

In *Crawford Fitting,* the Court rejected an argument very similar to respondents' argument that the term "costs" in § 1415(i)(3)(B) should be construed as an open-ended reference to prevailing parents' expenses. It was argued in *Crawford Fitting* that Federal Rule of Civil Procedure 54(d), which provides for the award of "costs" to a prevailing party, authorizes the award of costs not listed in 28 U.S.C. § 1821. The Court held, however, that Rule 54(d) does not give a district judge "discretion to tax whatever costs may seem appropriate"; rather, the term "costs" in Rule 54(d) is defined by the list set out in § 1920. Because the recovery of witness fees is strictly limited by § 1821, the Court observed, a broader interpretation of Rule 54(d) would mean that the Rule implicitly effected a partial repeal of those provisions. But, the Court warned, "[w]e will not lightly infer that Congress has repealed §§ 1920 and 1821, either through Rule 54(d) or any other provision not referring explicitly to witness fees."

The reasoning of *Crawford Fitting* strongly supports the conclusion that the term "costs" in 20 U.S.C. § 1415(i)(3)(B), like the same term in Rule 54(d), is defined by the categories of expenses enumerated in 28 U.S.C. § 1920. This conclusion is buttressed by the principle, recognized in *Crawford Fitting,* that no statute will be construed as authorizing the taxation of witness fees as costs unless the statute "refer[s] explicitly to witness fees." ...

Our decision in *Casey* confirms even more dramatically that the IDEA does not authorize an award of expert fees. In *Casey,* as noted above, we interpreted a fee-shifting provision, 42 U.S.C. § 1988, the relevant wording of which was virtually identical to the wording of 20 U.S.C. § 1415(i)(3)(B). ... We held that § 1988 did not empower a district court to award expert fees to a prevailing party. To decide in favor of respondents here, we would have to interpret the virtually identical language in 20 U.S.C. § 1415 as having exactly the opposite meaning. Indeed, we would have to go further and hold that the relevant language in the IDEA *unambiguously means* exactly the opposite of what the nearly identical language in 42 U.S.C. § 1988 was held to mean in *Casey.*

... Thus, *Crawford Fitting* and *Casey* strongly reinforce the conclusion that the IDEA does not unambiguously authorize prevailing parents to recover expert fees.

V

Respondents make several arguments that are not based on the text of the IDEA, but these arguments do not show that the IDEA provides clear notice regarding the award of expert fees.

Respondents argue that their interpretation of the IDEA furthers the Act's overarching goal of "ensur[ing] that all children with disabilities have available to them a free appropriate public education," as well as the goal of "safeguard[ing] the rights of parents to challenge school decisions that adversely affect their child." These goals, however, are too general to provide much support for respondents' reading of the terms of the IDEA. The IDEA obviously does not seek to promote these goals at the expense of all other considerations, including fiscal considerations. Because the IDEA is not intended in all instances to further the broad goals identified by respondents at the expense of fiscal considerations, the goals cited by respondents do little to bolster their argument on the narrow question presented here.

Finally, respondents vigorously argue that Congress clearly intended for prevailing parents to be compensated for expert fees. They rely on the legislative history of § 1415 and in particular on the following statement in the Conference Committee Report, discussed above: "The conferees intend that the term 'attorneys' fees as part of the costs' include reasonable expenses and fees of expert witnesses and the reasonable costs of any test or evaluation which is found to be necessary for the preparation of the ... case." H.R. Conf. Rep. No. 99–687, at 5.

Whatever weight this legislative history would merit in another context, it is not sufficient here. Putting the legislative history aside, we see virtually no support for respondents' position. Under these circumstances, where everything other than the legislative history overwhelmingly suggests that expert fees may not be recovered, the legislative history is simply not enough. In a Spending Clause case, the key is not what a majority of the Members of both Houses intend but what the States are clearly told regarding the conditions that go along with the acceptance of those funds. Here, in the face of the unambiguous text of the IDEA and the reasoning in *Crawford Fitting* and *Casey,* we cannot say that the legislative history on which respondents rely is sufficient to provide the requisite fair notice.

We reverse the judgment of the Court of Appeals for the Second Circuit and remand the case for further proceedings consistent with this opinion.

It is so ordered.

Justice Ginsburg filed opinion concurring in part and concurring in the judgment.

Justice Souter filed dissenting opinion.

Justice Breyer filed dissenting opinion joined by Justices Stevens and Souter.

WINKELMAN v. PARMA CITY SCHOOL DISTRICT, 550 U.S. 516 (2007).

Justice Kennedy delivered the opinion of the Court.

Some four years ago, Mr. and Mrs. Winkelman, parents of five children, became involved in lengthy administrative and legal proceedings. They had sought review related to concerns they had over whether their youngest child, 6–year–old Jacob, would progress well at Pleasant Valley Elementary School, which is part of the Parma City School District in Parma, Ohio.

Jacob has autism spectrum disorder and is covered by the Individuals with Disabilities Education Act (Act or IDEA), 20 U.S.C. § 1400 *et seq.* His parents worked with the school district to develop an individualized education program (IEP), as required by the Act. All concede that Jacob's parents had the statutory right to contribute to this process and, when agreement could not be reached, to participate in administrative proceedings including what the Act refers to as an "impartial due process hearing."

The disagreement at the center of the current dispute concerns the procedures to be followed when parents and their child, dissatisfied with the outcome of the due process hearing, seek further review in a United States District Court. The question is whether parents, either on their own behalf or as representatives of the child, may proceed in court unrepresented by counsel though they are not trained or licensed as attorneys. Resolution of this issue requires us to examine and explain the provisions of IDEA to determine if it accords to parents rights of their own that can be vindicated in court proceedings, or alternatively, whether the Act allows them, in their status as parents, to represent their child in court proceedings.

I

Respondent Parma City School District, a participant in IDEA's educational spending program, accepts federal funds for assistance in the education of children with disabilities. As a condition of receiving funds, it must comply with IDEA's mandates. IDEA requires that the school district provide Jacob with a "free appropriate public education," which must operate in accordance with the IEP that Jacob's parents, along with school officials and other individuals, develop as members of Jacob's "IEP Team."

The school district proposed an IEP for the 2003–2004 school year that would have placed Jacob at a public elementary school. Regarding this IEP as deficient under IDEA, Jacob's nonlawyer parents availed themselves of the administrative review provided by IDEA. They filed a complaint alleging respondent had failed to provide Jacob with a free appropriate public education; they appealed the hearing officer's rejection of the claims in this complaint to a state-level review officer; and after losing that appeal they filed, on their own behalf and on behalf of Jacob, a complaint in the United States District Court for the Northern District of Ohio. In reliance upon 20 U.S.C. § 1415(i)(2) they challenged the administrative decision, alleging, among other matters: that Jacob had not been provided with a free appropriate public education; that his IEP was inadequate; and that the school district had failed to follow procedures mandated by IDEA. Pending the resolution of these challenges, the Winkelmans had enrolled Jacob in a private school at their own expense. They had also obtained counsel to assist them with certain aspects of the proceedings, although they filed their federal complaint, and later their appeal, without the aid of an attorney. The Winkelmans' complaint sought reversal of the administrative decision, reimbursement for private-school expenditures and attorney's fees already incurred, and, it appears, declaratory relief.

The District Court granted respondent's motion for judgment on the pleadings, finding it had provided Jacob with a free appropriate public education. Petitioners, proceeding without counsel, filed an appeal with the Court of Appeals for the Sixth Circuit. ... [T]he Court of Appeals entered an order dismissing the Winkelmans' appeal unless they obtained counsel to represent Jacob. ...[T]the Court of Appeals had rejected the proposition that IDEA allows nonlawyer parents raising IDEA claims to proceed *pro se* in federal court. The court ruled that the right to a free appropriate public education "belongs to the child alone," not to both the parents and the child. It followed, the court held, that "any right on which the [parents] could proceed on their own behalf would be derivative" of the child's right, so that parents bringing IDEA claims were not appearing on their own behalf. As for the parents' alternative argument, the court held, nonlawyer parents cannot litigate IDEA claims on behalf of their child because IDEA does not abrogate the common-law rule prohibiting nonlawyer parents from representing minor children. ...[I]ts decision brought the Sixth Circuit in direct conflict with the First Circuit, which had concluded, under a theory of "statutory joint rights," that the Act accords to parents the right to assert IDEA claims on their own behalf.

Petitioners sought review in this Court. In light of the disagreement among the Courts of Appeals as to whether a nonlawyer parent of a child with a disability may prosecute IDEA actions *pro se* in federal court, we granted certiorari.

II

Our resolution of this case turns upon the significance of IDEA's interlocking statutory provisions. Petitioners' primary theory is that the Act makes parents real parties in interest to IDEA actions, not "mer[e] guardians of their children's rights." If correct, this allows Mr. and Mrs. Winkelman back into court, for there is no question that a party may represent his or her own interests in federal court without the aid of counsel. Petitioners cannot cite a specific provision in IDEA mandating in direct and explicit terms that parents have the status of real parties in interest. They instead base their argument on a comprehensive reading of IDEA. Taken as a whole, they contend, the Act leads to the necessary conclusion that parents have independent, enforceable rights. Respondent, accusing petitioners of "knit[ting] together various provisions pulled from the crevices of the statute" to support these claims, reads the text of IDEA to mean that any redressable rights under the Act belong only to children.

We agree that the text of IDEA resolves the question presented. We recognize, in addition, that a proper interpretation of the Act requires a consideration of the entire statutory scheme. Turning to the current version of IDEA, which the parties agree governs this case, we begin with an overview of the relevant statutory provisions.

A

The goals of IDEA include "ensur[ing] that all children with disabilities have available to them a free appropriate public education" and "ensur[ing] that the rights of children with disabilities and parents of such children are protected." To this end, the Act includes provisions governing four areas of particular relevance to the Winkelmans' claim: procedures to be followed when developing a child's IEP; criteria governing the sufficiency of an education provided to a child; mechanisms for review that must be made available when there are objections to the IEP or to other aspects of IDEA proceedings; and the requirement in certain circumstances that States reimburse parents for various expenses. Although our discussion of these four areas does not identify all the illustrative provisions, we do take particular note of certain terms that mandate or otherwise describe parental involvement.

IDEA requires school districts to develop an IEP for each child with a disability, with parents playing "a significant role" in this process. Parents serve as members of the team that develops the IEP. The "concerns" parents have "for enhancing the education of their child" must be considered by the team. IDEA accords parents additional protections that apply throughout the IEP process. ...The statute also sets up general procedural safeguards that protect the informed involvement of parents in the development of an education for their child. ...A central purpose of the parental protections is to facilitate the provision of a " 'free appropriate public education,' " which must be made available to the child "in conformity with the [IEP]."

The Act defines a "free appropriate public education" pursuant to an IEP to be an educational instruction "specially designed ... to meet the unique needs of a child with a disability," coupled with any additional " 'related services' " that are "required to assist a child with a disability to benefit from [that instruction]." The education must, among other things, be provided "under public supervision and direction," "meet the standards of the State educational agency," and "include an appropriate preschool, elementary school, or secondary school education in the State involved." The instruction must, in addition, be provided at "no cost to parents."

When a party objects to the adequacy of the education provided, the construction of the IEP, or some related matter, IDEA provides procedural recourse: It requires that a State provide "[a]n opportunity for any party to present a complaint ... with respect to any matter relating to the identification, evaluation, or educational placement of the child, or the provision of a free appropriate public education to such child." § 1415(b)

(6). By presenting a complaint a party is able to pursue a process of review that, as relevant, begins with a preliminary meeting "where the parents of the child discuss their complaint" and the local educational agency "is provided the opportunity to [reach a resolution]." § 1415(f)(1)(B)(i)(IV). If the agency "has not resolved the complaint to the satisfaction of the parents within 30 days," the parents may request an "impartial due process hearing," § 1415(f)(1)(A), which must be conducted either by the local educational agency or by the state educational agency, and where a hearing officer will resolve issues raised in the complaint.

IDEA sets standards the States must follow in conducting these hearings. Among other things, it indicates that the hearing officer's decision "shall be made on substantive grounds based on a determination of whether the child received a free appropriate public education," and that, "[i]n matters alleging a procedural violation," the officer may find a child "did not receive a free appropriate public education," only if the violation

> "(I) impeded the child's right to a free appropriate public education;

> "(II) significantly impeded the parents' opportunity to participate in the decisionmaking process regarding the provision of a free appropriate public education to the parents' child; or

> "(III) caused a deprivation of educational benefits."

If the local educational agency, rather than the state educational agency, conducts this hearing, then "any party aggrieved by the findings and decision rendered in such a hearing may appeal such findings and decision to the State educational agency." § 1415(g)(1). Once the state educational agency has reached its decision, an aggrieved party may commence suit in federal court: "Any party aggrieved by the findings and decision made [by the hearing officer] shall have the right to bring a civil action with respect to the complaint." § 1415(i)(2)(A); see also § 1415(i)(1).

IDEA, finally, provides for at least two means of cost recovery that inform our analysis. First, in certain circumstances it allows a court or hearing officer to require a state agency "to reimburse the parents [of a child with a disability] for the cost of [private–school] enrollment if the court or hearing officer finds that the agency had not made a free appropriate public education available to the child." § 1412(a)(10)(C)(ii). Second, it sets forth rules governing when and to what extent a court may award attorney's fees. Included in this section is a provision allowing an award "to a prevailing party who is the parent of a child with a disability."

B

Petitioners construe these various provisions to accord parents independent, enforceable rights under IDEA. We agree. The parents enjoy enforceable rights at the administrative stage, and it would be inconsistent with the statutory scheme to bar them from continuing to assert these rights in federal court.

The statute sets forth procedures for resolving disputes in a manner that, in the Act's express terms, contemplates parents will be the parties bringing the administrative complaints. In addition to the provisions we have cited, we refer also to § 1415(b)(8) (requiring a state educational agency to "develop a model form to assist parents in filing a complaint"); § 1415(c)(2) (addressing the response an agency must provide to a "parent's due process complaint notice"); and § 1415(i)(3)(B)(i) (referring to "the parent's complaint"). A wide range of review is available: Administrative complaints may be brought with respect to "any matter relating to ... the provision of a free appropriate public education." Claims raised in these complaints are then resolved at impartial due process hearings, where, again, the statute makes clear that parents will be participating as parties. ... The statute then grants "[a]ny party aggrieved by the findings and decision made [by the hearing officer] ... the right to bring a civil action with respect to the complaint."

Nothing in these interlocking provisions excludes a parent who has exercised his or her own rights from statutory protection the moment the administrative proceedings end. Put another way, the Act does not *sub silentio* or by implication bar parents from seeking to vindicate the rights accorded to them once the time comes to file a civil action. Through its provisions for expansive review and extensive parental involvement, the statute leads to just the opposite result.

Respondent, resisting this line of analysis, asks us to read these provisions as contemplating parental involvement only to the extent parents represent their child's interests. In respondent's view IDEA accords parents nothing more than "collateral tools related to the child's underlying substantive rights—not freestanding or independently enforceable rights."

This interpretation, though, is foreclosed by provisions of the statute. IDEA defines one of its purposes as seeking "to ensure that the rights of children with disabilities and parents of such children are protected." The word "rights" in the quoted language refers to the rights of parents as well as the rights of the child; otherwise the grammatical structure would make no sense.

Further provisions confirm this view. IDEA mandates that educational agencies establish procedures "to ensure that children with disabilities and their parents are guaranteed procedural safeguards with respect to the provision of a free appropriate public education." It presumes parents have rights of their own when it defines how States might provide for the transfer of the "rights accorded to parents" by IDEA, and it prohibits the raising of certain challenges "[n]otwithstanding any other individual right of action that a parent or student may maintain under [the relevant provisions of IDEA]". To adopt respondent's reading of the statute would require an interpretation of these statutory provisions (and others) far too strained to be correct.

Defending its countertextual reading of the statute, respondent cites a decision by a Court of Appeals concluding that the Act's "references to parents are best understood as accommodations to the fact of the child's incapacity." *Doe v. Board of Ed. of Baltimore Cty.*, 165 F.3d 260, 263 (4th Cir. 1998). This, according to respondent, requires us to interpret all references to parents' rights as referring in implicit terms to the child's rights—which, under this view, are the only enforceable rights accorded by IDEA. Even if we were inclined to ignore the plain text of the statute in considering this theory, we disagree that the sole purpose driving IDEA's involvement of parents is to facilitate vindication of a child's rights. It is not a novel proposition to say that parents have a recognized legal interest in the education and upbringing of their child. ...There is no necessary bar or obstacle in the law, then, to finding an intention by Congress to grant parents a stake in the entitlements created by IDEA. Without question a parent of a child with a disability has a particular and personal interest in fulfilling "our national policy of ensuring equality of opportunity, full participation, independent living, and economic self-sufficiency for individuals with disabilities." § 1400(c)(1).

We therefore find no reason to read into the plain language of the statute an implicit rejection of the notion that Congress would accord parents independent, enforceable rights concerning the education of their children. We instead interpret the statute's references to parents' rights to mean what they say: that IDEA includes provisions conveying rights to parents as well as to children.

A variation on respondent's argument has persuaded some Courts of Appeals. The argument is that while a parent can be a "party aggrieved" for aspects of the hearing officer's findings and decision, he or she cannot be a "party aggrieved" with respect to all IDEA-based challenges. Under this view the causes of action available to a parent might relate, for example, to various procedural mandates and reimbursement demands. The argument supporting this conclusion proceeds as follows: Because a "party aggrieved" is, by definition, entitled to a remedy, and parents are, under IDEA, only entitled to certain procedures and reimbursements as remedies, a parent cannot be a "party aggrieved" with regard to any claim not implicating these limited matters.

This argument is contradicted by the statutory provisions we have recited. True, there are provisions in IDEA stating parents are entitled to certain procedural protections and reimbursements; but the statute prevents us from placing too much weight on the implications to be drawn when other entitlements are accorded in less clear language. We find little support for the inference that parents are excluded by implication whenever a child is mentioned, and vice versa. ...Without more, then, the language in IDEA confirming that parents enjoy particular procedural and reimbursement-related rights does not resolve whether they are also entitled to enforce IDEA's other mandates, including the one most fundamental to the Act: the provision of a free appropriate public education to a child with a disability.

We consider the statutory structure. The IEP proceedings entitle parents to participate not only in the implementation of IDEA's procedures but also in the substantive formulation of their child's educational program. Among other things, IDEA requires the IEP Team, which includes the parents as members, to take into account any "concerns" parents have "for enhancing the education of their child" when it formulates the IEP. The IEP, in turn, sets the boundaries of the central entitlement provided by IDEA: It defines a " 'free appropriate public education' " for that parent's child.

The statute also empowers parents to bring challenges based on a broad range of issues. The parent may seek a hearing on "any matter relating to the identification, evaluation, or educational placement of the child, or the provision of a free appropriate public education to such child." § 1415(b)(6)(A). To resolve these challenges a hearing officer must make a decision based on whether the child "received a free appropriate public education." When this hearing has been conducted by a local educational agency rather than a state educational agency, "any party aggrieved by the findings and decision rendered in such a hearing may appeal such findings and decision" to the state educational agency. Judicial review follows, authorized by a broadly worded provision phrased in the same terms used to describe the prior stage of review: "Any party aggrieved" may bring "a civil action."

These provisions confirm that IDEA, through its text and structure, creates in parents an independent stake not only in the procedures and costs implicated by this process but also in the substantive decisions to be made. We therefore conclude that IDEA does not differentiate, through isolated references to various procedures and remedies, between the rights accorded to children and the rights accorded to parents. As a consequence, a parent may be a "party aggrieved" for purposes of § 1415(i)(2) with regard to "any matter" implicating these rights. The status of parents as parties is not limited to matters that relate to procedure and cost recovery. To find otherwise would be inconsistent with the collaborative framework and expansive system of review established by the Act.

Our conclusion is confirmed by noting the incongruous results that would follow were we to accept the proposition that parents' IDEA rights are limited to certain nonsubstantive matters. The statute's procedural and reimbursement-related rights are intertwined with the substantive adequacy of the education provided to a child, and it is difficult to disentangle the provisions in order to conclude that some rights adhere to both parent and child while others do not. Were we nevertheless to recognize a distinction of this sort it would impose upon parties a confusing and onerous legal regime, one worsened by the absence of any express guidance in IDEA concerning how a court might in practice differentiate between these matters. It is, in addition, out of accord with the statute's design to interpret the Act to require that parents prove the substantive inadequacy of their child's education as a predicate for obtaining, for example, reimbursement, yet to prevent them from obtaining a judgment mandating that the school district provide their child with an educational program demonstrated to be an appropriate one. The adequacy of the educational program is, after all, the central issue in the litigation. The provisions of IDEA do not set forth these distinctions, and we decline to infer them.

***

We conclude IDEA grants parents independent, enforceable rights. These rights, which are not limited to certain procedural and reimbursement-related matters, encompass the entitlement to a free appropriate public education for the parents' child.

C

Respondent contends, though, that even under the reasoning we have now explained petitioners cannot prevail without overcoming a further difficulty. Citing our opinion in *Arlington Central School Dist. Bd. of Ed. v. Murphy,* 548 U.S. 291 (2006), respondent argues that statutes passed pursuant to the Spending Clause, such as IDEA, must provide " 'clear notice' " before they can burden a State with some new condition, obligation, or liability. Respondent contends that because IDEA is, at best, ambiguous as to whether it accords parents independent rights, it has failed to provide clear notice of this condition to the States.

Respondent's reliance on *Arlington* is misplaced. In *Arlington* we addressed whether IDEA required States to reimburse experts' fees to prevailing parties in IDEA actions. "[W]hen Congress attaches conditions to a State's acceptance of federal funds," we explained, "the conditions must be set out 'unambiguously.' " The question to be answered in *Arlington,* therefore, was whether IDEA "furnishes clear notice regarding the liability at issue." We found it did not.

The instant case presents a different issue, one that does not invoke the same rule. Our determination that IDEA grants to parents independent, enforceable rights does not impose any substantive condition or obligation on States they would not otherwise be required by law to observe. The basic measure of monetary recovery, moreover, is not expanded by recognizing that some rights repose in both the parent and the child. Were we considering a statute other than the one before us, the Spending Clause argument might have more force: A determination by the Court that some distinct class of people has independent, enforceable rights might result in a change to the States' statutory obligations. But that is not the case here.

Respondent argues our ruling will, as a practical matter, increase costs borne by the States as they are forced to defend against suits unconstrained by attorneys trained in the law and the rules of ethics. Effects such as these do not suffice to invoke the concerns under the Spending Clause. Furthermore, IDEA does afford relief for the States in certain cases. The Act empowers courts to award attorney's fees to a prevailing educational agency whenever a parent has presented a "complaint or subsequent cause of action ... for any improper purpose, such as to harass, to cause unnecessary delay, or to needlessly increase the cost of litigation." This provision allows some relief when a party has proceeded in violation of these standards.

III

The Court of Appeals erred when it dismissed the Winkelmans' appeal for lack of counsel. Parents enjoy rights under IDEA; and they are, as a result, entitled to prosecute IDEA claims on their own behalf. The decision by Congress to grant parents these rights was consistent with the purpose of IDEA and fully in accord with our social and legal traditions. It is beyond dispute that the relationship between a parent and child is sufficient to support a legally cognizable interest in the education of one's child; and, what is more, Congress has found that "the education of children with disabilities can be made more effective by ... strengthening the role and responsibility of parents and ensuring that families of such children have meaningful opportunities to participate in the education of their children at school and at home."

In light of our holding we need not reach petitioners' alternative argument, which concerns whether IDEA entitles parents to litigate their child's claims *pro se*.

The judgment of the Court of Appeals is reversed, and the case is remanded for further proceedings consistent with this opinion.

It is so ordered.

Justice Scalia concurred in judgment in part and dissented in part, and filed opinion in which Justice Thomas joined.

FOREST GROVE SCHOOL DISTRICT v. T.A.,
557 U.S. 230 (2009).

Justice Stevens delivered the opinion of the Court.

The Individuals with Disabilities Education Act (IDEA or Act), 20 U.S.C. § 1400 *et seq.*, requires States receiving federal funding to make a "free appropriate public education" (FAPE) available to all children with disabilities residing in the State. We have previously held that when a public school fails to provide a FAPE and a child's parents place the child in an appropriate private school without the school district's consent, a court may require the district to reimburse the parents for the cost of the private education. See *School Comm. of Burlington v. Department of Ed. of Mass.,* 471 U.S. 359, 370 (1985). The question presented in this case is whether the IDEA Amendments of 1997 (Amendments) categorically prohibit reimbursement for private-education costs if a child has not "previously received special education and related services under the authority of a public agency." § 1412(a)(10)(C)(ii). We hold that the Amendments impose no such categorical bar.

I

Respondent T.A. attended public schools in the Forest Grove School District (School District or District) from the time he was in kindergarten through the winter of his junior year of high school. From kindergarten through eighth grade, respondent's teachers observed that he had trouble paying attention in class and completing his assignments. When respondent entered high school, his difficulties increased.

In December 2000, during respondent's freshman year, his mother contacted the school counselor to discuss respondent's problems with his schoolwork. At the end of the school year, respondent was evaluated by a school psychologist. After interviewing him, examining his school records, and administering cognitive ability tests, the psychologist concluded that respondent did not need further testing for any learning disabilities or other health impairments, including attention deficit hyperactivity disorder (ADHD). The psychologist and two other school officials discussed the evaluation results with respondent's mother in June 2001, and all agreed that respondent did not qualify for special-education services. Respondent's parents did not seek review of that decision, although the hearing examiner later found that the School District's evaluation was legally inadequate because it failed to address all areas of suspected disability, including ADHD.

With extensive help from his family, respondent completed his sophomore year at Forest Grove High School, but his problems worsened during his junior year. In February 2003, respondent's parents discussed with the School District the possibility of respondent completing high school through a partnership program with the local community college. They also sought private professional advice, and in March 2003 respondent was diagnosed with ADHD and a number of disabilities related to learning and memory. Advised by the private specialist that respondent would do best in a structured, residential learning environment, respondent's parents enrolled him at a private academy that focuses on educating children with special needs.

Four days after enrolling him in private school, respondent's parents hired a lawyer to ascertain their rights and to give the School District written notice of respondent's private placement. A few weeks later, in April 2003, respondent's parents requested an administrative due process hearing regarding respondent's eligibility for special-education services. In June 2003, the District engaged a school psychologist to assist in determining whether respondent had a disability that significantly interfered with his educational performance. Respondent's parents cooperated with the District during the evaluation process. In July 2003, a multidisciplinary team met to discuss whether respondent satisfied IDEA's disability criteria and concluded that he did not because his ADHD did not have a sufficiently significant adverse impact on his educational performance. Because the School District maintained that respondent was not eligible for special-education services and therefore declined to provide an individualized education program (IEP), respondent's parents left him enrolled at the private academy for his senior year.

The administrative review process resumed in September 2003. After considering the parties' evidence, including the testimony of numerous experts, the hearing officer issued a decision in January 2004 finding that respondent's ADHD adversely affected his educational performance and that the School District failed to meet its obligations under IDEA in not identifying respondent as a student eligible for special-education services. Because the District did not offer respondent a FAPE and his private-school placement was appropriate under IDEA, the hearing officer ordered the District to reimburse respondent's parents for the cost of the private-school tuition.

The School District sought judicial review pursuant to § 1415(i)(2), arguing that the hearing officer erred in granting reimbursement. The District Court accepted the hearing officer's findings of fact but set aside the reimbursement award after finding that the 1997 Amendments categorically bar reimbursement of private-school tuition for students who have not "previously received special education and related services under the authority of a public agency." 20 U.S.C. § 1412(a)(10)(C)(ii). The District Court further held that, "[e]ven assuming that tuition reimbursement may be ordered in an extreme case for a student not receiving special education services, under general principles of equity where the need for special education was obvious to school authorities," the facts of this case do not support equitable relief.

The Court of Appeals for the Ninth Circuit reversed and remanded for further proceedings. The court first noted that, prior to the 1997 Amendments, "IDEA was silent on the subject of private school reimbursement, but courts had granted such reimbursement as 'appropriate' relief under principles of equity pursuant to 20 U.S.C. § 1415(i)(2)(C)." It then held that the Amendments do not impose a categorical bar to reimbursement when a parent unilaterally places in private school a child who has not previously received special-education services through the public school. Rather, such students "are eligible for reimbursement, to the same extent as before the 1997 amendments, as 'appropriate' relief pursuant to § 1415(i)(2)(C)."

The Court of Appeals also rejected the District Court's analysis of the equities as resting on two legal errors. First, because it found that § 1412(a)(10)(C)(ii) generally bars relief in these circumstances, the District Court wrongly stated that relief was appropriate only if the equities were sufficient to " 'override' " that statutory limitation. The District Court also erred in asserting that reimbursement is limited to " 'extreme' " cases. The Court of Appeals therefore remanded with instructions to reexamine the equities, including the failure of respondent's parents to notify the School District before removing respondent from public school. In dissent, Judge Rymer stated her view that reimbursement is not available as an equitable remedy in this case because respondent's parents did not request an IEP before removing him from public school and respondent's right to a FAPE was therefore not at issue.

Because the Courts of Appeals that have considered this question have reached inconsistent results, we granted certiorari to determine whether § 1412(a)(10)(C) establishes a categorical bar to tuition reimbursement for students who have not previously received special-education services under the authority of a public education agency.

II

Justice Rehnquist's opinion for a unanimous Court in *Burlington* provides the pertinent background for our analysis of the question presented. In that case, respondent challenged the appropriateness of the IEP developed for his child by public-school officials. The child had previously received special-education services through the public school. While administrative review was pending, private specialists advised respondent that the child would do best in a specialized private educational setting, and respondent enrolled the child in private school without the school district's consent. The hearing officer concluded that the IEP was not adequate to meet the child's educational needs and that the school district therefore failed to provide the child a FAPE. Finding also that the private-school placement was appropriate under IDEA, the hearing officer ordered the school district to reimburse respondent for the cost of the private-school tuition.

We granted certiorari in *Burlington* to determine whether IDEA authorizes reimbursement for the cost of private education when a parent or guardian unilaterally enrolls a child in private school because the public school has proposed an inadequate IEP and thus failed to provide a FAPE. The Act at that time made no express reference to the possibility of reimbursement, but it authorized a court to "grant such relief as the court determines is appropriate." In determining the scope of the relief authorized, we noted that "the ordinary meaning of these words confers broad discretion on the court" and that, absent any indication to the contrary, what relief is "appropriate" must be determined in light of the Act's broad purpose of providing children with disabilities a FAPE, including through publicly funded private-school placements when necessary. Accordingly, we held that the provision's grant of authority includes "the power to order school authorities to reimburse parents for their expenditures on private special-education services if the court ultimately determines that such placement, rather than a proposed IEP, is proper under the Act."

Our decision rested in part on the fact that administrative and judicial review of a parent's complaint often takes years. We concluded that, having mandated that participating States provide a FAPE for every student, Congress could not have intended to require parents to either accept an inadequate public-school education pending adjudication of their claim or bear the cost of a private education if the court ultimately determined that the private placement was proper under the Act. Eight years later, we unanimously reaffirmed the availability of reimbursement in *Florence County School Dist. Four v. Carter*, 510 U.S. 7 (1993) (holding that reimbursement may be appropriate even when a child is placed in a private school that has not been approved by the State).

The dispute giving rise to the present litigation differs from those in *Burlington* and *Carter* in that it concerns not the adequacy of a proposed IEP but the School District's failure to provide an IEP at all. And, unlike respondent, the children in those cases had previously received public special-education services. These differences are insignificant, however, because our analysis in the earlier cases depended on the language and purpose of the Act and not the particular facts involved. Moreover, when a child requires special-education services, a school district's failure to propose an IEP of any kind is at least as serious a violation of its responsibilities under IDEA as a failure to provide an adequate IEP. It is thus clear that the reasoning of *Burlington* and *Carter* applies equally to this case. The only question is whether the 1997 Amendments require a different result.

<h1 style="text-align:center">III</h1>

Congress enacted IDEA in 1970 [then titled the Education for the Handicapped Act] to ensure that all children with disabilities are provided " 'a free appropriate public education which emphasizes special education and related services designed to meet their unique needs [and] to assure that the rights of [such] children and their parents or guardians are protected.' " After examining the States' progress under IDEA, Congress found in 1997 that substantial gains had been made in the area of special education but that more needed to be done to guarantee children with disabilities adequate access to appropriate services. The 1997 Amendments were intended "to place greater emphasis on improving student performance and ensuring that children with disabilities receive a quality public education."

Consistent with that goal, the Amendments preserved the Act's purpose of providing a FAPE to all children with disabilities. And they did not change the text of the provision we considered in *Burlington*, which gives courts broad authority to grant "appropriate" relief, including reimbursement for the cost of private special education when a school district fails to provide a FAPE. "Congress is presumed to be aware of an administrative or judicial interpretation of a statute and to adopt that interpretation when it re-enacts a statute without change." *Lorillard v. Pons,* 434 U.S. 575, 580 (1978). Accordingly, absent a clear expression elsewhere in the Amendments of Congress' intent to repeal some portion of that provision or to abrogate our decisions in *Burlington* and *Carter,* we will continue to read § 1415(i)(2)(C)(iii) to authorize the relief respondent seeks.

The School District and the dissent argue that one of the provisions enacted by the Amendments, § 1412(a)(10)(C), effects such a repeal. Section 1412(a)(10)(C) is entitled "Payment for education of children enrolled in private schools without consent of or referral by the public agency," and it sets forth a number of principles applicable to public reimbursement for the costs of unilateral private-school placements. Section 1412(a)(10)(C)(i) states that IDEA "does not require a local educational agency to pay for the cost of education ... of a child with a disability at a private school or facility if that agency made a free appropriate public education available to the child" and his parents nevertheless elected to place him in a private school. Section 1412(a)(10)(C)(ii) then provides that a "court or hearing officer may require [a public] agency to reimburse the parents for the cost of [private-school] enrollment if the court or hearing officer finds that the agency had not made a free appropriate public education available" and the child has "previously received special education and related services under the authority of [the] agency." Finally, § 1412(a)(10)(C)(iii) discusses circumstances under which the "cost of reimbursement described in clause (ii) may be reduced or denied," as when a parent fails to give 10 days' notice before removing a child from public school or refuses to make a child available for evaluation, and § 1412(a)(10)(C)(iv) lists circumstances in which a parent's failure to give notice may or must be excused.

Looking primarily to clauses (i) and (ii), the School District argues that Congress intended § 1412(a)(10)(C) to provide the exclusive source of authority for courts to order reimbursement when parents unilaterally enroll a child in private school. According to the District, clause (i) provides a safe harbor for school districts that provide a FAPE by foreclosing reimbursement in those circumstances. Clause (ii) then sets forth the circumstance in which reimbursement is appropriate—namely, when a school district fails to provide a FAPE to a child who has previously received special-education services through the public school. The District contends that because § 1412(a)(10)(C) only discusses reimbursement for children who have previously received special-education services through the public school, IDEA only authorizes reimbursement in that circumstance. The dissent agrees.

For several reasons, we find this argument unpersuasive. First, the School District's reading of the Act is not supported by its text and context, as the 1997 Amendments do not expressly prohibit reimbursement under the circumstances of this case, and the District offers no evidence that Congress intended to supersede our decisions in *Burlington* and *Carter*. Clause (i)'s safe harbor explicitly bars reimbursement only when a school district makes a FAPE available by correctly identifying a child as having a disability and proposing an IEP adequate to meet the child's needs. The clause says nothing about the availability of reimbursement when a school district fails to provide a FAPE. Indeed, its statement that reimbursement *is not* authorized when a school district provides a FAPE could be read to indicate that reimbursement *is* authorized when a school district does not fulfill that obligation.

Clause (ii) likewise does not support the District's position. Because that clause is phrased permissively, stating only that courts "may require" reimbursement in those circumstances, it does not foreclose reimbursement awards in other circumstances. Together with clauses (iii) and (iv), clause (ii) is best read as elaborating on the general rule that courts may order reimbursement when a school district fails to provide a FAPE by listing factors that may affect a reimbursement award in the common situation in which a school district has provided a child with some special-education services and the child's parents believe those services are inadequate. Referring as they do to students who have previously received special-education services through a public school, clauses (ii) through (iv) are premised on a history of cooperation and together encourage school districts and parents to continue to cooperate in developing and implementing an appropriate IEP before resorting to a unilateral private placement. The clauses of § 1412(a)(10)(C) are thus best read as elucidative rather than exhaustive.

This reading of § 1412(a)(10)(C) is necessary to avoid the conclusion that Congress abrogated *sub silentio* our decisions in *Burlington* and *Carter*. In those cases, we construed § 1415(i)(2)(C)(iii) to authorize reimbursement when a school district fails to provide a FAPE and a child's private-school placement is appropriate, without regard to the child's prior receipt of services. It would take more than Congress' failure to comment on the category of cases in which a child has not previously received special-education services for us to conclude that the Amendments substantially superseded our decisions and in large part repealed § 1415(i)(2)(C)(iii). We accordingly adopt the reading of § 1412(a)(10)(C) that is consistent with those decisions.

The School District's reading of § 1412(a)(10)(C) is also at odds with the general remedial purpose underlying IDEA and the 1997 Amendments. The express purpose of the Act is to "ensure that all children with disabilities have available to them a free appropriate public education that emphasizes special education and related services designed to meet their unique needs,"—a factor we took into account in construing the scope of § 1415(i)(2)(C)(iii). Without the remedy respondent seeks, a "child's right to a *free* appropriate education ... would be less than complete." The District's position similarly conflicts with IDEA's "child find" requirement, pursuant to which States are obligated to "identif [y], locat[e], and evaluat[e]" "[a]ll children with disabilities residing in the State" to ensure that they receive needed special-education services. A reading of the Act that left parents without an adequate remedy when a school district unreasonably failed to identify a child with disabilities would not comport with Congress' acknowledgment of the paramount importance of properly identifying each child eligible for services.

Indeed, by immunizing a school district's refusal to find a child eligible for special-education services no matter how compelling the child's need, the School District's interpretation of § 1412(a)(10)(C) would produce a rule bordering on the irrational. It would be particularly strange for the Act to provide a remedy, as all agree it does, when a school district offers a child inadequate special-education services but to leave parents without relief in the more egregious situation in which the school district unreasonably denies a child access to such services altogether. That IDEA affords parents substantial procedural safeguards, including the right to challenge a school district's eligibility determination and obtain prospective relief is no answer. We roundly rejected that argument in *Burlington,* observing that the "review process is ponderous" and therefore inadequate to ensure that a school's failure to provide a FAPE is remedied with the speed necessary to avoid detriment to the child's education. Like *Burlington,* this case vividly demonstrates the problem of delay, as respondent's parents first sought a due process hearing in April 2003, and the District Court issued its decision in May 2005—almost a year after respondent graduated from high school. The dissent all but ignores these shortcomings of IDEA's procedural safeguards.

IV

The School District advances two additional arguments for reading the Act to foreclose reimbursement in this case. First, the District contends that because IDEA was an exercise of Congress' authority under the Spending Clause, any conditions attached to a State's acceptance of funds must be stated unambiguously. Applying that principle, we held in *Arlington Central School Dist. Bd. of Ed. v. Murphy,* 548 U.S. 291, 304 (2006), that IDEA's fee-shifting provision, § 1415(i)(3)(B), does not authorize courts to award expert-services fees to prevailing parents in IDEA actions because the Act does not put States on notice of the possibility of such awards. But *Arlington* is readily distinguishable from this case. In accepting IDEA funding, States expressly agree to provide a FAPE to all children with disabilities. An order awarding reimbursement of private-education costs when a school district fails to provide a FAPE merely requires the district "to belatedly pay expenses that it should have paid all along." *Burlington,* 471 U.S., at 370–371. And States have in any event been on notice at least since our decision in *Burlington* that IDEA authorizes courts to order reimbursement of the costs of private special-education services in appropriate circumstances. ...

Finally, the District urges that respondent's reading of the Act will impose a substantial financial burden on public school districts and encourage parents to immediately enroll their children in private school without first endeavoring to cooperate with the school district. The dissent echoes this concern. For several reasons, those fears are unfounded. Parents "are entitled to reimbursement *only* if a federal court concludes both that the public placement violated IDEA and the private school placement was proper under the Act." *Carter,* 510 U.S., at 15. And even then courts retain discretion to reduce the amount of a reimbursement award if the equities so warrant—for instance, if the parents failed to give the school district adequate notice of their intent to enroll the child in private school. In considering the equities, courts should generally presume that public-school officials are properly performing their obligations under IDEA. As a result of these criteria and the fact that parents who " 'unilaterally change their child's placement during the pendency of review proceedings, without the consent of state or local school officials, do so at their own financial risk,'" *Carter,* 510 U.S., at 15, the incidence of private-school placement at public expense is quite small.

V

The IDEA Amendments of 1997 did not modify the text of § 1415(i)(2)(C)(iii), and we do not read § 1412(a)(10)(C) to alter that provision's meaning. Consistent with our decisions in *Burlington* and *Carter,* we conclude that IDEA authorizes reimbursement for the cost of private special-education services when a school district fails to provide a FAPE and the private-school placement is appropriate, regardless of whether the child previously received special education or related services through the public school.

When a court or hearing officer concludes that a school district failed to provide a FAPE and the private placement was suitable, it must consider all relevant factors, including the notice provided by the parents and the school district's opportunities for evaluating the child, in determining whether reimbursement for some or all of the cost of the child's private education is warranted. As the Court of Appeals noted, the District Court did not properly consider the equities in this case and will need to undertake that analysis on remand. Accordingly, the judgment of the Court of Appeals is affirmed.

It is so ordered.

Justice Souter filed a dissenting opinion, in which Justice Scalia and Justice Thomas joined.

FRY v. NAPOLEON COMMUNITY SCHOOLS,
580 U.S. ___, 137 S.Ct. 743 (2017).

Justice Kagan delivered the opinion of the Court.

The Individuals with Disabilities Education Act (IDEA or Act) ensures that children with disabilities receive needed special education services. One of its provisions, § 1415(*l*), addresses the Act's relationship with other laws protecting those children. Section 1415(*l*) makes clear that nothing in the IDEA "restrict[s] or limit[s] the rights [or] remedies" that other federal laws, including antidiscrimination statutes, confer on children with disabilities. At the same time, the section states that if a suit brought under such a law "seek[s] relief that is also available under" the IDEA, the plaintiff must first exhaust the IDEA's administrative procedures. In this case, we consider the scope of that exhaustion requirement. We hold that exhaustion is not necessary when the gravamen of the plaintiff's suit is something other than the denial of the IDEA's core guarantee—what the Act calls a "free appropriate public education."

I

A

The IDEA offers federal funds to States in exchange for a commitment: to furnish a "free appropriate public education"—more concisely known as a FAPE—to all children with certain physical or intellectual disabilities. As defined in the Act, a FAPE comprises "special education and related services"—both "instruction" tailored to meet a child's "unique needs" and sufficient "supportive services" to permit the child to benefit from that instruction. §§ 1401(9); see *Board of Ed. of Hendrick Hudson Central School Dist., Westchester Cty. v. Rowley,* 458 U.S. 176 (1982). An eligible child, as this Court has explained, acquires a "substantive right" to such an education once a State accepts the IDEA's financial assistance. *Smith v. Robinson,* 468 U.S. 992 (1984).

Under the IDEA, an "individualized education program," called an IEP for short, serves as the "primary vehicle" for providing each child with the promised FAPE. (Crafted by a child's "IEP Team"—a group of school officials, teachers, and parents— the IEP spells out a personalized plan to meet all of the child's "educational needs."). Most notably, the IEP documents the child's current "levels of academic achievement," specifies "measurable annual goals" for how she can "make progress in the general education curriculum," and lists the "special education and related services" to be provided so that she can "advance appropriately toward [those] goals."

Because parents and school representatives sometimes cannot agree on such issues, the IDEA establishes formal procedures for resolving disputes. To begin, a dissatisfied parent may file a complaint as to any matter concerning the provision of a FAPE with the local or state educational agency (as state law provides). That pleading generally triggers a "[p]reliminary meeting" involving the contending parties; at their option, the parties may instead (or also) pursue a full-fledged mediation process. Assuming their impasse continues, the matter proceeds to a "due process hearing" before an impartial hearing officer. Any decision of the officer granting substantive relief must be "based on a determination of whether the child received a [FAPE]." If the hearing is initially conducted at the local level, the ruling is appealable to the state agency. Finally, a parent unhappy with the outcome of the administrative process may seek judicial review by filing a civil action in state or federal court.

Important as the IDEA is for children with disabilities, it is not the only federal statute protecting their interests. Of particular relevance to this case are two antidiscrimination laws—Title II of the Americans with Disabilities Act (ADA), 42 U.S.C. § 12131, and § 504 of the Rehabilitation Act, 29 U.S.C. § 794—which cover both adults and children with disabilities, in both public schools and other settings. Title II forbids any "public entity" from discriminating based on disability; Section 504 applies the same prohibition to any federally funded "program or activity." A regulation implementing Title II requires a public entity to make "reasonable modifications" to its "policies, practices, or procedures" when necessary to avoid such discrimination. 28 C.F.R. § 35.130(b)(7) (2016)… And both statutes authorize individuals to seek redress for violations of their substantive guarantees by bringing suits for injunctive relief or money damages.

This Court first considered the interaction between such laws and the IDEA in *Smith v. Robinson.* The plaintiffs there sought "to secure a 'free appropriate public education' for [their] handicapped child But instead of bringing suit under the IDEA alone, they appended "virtually identical" claims (again alleging the denial of a "free appropriate public education") under § 504 of the Rehabilitation Act and the Fourteenth Amendment's Equal Protection Clause.. The Court held that the IDEA altogether foreclosed those additional claims: With its "comprehensive" and "carefully tailored" provisions, the Act was "the exclusive avenue" through which a child with a disability (or his parents) could challenge the adequacy of his education.

Congress was quick to respond. In the Handicapped Children's Protection Act of 1986, 100 Stat. 796, it overturned *Smith*'s preclusion of non-IDEA claims while also adding a carefully defined exhaustion requirement. Now codified at 20 U.S.C. § 1415(*l*), the relevant provision of that statute reads:

"Nothing in [the IDEA] shall be construed to restrict or limit the rights, procedures, and remedies available under the Constitution, the [ADA], title V of the Rehabilitation Act [including § 504], or other Federal laws protecting the rights of children with disabilities, except that before the filing of a civil action under such laws seeking relief that is also available under [the IDEA], the [IDEA's administrative procedures] shall be exhausted to the same extent as would be required had the action been brought under [the IDEA]."

The first half of § 1415(*l*) (up until "except that") "reaffirm[s] the viability" of federal statutes like the ADA or Rehabilitation Act "as separate vehicles," no less integral than the IDEA, "for ensuring the rights of handicapped children." H.R.Rep. No. 99–296, p. 4 (1985) According to that opening phrase, the IDEA does not prevent a plaintiff from asserting claims under such laws even if, as in *Smith* itself, those claims allege the denial of an appropriate public education (much as an IDEA claim would). But the second half of § 1415(*l*) (from "except that" onward) imposes a limit on that "anything goes" regime, in the form of an exhaustion provision. According to that closing phrase, a plaintiff bringing suit under the ADA, the Rehabilitation Act, or similar laws must in certain circumstances—that is, when "seeking relief that is also available under" the IDEA—first exhaust the IDEA's administrative procedures. The reach of that requirement is the issue in this case.

B

Petitioner E.F. is a child with a severe form of cerebral palsy, which "significantly limits her motor skills and mobility." When E.F. was five years old, her parents—petitioners Stacy and Brent Fry—obtained a trained service dog for her, as recommended by her pediatrician. The dog, a goldendoodle named Wonder, "help[s E.F.] to live as independently as possible" by assisting her with various life activities. In particular, Wonder aids E.F. by "retrieving dropped items, helping her balance when she uses her walker, opening and closing doors, turning on and off lights, helping her take off her coat, [and] helping her transfer to and from the toilet."

But when the Frys sought permission for Wonder to join E.F. in kindergarten, officials at Ezra Eby Elementary School refused the request. Under E.F.'s existing IEP, a human aide provided E.F. with one-on-one support throughout the day; that two-legged assistance, the school officials thought, rendered Wonder superfluous. In the words of one administrator, Wonder should be barred from Ezra Eby because all of E.F.'s "physical and academic needs [were] being met through the services/programs/accommodations" that the school had already agreed to. Later that year, the school officials briefly allowed Wonder to accompany E.F. to school on a trial basis; but even then, "the dog was required to remain in the back of the room during classes, and was forbidden from assisting [E.F.] with many tasks he had been specifically trained to do." And when the trial period concluded, the administrators again informed the Frys that Wonder was not welcome. As a result, the Frys removed E.F. from Ezra Eby and began homeschooling her.

In addition, the Frys filed a complaint with the U.S. Department of Education's Office for Civil Rights (OCR), charging that Ezra Eby's exclusion of E.F.'s service animal violated her rights under Title II of the ADA and § 504 of the Rehabilitation Act. Following an investigation, OCR agreed. The office explained in its decision letter that a school's obligations under those statutes go beyond providing educational services: A school could offer a FAPE to a child with a disability but still run afoul of the laws' ban on discrimination. And here, OCR found, Ezra Eby had indeed violated that ban, even if its use of a human aide satisfied the FAPE standard. OCR analogized the school's conduct to "requir[ing] a student who uses a wheelchair to be carried" by an aide or "requir[ing] a blind student to be led [around by a] teacher" instead of permitting him to use a guide dog or cane. Regardless whether those—or Ezra Eby's—policies denied a FAPE, they violated Title II and § 504 by discriminating against children with disabilities.

In response to OCR's decision, school officials at last agreed that E.F. could come to school with Wonder. But after meeting with Ezra Eby's principal, the Frys became concerned that the school administration "would resent [E.F.] and make her return to school difficult." Accordingly, the Frys found a different public school, in a different district, where administrators and teachers enthusiastically received both E.F. and Wonder.

C

The Frys then filed this suit in federal court against the local and regional school districts in which Ezra Eby is located, along with the school's principal (collectively, the school districts). The complaint alleged that the school districts violated Title II of the ADA and § 504 of the Rehabilitation Act by "denying [E.F.] equal access" to Ezra Eby and its programs, "refus[ing] to reasonably accommodate" E.F.'s use of a service animal, and otherwise "discriminat[ing] against [E.F.] as a person with disabilities." According to the complaint, E.F. suffered harm as a result of that discrimination, including "emotional distress and pain, embarrassment, [and] mental anguish." In their prayer for relief, the Frys sought a declaration that the school districts had violated Title II and § 504, along with money damages to compensate for E.F.'s injuries.

The District Court granted the school districts' motion to dismiss the suit, holding that § 1415(*l*) required the Frys to first exhaust the IDEA's administrative procedures. A divided panel of the Court of Appeals for the Sixth Circuit affirmed on the same ground. In that court's view, § 1415(*l*) applies if "the injuries [alleged in a suit] relate to the specific substantive protections of the IDEA." And that means, the court continued, that exhaustion is necessary whenever "the genesis and the manifestations" of the complained-of harms were "educational" in nature. On that understanding of § 1415(*l*), the Sixth Circuit held, the Frys' suit could not proceed: Because the harms to E.F. were generally "educational"—most notably, the court reasoned, because "Wonder's absence hurt her sense of independence and social confidence at school"—the Frys had to exhaust the IDEA's procedures. Judge Daughtrey dissented, emphasizing that in bringing their Title II and § 504 claims, the Frys "did not allege the denial of a FAPE" or "seek to modify [E.F.'s] IEP in any way.

We granted certiorari to address confusion in the courts of appeals as to the scope of § 1415(*l*)'s exhaustion requirement. We now vacate the Sixth Circuit's decision.

II

Section 1415(*l*) requires that a plaintiff exhaust the IDEA's procedures before filing an action under the ADA, the Rehabilitation Act, or similar laws when (but only when) her suit "seek[s] relief that is also available" under the IDEA. We first hold that to meet that statutory standard, a suit must seek relief for the denial of a FAPE, because that is the only "relief" the IDEA makes "available." We next conclude that in determining whether a suit indeed "seeks" relief for such a denial, a court should look to the substance, or gravamen, of the plaintiff's complaint.

A

In this Court, the parties have reached substantial agreement about what "relief" the IDEA makes "available" for children with disabilities—and about how the Sixth Circuit went wrong in addressing that question. The Frys maintain that such a child can obtain remedies under the IDEA for decisions that deprive her of a FAPE, but none for those that do not. So in the Frys' view, § 1415(*l*)'s exhaustion requirement can come into play only when a suit concerns the denial of a FAPE—and not, as the Sixth Circuit held, when it merely has some articulable connection to the education of a child with a disability. The school districts, for their part, also believe that the Sixth Circuit's exhaustion standard "goes too far" because it could mandate exhaustion when a plaintiff is "seeking relief that is *not* in substance available" under the IDEA. And in particular, the school districts acknowledge that the IDEA makes remedies available only in suits that "directly implicate[ ]" a FAPE—so that only in those suits can § 1415(*l*) apply. For the reasons that follow, we agree with the parties' shared view: The only relief that an IDEA officer can give—hence the thing a plaintiff must seek in order to trigger § 1415(*l*)'s exhaustion rule—is relief for the denial of a FAPE.

We begin, as always, with the statutory language at issue, which (at risk of repetition) compels exhaustion when a plaintiff seeks "relief" that is "available" under the IDEA. The ordinary meaning of "relief" in the context of a lawsuit is the "redress[ ] or benefit" that attends a favorable judgment. Black's Law Dictionary 1161 (5th ed. 1979). And such relief is "available," as we recently explained, when it is "accessible or may be obtained." *Ross v. Blake,* 578 U.S. ——,136 S.Ct. 1850, 1858 (2016). So to establish the scope of § 1415(*l*), we must identify the circumstances in which the IDEA enables a person to obtain redress (or, similarly, to access a benefit).

That inquiry immediately reveals the primacy of a FAPE in the statutory scheme. In its first section, the IDEA declares as its first purpose "to ensure that all children with disabilities have available to them a free appropriate public education." That principal purpose then becomes the Act's principal command: A State receiving federal funding under the IDEA must make such an education "available to all children with disabilities. The guarantee of a FAPE to those children gives rise to the bulk of the statute's more specific provisions. For example, the IEP— "the centerpiece of the statute's education delivery system"—serves as the "vehicle" or "means" of providing a FAPE. *Honig,* 484 U.S., [305] at 311 (1988). And finally, as all the above suggests, the FAPE requirement provides the yardstick for measuring the adequacy of the education that a school offers to a child with a disability: Under that standard, this Court has held, a child is entitled to "meaningful" access to education based on her individual needs.

The IDEA's administrative procedures test whether a school has met that obligation—and so center on the Act's FAPE requirement. As noted earlier, any decision by a hearing officer on a request for substantive relief "shall" be "based on a determination of whether the child received a free appropriate public education." Or said in Latin: In the IDEA's administrative process, a FAPE denial is the *sine qua non*. Suppose that a parent's complaint protests a school's failure to provide some accommodation for a child with a disability. If that accommodation is needed to fulfill the IDEA's FAPE requirement, the hearing officer must order relief. But if it is not, he cannot—even though the dispute is between a child with a disability and the school she attends. There might be good reasons, unrelated to a FAPE, for the school to make the requested accommodation. Indeed, another federal law (like the ADA or Rehabilitation Act) might *require* the accommodation on one of those alternative grounds. But still, the hearing officer cannot provide the requested relief. His role, under the IDEA, is to enforce the child's "substantive right" to a FAPE. And that is all.

For that reason, § 1415(*l*)'s exhaustion rule hinges on whether a lawsuit seeks relief for the denial of a free appropriate public education. If a lawsuit charges such a denial, the plaintiff cannot escape § 1415(*l*) merely by bringing her suit under a statute other than the IDEA—as when, for example, the plaintiffs in *Smith* claimed that a school's failure to provide a FAPE also violated the Rehabilitation Act. Rather, that plaintiff must first submit her case to an IDEA hearing officer, experienced in addressing exactly the issues she raises. But if, in a suit brought under a different statute, the remedy sought is not for the denial of a FAPE, then exhaustion of the IDEA's procedures is not required. After all, the plaintiff could not get any relief from those procedures: A hearing officer, as just explained, would have to send her away empty-handed. And that is true even when the suit arises directly from a school's treatment of a child with a disability—and so could be said to relate in some way to her education. A school's conduct toward such a child—say, some refusal to make an accommodation—might injure her in ways unrelated to a FAPE, which are addressed in statutes other than the IDEA. A complaint seeking redress for those other harms, independent of any FAPE denial, is not subject to § 1415(*l*)'s exhaustion rule because, once again, the only "relief" the IDEA makes "available" is relief for the denial of a FAPE.

B

Still, an important question remains: How is a court to tell when a plaintiff "seeks" relief for the denial of a FAPE and when she does not? Here, too, the parties have found some common ground: By looking, they both say, to the "substance" of, rather than the labels used in, the plaintiff's complaint. And here, too, we agree with that view: What matters is the crux—or, in legal-speak, the gravamen—of the plaintiff's complaint, setting aside any attempts at artful pleading.

That inquiry makes central the plaintiff's own claims, as § 1415(*l*) explicitly requires. The statutory language asks whether a lawsuit in fact "seeks" relief available under the IDEA—not, as a stricter exhaustion statute might, whether the suit "could have sought" relief available under the IDEA (or, what is much the same, whether any remedies "are" available under that law). In effect, § 1415(*l*) treats the plaintiff as "the master of the claim": She identifies its remedial basis—and is subject to exhaustion or not based on that choice. A court deciding whether § 1415(*l*) applies must therefore examine whether a plaintiff's complaint—the principal instrument by which she describes her case—seeks relief for the denial of an appropriate education.

But that examination should consider substance, not surface. The use (or non-use) of particular labels and terms is not what matters. The inquiry, for example, does not ride on whether a complaint includes (or, alternatively, omits) the precise words "FAPE" or "IEP." After all, § 1415(*l*)'s premise is that the plaintiff is suing under a statute *other than* the IDEA, like the Rehabilitation Act; in such a suit, the plaintiff might see no need to use the IDEA's distinctive language—even if she is in essence contesting the adequacy of a special education program. And still more critically, a "magic words" approach would make § 1415(*l*)'s exhaustion rule too easy to bypass. Just last Term, a similar worry led us to hold that a court's jurisdiction under the Foreign Sovereign Immunities Act turns on the "gravamen," or "essentials," of the plaintiff's suit. *OBB Personenverkehr AG v. Sachs,* 577 U.S. ——, 136 S.Ct. 390, 395, 396, 397 (2015). "[A]ny other approach," we explained, "would allow plaintiffs to evade the Act's restrictions through artful pleading." So too here. Section 1415(*l*) is not merely a pleading hurdle. It requires exhaustion when the gravamen of a complaint seeks redress for a school's failure to provide a FAPE, even if not phrased or framed in precisely that way.

In addressing whether a complaint fits that description, a court should attend to the diverse means and ends of the statutes covering persons with disabilities—the IDEA on the one hand, the ADA and Rehabilitation Act (most notably) on the other. The IDEA, of course, protects only "children" (well, really, adolescents too) and concerns only their schooling. And as earlier noted, the statute's goal is to provide each child with meaningful access to education by offering individualized instruction and related services appropriate to her "unique needs." By contrast, Title II of the ADA and § 504 of the Rehabilitation Act cover people with disabilities of all ages, and do so both inside and outside schools. And those statutes aim to root out disability-based discrimination, enabling each covered person (sometimes by means of reasonable accommodations) to participate equally to all others in public facilities and federally funded programs. In short, the IDEA guarantees individually tailored educational services, while Title II and § 504 promise non-discriminatory access to public institutions. That is not to deny some overlap in coverage: The same conduct might violate all three statutes—which is why, as in *Smith,* a plaintiff might seek relief for the denial of a FAPE under Title II and § 504 as well as the IDEA. But still, the statutory differences just discussed mean that a complaint brought under Title II and § 504 might instead seek relief for simple discrimination, irrespective of the IDEA's FAPE obligation.

One clue to whether the gravamen of a complaint against a school concerns the denial of a FAPE, or instead addresses disability-based discrimination, can come from asking a pair of hypothetical questions. First, could the plaintiff have brought essentially the same claim if the alleged conduct had occurred at a public facility that was *not* a school—say, a public theater or library? And second, could an *adult* at the school—say, an employee or visitor—have pressed essentially the same grievance? When the answer to those questions is yes, a complaint that does not expressly allege the denial of a FAPE is also unlikely to be truly about that subject; after all, in those other situations there is no FAPE obligation and yet the same basic suit could go forward. But when the answer is no, then the complaint probably does concern a FAPE, even if it does not explicitly say so; for the FAPE requirement is all that explains why only a child in the school setting (not an adult in that setting or a child in some other) has a viable claim.

Take two contrasting examples. Suppose first that a wheelchair-bound child sues his school for discrimination under Title II (again, without mentioning the denial of a FAPE) because the building lacks access ramps. In some sense, that architectural feature has educational consequences, and a different lawsuit might have alleged that it violates the IDEA: After all, if the child cannot get inside the school, he cannot receive instruction there; and if he must be carried inside, he may not achieve the sense of independence conducive to academic (or later to real-world) success. But is the denial of a FAPE really the gravamen of the plaintiff's Title II complaint? Consider that the child could file the same basic complaint if a municipal library or theater had no ramps. And similarly, an employee or visitor could bring a mostly identical complaint against the school. That the claim can stay the same in those alternative scenarios suggests that its essence is equality of access to public facilities, not adequacy of special education. And so § 1415(*l*) does not require exhaustion.

But suppose next that a student with a learning disability sues his school under Title II for failing to provide remedial tutoring in mathematics. That suit, too, might be cast as one for disability-based discrimination, grounded on the school's refusal to make a reasonable accommodation; the complaint might make no reference at all to a FAPE or an IEP. But can anyone imagine the student making the same claim against a public theater or library? Or, similarly, imagine an adult visitor or employee suing the school to obtain a math tutorial? The difficulty of transplanting the complaint to those other contexts suggests that its essence—even though not its wording—is the provision of a FAPE, thus bringing § 1415(*l*) into play.

A further sign that the gravamen of a suit is the denial of a FAPE can emerge from the history of the proceedings. In particular, a court may consider that a plaintiff has previously invoked the IDEA's formal procedures to handle the dispute—thus starting to exhaust the Act's remedies before switching midstream. Recall that a parent dissatisfied with her child's education initiates those administrative procedures by filing a complaint, which triggers a preliminary meeting (or possibly mediation) and then a due process hearing. A plaintiff's initial choice to pursue that process may suggest that she is indeed seeking relief for the denial of a FAPE—with the shift to judicial proceedings prior to full exhaustion reflecting only strategic calculations about how to maximize the prospects of such a remedy. Whether that is so depends on the facts; a court may conclude, for example, that the move to a courtroom came from a late-acquired awareness that the school had fulfilled its FAPE obligation and that the grievance involves something else entirely. But prior pursuit of the IDEA's administrative remedies will often provide strong evidence that the substance of a plaintiff's claim concerns the denial of a FAPE, even if the complaint never explicitly uses that term.

III

The Court of Appeals did not undertake the analysis we have just set forward. As noted above, it asked whether E.F.'s injuries were, broadly speaking, "educational" in nature. That is not the same as asking whether the gravamen of E.F.'s complaint charges, and seeks relief for, the denial of a FAPE. And that difference in standard may have led to a difference in result in this case. Understood correctly, § 1415(*l*) might not require exhaustion of the Frys' claim. We lack some important information on that score, however, and so we remand the issue to the court below.

The Frys' complaint alleges only disability-based discrimination, without making any reference to the adequacy of the special education services E.F.'s school provided. The school districts' "refusal to allow Wonder to act as a service dog," the complaint states, "discriminated against [E.F.] as a person with disabilities ... by denying her equal access" to public facilities. The complaint contains no allegation about the denial of a FAPE or about any deficiency in E.F.'s IEP. More, it does not accuse the school even in general terms of refusing to provide the educational instruction and services that E.F. needs. As the Frys explained in this Court: The school districts "have said all along that because they gave [E.F.] a one-on-one [human] aide, that all of her ... educational needs were satisfied. And we have not challenged that, and it would be difficult for us to challenge that." The Frys instead maintained, just as OCR had earlier found, that the school districts infringed E.F.'s right to equal access—even if their actions complied in full with the IDEA's requirements.

And nothing in the nature of the Frys' suit suggests any implicit focus on the adequacy of E.F.'s education. Consider, as suggested above, that the Frys could have filed essentially the same complaint if a public library or theater had refused admittance to Wonder. Or similarly, consider that an adult visitor to the school could have leveled much the same charges if prevented from entering with his service dog. In each case, the plaintiff would challenge a public facility's policy of precluding service dogs (just as a blind person might challenge a policy of barring guide dogs) as violating Title II's and § 504's equal access requirements. The suit would have nothing to do with the provision of educational services. From all that we know now, that is exactly the kind of action the Frys have brought.

But we do not foreclose the possibility that the history of these proceedings might suggest something different. As earlier discussed, a plaintiff's initial pursuit of the IDEA's administrative remedies can serve as evidence that the gravamen of her later suit is the denial of a FAPE, even though that does not appear on the face of her complaint. The Frys may or may not have sought those remedies before filing this case: None of the parties here have addressed that issue, and the record is cloudy as to the relevant facts. Accordingly, on remand, the court below should establish whether (or to what extent) the Frys invoked the IDEA's dispute resolution process before bringing this suit. And if the Frys started down that road, the court should decide whether their actions reveal that the gravamen of their complaint is indeed the denial of a FAPE, thus necessitating further exhaustion.

With these instructions and for the reasons stated, we vacate the judgment of the Court of Appeals and remand the case for further proceedings consistent with this opinion.

It is so ordered.

Justice Alito filed an opinion concurring in part and concurring in the judgment, in which Justice Thomas joined.

**ENDREW F. v. DOUGLAS COUNTY SCHOOL DISTRICT RE–1.,
580 U.S. ___, 137 S.Ct. 988 (2017).**

Chief Justice Roberts delivered the opinion of the Court.

Thirty-five years ago, this Court held that the Individuals with Disabilities Education Act establishes a substantive right to a "free appropriate public education" for certain children with disabilities. *Board of Ed. of Hendrick Hudson Central School Dist., Westchester Cty. v. Rowley,* 458 U.S. 176 (1982). We declined, however, to endorse any one standard for determining "when handicapped children are receiving sufficient educational benefits to satisfy the requirements of the Act." That "more difficult problem" is before us today.

I

A

The Individuals with Disabilities Education Act (IDEA or Act) offers States federal funds to assist in educating children with disabilities. In exchange for the funds, a State pledges to comply with a number of statutory conditions. Among them, the State must provide a free appropriate public education—a FAPE, for short—to all eligible children.

A FAPE, as the Act defines it, includes both "special education" and "related services." "Special education" is "specially designed instruction ... to meet the unique needs of a child with a disability"; "related services" are the support services "required to assist a child ... to benefit from" that instruction. A State covered by the IDEA must provide a disabled child with such special education and related services "in conformity with the [child's] individualized education program," or IEP.

The IEP is "the centerpiece of the statute's education delivery system for disabled children." *Honig v. Doe,* 484 U.S. 305 (1988). A comprehensive plan prepared by a child's "IEP Team" (which includes teachers, school officials, and the child's parents), an IEP must be drafted in compliance with a detailed set of procedures. These procedures emphasize collaboration among parents and educators and require careful consideration of the child's individual circumstances. The IEP is the means by which special education and related services are "tailored to the unique needs" of a particular child.

The IDEA requires that every IEP include "a statement of the child's present levels of academic achievement and functional performance," describe "how the child's disability affects the child's involvement and progress in the general education curriculum," and set out "measurable annual goals, including academic and functional goals," along with a "description of how the child's progress toward meeting" those goals will be gauged. The IEP must also describe the "special education and related services ... that will be provided" so that the child may "advance appropriately toward attaining the annual goals" and, when possible, "be involved in and make progress in the general education curriculum."

Parents and educators often agree about what a child's IEP should contain. But not always. When disagreement arises, parents may turn to dispute resolution procedures established by the IDEA. The parties may resolve their differences informally, through a "[p]reliminary meeting," or, somewhat more formally, through mediation. If these measures fail to produce accord, the parties may proceed to what the Act calls a "due process hearing" before a state or local educational agency. And at the conclusion of the administrative process, the losing party may seek redress in state or federal court.

B

This Court first addressed the FAPE requirement in *Rowley*. Plaintiff Amy Rowley was a first grader with impaired hearing. Her school district offered an IEP under which Amy would receive instruction in the regular classroom and spend time each week with a special tutor and a speech therapist. The district proposed that Amy's classroom teacher speak into a wireless transmitter and that Amy use an FM hearing aid designed to amplify her teacher's words; the district offered to supply both components of this system. But Amy's parents argued that the IEP should go further and provide a sign-language interpreter in all of her classes. Contending that the school district's refusal to furnish an interpreter denied Amy a FAPE, Amy's parents initiated administrative proceedings, then filed a lawsuit under the Act.

The District Court agreed that Amy had been denied a FAPE. The court acknowledged that Amy was making excellent progress in school: She was "perform[ing] better than the average child in her class" and "advancing easily from grade to grade." At the same time, Amy "under[stood] considerably less of what goes on in class than she could if she were not deaf." Concluding that "it has been left entirely to the courts and the hearings officers to give content to the requirement of an 'appropriate education,'" the District Court ruled that Amy's education was not "appropriate" unless it provided her "an opportunity to achieve [her] full potential commensurate with the opportunity provided to other children." The Second Circuit agreed with this analysis and affirmed.

In this Court, the parties advanced starkly different understandings of the FAPE requirement. Amy's parents defended the approach of the lower courts, arguing that the school district was required to provide instruction and services that would provide Amy an "equal educational opportunity" relative to children without disabilities. The school district, for its part, contended that the IDEA "did not create substantive individual rights"; the FAPE provision was instead merely aspirational.

Neither position carried the day. On the one hand, this Court rejected the view that the IDEA gives "courts *carte blanche* to impose upon the States whatever burden their various judgments indicate should be imposed." After all, the statutory phrase "free appropriate public education" was expressly defined in the Act, even if the definition "tend[ed] toward the cryptic rather than the comprehensive." This Court went on to reject the "equal opportunity" standard adopted by the lower courts, concluding that "free appropriate public education" was a phrase "too complex to be captured by the word 'equal' whether one is speaking of opportunities or services. The Court also viewed the standard as "entirely unworkable," apt to require "impossible measurements and comparisons" that courts were ill suited to make.

On the other hand, the Court also rejected the school district's argument that the FAPE requirement was actually no requirement at all. Instead, the Court carefully charted a middle path. Even though "Congress was rather sketchy in establishing substantive requirements" under the Act, the Court nonetheless made clear that the Act guarantees a substantively adequate program of education to all eligible children... We explained that this requirement is satisfied, and a child has received a FAPE, if the child's IEP sets out an educational program that is "reasonably calculated to enable the child to receive educational benefits." For children receiving instruction in the regular classroom, this would generally require an IEP "reasonably calculated to enable the child to achieve passing marks and advance from grade to grade."

In view of Amy Rowley's excellent progress and the "substantial" suite of specialized instruction and services offered in her IEP, we concluded that her program satisfied the FAPE requirement. But we went no further. Instead, we expressly "confine[d] our analysis" to the facts of the case before us. Observing that the Act requires States to "educate a wide spectrum" of children with disabilities and that "the benefits obtainable by children at one end of the spectrum will differ dramatically from those obtainable by children at the other end," we declined "to establish any one test for determining the adequacy of educational benefits conferred upon all children covered by the Act."

C

Petitioner Endrew F. was diagnosed with autism at age two. Autism is a neurodevelopmental disorder generally marked by impaired social and communicative skills, "engagement in repetitive activities and stereotyped movements, resistance to environmental change or change in daily routines, and unusual responses to sensory experiences." A child with autism qualifies as a "[c]hild with a disability" under the IDEA, and Colorado (where Endrew resides) accepts IDEA funding. Endrew is therefore entitled to the benefits of the Act, including a FAPE provided by the State.

Endrew attended school in respondent Douglas County School District from preschool through fourth grade. Each year, his IEP Team drafted an IEP addressed to his educational and functional needs. By Endrew's fourth grade year, however, his parents had become dissatisfied with his progress. Although Endrew displayed a number of strengths—his teachers described him as a humorous child with a "sweet disposition" who "show[ed] concern[ ] for friends"—he still "exhibited multiple behaviors that inhibited his ability to access learning in the classroom." Endrew would scream in class, climb over furniture and other students, and occasionally run away from school. He was afflicted by severe fears of commonplace things like flies, spills, and public restrooms. As Endrew's parents saw it, his academic and functional progress had essentially stalled: Endrew's IEPs largely carried over the same basic goals and objectives from one year to the next, indicating that he was failing to make meaningful progress toward his aims. His parents believed that only a thorough overhaul of the school district's approach to Endrew's behavioral problems could reverse the trend. But in April 2010, the school district presented Endrew's parents with a proposed fifth grade IEP that was, in their view, pretty much the same as his past ones. So his parents removed Endrew from public school and enrolled him at Firefly Autism House, a private school that specializes in educating children with autism.

Endrew did much better at Firefly. The school developed a "behavioral intervention plan" that identified Endrew's most problematic behaviors and set out particular strategies for addressing them. Firefly also added heft to Endrew's academic goals. Within months, Endrew's behavior improved significantly, permitting him to make a degree of academic progress that had eluded him in public school.

In November 2010, some six months after Endrew started classes at Firefly, his parents again met with representatives of the Douglas County School District. The district presented a new IEP. Endrew's parents considered the IEP no more adequate than the one proposed in April, and rejected it. They were particularly concerned that the stated plan for addressing Endrew's behavior did not differ meaningfully from the plan in his fourth grade IEP, despite the fact that his experience at Firefly suggested that he would benefit from a different approach.

In February 2012, Endrew's parents filed a complaint with the Colorado Department of Education seeking reimbursement for Endrew's tuition at Firefly. To qualify for such relief, they were required to show that the school district had not provided Endrew a FAPE in a timely manner prior to his enrollment at the private school. Endrew's parents contended that the final IEP proposed by the school district was not "reasonably calculated to enable [Endrew] to receive educational benefits" and that Endrew had therefore been denied a FAPE. An Administrative Law Judge (ALJ) disagreed and denied relief.

Endrew's parents sought review in Federal District Court. Giving "due weight" to the decision of the ALJ, the District Court affirmed. The court acknowledged that Endrew's performance under past IEPs "did not reveal immense educational growth." But it concluded that annual modifications to Endrew's IEP objectives were "sufficient to show a pattern of, at the least, minimal progress." Because Endrew's previous IEPs had enabled him to make this sort of progress, the court reasoned, his latest, similar IEP was reasonably calculated to do the same thing. In the court's view, that was all *Rowley* demanded.

The Tenth Circuit affirmed. The Court of Appeals recited language from *Rowley* stating that the instruction and services furnished to children with disabilities must be calculated to confer "*some* educational benefit." The court noted that it had long interpreted this language to mean that a child's IEP is adequate as long as it is calculated to confer an "educational benefit [that is] merely ... more than *de minimis*." Applying this standard, the Tenth Circuit held that Endrew's IEP had been "reasonably calculated to enable [him] to make *some* progress." Accordingly, he had not been denied a FAPE.

We granted certiorari.

II

A

The Court in *Rowley* declined "to establish any one test for determining the adequacy of educational benefits conferred upon all children covered by the Act." The school district, however, contends that *Rowley* nonetheless established that "an IEP need not promise any particular *level* of benefit," so long as it is "'reasonably calculated' to provide *some* benefit, as opposed to *none*."

The district relies on several passages from *Rowley* to make its case. It points to our observation that "any substantive standard prescribing the level of education to be accorded" children with disabilities was "[n]oticeably absent from the language of the statute." The district also emphasizes the Court's statement that the Act requires States to provide access to instruction "sufficient to confer *some* educational benefit," reasoning that any benefit, however minimal, satisfies this mandate. Finally, the district urges that the Court conclusively adopted a "some educational benefit" standard when it wrote that "the intent of the Act was more to open the door of public education to handicapped children ... than to guarantee any particular level of education."

These statements in isolation do support the school district's argument. But the district makes too much of them. Our statement that the face of the IDEA imposed no explicit substantive standard must be evaluated alongside our statement that a substantive standard was "implicit in the Act." Similarly, we find little significance in the Court's language concerning the requirement that States provide instruction calculated to "confer some educational benefit." The Court had no need to say anything more particular, since the case before it involved a child whose progress plainly demonstrated that her IEP was designed to deliver more than adequate educational benefits. The Court's principal concern was to correct what it viewed as the surprising rulings below: that the IDEA effectively empowers judges to elaborate a federal common law of public education, and that a child performing *better* than most in her class had been denied a FAPE. The Court was not concerned with precisely articulating a governing standard for closer cases. And the statement that the Act did not "guarantee any particular level of education" simply reflects the unobjectionable proposition that the IDEA cannot and does not promise "any particular [educational] outcome." No law could do that—for any child.

More important, the school district's reading of these isolated statements runs headlong into several points on which *Rowley* is crystal clear. For instance—just after saying that the Act requires instruction that is "sufficient to confer some educational benefit"—we noted that "[t]he determination of when handicapped children are receiving *sufficient* educational benefits ... presents a ... difficult problem." And then we expressly declined "to establish any one test for determining the *adequacy* of educational benefits" under the Act. It would not have been "difficult" for us to say when educational benefits are sufficient if we had just said that *any* educational benefit was enough. And it would have been strange to refuse to set out a test for the adequacy of educational benefits if we had just done exactly that. We cannot accept the school district's reading of *Rowley.*

B

While *Rowley* declined to articulate an overarching standard to evaluate the adequacy of the education provided under the Act, the decision and the statutory language point to a general approach: To meet its substantive obligation under the IDEA, a school must offer an IEP reasonably calculated to enable a child to make progress appropriate in light of the child's circumstances.

The "reasonably calculated" qualification reflects a recognition that crafting an appropriate program of education requires a prospective judgment by school officials. The Act contemplates that this fact-intensive exercise will be informed not only by the expertise of school officials, but also by the input of the child's parents or guardians. Any review of an IEP must appreciate that the question is whether the IEP is *reasonable,* not whether the court regards it as ideal.

The IEP must aim to enable the child to make progress. After all, the essential function of an IEP is to set out a plan for pursuing academic and functional advancement. This reflects the broad purpose of the IDEA, an "ambitious" piece of legislation enacted "in response to Congress' perception that a majority of handicapped children in the United States 'were either totally excluded from schools or [were] sitting idly in regular classrooms awaiting the time when they were old enough to "drop out." '" *Rowley,* 458 U.S., at 179. A substantive standard not focused on student progress would do little to remedy the pervasive and tragic academic stagnation that prompted Congress to act.

That the progress contemplated by the IEP must be appropriate in light of the child's circumstances should come as no surprise. A focus on the particular child is at the core of the IDEA. The instruction offered must be *"specially* designed" to meet a child's *"unique* needs" through an *"[i]ndividualized* education program." §§ 1401(29), (14) (emphasis added). An IEP is not a form document. It is constructed only after careful consideration of the child's present levels of achievement, disability, and potential for growth. As we observed in *Rowley,* the IDEA "requires participating States to educate a wide spectrum of handicapped children," and "the benefits obtainable by children at one end of the spectrum will differ dramatically from those obtainable by children at the other end, with infinite variations in between."

Rowley sheds light on what appropriate progress will look like in many cases. There, the Court recognized that the IDEA requires that children with disabilities receive education in the regular classroom "whenever possible." When this preference is met, "the system itself monitors the educational progress of the child." *Id.,* at 202–203. "Regular examinations are administered, grades are awarded, and yearly advancement to higher grade levels is permitted for those children who attain an adequate knowledge of the course material." Progress through this system is what our society generally means by an "education." And access to an "education" is what the IDEA promises. Accordingly, for a child fully integrated in the regular classroom, an IEP typically should, as *Rowley* put it, be "reasonably calculated to enable the child to achieve passing marks and advance from grade to grade."

This guidance is grounded in the statutory definition of a FAPE. One of the components of a FAPE is "special education," defined as "specially designed instruction ... to meet the unique needs of a child with a disability." §§ 1401(9), (29). In determining what it means to "meet the unique needs" of a child with a disability, the provisions governing the IEP development process are a natural source of guidance: It is through the IEP that "[t]he 'free appropriate public education' required by the Act is tailored to the unique needs of" a particular child.

The IEP provisions reflect *Rowley*'s expectation that, for most children, a FAPE will involve integration in the regular classroom and individualized special education calculated to achieve advancement from grade to grade. Every IEP begins by describing a child's present level of achievement, including explaining "how the child's disability affects the child's involvement and progress in the general education curriculum." It then sets out "a statement of measurable annual goals ... designed to ... enable the child to be involved in and make progress in the general education curriculum," along with a description of specialized instruction and services that the child will receive. The instruction and services must likewise be provided with an eye toward "progress in the general education curriculum." Similar IEP requirements have been in place since the time the States began accepting funding under the IDEA.

The school district protests that these provisions impose only procedural requirements—a checklist of items the IEP must address—not a substantive standard enforceable in court. But the procedures are there for a reason, and their focus provides insight into what it means, for purposes of the FAPE definition, to "meet the unique needs" of a child with a disability. When a child is fully integrated in the regular classroom, as the Act prefers, what that typically means is providing a level of instruction reasonably calculated to permit advancement through the general curriculum.

Rowley had no need to provide concrete guidance with respect to a child who is not fully integrated in the regular classroom and not able to achieve on grade level. That case concerned a young girl who was progressing smoothly through the regular curriculum. If that is not a reasonable prospect for a child, his IEP need not aim for grade-level advancement. But his educational program must be appropriately ambitious in light of his circumstances, just as advancement from grade to grade is appropriately ambitious for most children in the regular classroom. The goals may differ, but every child should have the chance to meet challenging objectives.

Of course this describes a general standard, not a formula. But whatever else can be said about it, this standard is markedly more demanding than the "merely more than *de minimis*" test applied by the Tenth Circuit. It cannot be the case that the Act typically aims for grade-level advancement for children with disabilities who can be educated in the regular classroom, but is satisfied with barely more than *de minimis* progress for those who cannot.

When all is said and done, a student offered an educational program providing "merely more than *de minimis*" progress from year to year can hardly be said to have been offered an education at all. For children with disabilities, receiving instruction that aims so low would be tantamount to "sitting idly ... awaiting the time when they were old enough to 'drop out.'" *Rowley,* 458 U.S., at 179. The IDEA demands more. It requires an educational program reasonably calculated to enable a child to make progress appropriate in light of the child's circumstances.

C

Endrew's parents argue that the Act goes even further. In their view, a FAPE is "an education that aims to provide a child with a disability opportunities to achieve academic success, attain self-sufficiency, and contribute to society that are substantially equal to the opportunities afforded children without disabilities."

This standard is strikingly similar to the one the lower courts adopted in *Rowley,* and it is virtually identical to the formulation advanced by Justice Blackmun in his separate writing in that case. But the majority rejected any such standard in clear terms. Mindful that Congress (despite several intervening amendments to the IDEA) has not materially changed the statutory definition of a FAPE since *Rowley* was decided, we decline to interpret the FAPE provision in a manner so plainly at odds with the Court's analysis in that case.

D

We will not attempt to elaborate on what "appropriate" progress will look like from case to case. It is in the nature of the Act and the standard we adopt to resist such an effort: The adequacy of a given IEP turns on the unique circumstances of the child for whom it was created. This absence of a bright-line rule, however, should not be mistaken for "an invitation to the courts to substitute their own notions of sound educational policy for those of the school authorities which they review." *Rowley,* 458 U.S., at 206.

At the same time, deference is based on the application of expertise and the exercise of judgment by school authorities. The Act vests these officials with responsibility for decisions of critical importance to the life of a disabled child. The nature of the IEP process, from the initial consultation through state administrative proceedings, ensures that parents and school representatives will fully air their respective opinions on the degree of progress a child's IEP should pursue. By the time any dispute reaches court, school authorities will have had a complete opportunity to bring their expertise and judgment to bear on areas of disagreement. A reviewing court may fairly expect those authorities to be able to offer a cogent and responsive explanation for their decisions that shows the IEP is reasonably calculated to enable the child to make progress appropriate in light of his circumstances.

The judgment of the United States Court of Appeals for the Tenth Circuit is vacated, and the case is remanded for further proceedings consistent with this opinion.

It is so ordered.

Topical Index